Praise for *Faith and Learning on the Edge*

There is a wonderful passion in this book: a passionate critique of a lot of educational nonsense, a passionate call for a higher education into which Christianity has been integrated rather than to which it has merely been added. But not just passion; also intelligence, scope, and wide reading. All in all, a vivid and eloquent contribution to the current discussion on Christian higher education.

Nicholas Wolterstorff
Noah Porter Professor Emeritus of Philosophical Theology, Yale University

Claerbaut is surely right to think that naturalist ideology has sought to exclude thoughtful Christianity from the university at least as ardently as it has sought to exclude biblical perspectives from the schools and the courts. Modernism's most cherished myth—that educated people "outgrow" God—apparently requires to be protected by excluding the possibility of contrary witnesses. But Claerbaut sounds a still more sober warning to the church: too many Christian intellectuals have, in the face of growing secularist hostility, fallen silent or taken on protective coloration. Thus, at precisely that moment when America most needs from Christians a full obedience to love God with the mind, subcultural ghettoization and shallow piety divorced from thought and work in the world undermine our claim to be Christian in any meaningful sense of the word. Claerbaut's book should help stimulate a thoughtful examination of conscience in respect of these realities.

David Lyle Jeffrey
Senior Vice-Provost and Distinguished Professor
of Literature and the Humanities, Baylor University

Based on wide experience in learning and teaching and on years of reflection, Claerbaut, despite his topic's demand that he simplify and summarize, surprises the reader again and again with thought-provoking commentary. Teachers, college and graduate students, parents, pastors, and professionals can read it with profit. Books on education abound and books on the crisis in education proliferate, yet, arising from the Evangelical world, Claerbaut's wide-ranging and wise book deserves consideration by thoughtful Christians whatever their confessional commitments.

Dennis D. Martin
Associate Professor of Historical Theology, Loyola University Chicago

David Claerbaut has thought long and hard about the many subjects—and many levels of subject matter—treated in this book. It is a positive sign of maturing Christian reflection on the enterprise of American higher education that Claerbaut's book pays off with so many valuable insights on so many topics.

Mark A. Noll
McManis Professor of Christian Thought, Wheaton College

In recent years, Evangelicals and Roman Catholics have found important common ground on a number of fronts, including fundamental affirmations of Christian faith and morality. David Claerbaut's new book represents still another important initiative by an Evangelical to establish more such common ground: namely, the legitimate and necessary place Christian intellectual traditions should have in the academy.

Rev. James L. Heft, S. M.
University Professor of Faith and Culture and
Chancellor, University of Dayton, Dayton, Ohio

FAITH AND LEARNING

on the EDGE

A BOLD NEW LOOK
AT RELIGION IN
HIGHER EDUCATION

DAVID CLAERBAUT

ZONDERVAN™

GRAND RAPIDS, MICHIGAN 49530 USA

Faith and Learning on the Edge
Copyright © 2004 by David Claerbaut

Requests for information should be addressed to:
Zondervan, *Grand Rapids, Michigan 49530*

Library of Congress Cataloging-in-Publication Data

Claerbaut, David.
    Faith and learning on the edge : a bold new look at religion in higher
education / David Claerbaut.
        p. cm.
    Includes index.
    ISBN 0-310-25317-9
    1. Church and college—United States. 2. Postmodernism and higher education—United
States. I. Title.
    LC383.C56 2004
    378'.071—dc22
                                                                                    2004001546

This edition printed on acid-free paper.

The website addresses recommended throughout this book are offered as a resource to you. These websites are not intended in any way to be or imply an endorsement on the part of Zondervan, nor do we vouch for their content for the life of this book.

Interior design by Beth Shagene

Printed in the United States of America

04 05 06 07 08 09 10 /❖ DC/ 10 9 8 7 6 5 4 3 2 1

To Rochelle, James, Chris, and Mike, four of my precious children
But most of all, to Rita, whose love sustains me

CONTENTS

Acknowledgments   9

PART ONE: UNDERSTANDING FAITH AND LEARNING

1. Christian Education or Baptized Paganism?   13
2. The Artificial Lighting of the Academic Mainstream   25
3. The Relatives of Naturalism   41
4. Down the Intellectual Cul de Sac of Postmodernism   53
5. The High Stakes Politics of the Academic Mainstream   62
6. How Does Christian Scholarship Fit into the Academic Mainstream?   77
7. What Is Faith and Learning?   92
8. How Can We Be True to the Role of Learning in Christian Scholarship?   106
9. Where Does Reason End and Faith Begin?   115
10. What Are the Components of Faith and Learning?   125

PART TWO: APPLYING FAITH AND LEARNING IN THE CLASSROOM AND IN RESEARCH

11. Interpassage: Stimulating the Dialogue   139
12. Why Is Creation Central to the Faith-and-Learning Enterprise?   146

THE PHYSICAL SCIENCES

13. What Is the Mind-set of the Christian in the Physical Sciences?   163
14. Christian Implications in the Physical Sciences   171

THE ARTS AND HUMANITIES

15. How Do We Look at Art through Christian Eyes?   181

16. Some Guidelines for the Christian Artist   188

17. How Do We Teach Literature in a Postmodern World?   194

18. Philosophy under a Christian Lens   200

19. Atheist vs. Christian: Freud and Lewis Debate
    the Great Philosophical Questions   213

20. Education: The Battleground   224

21. What Is a Christian Historian?   234

THE BEHAVIORAL SCIENCES

22. Reflections for the Christian Political Scientist   245

23. Psychology: Need Theory—A Place Where Faith Meets Learning   258

24. Faith Meets the Mental Health Models   270

25. Sociology: Faith in the Eye of Naturalism   279

26. Economics: Some Christian Views on the "Dismal" Science   295

Conclusion   307

Name Index   309

Subject Index   313

ACKNOWLEDGMENTS

I am grateful to Stan Gundry, Tim Beals, and Mark Doty, each of whom has a passion for faith and learning.

A very special thanks to another writer—my wonderful daughter, Rochelle—who was instrumental in reading and editing much of this work.

PART ONE

UNDERSTANDING
FAITH AND LEARNING

1

CHRISTIAN EDUCATION
OR
BAPTIZED PAGANISM?

A Christian college at which I once lectured held an annual "Festival of Faith" week. To heighten interest, the seven-day event often featured a unifying theme and a well-known guest speaker. Much was made of the week. Signage abounded, student volunteers facilitated the implementation of activities, and faculty members were enjoined to promote the events in their classrooms. Despite noble intentions, the week rarely proved to be a raging success. Sometimes this was due to the theme. A week focusing on what is now euphemistically termed "racial reconciliation," for example, engendered fierce, divisive controversy.

One year the theme was "Faith and Learning," certainly an appropriate topic for a Christian college. The outcome was, in a word, calamitous. A cynical columnist offered a witty summation of the week in the student newspaper, writing something to the effect of "Faith and learning met on campus last week, and they didn't hit it off very well."

Regrettably, this columnist's cryptic comment sums up much of my experience in higher education. My career has exposed me to nearly the entire spectrum of American higher educational institutions—conservative evangelical, mainline Protestant, Roman Catholic, private nonsectarian, as well as the mainstream state university setting. If my experience is at all typical—and I fear that it is—faith and learning often do not hit it off very well on many campuses, even Christian ones.

▸▸ Faith and Learning: A Memoir

Having graduated from a public high school, my faith-and-learning odyssey began in the late 1960s at a Christian college that marketed itself without apology as one that taught its courses "from a Christian perspective." Apparently, most of that teaching occurred during classes I cut or slept through, because I recall scarcely a single class session devoted entirely to providing an overtly Christian perspective from which to view the material studied. I am not talking about the "hard sciences" here—chemistry, physics, mathematics, and the like. I am referring to English, psychology, and even philosophy classes.

I was disappointed. And unprepared. Rebellious, agnostic students—many of whom had been forced by their parents to attend a Christian college—boldly proclaimed their unbelieving views in dormitory bull sessions. "There is no true altruism," stated one cynical student in one late-night verbal free-for-all. His point was that all behavior is somehow self-motivated. Though specifically a theological point, he was taking a shot at the Christian notion of self-denial. Whether or not he was correct was not important at the time. What I recall was how immobilized I was by his ideological challenge. I felt intellectually unarmed, devoid of any ammunition to answer this and other examples of unbelief, from the nihilism of Nietzsche to the scoffing atheism of Marx.

I would have settled for an occasional "Why I'm a Christian" profession of faith from one of the learned faculty. Though hardly academic in nature, it would certainly have been helpful to have at least one of these genuinely impressive minds express the reason for his or her life commitment. No such testimonies were rendered in my hearing. In fact, issues of the faith were invariably dealt with in distancing, cognitive terms. It seemed the faculty members were uncomfortable with the faith side of the faith-and-learning nexus. The college's academic atmosphere, suffused with efforts to appear intellectually sophisticated, stood in sharp contrast to the institution's efforts to promote its Christian identity. Although terms such as "world-and-life view" were tossed about, I do not recall one memorable personal or intellectual expression as to why these scholars had adopted a Christian perspective on reality.

While I do remember a beloved English professor, who worshiped in the same church I attended, pointing out that Hemingway was a nihilist, I do not remember any Christian critique of this famous but depressing author. In fact, when in a term paper I attacked the celebrated author for feeding his readers "the bread of despair," the professor commented that I was perhaps being a bit unfair to Hemingway. Another English professor, a man whose dyspeptic disposition seemed more reflective of Hemingway's worldview than that of a grateful Christian's, made no secret of his disdain for "come-to-Jesus talk" in the classroom. He found such testimonials anti-intellectual, even embarrassing, well beneath the elevated academic bar he proudly set for his classroom. This esteemed professor seemed far more comfortable chortling about how Chaucer's, Miller's, and Reeve's tales "held up a mirror to human nature," as he put it mirthfully, than examining the life philosophies of Chaucer and how they were expressed in his writings. Yet another professor seemed to glory in the bawdiness of Donne's early poetry but said little about the world-and-life views of the seventeenth-century poets under study.

James Orr, in his book *The Christian View of God and the World,* claims there is a coherent, unified Christian view of reality clearly distinguishable from other theories and notions.[1] If so, I would have liked to have such a worldview applied to literature. I wondered why certain basic questions were not addressed in such a self-proclaimed Christian college. For example, why should a Christian scholar study English? What seeming universal truths and symbols did the "better" authors employ that could inform the Christian thinker? What cunning assumptions were kneaded into the literature of some of the most celebrated writers? What guidelines, if any, might a Christian follow if he or she aspired to become a novelist?

The foregoing questions are merely suggestive. Other students, many of whom had to be experiencing their own crises of faith, almost certainly had some questions of their own. We remained silent, I suspect, out of fear of appearing simplistic and naïve. The atmosphere simply did not seem to invite such blatant workings out of faith and learning. But it should have. I think it is reasonable to expect that an institution that proudly and unabashedly asserts that the instruction carried on within its walls is uniquely Christian would have engaged at least some questions of this nature.

It was much the same in other classes. The basic psychology course was indistinguishable from that taught in any of the neighboring state universities, albeit at a far lower cost. One merely read the textbook—a typical survey of the discipline, running from monkey psychology to abnormal behavioral states—and passed the tests. There was nary a mention of the challenges for the Christian within a discipline that is founded in large part on a naturalist worldview that regards humans as merely advanced forms of life, rather than as beings molded in the image of God.

Clearly, there was much faith-and-learning grist available here. Again, some questions come to mind. What are the limits of the discipline? What were the world-and-life views of psychology's "founding fathers"? How do those views shape the discipline's direction even now? Where does the discipline's claim to being a science end and theory begin? In the absence of any attempt at a synthesis of psychology and faith, I suspect that some students who came from more rural, reactionary backgrounds, felt they had to choose between their faith and the discipline.

Later, when teaching social psychology at the college level, I eagerly joined a Christian psychological organization, even presenting a paper at one of its conferences. Here again, genuinely Christian thinking seemed in short supply. Much of the research amounted to little more than dubious reformulations of scriptural views on matters of current concern. In one session, labeling the "such a worm as I" theology as harmful to the fragile self-esteem of believers seemed to be a major purpose. The presenter, an earnest and amiable soul, valiantly attempted to reconfigure Paul's writings to cohere with those of the prevailing proponents of self-esteem. He earnestly presented what seemed to me a complete misunderstanding of Paul's writings.

Although the presenter failed to understand that "worm" theology is not an attempt to debase humanity, but rather a celebration of grace coming from an all-loving, infinite God to a finite, fallen species, his presentation was at least an attempt at merging faith and learning. As such, it was far superior to presentations that degenerated into arrogant and sarcastic critiques—carried on in the absence of any alternative theories or convincing research—of some of the more conservative views published by Christian practitioners in the mental health field.

Let me drop in an aside here. That initial attempts at a "Christian sociology" or "Christian economics" may not be particularly "good" sociology or economics is no reason to dismiss them. They are what academics call "first approximations"—models to be improved upon. Consider that the first mainstream formulations in medicine, sociology, and psychology were incredibly crude attempts. The Swiss cheese–like holes in these theories and practices—applying leeches, engaging in phrenology as a way of identifying deviants, and performing frontal lobotomies—are now obvious. Nonetheless, those early efforts at theory building were an important start. So also, I believe, is the case with faith and learning. Reviewers need to realize that we are, in many cases, still in the intellectual starting blocks. Critiques need to be constructive and illuminating rather than mean-spirited. Constructive critiques will often serve to stimulate further attempts at integrating faith and learning.

Returning to my undergraduate experience, I recall no models of Christian thought available for even mean-spirited critique. The basic philosophy courses were largely uncritical examinations of the intellectual rudiments of famous philosophers. Although one professor stated, in response to the anti-Christian views of a cynical philosopher, that Christianity was a "commitment of the heart, not a mere assent to propositions," I needed more. I dearly wanted a bit of Christian critique of some cynic's "propositions." Here again, I was left to wonder: What philosophical "truths" are basic to life, whether emanating from

Christian or secular thinkers? What theoretical foundations make a philosophy clearly Christian or non-Christian? How can a Christian assess the soundness of a philosophical formulation?

The problem extended even to classes in religion. I remember one theology professor saying, "It takes more courage in some small towns not to join the church as a young adult than to do so." Though this was indeed true in some of the rural hamlets from which certain of the students hailed, there was no counterpresentation stressing the courage necessary to declare one's faith in an intellectually hostile setting. In another course, the professor focused on Calvin's notion of sphere sovereignty. The pedagogue busily drew a series of parallel circles representing the various spheres of Western culture—education, government, business, and so forth—presenting them as largely autonomous sectors. Although the very sociological soundness of the doctrine seems questionable, given its complete denial of the interaction among these supposedly sovereign social institutions, I found myself drawn to it. It did make for a rather intellectually tidy design, typical of Calvin's brilliant systematic theology. Nevertheless, I wondered just where exactly God fit into this nicely designed structure. Upon closer examination, there he was, all alone at the top of the organizational chart, busy controlling and redeeming these spheres with his ultimate sovereignty. God as CEO.

The point was that God—through his human servants—permeates and hence redeems these institutions of his creation. It was hard to see, given the turbulence in the nation at the time: a country torn asunder by a war in Southeast Asia, a burgeoning civil rights struggle, assassinations of major social and political leaders, and an ever more aggressive sexual revolution and youth drug culture. In short, it didn't seem he or we were doing a very good job of permeation, much less of redemption. Moreover, I recall no direction as to just how this reforming activity was to be accomplished. The whole theory was presented rather casually, as if it derived from deism (the belief that God created the universe and has since let it play out in a laissez-faire fashion). In brief, the professor's presentation left me feeling that, despite the apparent godlessness and rebellion all around me, indeed his was the God of Romantic poet Robert Browning—in heaven, with all being right with the world—and that redemption was doing rather well, although not very visibly.

At most, issues of faith were additive rather than integrative. Religion classes were simply parallel to the other subjects, added to the otherwise secular curriculum. This arrangement of the subject matter resulted in a series of mixed ideological messages. One could learn about the sovereignty of God and the purpose of humankind in a theology course, only to find that psychology taught as if all one "needs for personal well-being is to grow like a tree or bound about self-expressively like a deer."[2] Similarly, while this very academic institution was founded on the belief that all reality is grounded in God and his divine plans, literature courses proclaimed the brilliant writing of some of the famous nihilists.

Charles Colson and Nancy Pearcey offer a specific and explicit definition of Christian education. They assert that it is more than devotionals coupled with teaching out of secular textbooks. "It consists," they say, "of teaching everything, from science and mathematics to literature and the arts, within the framework of an integrated biblical worldview." They then tighten the definition. "It means teaching students to relate every academic discipline to God's truth and his self-revelation in Scripture, while detecting and critiquing nonbiblical worldview assumptions."[3] That did not happen in my undergraduate experience.

The Christian college marketing pieces, trumpeting the Christian character of the instruction (I believe the words used were *uniquely* and *distinctly*), in no way resembled my experience at the institution. The Christian faith was not used to "salt" my learning experiences, nor was the light of revelation employed to illuminate my understanding of the subjects studied.

There is a distinctly Christian view of what life is all about, about the nature of humankind, about what our purposes ought to be, and about where we are headed eternally.[4] To dance away from these distinctives is to marginalize faith as an element in the learning process. It was as if the college faculty—all supposedly active, professing Christians—instead of searching for points of Christian permeation of the matters under study, wanted to fly as close to the secular, intellectual flame as possible, yet without stepping over any uncrossable lines of apostasy. In short, I felt I was receiving a type of "baptized paganism," an essentially secular education delivered by a faculty comprised of Christians. It seemed as if I was being taught by professors who happened to be Christians, rather than Christian professors. In short, nothing in my undergraduate academic experience overtly strengthened my faith.

Certainly, this is not to say there were no sincere attempts at fusing faith and learning at my college. My exposure was by no means total. Indeed, there were many courses I did not take and many faculty members under whom I did not study. Nonetheless, I greatly doubt that myriad meshings of faith and learning went on at that academically excellent institution, all rather coincidentally out of my earshot or without penetrating my awareness.

My expectations were not high. I would have settled for much less than the high-voltage Colson-Pearcey approach. But I did want something. By my senior year I had had enough. Plagued by intellectual doubt, a troubled love life, and a serious illness in my family, I acted out my frustration. In a somewhat rambling discourse, I raged at the institution in my final term paper. All but charging the institution with false advertising, I attacked those members of the faculty "who seemed ashamed to name the name of Jesus Christ in the classroom." Apparently, the professor was shaken. Perhaps realizing that I had counted him among the culprits, he invited me to discuss my perceptions with him. Although I remember little of my conference with him, I appreciated his caring, sensitive manner.

That was my undergraduate experience with faith and learning. I have since come to the conclusion that every Christian college should require at least one course in apologetics so students understand that personal Christian faith can have a solid intellectual dimension. There are two reasons for this. First, late adolescence is a time of physical and psychological change and even upheaval; it is therefore a time in a person's life when there is a higher than normal likelihood of a faith crisis. Second, for many students who come from less than highly intellectual backgrounds, the heavy onslaught of mainstream, secular bodies of knowledge can be overwhelming. Unless the Christian college—or a professor— truly engages the faith-and-learning challenge, one cannot be certain that the spiritually troubled student will be ministered to effectively. Conversely, one could argue that if a college really did provide a quality faith-and-learning experience throughout its curriculum, there might be little need to include courses in religion and philosophy in its general education requirements.

Graduate school was different. At one large Jesuit university, in which I later taught graduate courses, Father Thomas Gannon, chair of the sociology department, pointed out to me in an individual conference how one of the discipline's basic theories unintentionally reinforced the Christian concept of immortality. Another renowned professor began his class with a group recitation of the Lord's Prayer and wore his Catholic faith comfortably and openly in the classroom. At another university, I even found some graduate professors who were hostile to Christian faith helpful in a paradoxical way. One of my favorites, David Angus, a self-professed atheist humanist philosopher, proclaimed Albert Camus's writings, claiming that life was simply "a mass of absurdities." Angus was, nonetheless, comfortable in dialogue with Christian students on issues of faith. That openness, coupled with his acknowledgment that there were indeed quality scholars who did embrace religious faith, was encouraging to me.

After graduate school, I taught at a Christian (though not overtly evangelical) college. I often devoted the final class session of the term to looking at some Christian approaches to the social sciences. It was hardly an intense immersion into faith and learning. That some students praised me in their reviews for working in this bit of faith-and-learning interaction was gratifying. That they often mentioned that I was the only faculty member that did so was not.

Although the credo of the college was, "In thy light, shall we see light," not much light seemed to be derived from many of the religion courses. Reportedly, religion professors routinely indulged in biblical criticism. The school did not require a faith statement as a condition for admission. Moreover, students from the sponsoring denomination often entered these classes with a rather simple pietistic faith, one based on a personal experience with God. Others came with little or no faith at all. Neither group was prepared to have religion instructors undermine any vestiges of childlike faith by challenging the validity (infallibility) of certain passages of Scripture, suggesting the presence of redactors (editors) throughout the Bible, and questioning the authorship of certain of its books. It is not as if these matters need be off-limits in a Christian college that values academic freedom. On the contrary, open inquiry and thorough investigation should typify a liberal education. What was going on, however, seemed to be something much different from earnest inquiry. The simple faith of the students was being assaulted by these learned, allegedly Christian teachers.

▸▸ Resistance from Within

The president of the college where I taught was a registered psychologist adept at faith-and-learning interchanges, whose charge included returning the institution to its more pure, orthodox Christian roots. Given that the statements of faith the faculty signed in this college were not very restrictive, his charge was rather daunting. In any case, the president urged the faculty to invest their energies in faith-and-learning syntheses in their respective fields. One could say he was met with bridled enthusiasm. His faith-and-learning entreaties were frequently met with derisive references to the seeming absurdity of "Christian mathematics" and other hostile remarks.

One nationally celebrated Christian lecturer in the humanities, a Roman Catholic scholar whose academic credentials fairly towered over those of his audience, was given a less than hospitable hearing. When he referred to the "received tradition" of beliefs that we Christians have, one aged faculty member openly proclaimed, "Dogma is dead," at a later discussion. Another guest lecturer, an internationally renowned Ivy League philosopher, was dismissed as being too geometric in his Christian thinking. It seemed as if my colleagues' critiques had a vested interest in trivializing the ideas of these thinkers. Perhaps my professional peers were either too insecure in their ability to do genuine Christian scholarship or simply unwilling to engage in the effort.

Other efforts made by the president to get the faculty to do what the college proclaimed it did routinely—teach in the context of a Christian perspective—

elicited almost sophomoric resistance. At a faculty retreat dedicated to faith and learning, the philosophy professor charged with leading the session deftly avoided any real engagement of the matter by routing the discussion toward the larger question, "What is a Christian college?" It was clear that the chief purpose of this deflection was to derail the president's attempts to focus on faith and learning. It was successful. The incredible diversity of opinion that surfaced submerged the retreat in an ocean of confusion. This then became a permission-giver for each faculty member to handle the matter of Christian teaching the way he or she saw fit. Most chose not to handle it at all.

The academic dean arranged a joint conference on the matter of faith and learning with another, more overtly evangelical Christian college. Though well structured, the conference was an embarrassing flop. The only obvious point of agreement among our faculty seemed to be that no one had the right to direct them in their teaching. Moreover, the attitude seemed to be that to work within a Christian context in one's teaching was to lower the academic quality of the pedagogy. Christian education was to be left to Sunday school teachers and Bible colleges, while the real academic heavy lifting went far beyond such fluff.

Some faculty members felt it sufficient simply to conduct oneself in a Christian fashion with students. Another common defense went like this: "I believe I fulfill the matter of being a Christian teacher by doing the best job possible in teaching the material in my discipline." Nothing more than baptized paganism, this attitude suggests that one's faith should have nothing at all to do with how he or she works in an academic discipline; whether or not God exists is irrelevant to the education process. Given that many of these people were hardly luminaries in their field, many of my professors who were self-proclaimed agnostics were far better "Christian teachers" than some of my believing colleagues if one were to use this secular criterion of Christian teaching.

Such was my experience with Christian colleges. Realizing that courses focused on Christian approaches to learning now exist in Christian colleges, I thought things might have changed. Perhaps my experience was atypical or at least badly dated. I have discovered it is neither. When I began working on this book, I spoke with others who had extensive involvement with Christian colleges. Their experiences were disturbingly similar. One exchange in particular stands out. I spent a day with a renowned Christian scholar, a textbook-writing full professor at a major research university, who never tires of looking at Christian approaches to learning. This faith-and-learning zeal led him to spend a semester as a visiting professor at a high-profile Christian college, exchanging the prestige of working with graduate students for a heavier undergraduate teaching load.

Although he found the academic standards, the intellectual acumen of the students, and the quality of teaching impressive, he found nothing approaching the level of faith-and-learning integration he had expected. "I decided to spend a semester there to find out how different it is at a Christian college," he explained. "Regrettably, I found out how different it isn't."

It needs to be different if Christians are truly to be a force of light and salt in the world of the twenty-first century. A genuine passion for the integration of faith and learning needs to develop among Christian thinkers everywhere if we are truly serious about our call as servants of Christ.

▸▸ The Christian Mind

In 1963, British intellectual Harry Blamires began marking out some sharp boundaries relevant to the faith-and-learning relationship. Employing a rather shrill style and given to the occasional overstatement, Blamires opens one of his books by stating, "There is no longer a Christian mind."[5] Blamires observes a sort of schizoid or compartmentalized Christianity in operation. It is one in which Christians, while often clearly distinguishable from the larger society in areas of faith and personal conduct, are not at all distinct when it comes to matters of thought. Instead, they think secularly. "To think secularly is to think within a frame of reference bounded by the limits of our life on earth; it is to keep one's calculations rooted in this-worldly criteria."[6] It is, in effect, to dismiss the reality that humans are spiritual, rather than merely physical, beings.

Using analyses of political and social issues as examples, Blamires has observed that believers simply do not employ a Christian vocabulary or Christian values in discussing these issues. "Because the subject was social or political, we left our well-tried and well-grounded Christian concepts behind us, and adopted the vocabulary of secularism."[7] In many cases, Christians have trained and disciplined themselves—perhaps out of a desire to communicate with relevance in the larger society—to think secularly about secular (nonspiritual) matters.[8]

For those who doubt his case, Blamires challenges his readers to take any political topic and determine the *right* policy with regard to it, but to do so without reference to any prevailing political alignment or bias. In short, one is to found one's conclusions on solely Christian thinking. With the exception of emotionally charged issues such as abortion or capital punishment, many believers will hit an intellectual wall trying to do this. For those who do succeed, however, Blamires pushes the bar higher, suggesting they attempt to discuss their formulations with other believers. That, he suspects, will prove to be a very unsatisfying experience, resulting in an awareness of how alone one is when involved in Christian thinking.[9]

Much has happened since 1963, and some might feel Blamires has overstated the matter a bit. He does, however, make a strong case for his thesis that Christian thinking is in rather short supply. What is particularly troubling to Blamires is that it has often been secularist humanists—D. H. Lawrence, George Orwell, Henry Miller, and Samuel Beckett, to name a few—rather than Christians who have rendered the most prophetic critiques of the indignities heaped on the human spirit in contemporary life. Christians are often too invested in the current social and political structures to critique injustices and social ills in the prevailing culture from the perspective of Christian values and theology. In the instances in which Christians do examine their society, they too often do so by thinking secularly, analyzing and evaluating data from the temporal, this-worldly point of view employed by the non-Christian scholar.[10] When we engage consistently in secular examinations and analyses, we imperil the very survival of faith and learning.

Again, the issue here is not about one's personal commitment to Christ or one's willingness to live the life of the Spirit; those are matters of faith, will, and conduct. It is about viewing life mentally through Christian lenses, just as the zealous political partisan will view almost any matter in the light of his or her liberal or conservative commitment. It is about thinking things through, using Christian criteria in making assessments. It is about moving the faith-and-learning endeavor off the back shelf and taking it to the edge. It is about having a Christian mind. "To think Christianly," notes Blamires, "is to accept all things with the mind as related, directly or indirectly, to man's eternal destiny as the redeemed and chosen child of God."[11]

The importance of developing the Christian mind is inescapably obvious. It is basic to the call of the Christian life. The first great commandment is to love God with all of one's heart, soul, and *mind.* The primary mission of Christian higher education, then, should be to develop the Christian mind. That is the reason for its existence. The Christian mind develops no differently from other areas of the Christian life. It is a matter of practice and discipline. More particularly, it is the result of a healthy meeting of faith and learning. It most certainly can be done. The intellectual talent to develop fresh faith-and-learning integrations among the academic disciplines is abundantly present among Christian scholars. I have found some of the finest, most conscientious and disciplined minds in higher education among this group. That talent needs to be put to work, and with a sense of urgency.

The title of this book, *Faith and Learning on the Edge,* can be looked at from several vantage points. In one sense, to neglect the development of the Christian mind places the very existence of the faith-and-learning enterprise on the edge of extinction. In another, the call of the Christian life is to sharpen our minds and to bring faith and learning to the edge as we look at the world through educated, Christian eyes.

In any case, the stakes are high. Not to engage the challenge, not to answer the call, not to shine the light of Christian insight across our disciplines, is to make the education we offer indistinguishable from the artificial lighting of the secular mainstream.

Notes

1. James Orr, *The Christian View of God and the World* (Grand Rapids: Kregel, 1989), 16; David S. Dockery, "Introduction: Shaping a Christian Worldview," in *Shaping a Christian Worldview,* ed. David S. Dockery and Gregory Alan Thornbury (Nashville: Broadman and Holman, 2002), 2.
2. Harry Blamires, *Where Do We Stand?* (Ann Arbor, MI: Servant, 1980), 54–55.
3. Charles Colson and Nancy Pearcey, *How Now Shall We Live?* (Wheaton, IL: Tyndale, 1999), 338, quoted in Antonio A. Chiareli, "Christian Worldview and the Social Sciences," in Dockery and Thornbury, *Shaping a Christian Worldview,* 261.
4. Blamires, *Where Do We Stand?* 46.
5. Harry Blamires, *The Christian Mind* (Ann Arbor, MI: Servant, 1997), 3.
6. Ibid., 44.
7. Ibid., 38.
8. Ibid., 39.
9. Ibid., 14.
10. Ibid., 5–12, 48–49.
11. Ibid., 44.

2

THE ARTIFICIAL LIGHTING
OF THE ACADEMIC MAINSTREAM

There are three basic reasons we do Christian scholarship. The first is spiritual. We are instructed to do all things—whether we eat or drink, says Paul in 1 Corinthians 10:31—to the glory of God and, as his stewards, in partnership with God. Our mandate—rooted in the basic Christian doctrine that we are trustees of God's creation—is to bring all things under his power, including what we call learning. Christian scholarship is part of developing the Christian mind—the mind of Christ. If we were to use the Westminster Catechism's assertion that our chief purpose is to glorify and enjoy God forever, a case can be made for the acquisition of knowledge in and of itself. It is part of knowing and enjoying the Creator. Knowledge is truth. Therefore, it is from God, who is truth. Knowing truth both vivifies our understanding and sharpens our perception of reality. It is part of God's revelation made available to us.

The second reason is both spiritual and practical. If Christianity is truth, then Christian education is the only true education and therefore the only practical education. There is no education, no truth—nothing—without God, the eternal author of reality. To be educated, then, is to know that eternal author. He is infinitely larger than the mind that searches for truth. Descartes said, "I think, therefore I am." For the Christian, it is exactly the opposite. "I am (a creation of God), therefore I think." Thinking is a part of being. Were I born without a mind, I would still *be*. I would be a child of God. Furthermore, the practical aspects of education have spiritual value. Philosopher Nicholas Wolterstorff suggests that the purpose of Christian scholarship is to contribute to what he calls *justice-in-shalom*.[1] Wolterstorff's point merits attention. The second great commandment—that we love our neighbor as ourselves—is also critical here. Peace, justice, liberation, and reconciliation—whether it be among races, income groups, or nations—are part of the Christian's responsibility. As such, the Christian who sees her scholarship in the context of accomplishing those goals is well focused.

The third reason is largely practical. It is virtually impossible to exaggerate the impact of education. No institution wields a more powerful influence in a techno-industrial society than does education. It could well be argued that educational institutions shape a society rather than the converse. Education not only molds an ever-growing segment of the population; almost every one of society's leaders is a product of the American higher educational system. Moreover, Americans hold education (particularly in our informational, knowledge-driven era) in such high esteem that they rarely question any of what is taught as fact in the nation's classrooms. Due to academic freedom, it could be argued that nowhere in our society are there fewer checks on an institution's functions than in education. Hence, there are few needs greater than the presence of Christian minds and sharp Christian thinking infusing this potent Western institution. Yet this is not happening.

No one, not even Blamires, disputes that Christianity has rightly focused on the commitment of the heart and soul to Christ and on the importance of conducting oneself in a Christian fashion. Developing the mind of Christ—the ability to apply Christian values and analyses to what one studies and learns—however, is what is at issue. In an education-driven culture, the mind has become the spiritual battlefield. It is so important that some believe Christian philosophers need to be valued similar to ministers and church leaders.[2] Failure to educate the mind's eye to see life through a Christian lens—no different from a feminist's viewing reality through a feminist prism—is to cede an absolutely critical mission field to secularism.

▶▶ Enlightenment

Simply stated, given the culture-defining power of education, there is an ever more pressing need to educate with the light on. John begins his gospel by saying, "In the beginning was the Word, and the Word was with God, and the Word was God." He goes on to assert that in this Word (Jesus) "was life, and that life was the light of men. The light shines in the darkness, but the darkness has not understood it" (John 1:4–5).

There it is. Reality, truth—enlightenment—is found in a person, Jesus Christ. Without that person, there may well be some knowledge but there is no real light, no real understanding of life. I use the word *enlightenment* deliberately, because to understand the current academic mainstream, one has to understand the importance of the period by the same name.

The Enlightenment period, begun by a group of French intellectuals near the end of the seventeenth century, emerged from three central beliefs: (1) the power of order over disorder, (2) the value of reason over the forces of ignorance, and (3) a reliance on science as opposed to superstition and religion. The order-over-disorder doctrine was much fueled by the organizing impact of modern industrialization and capitalist economic structures. The every-family-for-itself nature of agrarian life was being replaced by large cities, divisions of labor, and set patterns regarding the distribution of goods and services.[3] The latter two beliefs—the primacy of reason and science—are pivotal to our discussion. Reason here refers to human reason, not reason in the context of God's illuminating presence. Furthermore, this reason was much rooted in science that, of course, was to triumph over superstition and religion. In a word, God was out of the equation. The logo of the Enlightenment might well have been "In the light of human reason and science shall we find truth." Religion was viewed as a division or form of superstition, filled with scientifically unverifiable notions about reality, ideas that do not comport with reason.

So began what is called the modern era.

The Enlightenment way of thinking was itself a religion in that its adherents believed in it with worshipful respect. They felt that humans would wipe away poverty, violence, and insecurity en route to a peaceful and prosperous world of ever-increasing progress. People's commitment to Enlightenment thinking runs parallel to the Genesis 3 account of the Fall. Whether read literally or figuratively, the message is the same: the serpent manipulates Adam and Eve into thinking that by violating God's laws, taking him out of the equation, they will be "as gods" themselves. Similarly, by Enlightenment logic, humans do not need God to comprehend truth and reality. In fact, he often gets in the way of the process. This getting-in-the-way mentality is basic to the mind-set that emerged from the Enlightenment: *secularism.* Secularism is not necessarily characterized by a thrusting of the middle finger skyward in rebellion against God. Rather, it is living as if God does not exist. God may as well be that irrelevant grandfather who lives several states away. We rarely if ever visit him, call him, write him, or even drop him an email message. He is there, but we live as if he does not exist. So it is with secularism.

The bright light offered by the Enlightenment has proven to be artificial. Two world wars; the totalitarianism of Stalin and Hitler; the Holocaust; the forces of colonialism, racism, and economic exploitation that give rise to world hunger and genocide; and a host of other maladies have dashed its glittering promises of human perfectibility. By the end of the late 1970s, the idealism of the Enlightenment had pretty well devolved into a spirit of disillusionment and a new mind-set called postmodernism, something we will discuss in the next chapter.

The academic mainstream, however, remains very much a continuing product of the Enlightenment. It is a secularist entity that seeks truth, but by emphasizing the primacy of human reason and science over religion as the sole revelation of that truth.

▸▸ The Rise of Secularism

That the academic mainstream was not always that way is brilliantly chronicled by George Marsden in *The Soul of the American University*.[4] The American university was a product of an avowedly Protestant culture that emphasized at least the moral aspects of traditional Christianity, if not its basic doctrines. In fact, the training of an educated clergy was among its primary missions. Nation building, rooted in moral principles and technological advancement, was the aim of its largely New England founders in the late nineteenth and early twentieth centuries. No value was more cherished than freedom, including freedom from religious authoritarianism as practiced by the Roman Catholic Church. There was much support for free scientific inquiry, in part because it was assumed that solid scientific effort would advance the Christian civilization it was to serve. Faith and learning, though looking like happy partners, were actually on a collision course, largely because they were moving on separate tracks in this freedom-seeking atmosphere.

This quest for freedom gave rise to a growing nonsectarianism, a force that by virtual definition assured a distancing of institutions from biblical authority and theological orthodoxy. With a general though nondoctrinal Christian outlook still accepted as a given, little thought was put into developing explicitly Christian perspectives in the various disciplines. Hence, by the time Darwinian thinking began to challenge the necessity of Christian notions about reality, there were no established Christian schools of thought to counter it. All the while, the university system was moving toward a unified cultural ideal, one aimed at building a national culture, one with an ever less defined Christian common denominator.

Though regarded as Christian in the broadest, nondefinitive sense, the university was now a place in which much scholarship was freed from the restraints of Christian doctrine. Religion's value lay in its temporal, nonsupernatural aspect. Seen as a benign force having moral impact and a civilizing effect, it had no authority. Charles Seymour's 1937 inaugural address as Yale's president is illustrative of this. "I call on all members of the faculty, as members of a thinking body, freely to recognize the tremendous validity and power of the teachings of Christ in our life-and-death struggle against the forces of selfish materialism. If we lose that struggle, judging from present events abroad, scholarship as well as religion will disappear."[5]

A careful look at Seymour's words indicates that religion was to serve as a security device for scholarship and the preservation of a humanistic society. In fact, Seymour fears that religion itself will disappear if humankind does not keep it alive by affirming the teachings of Jesus; God dependent on humankind—the ultimate role reversal. In the spirit of the times, Woodrow Wilson sent a curious mixed message when president at Princeton. He reined in openly Christian teaching on one hand, while proclaiming the value of a moral and democratic Christian civilization on the other. In short, the faith had no inherent valid truths. Its worth resided in its capacity to tranquilize humanity's savage tendencies.

The secularization of the American university continued to accelerate in the 1950s as the term *Christian* gave way to *Judeo-Christian* or *Western*. Religion was no longer integrated into the general academic subjects but became a separate area of study, in addition to functioning as an extracurricular activity for students. Over the ensuing decades, religion has continuously become marginalized, even trivialized, in the culture of the academic mainstream and is often regarded as hardly more substantive than a hobby. The behavioral sciences rather than faith were now regarded as the vehicle by which humankind could maintain a civilized society. Religious studies themselves no longer focused on the transcendent and uplifting value of faith, but rather on scientific approaches to the study of religion.

One of the first to blow the whistle on the secularizing of the American academic scene was none other than the ever-provocative William F. Buckley Jr. in 1951. Buckley rocked the academic world with *God and Man at Yale,* charging that his alma mater—once a self-proclaimed Christian institution—was no longer faithful to its charter. Buckley set off a firestorm of denial when he wrote, "I propose, simply, to expose what I regard as an extraordinarily irresponsible educational attitude that, under the protective label 'academic freedom,' [Yale] has produced one of the most extraordinary incongruities of our time: the institution derives its moral and financial support from Christian individualists and then addresses itself to the task of persuading the sons of these supporters to be atheistic socialists."[6]

Not only was Buckley charging Yale with being inadequately Christian in nature, he was all but indicting the university for fraud by deception. Though far better known for his conservative political commentary and acerbic wit, Buckley has for decades been a consistently vigilant and insightful critic of the agnostic and postmodern drifts in higher education. In any case, his initial charge would scarcely set off even a flicker of defensive protest today. In fact, were the current president of Yale to claim the institution to be Christian, he would likely provoke belly laughs of derision among his own faculty. Yale is but one of many institutions that were once mainline Protestant bastions of religious orthodoxy but are thoroughly secular entities today.

The Bible describes the serpent, the symbol of evil, in Genesis 3 as subtle and cunning. Throughout Scripture, evil is consistently characterized as deceptive and deceitful, with its personification, Satan, called the father of lies. Such is the nature of spiritual error. It rarely occurs overnight, or even blatantly. It evolves slowly, if not imperceptibly. Such was the case in the secularizing of once-Christian institutions of higher learning. Again, many such institutions began with Scripture as central to the learning process, the unquestioned source of ultimate revelation, but over time the spiritual controls were loosened, with secularism filling the vacuum.

Much of this secularizing of the American university can be traced to the latter portion of the nineteenth century. It was then that science, with its startling advances, began accelerating and began offering alternatives to the Christian worldview. Those governing the universities then started to cede control of their institutions to the forces of unbelief. With science taking a position at least parallel to Scripture as an arbiter of truth, and with differences between science and Scripture becoming more evident and more difficult to reconcile (as in the case of evolution and naturalism), these administrators remained passive.

The leaders of these institutions did not insist on working at syntheses between science and religion through faith-and-learning dialogues in which scriptural doctrines such as creation were to be accepted as transcendent truths to guide human inquiry. Instead, they attempted to separate these ideological combatants. From there, science took over as the preeminent dispenser of truth, while religion, taught in the context of Western civilization and culture, became politically impotent. Faith statements began disappearing as a part of the hiring process, making faculties more agnostic and atheistic in nature. Moreover, academic freedom prevented university officials from insisting that Scripture be used as a corrective guide in the teaching/learning process.

Gregory Alan Thornbury cites the case of Baptist-founded Bucknell University in tracing the secularization of once-Christian institutions of higher education. When it began classes in 1846 in Lewisburg, Pennsylvania, this denominational school required regular attendance at daily chapel as well as Sunday service attendance from its students. Over time, however, Bucknell drifted away from its denominational commitment. It did not require confessional statements from its faculty or board of trustees. By opening up the school, Bucknell grew in enrollment, dollars, and secularism. By 1953, the school dismissed any responsibility to the American Baptist Convention, and today it claims no religious heritage at all.[7] Thornbury attributes the secularization of once-Christian colleges to three factors. First, the gradual disconnection of the institution from the church; second, the absence of any binding theological standard to regulate it; and finally the abandonment of a commitment to an evangelical mandate.[8] In every case, however, the process by which modern universities became secularized was a subtle one.

This secularism is most certainly not spiritually benign. Often it begins by slowly pushing God out of the classroom, in effect trivializing the import of religion as to make it irrelevant to the life of the thinking person. Will Herberg, a Jewish sociologist and philosopher, accurately concludes that "the prohibition against paying any classroom attention at all to God ... has the effect of removing from the students' intellectual consciousness the entire supernatural dimension."[9]

Foundational to the secularist's worldview is humanism—the belief that humans are the only "gods." And it is everywhere. According to Richard Bennett in *Your Quest for God,* "Humanism is proclaimed in the universities, newspapers, multinational corporate seminars, popular magazines, and on radio and television. 'Pamper yourself' is the selfish theme popularized by the advertising world."[10] This secular humanism is, says Bennett, "nothing more than the worshiping of man."[11] Part of that worship resides in the notion of control. "It is a self-sufficient world," writes Blamires. "It is a world whose temporality is conclusive and final, whose comprehensiveness of experience embraces all that is and that will ever be. It is a world run by men, its course determined by men. It is a world in which men have got things taped. The secular feels things are, on the whole, under control."[12] Occasionally, the tape comes a bit undone, as was the case on September 11, 2001. Soon, however, there is a return to the illusion of humankind's mastery. This is because the boundaries of the secularist's world are natural, tangible, and material. Moreover, because humans are the highest of the life forms, what humans experience with their senses is seen to constitute the totality of all that is.

Christianity and secularism are forever on an ideological collision course. It can be no other way. For the Christian, the world is spiritual and eternal, with planet Earth populated by fallen humans desperately in need of the grace of a loving God. In addition, the Christian sees secularist notions of human control as illusory. Instead, we humans are seen as impotent creatures, scurrying about and living in the illusion that we can live without God or that he does not even exist, all the while "making an appalling mess of things."[13]

Christianity holds that humans, far from being the final arbiters of reality, are created beings dependent on and subject to the will of a supernatural being. Furthermore, that divine being lovingly intervenes in human affairs. The Incarnation is the ultimate example of such intervention. For the secularist to acknowledge even the very existence of such a divine, infinite, intervening being would necessitate that he or she worship—honor and submit to—that God.[14] To do so would be to give up control of one's life, which is alien to the proud nature of humankind.

Bennett illustrates this disinclination to submit in the story of a noted European psychiatrist with whom Bennett's wife shared her faith. After reminding the psychiatrist of how several of his patients had been restored to healthy mental functioning through spiritual transformation after being adjudged to be beyond the reach of standard psychiatric intervention, this professional agreed to read the Bible. Seven weeks later, he told Bennett's wife that he was no longer an atheist. Still, it took him nearly a decade to embrace the Christian faith because he did not want to submit to God. "My problem is no longer intellectual," he acknowledged, "but I find that I am unwilling to accept the changes that would occur if I were to become a committed believer."[15] So the ideological gang war continues to rage, with the turf being the mind of the student.

The basis of the Christian/secular clash is the orientation of supernatural versus natural. From creationism in biology to views of human nature in sociology, from nihilism in literature to matters of justice in political science, this is true at every scholarly level.[16] The Christian and the secularist do share much knowledge, particularly in the tightly defined world of the physical sciences. Indeed, two plus two equals four on both of their calculators, and the elemental chart is identical for each. Even in the social and behavioral sciences, they agree on many concepts and theories, affirming common standards of scholarship. Despite these points of agreement, however, the irreconcilable differences that remain are, in a word, *profound*. They involve the most salient of issues, including one's orientation toward reality (supernatural, spiritual, and eternal for the Christian; natural, material, and temporal for the secularist) and one's source of truth—scriptural revelation and scientific discovery for the believer as opposed to science alone for the secularist.

Unlike much of postmodern culture that is largely indifferent to faith, secular education does not peacefully coexist with faith-centered learning. Rather, secularism is, of ideological necessity, antagonistic to faith and is largely characterized by a virulent, almost militant agnosticism, one that attacks the very faith tenets on which the American university was founded. Moreover, as more and more students are proselytized into a secularist, nontheistic mind-set, the de-Christianizing effect on the culture is escalated. Moreover, education molds an ever-growing segment of the population. Almost every one of society's leaders is a product of the nation's higher educational system.

►► Scientism: A Philosophy

The academic mainstream venerates as its supreme ruler the scientific method, which involves the following five steps:

1. making observations and collecting data in the absence of any preconceived notions;
2. forming a hypothesis (an educated guess) of how things happen;
3. testing the hypothesis;
4. using the results to accept or reject the hypothesis;
5. if the hypotheses is confirmed, having it accepted as valid after other scientists repeat the process and gain the same results.

Leaders of the academic mainstream have long worshiped at the altar of the scientific method. Harvard University president Charles William Eliot, marking the expansion of the American Museum of Natural History in 1877, stated: "In every field of study, in history, philosophy, and theology as well as in natural history and physics, it is now the scientific spirit, the scientific method which prevails."[17] Note Eliot's extension of the scientific method beyond the physical sciences. In the true spirit of the Enlightenment, Eliot went on to claim that social problems such as the prison system necessitated the scientific mind-set, which would "guide wisely the charitable action of the community; give a rational basis for penal legislation."[18]

Critical to the scientific method is that no respect is accorded any assumptions or beliefs derived from any other source. Such veneration of this single method becomes not science, but scientism, a philosophical worldview that views reality only in terms of that which is verifiable by this method. Because the practice of science is limited to the natural and temporal, there is no room even to entertain the supernatural. Scientism resembles a religion in its faith in the scientific method as the supreme revelation of truth.[19] It operates from the position that if a belief cannot be proven by employing the scientific method (or through unimpeachable linear logic), it is of no value. Furthermore, it implies that whatever cannot be measured does not exist, or at least should be regarded as not existing. By this standard, to base one's life on a transcendent reality—God—is more than folly; it is unscientific and, in short, unintellectual.

Although for many people, science is the way, the truth, and the life, it yields provisional rather than final truth. Philosopher David Hull points out its limits: "Scientists are not infallible. Science . . . is a process by which scientists go from some knowledge to more knowledge. . . . In general, scientists regard their empirical approach as a way of moving toward a closer approximation of reality. To claim more than that is to move beyond the limits of science into philosophy."[20]

But that is exactly what secularism and scientism are: philosophy. The unspoken but patently obvious implication that, more than being merely descriptions of reality, scientific statements are all there is to reality crosses the boundary of science into the world of philosophy. It enters the philosophical arena as certainly as does any dialogue on ethics in science. This foray into philosophy commits the same academic sin that theists are accused of when charged with "corrupting science" through their beliefs in a nonscientifically verifiable divine creator.

Nonetheless, for many students the high-voltage, agnostic nature of the academic environment can make retaining even the simplest elements of one's faith challenging. It is hardly surprising that many come to regard the faith of their parents as nothing more than ignorant, naïve ventures into unsophisticated, unscientific modes of thinking.

In a world suffused with scientism, notions of heaven and hell, angels and demons, a personal God and a holy book, begin to seem foolishly ludicrous—intellectual embarrassments—in the glare of educated doubt and questioning. To retain such "magical thinking" is regarded in the academic culture as the intellectual equivalent of wearing a bowling shirt to a formal occasion in midtown Manhattan. By these standards, the gospel is indeed foolishness, as the apostle Paul (who atheist Sigmund Freud cited as one of the world's truly brilliant figures) put it. In fact, the very specter of a member of a community of scholars believing in such unempirical rubbish is scarcely entertained. Eighteenth-century philosopher David Hume put it rather bluntly: "The Christian religion not only was first attended with miracles, but even at this day cannot be believed by any reasonable person without one."[21]

Though most of these secular institutions are served by various campus clergy, the latter are widely viewed as obsequious fools indulging in fairy-tale thinking, who help students feel better about themselves with God-talk. Their critics, however, are equally devoid of sophistication in religious matters, making them hardly qualified to comment. According to famed University of California anthropologist Robert Lowie, "Modern intellectuals are really poor judges of religion since it is so remote to their experience—they are, in actual fact, 'spiritual illiterates.'"[22]

Notwithstanding, faith-based concepts—the very bedrock of many students' formative belief systems—are objects of ridicule and indicators of a lack of educational refinement. Intellectual discrimination is common in the classroom, notes anthropologist Jacob Loewen. "This may be very benign, as when a professor says: 'I have no intentions of hurting anyone's faith,' but then launches into a rather unsubtle ridicule of belief in the supernatural."[23]

Adherents of faith often risk the siege of active attack. Ravi Zacharias illustrates this by relating an experience at a major university in which he was to play the token theist's role in a presentation on ethics. After the event, a student approached him with a dilemma. She told Zacharias that her professor had assigned her the task of critiquing his presentation, but that she found herself actually agreeing with Zacharias's points. When Zacharias suggested the student acknowledge this accord in her paper, the student quickly dismissed the idea as a feasible option, stating that her grade would be "docked" were she to concur with his theistic framework.[24]

Such is the mind-set of secular academe. To entertain the idea that the universe was created by a holy, almighty, triune God, that he is to be worshiped and related to personally through the historical yet divine Jesus of Nazareth, is to invite a megadose of humiliation and intellectual annihilation from many in the academic community. That was the experience of Marvin Olasky, professor of journalism at the University of Texas, a scholar who has contributed 11 books and over 350 articles to the learning enterprise.

A onetime member of the Communist Party USA, Olasky came to faith in 1976 while pursuing his Ph.D., almost losing his academic career in the process. Olasky and his communist views were regaled when he left the *Boston Globe* for life as a graduate student at the University of Michigan in 1973. "Professors there were so impressed by my theorizing that they wrote recommendations citing my 'brilliance' and 'genius.' They also increased my fellowship. (Get Marx. It pays.)," quips Olasky.[25] He also notes satirically that these faculty members revised their estimate of his genius downward after his conversion. The original chairperson of his dissertation committee who "had written glowingly about my intellect when I was spouting communist dialectic, decided that I had suddenly become stupid," Olasky relates. "Because the academic environment had grown so politically hostile toward me, I left to join the DuPont public affairs department in 1978."[26]

In brief, the intellectual arena is not one in which truth is measured against one's religious belief system, but one ruled solely by the measure of science. Though rarely carried out in practice, all quests for knowledge are to begin with the null hypothesis, the notion that there is nothing until something verifiable emerges. Assumptions, givens, presuppositions—other than that the scientific method is the infallible guide to knowledge—are to be eliminated. Gone now is the certainty of Scripture, the Apostle's Creed, and the catechisms. They count for nothing. In fact, the thing to do is either to get one's intellectual union card punched by joining the community of doubt or to simply live in a world of quiet, intellectual uncertainty.

▸▸ Naturalism

There is more than doubt operating here. A subtle, cunning, insidious philosophy called naturalism is being advanced. Naturalism, by any standard, is diametrically opposed to the supernaturalism of a Christian worldview. It regards humans as nothing more or less than objects of nature. Human distinctiveness is not the work of a master creator but merely the result of purposeless processes—random genetic mutations and the process of natural selection. No activity, no human emotion, no behavior, is viewed as existing outside of these chance processes.

According to the doctrines of naturalism, for example, love does not reflect the nature of the creator but is the result of male and female humans getting together to spawn children and remaining together, points out philosopher Alvin Plantinga in his critique. There is even a naturalistic explanation for altruism. Far from being a higher order of functioning, some naturalists regard it as likely the result of a genetic defect. The thinking goes like this: While the rational functioning human organizes her behavior around self-preservation and enhancement, altruists unthinkingly behave according to what the society directs them to do. Their altruism indicates a failure to distinguish between behavior that benefits their own selves and behavior that does not.[27]

Indeed, any pursuit of the truth in higher education ignores the possibility of the transcendent. Darel Rex Finley, a scientist who has come to reject naturalistic evolution on research-based scientific grounds, describes the plight of those who do not commit to the agnostic perspective: "Unbelievers are treated very poorly.... Insinuations are made that the only reason to doubt (much less disbelieve) evolution is that a religious bias requires the doubter to stick to one rigid scenario regardless of what the evidence holds." All the while, evolutionists are regarded as "objective scientists with no biases, who are willing to consider any possibility, but are required by the provable evidence to believe in evolution."[28]

Yet the history of science is littered with commitments to false theory. Jimmy Davis of Union University relates the story Joseph Priestley, an accomplished scientist who in his experimental research identified seven gases, including oxygen.[29] For many years, combustion was explained according to the "phlogiston theory" of German scientists Johann Bechler and Georg Stah. In 1702, these scientists proposed that when a substance burns, a chemical called phlogiston escapes into the air. Plants absorb phlogiston, which accounts for why dried plants are highly combustible. The phlogiston theory held sway in chemistry for eighty years. It was a fruitful theory leading to the isolation and study of hydrogen, nitrogen, nitrous oxide, nitric oxide, carbon dioxide, sulfur dioxide, hydrogen chloride, ammonia, and oxygen gases. It ignored, however, the issues involved in mass changes.

Another chemist, Frenchman Antoine Lavoisier, determined that phlogiston did not exist and that combustion emerged from a reaction of oxygen with material. He also found that the mass of the products is equal to the mass of the reactants (called the Law of Conservation of Mass). Although Lavoisier has been immortalized as a father of modern chemistry, chemistry was not his day job. A tax collector, he was guillotined during the French Revolution. Lavoisier's discoveries amounted to what is called a paradigm shift in the discipline, one not all his contemporaries were able to accept. Among them was the able Priestley. Both he and Lavoisier performed the same reactions, but because of their different assumptions, the two collected and interpreted the data differently. Clearly, the brilliant Priestley was in error. "As the example of Priestley shows," says Davis, "going from information to knowledge is much more than just the facts. One's worldview will color how information is processed into knowledge."[30]

Scientists are not always open-minded. In that vein, Finley finds the evolutionists' charge as to the bias-driven closed-mindedness of creationists fallacious: "The truth is usually the reverse. Creationists . . . are open to many possible ways that God might have chose to create life. . . . Evolutionists, guided by a bias in favor of atheism are locked into a single scenario, naturalistic evolution, and must defend it regardless of what the evidence shows."[31]

Make no mistake, in the academic mainstream, naturalism is the lion king of the intellectual jungle. Stanley Fish, Dean of the College of Liberal Arts and Sciences at the University of Illinois, Chicago, professing no religious belief, states the case in an unvarnished fashion: "Academic freedom, rather than being open to all points of view, is open to all points of view only so long as they offer themselves with the reserve and diffidence appropriate to Enlightenment decorums, only so long as they offer themselves for correction."[32]

"There is not enough room for the New Social Order *and* religion," concludes Buckley. "The New Order is philosophically wedded to the doctrine that the test of truth is its ability to win acceptance by the majority."[33] Genuine liberalism ends among the adherents of academic freedom the moment one asserts the existence of God and his immutable truths. While on the face of it the scientific majority wants to purge the academic community of those who engage in unscholarly thinking, more is going on. "They really mean that those people who disagree with their version of truth, who disagree that pragmatism, positivism, and materialism are the highest values, are in error. And with characteristic intolerance toward differing creeds, they seek to liquidate their opponents by talking about such things as democracy and divisiveness."[34]

Short of possessing singularly impressive preinterview academic credentials, it is difficult to imagine an openly evangelical scholar not facing severe opposition were she to seek an appointment to the faculty of a prestigious research university. In fact, a friend of mine who is a senior professor at a large state university was involved in assessing a candidate for his department's faculty. During the interview the candidate—not a religious person himself—made a passing reference to a religious community near the campus.

"With that," said my friend, "the usually cerebral academic dean flew into an emotional tirade, lambasting anyone and everyone who might entertain the slightest shred of religious belief as being moronic."

The late Carl Sagan, in the opening of his famous television series *Cosmos,* put it succinctly: "The Cosmos is all there is or ever was or ever will be." Richard Dawkins reflected the near adrenaline-like fervor of the proponents of naturalistic evolution. "It is absolutely safe to say that if you meet someone who claims not to believe in evolution," says Dawkins, "that person is ignorant, stupid, or insane (or wicked, but I'd rather not consider that)."[35]

The reigning plausibility structure in mainstream academe has been and continues to be naturalism—an outgrowth of the Enlightenment—particularly in the physical sciences. But naturalism has tentacles that extend well into other areas of inquiry.

Notes

1. Nicholas Wolterstorff, *Reason within the Bounds of Religion* (Grand Rapids: Eerdmans, 1984), 113–16. Wolterstorff builds a careful and excellent case for the purpose of Christian scholarship, one that goes beyond elitism to service.

2. David S. Dockery and Gregory Alan Thornbury, "Shaping the Academic Enterprise: An Interview with Carla Sanderson, Provost, Union University," in *Shaping a Christian Worldview,* ed. David S. Dockery and Gregory Alan Thornbury (Nashville: Broadman and Holman, 2002), 388.

3. Barry Burke, "Post-Modernism and Post-Modernity," http://www.infed.org/biblio/b-postmd.htm (accessed July 17, 2002). Burke reviews Enlightenment thinking in the context of postmodernism.

4. George M. Marsden, *The Soul of the American University* (New York: Oxford University Press, 1994). Marsden traces the history of unbelief in the mainstream university system in his book *The Outrageous Idea of Christian Scholarship* (New York: Oxford University Press, 1997), 14–23.

5. Charles Seymour, quoted in William F. Buckley Jr., *Nearer, My God* (San Diego: Harvest, 1998), 29–30.

6. William F. Buckley Jr., *God and Man at Yale* (Chicago: Regnery, 1951), xv–xvi.

7. Gregory Alan Thornbury, "The Lessons of History," in Dockery and Thornbury, *Shaping a Christian Worldview*, 44–47.

8. Ibid., 50.

9. Will Herberg, quoted in Buckley, *Nearer, My God,* 227.

10. Richard A. Bennett, *Your Quest for God* (Franklin, TN: Providence, 1998), 82.

11. Ibid.

12. Harry Blamires, *The Christian Mind* (Ann Arbor, MI: Servant, 1997), 73.

13. Ibid.

14. Ibid., 68.

15. Bennett, *Your Quest for God,* 18.

16. Blamires, *The Christian Mind,* 74–75.

17. Charles William Eliot, "Address on the Opening of the New Building," in *American Museum of Natural History, 8th and 9th Annual Reports* (1878), 49–52, quoted in Jimmy H. Davis, "Faith and Learning," in Dockery and Thornbury, *Shaping a Christian Worldview,* 131.

18. Ibid.

19. George W. Andrews, "Geology," in *Christ and the Modern Mind,* ed. Robert W. Smith (Downers Grove, IL: InterVarsity, 1972), 264.

20. D. L. Hull, *Science as a Process: An Evolutionary Account of the Social and Conceptual Development of Science* (Chicago: University of Chicago Press, 1988), 26, quoted in Walter R. Hearn, *Being a Christian in Science* (Downers Grove, IL: InterVarsity, 1997), 19.

21. David Hume, "Of Miracles," *An Enquiry Concerning Human Understanding,* 1748.

22. Robert H. Lowie, "Religion in Human Life," *American Anthropologist* 65 (1963): 532–42, quoted in Jacob A. Loewen, "Anthropology," in Smith, *Christ and the Modern Mind,* 139.

23. Jacob Loewen, "Anthropology," in Smith, *Christ and the Modern Mind,* 140.

24. Ravi Zacharias, *Jesus among Other Gods* (Nashville: Word, 2000), 145–46.

25. Marvin Olasky, "Marxism and Me," in *Professors Who Believe,* ed. Paul M. Anderson (Downers Grove, IL: InterVarsity, 1998), 175.

26. Ibid., 176–77.

27. Alvin Plantinga, "Christian Scholarship: Need," http://www.leaderu.com/aip/docs/plantec1.html (accessed July 16, 2002). Plantinga, a philosopher, is one of the foremost authorities on Christian scholarship. In these lecture notes published on the Internet, Plantinga critiques naturalism and relativism, among other things, from a Christian perspective.

28. Darel Rex Finley, "Why I Disbelieve Evolution," http://freeweb.pdq.net/smokin/evolution (accessed January 10, 2001). There are a number of excellent websites that critique naturalistic evolution intelligently, such as http://www.creationism.org and http://www.infidels.org/library/modern/science/creationism/index.shtml.

29. Davis, "Faith and Learning," in Dockery and Thornbury, *Shaping a Christian Worldview,* 133.

30. Ibid.

31. Finley, "Why I Disbelieve Evolution."

32. Alan Wolfe, "The Opening of the Evangelical Mind," pt. 4 of *The Loyalty-Oath Problem,* http://www.theatlantic.com/issues/2000/10/wolfe4.htm (accessed July 17, 2002). Wolfe published a four-part series on evangelical thinkers' attempts to "revitalize their tradition" in the *Atlantic Monthly.*

33. William F. Buckley Jr., *Let Us Talk of Many Things* (Roseville, CA: Prima, 2000), 9.

34. Ibid., 12.

35. Richard Dawkins, review of *Blueprints,* by Maitland Edey, *New York Times,* April 9, 1989, 35.

3

THE RELATIVES
OF NATURALISM

F lowing from the catechism of naturalism are several other powerful doctrines, including value freedom, reductionism, and empiricism.

⇥ The Myth of Value Freedom

One doctrine is that Western education is essentially value-free. Despite powerful philosophical challenges to this myth, it lingers on. Value freedom suggests
that scholarship be carried out in the absence of any preexisting values or theoretical frameworks. But it goes beyond that. It holds that such an approach is
the only valid form of education. Value-based education becomes an oxymoron
by this standard.

The commitment to value freedom is a value in itself, when one considers
it. It is based on the premise that to enter the scholarly fray with any preset values is to stain the objective purity of the scientific process by possibly prejudg-
ing whatever it is one is studying. Science, like a yardstick, is thought to be
value-neutral, amoral. According to this doctrine, the fear of God is not the
beginning of wisdom, as the writer of Proverbs (9:10) put it. It is a mental state
that corrupts any effort at gaining knowledge and understanding reality.

This primary doctrine is a relative of naturalism. It is also arrogant and
seductive. It is arrogant in its implication that contemporary scholarship is
essentially devoid of subjectivity and bias, its results needing to be accepted with
near-devout seriousness. This strain of arrogance is evident in graduate schools
in which the more celebrated research professors are accorded near-reverential
respect, regarded as the purveyors of the latest truth. Students are intellectually
seduced by the enormous prestige associated with academic expertise. Hence, a
near-castelike status system develops among both professors and students in
various graduate departments, with those at the top revered, even envied, by
their peers. Posturing is common, as students vie for the good opinion of the

professors in charge of the various fiefdoms within the kingdom. How can it not be so? With humans being the highest form of intelligent life, and knowledge thought to be objectively validated, those at the peak of the knowledge hierarchy quite understandably will be regarded as the finest of the species. This is the value system.

But it is nonsense. In reality, research and investigation are almost never carried on without some presuppositions. In the world of criminology, for example, the best detective work begins with a set of assumptions about the commission of a crime. These assumptions are then "tested" as evidence is gathered and assembled. This process parallels much of current practice in higher educational research. Make no mistake, almost without exception, researchers begin with a set of beliefs (often called a hypothesis) about a matter under study and then go about the task of validating or invalidating those preset notions. Furthermore, like Priestley and phlogiston, the hypotheses that precede the research process shape the very nature of the investigative endeavor—what variables are tested, how they are tested for, and how the data are interpreted.

Implicit in the value-free definition of science is that such scholarship is a nontheoretical exercise of observation and experimentation. It is focused largely on the physical world, looking for cause-and-effect relationships. As such, it ignores primary, ultimate, and certainly supernatural causes.[1] The unvarnished reality is that all branches of science involve theory as well as observation. Physicists, for example, tend to identify themselves either as experimentalists or theorists. That we now have hybrid fields such as geophysics and biochemistry suggests the presence of theoretical notions regarding interactions and relationships among these otherwise pure or "exact" sciences. Beyond hybrid science, there is historical science, which tries to establish what has already happened but cannot be repeated. Cosmology, historical geology, and macroevolutionary biology are examples of this jaunt out of certainty into theory.

To apply the scientific method itself involves several steps of faith. Among them is the belief or faith that the natural world is consistent and able to be understood through the use of rational analysis. In addition, scholars, though often projecting an air of intellectual objectivity, are frequently ideological captives of their own educational experience. Using personality theory in psychology as an example, Mansell Pattison points out that not only is any such theory "grounded in philosophy, whether the theorist is aware of it or not," but psychologists adopt "whatever metaphysical philosophy was popular in their graduate school experience and unwittingly incorporate it into their psychology."[2] Pattison makes a vital point here. Often a newly hired university professor will proudly proclaim his academic pedigree, telling one and all that he studied at XYZ university, under the direction of a foremost authority in the field. What that same professor is not say-ing (and perhaps not realizing) is that he almost certainly has internalized every theoretical bias of the mentors of which he is so proud.

Institutions and departments have known biases. One school of social work may be regarded as Freudian in its approach to psychiatric social work. Another may take a community focus, arising from a Jane Addams, Hull House tradi-tion. One department of economics may be tilted to the right, with Milton Fried-man's thinking front and center. Another may be more liberal, with John Kenneth Galbraith as its ideological patron saint. Political science departments are bastions of ideologies. I taught at a university in which the department was, for years, chaired by a leftist Quaker pacifist who taught every course in a tuto-rial fashion. Upon his retirement, a younger Ph.D. who was an ardent partici-pant in Republican politics replaced him. The student majors, caught in the middle of this transition, encountered a jarring academic experience.

In the spirit of Pattison's observation, Antonio Chiareli reminds us that "everyone is someone's disciple." For Chiareli, who is firmly convinced "that Christian higher education in general must go the distance in establishing the value of the Christian worldview in the liberal arts," the question becomes whose disciple we are, and whose disciples we are preparing our students to become.[3]

The very notion of a value-free education is preposterous, straining the credulity of a rational person. Inherent in one's decision to pursue knowledge is a personal value. "You have to be dead to be value-neutral," says writer Samuel Blumenfeld.[4] Values are basic to daily functioning, notes Al Gini. "Values—even bad values—guide how we make decisions and the kinds of decisions we make."[5]

The poet T. S. Eliot made the point in a lecture at the University of Chicago in 1950, stating, "But the moment we ask about the purpose of anything, we may be involving ourselves in asking about the purpose of everything." Simply by defining education, one is led to ask about the nature of humankind and its very purpose. There is, invariably, an implicit strain or philosophy or theology present.[6]

The existence of "special interest" studies (African American, gay, feminist, etc.) further repudiates the notion of value freedom. These culturally relative perspectives are based on sets of common values, shared world-and-life views, through which all of reality is interpreted. Moreover, simply to commit oneself to the scientific method as the only mode by which one pursues knowledge, then, is itself to act out a value. To select a field, much less a subject of inquiry, involves a value-based decision. When academics engage in conferences about the ethics of science and research, they cease to be scientists and become philoso-phers involved in a subject almost inextricably tied to religion.

It follows, then, that philosophically you either engage in your scholarship believing there is a God or you do not; you either believe that humans are spiritual and live beyond this life or you do not; you either regard life as having purpose or you do not.[7] Sociologist David Moberg believes that behind any person's "decisions lies ultimately a philosophy of life that provides the guiding values on the basis of which specific choices are made. This fact has led some philosophers, theologians, and social science theorists to say that every man has a religion or pseudo-religion of some kind."[8] If nothing else, realizing there is a measure of faith required in adopting any worldview should move the Christian thinker off the defensive when in dialogue with those of an atheistic or agnostic spiritual mind-set.

One can hardly overstate the importance of dispelling the myth of value freedom, because it is so often wielded as a weapon against believing scholars. By claiming that real science (using *science* as synonymous with verifiable fact) results from virgin-pure, value-free scholarship, the skeptic can then label every shred of Christian scholarship as invalid, because it is not sufficiently founded on such a base. In fact, much Christian scholarship is met with a sneering dismissal by secularists, because its scholars are regarded as coming from a subjective point of view. In reality, education's claim to be value-free is no more valid than a newspaper's claim to absolute objectivity in its coverage. In short, the secular university does not offer anything approaching value freedom. It offers an agnostic, if not atheistic, point of view. Buckley, in rebutting the ugly charge that value-based learning is not education but indoctrination, stated the case sharply:

> Just as it is almost impossible for an individual to be entirely neutral, so it is almost impossible for a department within a college to be entirely neutral, or even for a college to be entirely neutral. "Indoctrination," in the sense of the urging of one doctrine over another, goes on all the time; indeed, some of the most vociferous academic-freedomites are themselves the premier indoctrinators.[9]

One could say that much of this "value-free" bias is rooted in a spiritually rebellious attitude. There is nothing academics thirst for more ardently than to be revered as an "authority" in a given area of study, almost regardless of the trifling significance of the subject. Such a designation confers the near-godlike status on a scholar, to which we referred earlier. In Christian scholarship, there is only one authority: God. We do not create knowledge. We do not even contribute to it. We discover what already exists, placed there by the Creator. Glory, and therefore worship, goes not to the scholar but to God, the authority. Human pride, so endemic to intellectual endeavor, is necessarily removed from the formula. Not surprisingly, the more erudite and elite the mainstream academic institution, the more antagonistic it will often be to matters of faith. The reason is likely lodged in the greater presence of "authorities," human "creators of knowledge" who worship their own intellects as the final arbiters of truth.

▸ Reductionism

"Value-free" education is more accurately called reductionistic, because it claims to accept as valid only that which is observable or experimentally verifiable. It implies that what cannot be measured does not exist. One cannot equate the destruction of a Rembrandt to that of a soiled piece of paper, even though both consist of essentially the same material.[10] Glenn Marsch exposes the silly "scientific triumphalism" of reductionism: "Science cannot reduce the essence of a Monet painting to a prescribed orientation of paint blotches, each of which is defined by a specific absorption spectrum, and science cannot better introduce us to George Washington with a clone from his DNA than history can with his letters and the record of witnesses."[11]

As noted earlier, even statements based on tightly defined scientific standards are at best partial, incomplete descriptions of reality.[12] For example, a research psychologist's study of visual perception will differ greatly from a physicist's study of the same phenomenon. An astronomer, who, though interested in visual perceptions of electromagnetic radiation, is rather disinterested in the physiological and psychological findings because they are gained out of the range of the telescope.[13] Moreover, the more the "exact" physical sciences come into play, the more the very process by which knowledge is gained moves in precisely the opposite direction from holism. Hearn illustrates this in a fable in which a social scientist, noting a sheep on a Scottish hillside, casually remarks that the sheep in Scotland are black.

"What you mean," corrects the biologist, "is that at least one sheep in Scotland is black."

"No, no," interjects the physicist, "you need to be much more precise. All we can conclude from this observation is that there is at least one sheep in Scotland, one side of which is black."[14]

The reductionist perspective becomes one emphasizing limitation. "The totality of the universe is so vast and complex," says Moberg, "that man's mind and senses can comprehend but a small portion of its totality."[15] To make that search for reality manageable, scholars move away from holistic thinking toward reductionism. Major universities are constructed on a reductionist model. These institutions commonly contain a number of "colleges," as in the college of behavioral sciences, the college of physical sciences, and the college of human-ities. Within each college are a variety of departments, such as sociology and psychology, which are often located within a college of behavioral sciences. Within each department are specialties, such as experimental psychology and abnormal psychology. Within each specialty are subspecialties. In the case of abnormal psychology, these might include the study of psychoses and person-ality disorders. And so on.[16] Therefore, when one hears academic professionals make declarative and sweeping reality statements, it is wise to exercise the same skepticism toward these pronouncements as the reductionists express toward religious belief.

Scientific statements are also to some extent distorted because of their very incompleteness. Henry Morgenthau provides a succinct summary of the matter, stating, "Science will tell us what things are real but will refuse to say what is reality."[17] The late Donald M. MacKay, a brain physiologist, used the analogy of an electric sign to point out the absurdity of reductionism. An electrical engineer could render a thorough account of the operation of the sign, though one would hardly expect the engineer to discuss what the sign said. Were it to say Live Nude Girls, however, the sign takes on additional meaning. With that knowledge, a sociologist could lecture at great length as to its cultural significance, while an economist would likely focus on its marketing impact. Those involved in gen-der studies might suggest that the sign is nothing but a form of sexual exploita-tion, while political scientists may become enmeshed entirely in the legal ramifications regarding community standards. In sum, although each scholar could describe the sign at exhaustive length, doing so as if its significance lay totally in that scholar's area of expertise, each of these limited "it's nothing but" descriptions falls far short of an adequate explanation of the sign and its entire significance.[18]

This is what reductionism does. It provides a "nothing but" statement that most assuredly excludes God from the explanation. As such, religion is at best trivialized—made so insignificant as to be unworthy of being a part of the equa-tion—and at worst branded as utter nonsense.

▸▸ Empiricism

Because the roots of naturalism are in biology and in the work of Darwin and his disciples, many naïvely think its impact is confined to the physical sciences. It is not. To understand the pervasive power of naturalism, it is necessary to understand the doctrine of empiricism, which is derived from naturalism. Empiricism, much used in the behavioral or social sciences, centers on the belief that life is to be understood through the use of concrete observation, the classic scientific method, and the basic laws of logic. Empiricism is naturalism's closest relative.

Indisputably, empiricism has brought great value to humanity. Everything from air travel to computer capabilities has benefited from this method of attaining knowledge. In the physical sciences, virtually every medical advance has been generated by this approach. Moreover, in the social (or behavioral) sciences, this careful, disciplined methodology has freed us from ugly stereotypes and unexamined prejudices.

Nonetheless, in the world of empirical knowledge, all aspects of the universe, including humankind, are studied from a naturalistic perspective, as phenomena without purpose or meaning. Essentially, no concern is given to human nature, ultimate causes, or any other nonmaterial aspects. Because these matters are outside the scope of empirical verification, they are matters of "profound indifference." The problem with empiricism does not lie in its careful approach to scholarship, but rather in its tendency to dismiss as nonexistent the ultimate or nonmaterial, simply because they have no verifiable linkages to empiricism.[19] It is at this point that empiricism becomes an integral part of the naturalistic philosophy of scientism. Empirical research functions as a religious exercise in secular, materialistic society, says Hearn.[20] It indeed becomes a religion for those who continue to believe that as science continues to unravel the mysteries of the natural universe, it will eventually solve all human problems. The logical corollary to this belief is that philosophy and religion are impediments to those solutions because they introduce moral judgments and other nonmaterial concerns.[21]

Chiareli witnessed an event during his graduate experience at Northwestern University that illustrates this dismissal of the nonmaterial. An atheistic professor, while thumbing through the chapters of Smelser's *Handbook of Sociology,* boasted aloud how he had published in almost every area of the discipline discussed in the book. There was one exception: chapter 15 on the sociology of religion. "Well, I've never written anything on this. I just don't know why serious sociologists bother with such things," he remarked, much to the mirth of the graduate students in attendance.[22] Chiareli acknowledges the particularly antireligious bias on the part of this professor. "But the fact that not once during my graduate years did I encounter a Christian sociologist teaching in the discipline's mainstream, is some evidence of its overwhelmingly secular orientation."[23]

This negative attitude toward religion can come from unlikely sources. A graduate student at a major university experienced this firsthand within the school's religion department. "I quickly learned that some religious teachers were actively indoctrinating undergraduates against the Bible," he reported.

"When I talked at length with one professor about it, he argued that 'academic freedom' meant that he could attack Christianity and Judaism, and grade down biblically conservative students, if he liked. At the same time, he argued that any teacher who publicly acknowledged that he or she believed in God should be fired."[24]

Empiricism is the finger of naturalism that directs much scholarship in the humanities and social sciences. The test of validity, offered back in the eighteenth century by philosopher David Hume, continues to frame the empiricist's mind-set rather well. "If we take in our hand any volume: of, say, divinity or school of metaphysics, for instance; let us ask, Does it contain any abstract reasoning concerning quantity of number? No. Does it contain any experimental reasoning concerning matter of fact and existence? No. Commit it to the flames; For it can contain nothing but sophistry and illusion."[25]

Though no *stated* philosophical framework or perspective guides empiricism, as in the case of the scientific method, it is not without its own underlying beliefs or presuppositions. Among them are the existence of a material world, its consistent and rational nature, the validity of sensory perception (the ability to read data accurately), and the basic rules of logic. In addition, there is one moral precept: the importance of honesty in research. False, "fudged," or knowingly distorted data is unacceptable, and its perpetrators are condemned. This issue of academic honesty is not advanced as simply a pragmatic way of keeping the playing field level for competing researchers. It has a moral (nonscientific) tone, and violators are often dealt with severely, treated with near scarlet-letter judgment.

Even philosophy, a discipline generally thought to fall outside the boundaries of empiricism, has not escaped its impact. Theology, once the context in which philosophy was studied, is now regarded as a small subdiscipline of philosophy. The latter, in its focus on meaning, has tended to restrict itself to very tight laws of logic, removing many nonmaterial assumptions.

The "religious nature" of empiricism has a lengthy heritage. The nineteenth-century father of sociology, Auguste Comte, in his positivistic (or essentially empirical) stage of societal and scientific evolution, actually believed that the Christian clergy would eventually be replaced with a new type of moral teacher, one whose ideas would be scientifically verifiable.[26] The study of deviant or antisocial behavior provides an example of this very development. In previous eras, such behavior was defined as sinful, wrong, or immoral. Enlightenment thinking provided a different spin, with deviance largely viewed as unnatural and out of rhythm with the natural laws governing human behavior. In the empirical realm, individual responsibility may be partly or fully removed, with such behavior studied in terms of environmental, and even biological, determinants.

The social sciences—arising from what was called "social philosophy," practiced by Comte among others—have made an intense commitment to empiricism. These disciplines, particularly psychology and sociology, have long suffered from what might best be called an "intellectual inferiority complex," being regarded by those in the physical sciences as soft, inexact, "armchair" sciences. In response, these spheres of inquiry have exhibited what can best be described as a collective compensatory reaction, adopting tight empirical, statistical, and experimental methods in their study. A glance at the mainline scholarly journals in these disciplines will reveal a welter of empirical scholarship in the absence of thought-provoking, theoretical discourses.

▸▸ Sociologism

Basic sociology textbooks commonly devote as much as a chapter to the general topic of religion. The treatment of religion in these texts is typical of the bias toward empirical analyses. A review of sociology texts indicates that religion is commonly defined as "a set of behavior patterns dealing with the ultimate issues of life."[27] Behavior is stressed in the absence of personal commitment. Moreover, texts often lump all belief systems and spiritual quests—even references to magic—under the amorphous heading "Religion." No effort is made to distinguish among even the major religions. Hence, the notion that all religions are essentially the same is implied.

Students become all but immunized against making a genuine commitment to a religious faith, because they are directed to study religion in a wholly dispassionate and empirical fashion. Because the very possibility of there being a genuinely transcendent, supernatural entity is totally dismissed, there is no incentive to examine more deeply the truth or error of the various belief systems. Perhaps worse, the very study of religion is often denigrated because, as in the case of Chiareli's graduate professor, religion itself is unscientific and therefore of minimal import.

Sociology as discipline, however, despite its attempts to certify itself in the scientific community, is far from entirely scientific in nature. There is a vast amount of social behavior for which no explanation can be derived from empirical or even statistical data. Theories, often based on limited data, are used to account for such phenomena. These theories contain value judgments and perspectives of reality that are no more empirically verifiable than Christian notions. The same texts that fail to differentiate among religions and even trivialize the subject in general will examine subjects such as culture, deviance, majority-minority relations, and social change with extensive, wholly nonempirical explanations of major theories, treating the latter as fact.

This theoretical aspect is particularly evident in the "special interest" studies. Central to gender studies, for example, is the notion of sexism. While few would challenge its existence, sexism is difficult to define in empirical fashion, because it emanates from a state of mind. Like a foul in basketball, it is a judgment call. This notwithstanding, sexism is a label often attached to people and movements with little empirical support for the charge.

The sociology texts chide religions for their claims to ultimate truth. Instead, cultural relativism is promoted as objective fact, making one culture's religious beliefs no more valid than another. In addition, religion is regularly perceived as having little relevance to the secular aspects of one's life. It is, according to Blamires, intellectually emasculated.[28] Life is presented as compartmentalized, with religion occupying a compartment of decreasing import. In brief, religion is treated as a mere cultural element with attendant functions and dysfunctions for the society of which it is a part. It is studied factually in terms of ecclesia, denominations, and sects, correlated statistically with social class and political affiliation. Thus, religion is shredded from its supernatural grounding and is therefore stripped of its power. Although a scientific analysis of religion is appropriate in an academic discipline, there remains the unmistakable implication that such an analysis provides sufficient insight into all there is to religion, that for a thinking person to live life with God at the center would be utter folly.

When one views the nature of the sociological mind-set, one notices that there exists a sociological frame of reference, or view of reality, a secular theology that envelops every subject, including religion—one that is far more influential than any religion as a perspective on life. In this form of scientism, "sociologism" we will call it, religion is studied as a dependent, rather than independent, variable.[29] This empirically driven mind-set is so pervasive throughout the social sciences that one is likely to find fewer theists, much less Christians, there than in the physical sciences.

Quite apart from the matter of faith and learning, this commitment to empiricism has had some unfortunate consequences for the social sciences. Theory building has suffered due to the focus on complex research designs complete with rotating matrices and regression analyses. Form (or design) is elevated over substance (the relevance of the subject), giving rise to what a cynical conference colleague of mine called "systematizing the obvious." An aspiring scholar is more likely to get published by submitting an intricate, statistical examination of left-handedness among a subgroup of felons in a prison population than with a scintillating and creative theory as to social origins of criminal behavior. Microanalyses of social phenomena, because such endeavors can be experimentally controlled, predominate over larger reviews of accepted theoretical models.

Not surprisingly, liberal arts students who wish to study in the fields of sociology and psychology in hopes of understanding individual and collective behavior more fully, often find their academic experiences frustrating and unfulfilling. Pedantic research ventures and studies focused on minutiae, aimed at developing at least superficially intellectually respectable models (theories), are at best annoying and at worst intellectually stifling. In any case, they characterize the academic downside of the worship of empiricism.

Again, the reigning plausibility structure in much of mainstream academe has been and continues to be naturalism and its related doctrines. Pure and simple, it is the ultimate reality in the academic mainstream. Not to be a naturalist is not to be taken seriously in many intellectual communities. It may even mean being driven out of them. Despite the overwhelming theism in the nation, that such a paradigm is so universally accepted suggests that many Christians have divorced faith from learning (and science), abandoning the Christian mind. This allows them, in theory, to exist next to one another, while in fact permitting naturalism to be the final arbiter, the intellectual referee of what is deemed reality.

Notes

1. Walter R. Hearn, *Being a Christian in Science* (Downers Grove, IL: InterVarsity, 1997), 17.
2. E. Mansell Pattison, "Psychology," in *Christ and the Modern Mind,* ed. Robert W. Smith (Downers Grove, IL: InterVarsity, 1972), 188.
3. Antonio A. Chiareli, "Christian Worldview and the Social Sciences," in *Shaping a Christian Worldview,* ed. David S. Dockery and Gregory Alan Thornbury (Nashville: Broadman and Holman, 2002), 241.
4. Samuel Blumenfeld, quoted in Al Gini, "Do the Right Thing," *Loyola* (Summer 2001): 27.
5. Ibid.
6. Harry Blamires, *Where Do We Stand?* (Ann Arbor, MI: Servant, 1980), 53.
7. Ibid., 52.
8. David O. Moberg, "The Social Sciences," in Smith, *Christ and the Modern Mind,* 115.
9. William F. Buckley Jr., *Let Us Talk of Many Things* (Roseville, CA: Prima, 2000), 106.
10. Richard A. Bennett, *Your Quest for God* (Franklin, TN: Providence, 1998), 102.
11. Glenn A. Marsch, "Christian Worldview and Natural Science," in Dockery and Thornbury, *Shaping a Christian Worldview,* 165.
12. Hearn, *Being a Christian in Science,* 17.
13. Ibid.
14. Ibid., 18.
15. Moberg, "The Social Sciences," in Smith, *Christ and the Modern Mind,* 110.
16. Ibid.

17. Henry Morgenthau, quoted in Charles E. Hummel, "The Natural Sciences," in Smith, *Christ and the Modern Mind,* 242.

18. George M. Marsden, *The Outrageous Idea of Christian Scholarship* (New York: Oxford University Press, 1997), 75.

19. John Sanzoni, "Sociology," in Smith, *Christ and the Modern Mind,* 126.

20. Hearn, *Being a Christian in Science,* 42.

21. Charles E. Hummel, "The Natural Sciences," in Smith, *Christ and the Modern Mind,* 246.

22. Chiareli, "Christian Worldview and the Social Sciences," in Dockery and Thornbury, *Shaping a Christian Worldview,* 240.

23. Ibid., 240–41.

24. Craig Keener, letter to the editor, *InterVarsity Magazine,* Fall 1992, 2, quoted in Marsden, *The Outrageous Idea of Christian Scholarship,* 22.

25. David Hume, quoted in Ravi Zacharias, *Jesus among Other Gods* (Nashville: Word, 2000), 63.

26. Anthony Campolo, *A Reasonable Faith* (Waco, TX: Word, 1983), 30.

27. The material on how sociology studies religion is taken from David Claerbaut, "How Sociology Texts Treat Religion," *Universitas* (April 1974): 3.

28. Harry Blamires, *The Christian Mind* (Ann Arbor, MI: Servant, 1997), 16.

29. Claerbaut, "How Sociology Texts Treat Religion," 3; Gordon W. Allport, "Psychology," in Edward W. Hazen Foundation, *College Reading and Religion* (New Haven, CT: Yale University Press, 1948). Allport presents the notion of "psychologism" as applied to the discipline of psychology. See also Moberg, "The Social Sciences," in Smith, *Christ and the Modern Mind,* 120.

4

DOWN THE INTELLECTUAL CUL DE SAC
OF POSTMODERNISM

ndeed, the contributions of secular higher education, with its emphasis on reason and science, are myriad. Nonetheless, despite this, Enlightenment-driven scientism has fallen far short of solving all human problems. Charles Hummel, nearly three decades ago, noticed that problems have actually multiplied amid scientific progress. "Modern literature and art forms reflect this sense of frustration.... Ironically, anxiety matches affluence as our technological skills have reached peak efficiency in a climate of apparent meaninglessness, moral irresponsibility, and impersonal manipulation."[1]

The artificial light of the Enlightenment began dimming by the last quarter of the twentieth century. Endless wars, hunger epidemics, intense poverty, and social toxins such as racism and economic exploitation continued unabated, giving rise to an era of cynicism. Enlightenment thinking pretty much breathed its last gasp in the 1960s, when a disillusioned yet optimistic youth culture pushed mightily for a new social order throughout Europe and the United States, advocating peace, affirming sexual freedom, and engaging in drug experimentation.[2] The mind-set of that youth movement made its mark on Western intellectuals such that one of the best-selling books of the early 1970s was Charles Reich's *The Greening of America*.[3] In this book, the Yale professor described three types of consciousness. Consciousness I was characterized by a preindustrial ruralism. Consciousness II referred to the modern era, one of industrialization and economic productivity. Despite its promises of a better life, Consciousness II is depicted in near-Marxian terms — an existence in which humans become slaves to machines and organizations, draining daily life of all vitality. For Reich, all was not lost. Out of these two would evolve a more life-affirming, liberationist Consciousness III, a culture in which the importance of individual identity would triumph over the oppressive forces of materialism and industrialization.

Reich was half right. By the close of the 1970s, Consciousness II (modern era), with its focus on modernization and industrialization as the pathways to universal human betterment, was dying. Reich, however, was wrong. The post-modern era was not characterized by a Consciousness III utopianism. Instead, a skeptical mind-set began emerging, one characterized by a loss of idealism. Hope, through political change, was abandoned along with grand, macro ideologies. Although strains of postmodern thinking have been with us for generations, postmodernism became a major cultural force in the West by the close of the twentieth century.

▸▸ Postmodernism

Postmodern thinking is difficult to define. In fact, it defies general definition. It is characterized by fragmentation—bits and pieces rather than wholeness. Postmodernism rejects general theories and systematic approaches to truth and reality. According to postmodernism, there is no ultimate truth, no objective reality governing all of humanity. Truth is whatever is true in the experience of the individual or the culture of which the person is a member. It is completely subjective, a matter of individual and cultural interpretation.

Postmodern cynicism is evident in politics. Ideological and political "truth" is regarded satirically, defined as whatever "reality" those in power, those able to shape the culture, are able to force on those out of power. By controlling the social context, those with the power to manipulate and control the language, the symbols, the mass media, and the social structure, also define what is true (or at least real) for a population. In any case, truth is relative to a situational context. It does not exist independent of defining circumstances. It is a changing, subjective entity not grounded in an objective reality.

Postmodernism represents a movement from macro to micro thinking, from monolithic ideas to pluralistic notions. With no objective reality, there are only individual and cultural points of view, none of which is more valid than any other. Hence, if there is one universal value affirmed in postmodernism, it is multiculturalism. With truth always bounded by social context—a matter of cultural relativism—all cultures must be respected. In this world without rules, political correctness and its doctrine of according equal respect to all points of view is, then, postmodernism's only real commandment. When applied to religion, it means affirming individualistic, subjective, your-opinion-is-as-good-as-mine expressions based on personal experiences. Religious expressions of faith are tolerated to the extent that they are communicated as totally personal, subjective notions. In the parlance of postmodernism, Christianity "may be true for you, but not true for me."

Michael McConnell, accorded the Presidential Professorship at the University of Utah College of Law after more than a decade at the Law School at the University of Chicago, illuminates the spiritual essence of postmodernism: "A 'personal faith' means a faith that makes no claim on the intelligence of anyone else, a faith that offers no challenge to the world." By making faith personal—subjective—it is nonthreatening to anyone else and so removes the believer from threat. "The easiest way for believers to escape conflict," says McConnell, "is to wrap themselves in subjectivity."[4]

From an academic standpoint, the influence of postmodernism is much evident in the arts and humanities. Focusing on experience over substance, diversity in form and context triumph over depth and meaning. This "anything goes" absence of rules and organizing principles extends from postmodern painting and sculpture to architecture and music, even to drama and literature.

Much is made of language and symbolism. Postmodernists do not view language as a tool to describe, define, and communicate an objective reality. Rather, language is seen as a set of symbols used either to describe something in a wholly subjective fashion or perhaps to shape the experience of an individual or a cultural group. Postmodernism borders on being a world without nouns. "Image," to quote a popular marketing phrase of the 1980s, "is everything." In fact, it is the only thing. Substance, in the objective sense, is nothing. It does not exist. No single objective, transcendent reality is to be found amid this intellectual and artistic free-for-all. There is only a technological jungle of sounds, symbols, and images that form individual experience.

Philosophy has become deconstructionist and atomistic. Comprehensive systems of logic and thought, aimed at capturing a universal reality, have been discarded in favor of fragmentary and changing notions. The Baltimore Catechism and Calvin's systematic theology are of no standing to the postmodernist, while Marxism, liberalism, and Christianity are meaningless because they attempt to explicate a human reality that simply does not exist. Such macro constructions are regarded as forces used at various points in history to legitimate the power of their purveyors as means of controlling those under their power. Those who attempt to present unchanging, immutable truth are met with the charge of being "intolerant proselytizers."[5]

From an intellectual standpoint, postmodern humans are but free-floating balloons wafting aimlessly in an atmosphere of gurgling change and fragmentation. The individual is neither the source of truth nor its finder. She functions as a pinball-like entity, caroming off various forms of stimulation and images that generate her subjective experiences.

▸▸ Academic Freedom

In the university mainstream, postmodernism has gotten into bed with views of academic freedom. Academic freedom—rooted in the conviction that learning proceeds best in an atmosphere of open inquiry that does not restrict the scholar in her pursuit of knowledge—is a justifiably cherished value, having provided First Amendment–like protection for scholars who research controversial subjects such as evolution or espouse unpopular opinions. Without academic freedom, the pursuit of knowledge would have been severely thwarted, particularly in eras of heavy social, intellectual, and political censorship.

Since the 1950s, however, academic freedom has evolved to mean something much different from protection of open inquiry. Rather than simply ensuring freedom of expression and furthering the effort to find truth, it has taken a postmodern direction, one characterized by ideological neutrality. Buckley has long critiqued this application of academic freedom:

> Under academic freedom, the modern university is supposed to take a position of "neutrality" as among competing ideas. "A university does not take sides on the questions that are discussed in its halls," a committee of scholars and alumni of Yale reported in 1952. "In the ideal university all sides of any issue are presented as impartially as possible." To do otherwise, they are saying, is to prejudice the race, which if all the contestants are let strictly alone, truth is bound to win.[6]

"That is voodoo," says the ever-opinionated Buckley, because it fogs over the very purpose of the educational enterprise. "Academic freedom is conceived as a permanent instrument of doctrinal egalitarianism; it is always there to remind us that we can never know anything for sure—which I view as another way of saying we cannot really know what are the aims of education."[7] Academic freedom has evolved into a weapon to be used against those who may assert some claim to truth. From here, all direction is lost, and education bobs along like an impotent cork on an ocean of opinions, as noted by a student at the University of California. "Then I took a philosophy course which sent me spinning," he wrote. "How can one learn the Truth about something when he cannot know for sure if what he is told is the truth unless he knew beforehand what it is, in which case there would be no reason to ask questions?"[8]

The whole postmodern thinking process becomes intellectually immobilizing. Apply postmodern thinking to solving a problem in mathematics, for example. If one of twelve students were to arrive at the mathematically correct answer while the other eleven did not, it would make no sense for that student to average his or her answer with those of the other eleven. Yet by postmodern standards, that would most certainly be preferable to the student's asserting a claim to being right. Similarly, if one student were to think rationally about a given problem, and another student to think about it irrationally, it would be foolish for the rational student to corrupt her thinking with that of the irrational one. Nevertheless, in the wholly subjective postmodern universe, such a dilution would be more acceptable than for the rationalist to dismiss the irrational student's ideas.[9]

Ever the doctrinaire, Buckley attempts to break the gridlock by providing a mission statement for the academic mainstream. "The aims of education are to forward knowledge and right conduct—at the *expense* of some points of view."[10] Although a Christian might argue that the notion of arriving at truly "right conduct" in God's eyes is not possible without divine guidance, there is much to be said for Buckley's mission statement. Indeed, humans have been endowed with rational and logistical capacities that assist in finding certain truths. "What seems . . . self-evident is that in the process of history certain immutable truths have been revealed and discovered," argues Buckley, "and that their value is not subject to the limitations of time and space."[11]

In reality, pure academic freedom in the postmodern sense has scarcely, if ever, existed. Noting an internal campus survey indicating the faith-weakening effect of attending Harvard, Buckley suggested that the university must be acting on the assumption that to "indoctrinate students toward philosophical agnosticism is to lead them towards truth."[12] The issue here is not in what direction this bastion of mainstream academe is manipulating its students, but that "in violation of the precepts of academic freedom, it is taking any direction at all."[13]

▸▸ Intellectual Cul de Sac

Rather than advocating the Enlightenment doctrine of an evolving process by which humankind will build an ever better social order, postmodernism sees only a global village of varying cultures striving to find and enjoy their own "true" experiences. As such, it becomes an intellectual cul de sac. Instead of a journey ending in finding objective truth, one merely travels in and out of various kinds of truth. There is, for example, African American truth, Third World truth, and lesbian truth. Postmodernism has brought on a new type of darkness. By its standards, there is no one Word who is the life and the light of all humanity. Rather than being the way, the truth, and the life for the entire universe, Jesus is merely truth for the Christian.

Postmodernism is confusing and contradictory, filled with polarities. For example, postmodernists affirm individuality and cultural relativism, but do so while highlighting the collective global-village concept. Language is viewed as a culture-specific medium, yet in a larger context, a uniform language of technology is seen as dominating life. Difference and uniqueness are celebrated, but amid an intense search for community, oneness, and relationship. In a curiously logical way, postmodernism's disillusionment and rejection of traditional modes of seeking truth all but mandate this systematic chaos. Moreover, out of this logical illogic comes a commitment-averse spirit, because by postmodern standards, there is simply nothing to commit to. The New Age wisdom principle—"Always keep your mind open and attached to nothing"—advanced by popular philosopher Wayne Dyer in his PBS presentations, captures this spirit well.

If there is a conceptual trinity in postmodernism, it consists of multiculturalism, subjective reality, and aversion to commitment.

▶▶ Current Academic Mainstream

So where is the academic mainstream in all of this? Is it characterized by Enlightenment or postmodern thinking? It is a curious amalgam of both. While the dominant force is naturalism and its relatives, reductionism and empiricism, there is a powerful strain of postmodernism running through the academic world, particularly in the student culture.

Postmodernism is evident in the university's strong emphasis on multiculturalism and political correctness. Pluralism—the right of various subcultural groups to practice their distinctive patterns of feeling, thinking, and behavior, provided they do not disrupt the larger academic community—is not merely tolerated in the university community; it is celebrated. As such, universities are loath to make unequivocal, doctrinaire statements regarding belief or behavior, for fear of offending one or more of its publics. All religions, all philosophies, and almost all political notions are accorded at least superficial, public respect, provided each respects the existence of all the others, making no claim to an ultimate, objective truth that by consequence labels other belief systems as false. What is affirmed is that each is on her own life journey to personal meaning and truth—a sort of harmonious agnosticism.

From a behavioral standpoint, morality is not a fixed reality. Rather, it is whatever is consensual. What is immoral (or more contemporarily, *inappropriate*) behavior is defined as any conduct that overtly hurts or limits the freedom of another person. Moreover, rules of behavior are made by groups for the members of those groups only. They have no validity outside that context because they are not absolute, objective moral precepts. With God absent, or at least irrelevant, humans make their own rules. Nothing could be more postmodern than that.

In the spirit of multiculturalism, the word *spiritual* has replaced the word *religious* in the lexicon of academe. *Spiritual* is a looser, more expansive, less defining word, referring to some ethereal, nonmaterial, human experience rather than to transcendent deity. To appease the various belief communities, an academic institution may encourage "spiritual emphasis" events, deftly sidestepping any hint of favoring one belief system over another.

Using the example of Millbrook, the once-Christian prep school from which he graduated, Buckley exposed the absurdity of much of this. Millbrook commissioned a Spiritual Life Committee with the postmodern mission of "honoring and nurturing the development of the inner life, in whatever individual and communal ways that inner life is expressed." Buckley punctured this nonsense by stating, "One is required to observe that either that statement means nothing at all or else it is indefensible. Some inner lives . . . simply oughtn't to be encouraged whatever the inner glow they generate."[14]

Among the committee's goals was to provide at least one major spiritual event for the students annually. "How about Easter?" Buckley asks tongue-in-cheek.[15] Another was to present a "vehicle for reflection" in a spiritual vein. "Why not describe that vehicle?" queries Buckley sarcastically. "And while at it, explain why the Bible, which in the Christian world has more or less officially served that purpose since Constantine (d. AD 337), is no longer adequate to serve such purposes?"[16] Faithful to the creed of multiculturalism, Millbrook offered a "Sunday Evening Prayer Service for people of all faiths" that included "inter-religious reading, etc." "What *is* inter-religious reading, etc.?" asks Buckley. "Or did the committee intend the word *multi*religious? As in ten minutes Buddhism, ten Islam, ten Jewish, that sort of thing?" Moreover, Buckley wonders why committed Jews or Christians would even attend such a prayer service, "inasmuch as to do so as a participant would be to violate the commandment in both faiths which forbids the worship of false gods?"[17]

According to McConnell, "Postmodernism is, in essence, philosophical paganism: there are many gods (understandings of the good), and there is no way to choose between them." It is from this mind-set that interest in Hinduism and other Eastern religions and philosophies have arisen. It is then permissible for people to give particular attention to the god of their choice. "This produces a kind of tolerance," says McConnell. "You can worship pretty much the way you choose, and anything you choose, without running afoul of the logic of paganism. There is only one heresy within the pagan understanding: the insistence that one's own 'god' is God."[18]

Were one to apply postmodern thinking to biblical Christianity, it might go something like this: the Old Testament would be excised as too bloodthirsty and simply irrelevant to contemporary Western culture, and the New Testament would be rounded out a bit—augmented perhaps with insights from Plato, Confucius, and other philosophers. Certainly the notion of seeing oneself as a sinner in need of grace would need to be deleted in favor of a more affirming ethic.[19]

As for the academic mainstream, to the extent that it is postmodern, one could argue that a Christian could at least exist reasonably well within it. The pluralistic emphasis not only would allow the believer to practice her faith within a community of fellow Christians but would also provide the freedom to study the body of knowledge within her chosen discipline through a lens of faith. Indeed, believers would at minimum be a protected, respected minority, free to interpret truth as emanating from a sovereign creator. Evangelism would have to be carried on at considerable risk, however, with the gospel being presented in a less than authoritative fashion.

To the extent that religion is introduced into postmodern thinking, it is presented as an amorphous, undefined divine force that interacts with the human psyche as reality continues to be created. One will rarely hear the word *God* in postmodern conversation. You may hear the word *Intelligence* or even the term *Divine Intelligence,* but not as synonyms for the Jehovah of Scripture. Rather, these terms are used to describe some indefinable and nonmaterial forces within the universe, friendly forms of energy that bind us together as a human community with limitless capability to create personal and relational reality. There is no *One* with whom many can have a common fellowship and together build a unified, believing community, the bonds of which transcend the cultural limits of race, gender, and language.

Postmodernism, though not overtly naturalistic, does fit well within the naturalistic setting of the university for several reasons. First, many postmodernists would not regard naturalism as a grand or macro theory because of its reductionistic, nontranscendent quality. More important, however, naturalism affirms the postmodern rejection of ultimate truth and meaning. Furthermore, postmodernism's emphasis on subjective, personally created truth conflicts directly with Christianity. "You do not *make* the truth. You *reside* in the truth," states Blamires.[20] The impact of postmodernism is not to be casually dismissed as harmless fog. Renowned Christian philosopher Arthur Holmes, when asked what was the most challenging issue facing Christian higher education in the new millennium, replied that it was postmodern subjectivism as a way of perceiving reality.[21]

Whereas the naturalist finds Christianity illogical with its preposterous notions of the supernatural and an afterlife, the postmodernist finds the faith too logical with its systematic approach to one universal truth. Moreover, as it is for the naturalist, the notion that the chief end of humanity is the glorification of God is absolutely ludicrous to the postmodernist. There is no chief end, because truth has no ultimate author. It is continuously created in subjective microbits by the actions of humans and their reactions to their environments.

Notes

1. Charles E. Hummel, "The Natural Sciences," in *Christ and the Modern Mind,* ed. Robert W. Smith (Downers Grove, IL: InterVarsity, 1972), 228.
2. Barry Burke, "Post-Modernism and Post-Modernity," http://www.infed.org/biblio/ b-postmd.htm (accessed July 17, 2002). Burke does an excellent job of capturing and critiquing the impact of postmodernism in Western culture.
3. Charles A. Reich, *The Greening of America* (New York: Random House, 1970).
4. Michael W. McConnell, "We Worship the Same God You Do," in *Professors Who Believe,* ed. Paul M. Anderson (Downers Grove, IL: InterVarsity, 1998), 202.
5. John Eaves, director of Hephzibah House, conversation with author, New York City, February 3, 2003.
6. William F. Buckley Jr., *Let Us Talk of Many Things* (Roseville, CA: Prima, 2000), 104–5.
7. Ibid.
8. Ibid., 136.
9. Harry Blamires, *The Christian Mind* (Ann Arbor, MI: Servant, 1997), 8.
10. Buckley, *Let Us Talk of Many Things,* 104.
11. Ibid., 105.
12. Ibid., 106–7.
13. Ibid., 107.
14. William F. Buckley Jr., *Nearer, My God* (San Diego: Harvest, 1998), 287.
15. Ibid., 288.
16. Ibid.
17. Ibid., 289.
18. McConnell, "We Worship the Same God You Do," in Anderson, *Professors Who Believe,* 203.
19. Blamires, *The Christian Mind,* 115.
20. Ibid., 113.
21. Arthur Holmes, "Shaping the Academic Enterprise," in *Shaping a Christian Worldview,* ed. David S. Dockery and Gregory Alan Thornbury (Nashville: Broadman and Holman, 2002), 388.

5

THE HIGH STAKES POLITICS
OF THE ACADEMIC MAINSTREAM

My friend Charles was an honor student and a solid athlete in high school. Good-looking and popular, he was rarely vulgar or profane, having grown up in a strong Christian family. Charles attended morning and evening worship services, Sunday school, and catechism classes throughout his youth. As a teenager, he was the president of the church's youth organization. At eighteen, Charles professed his faith and joined the church. The pattern prescribed that he would go to college, pursue his engineering degree, get married, and start his own Christian family.

But it never happened.

In the fall, Charles went away to a major state university, and there he apparently lost his faith. The process was evident early on. After a year at the university, Charles returned home a different young man. His language was more coarse, his values more secular, and his friends not from Christian backgrounds. Charles had adopted a cynical air toward the unsophisticated provinciality of his home community and toward its unscientific, blind Christian faith. Eventually marrying a nonbeliever, Charles appeared to have recanted the faith and values of his youth.

▸▸ Turf Control

The secular transformation of Charles is not unusual. Students encounter an ever more powerful yet cunning force when entering the academic mainstream—one for which believers are often unprepared. It is not simply ideological. It is political. As such, it deserves attention.

The doctrines of naturalism and postmodernism have become institutionalized in Western culture such that they go unquestioned and are accepted as fact. Over time it has become obvious that those holding the intellectual reins of power have proven no more open-minded than their creationist forebears. In fact, the naturalists in particular carefully guard the turf of evolutionism, even in the face of legitimate academic and scientific challenges to its validity.

"In technical circles, where the empirical flaws are common knowledge," says Finley, who supports creationism on scientific grounds, "evolutionists debate the possibility that a new naturalistic explanation of life may be thought up, but in public presentations they preach doctrinaire evolution and pretend that the empirical problems do not exist."[1] Referring to the ape-to-man theory, another group of scholars note that these observations are assumed and go unchallenged.[2]

Absolutely no secret is made of this ideological commitment to naturalistic evolution. Recently, the American Association for the Advancement of Science offered a seminar titled "Good Science, Bad Science: Teaching Evolution in the States." Various states were graded on how favorably they handled evolution in the classroom. A's were given to states that carefully hewed the ideological line. Some received F's. One state, Kansas, was rated an F–, because it had the temerity to refuse to claim that Darwin's notion of evolution accounts for all major aspects of living things. The seminar, however, falsely accused Kansas of "removing all references to evolution."[3] Such is the hysteria surrounding any perceived challenge to naturalism.

Any critique of naturalistic evolution seems to elicit a forceful dismissal. When asked whether myriad scientific problems with naturalism should be cited in the teaching curriculum, noted evolutionist Stephen Jay Gould had a ready response: "We have no time to teach the conflicts."[4] Valid opposition to evolution is given no voice. Scholar Henry Creechan notes, "Any scientist who rejects evolution tends to be branded a religious fanatic, or similar. The media either ignores them or discredits them by disparagement."[5]

The commitment to naturalism is far more philosophical than scientific. In the face of indisputable scientific evidence to the contrary, naturalistic theories are stated as fact. And it doesn't end there. So committed are the devotees of naturalism that when some of its claims do not stand up to rigorous scrutiny, scholars have been willing to help the cause along in rather dubious ways.

►► Fraud

Jonathan Wells, author of *Icons of Evolution,* makes a powerful case for stipulating a nonscientific bias present among naturalists.[6] He points out that during his academic career at the University of California, the very prospect of questioning prevailing scientific paradigms was unthinkable. No longer so for Dr. Wells, once he noticed a set of drawings of vertebrate embryos (fish, chicken, humans, etc.) that were used to support the doctrine that all living organisms emanated from a common ancestor.

The drawings were fake. The renderings, known to be forgeries for over a century, were foundational to Charles Darwin, who wrote, "I view all beings not as special creations, but as the lineal descendants of some few beings." Darwin held that differentiation among species occurred over time as organisms adapted for survival. He rooted his theory of evolution in embryology, finding it to have "by far the strongest single class of facts" favoring his paradigm.[7]

Ernst Haeckel assisted Darwin by providing drawings of various vertebrates designed to indicate that they were virtually identical in their earliest stages of development. Haeckel "doctored his drawings to make embryos appear more alike than they really were."[8] Haeckel's drawings have lingered in academic circles despite critiques by his contemporaries. Even when in 1997 British embryologist Michael Richardson provided conclusive evidence that the drawings were contrived, the drawings still held firm in academe.[9] Beyond the fraudulent drawings, Haeckel omitted the earliest embryonic stages, in which differences among the vertebrates are more pronounced. As far back as 1976, embryologist William Ballard stated that "only by semantic tricks and subjective selection of evidence" and by "bending the facts of nature" could one claim that the earliest stages of embryonic development are more similar than their adult forms.[10] Richardson, comparing the textbook drawings with actual embryos, stated in the renown journal *Science,* "It looks like it's turning out to be one of the most famous fakes in biology."[11]

Such evidence did not dampen naturalistic spirits. At the 2000 conference, Eugenie Scott, executive director of the National Center for Science Education, boldly proclaimed that no one would seriously question "that embryos are more similar than the mature bodies."[12] Little wonder, then, that although convincingly debunked, Haeckel-like drawings are everywhere. Wells reviewed all his textbooks, finding such drawings "all obviously wrong."[13] Although naturalist Gould wrote that we should "be astonished and ashamed by a century of mindless recycling that has led to the persistence of these drawings in a large number, if not a majority, of modern textbooks," his scholarly hands were not clean.[14] Gould knew for decades that the drawings were false but remained silent, apparently to protect the general theory of naturalism against formidable attack.[15]

It only begins with Haeckel. "My search revealed a startling fact, however," notes Wells. "Far from being exceptions, such blatant misrepresentations are more often the rule." So common is this academic fraud that Wells called them "Icons of Evolution."[16]

Wells found many instances of fraud. In the 1950s, British physician Bernard Kettlewell theorized that peppered moths had gone from light to dark color over the past century to be camouflaged by darkened tree bark and hence spared from being eaten by birds. In the 1980s, it was determined that peppered moths do not rest on tree trunks, but rather they fly by night and hide in higher branches during daylight hours. Kettlewell had manufactured an artificial experimental situation. Moreover, he "proved" his hypothesis by having photographers actually glue dark-colored dead moths to the bark of trees and shamelessly presented the fabricated pictures as "Darwin's missing evidence."[17]

Kettlewell—who to this day is regarded as having made a powerful score, as his experiment is recounted in many introductory biology texts, often accompanied by photos of the moths on the tree trunks—has his defenders.[18] One academic administrator asserted, "You get a better picture if you glue the moth to the tree."[19] Moreover, Canadian textbook author and apologist Bob Ritter betrays the bias found in the politics of naturalism, arguing, "You have to look at the [high school] audience. How convoluted do you want to make it for the first-time learner? We want to get across the idea of selective adaptation. Later on, they can look at the work critically."[20]

Politics was also at work in the 1970s when Peter and Rosemary Grant found that the beaks of finches in the Galapagos Islands increased in size by 5 percent after a drought, assumedly because the beak structures were strengthened by having to crack hard seeds. This small finding was regaled in a 1999 booklet by the United States National Academy of Sciences as providing "a particularly compelling example" of the origin of the species. Given that the change in size occurred in a single year, the publication projected that "if droughts occur about once every 10 years on the islands, a new species of finch might arise in only about 200 years."[21]

What the booklet did not report, however, was that the beaks returned to pre-drought size after the rains came. "No net evolution occurred."[22]

Harvard biologist Louis Guenin was irate, believing that this suppression of evidence verges on scientific misconduct. Using the metaphor of the securities industry, Guenin stated in a 1999 issue of *Nature* that were a stockbroker to highlight a stock moving up 5 percent in a given year without telling the unsuspecting investor that that same stock dropped 5 percent the following year, he could well be charged with fraud.[23]

Other students of evolution have detected a centuries-old bias in the form of an intellectually rigged system. "Science, real science ... has been co-opted by an ancient philosophical/religious doctrine the origins of which can be traced back to at least 400–700 years before Christ."[24] These efforts to suppress "strong negative evidence ... are in gross violation of the scientific attitude," says Finley.[25]

Darwin was unbending on the critical matter of the origin of the human race in *The Descent of Man*. "My object is to show that there is no fundamental difference between man and the higher animals in their mental faculties," he wrote.[26] He extended this parallelism to religion, using a dog as an example. That a dog tends to imagine some hidden dimension to items moved by the wind was, to Darwin, similar to "the belief in the existence of one or more gods."[27]

Darwin's theory, however, lacked a missing link between humans and animals. Then in 1912, Charles Dawson uncovered what appeared to be the missing link—part of a human skull and part of the lower jaw of an ape—in a gravel pit in Piltdown, England. It wasn't until the 1950s that a group of scientists determined that "the jaw had been chemically treated to make it look like a fossil, and its teeth had been deliberately filed down to make them look human. Piltdown Man was a forgery."[28]

Modern texts rarely mention this fraud. If anything, Darwinians use the forged finding as illustrative of the self-correcting nature of science. This correction, however, took four decades.

In decrying the politics of naturalism, Wells reviewed ten popular high school biology textbooks, eight by established publishers. Similar to the American Association for the Advancement of Science, he evaluated them on an A–F scale. An A signified that a "book had full disclosure of the truth, discussion of relevant scientific controversies, and a recognition that Darwin's theories—like all scientific theories—might have to be revised or discarded if it doesn't fit the facts." An F "indicates the textbook uncritically relies on logical fallacy, dogmatically treats a theory as an unquestionable fact, or blatantly misrepresents published scientific evidence." Among the ten textbooks in question, none received an A, B, or C. One rated a D+, and two a D–. The remaining eight were accorded F's.[29]

The cooked evidence is "good propaganda," Bethell points out. "So they remain in the textbooks, even though no reputable scientists would stand behind them, and our children are taught misinformation in the name of a 'higher truth,' because . . . as every educated person knows, evolution must be true."[30]

▸▸ Public Acceptance of Evolutionism as Fact

The long-standing doctrine of evolutionism is currently called scientism or metaphysical naturalism, and it "has been so effectively interlaced with science that it is often difficult for the scientist, much less the layperson, to separate the two."[31] As recently as January 23, 2001, the evidence of public acceptance of evolution as fact jumped out at me as I watched Chris Matthews on his nightly *Hardball* program. Matthews, a practicing Roman Catholic, is a man of considerable intellectual sophistication. While in full debate over newly elected George

W. Bush's education proposals focusing on local control of schools, Matthews mused openly several times over the possibility of some rural districts seizing control of the curricula and teaching creationism as if the possibility were about as valid and intellectually defensible as advancing racial stereotypes. The words of this theist oozed an unthinking naturalistic bias, exemplifying the evolution-as-fact point of view.

Indeed *Time*'s "How Apes Became Human" headline left no doubt as to where it stood on the matter of evolution versus creation when Ethiopian fossil evidence of an ape that apparently walked upright and had teeth similar to those of humans was found. Immediately below the headline was an additional narrative: "What a New Discovery Tells Scientists about How Our Oldest Ancestors Stood on Two Legs and Made an Evolutionary Leap."[32] The subtitle of the article continued to proclaim naturalistic evolution as fact: "Meet Your Newfound Ancestor, a Chimplike Forest Creature That Stood Up and Walked 58 Million Years Ago."[33]

The article presented an evolutionary timeline with the following introduction: "The newest fossils have brought scientists tantalizingly close to the time when humans first walked upright—splitting off from chimpanzees."[34] No mention was ever made of the total absence of missing links. The possibility that this elusive "missing link" may prove to be something other than the clinching evidence that evolutionists hoped for was also not addressed.

Newsweek, though far less impressed with the newly found fossils and citing the host of problems with fossil research, did show its naturalistic bias in wondering if we would "ever find our oldest direct ancestor," implying a transitional is out there somewhere.[35] The zeal with which naturalism is advanced in education is evidenced by the near-hysterical reaction to the Kansas school board's determination to permit dissent in the teaching of evolution. "According to the news media," notes Wells, "only religious fundamentalists question Darwinian evolution. People who criticize Darwin, we are told, want to bomb science back to the Stone Age and replace it with the Bible."[36]

Despite its rock-ribbed public commitment to scientific purity, however, the naturalistic political agenda is antiscientific in practice. "The growing body of scientific evidence contradicting Darwinian claims is steadfastly ignored," Wells asserts.[37] Moreover, serious critics, like Michael Behe who reported in the *New York Times* that the embryo evidence was "faked," are lambasted. The aforementioned Gould, aware for decades of this intellectual atrocity, "accused Behe [falsely] of being a 'creationist' for pointing it out."[38]

Behe looms large. A professor of biological sciences at Lehigh University, his book *Darwin's Black Box: The Biochemical Challenge to Evolution* was published by

Simon and Schuster in 1996. Behe believes that certain cell structures are "irreducibly complex" in nature. These structures involve such a high degree of molecular interaction that they could not have developed in the step-by-step process advocated by Darwin. "I don't think something like that could have happened by simple, natural laws," he said.

▸▸ Political Agenda

Wells sees the advocacy of evolution as political. "I suspect that there's an agenda other than pure science at work here," he concludes. "My evidence is the more or less explicit materialist message woven into many textbook accounts."[39] He cites Douglas J. Futuyma's *Evolutionary Biology* as an example. Futuyma states that it was the work of Darwin and his theory of evolution, in addition to the work of Karl Marx in history and Sigmund Freud in psychology, "that provided a crucial plank to the platform of mechanism and materialism" that has become the foundation of Western thinking.[40] Naturalism is exalted as the only guide to knowledge. Wells notes that in one textbook Gould is quoted as stating "that humans are not created, but are merely fortuitous twigs on a 'contingent' (i.e. accidental) tree of life."[41]

Perceived dissidents are severely punished. The experience of William Dembski, a mathematician whose estimable credentials include a Ph.D. from the University of Chicago and a book, *Design Inference,* published by the prestigious Cambridge University in 1998, provides a strong case in point. Dembski, the director of the Michael Polanyi Center at Baylor University, developed mathematical methods "that can distinguish randomness from complexity designed by an intelligent agent."[42] His analysis of biochemical cell structures led him to conclude that "blind natural selection could not have created them."[43] "The intelligent design movement, of which Dembski is a prominent member," notes Fred Heeren, "is based on the theory that life, which is made up of interdependent parts, can be better explained as the product of mindful planning than chance."[44]

The key word in Dembski's research, of course, is *design*—the root word of the linguistic creation *designfulness.* The critics waged an all-out political attack on the unsuspecting Dembski, claiming that the notion of intelligent design is nothing more than "a disguised form of creationism."[45] Little wonder, because intelligent design theory seems to be rather threatening to the naturalists in academe. The front page of the Sunday, April 8, 2001, edition of the *New York Times* weighed in on the matter, blaring the headline, "Darwin vs. Design: Evolutionists' New Battle." In brief, the intelligent design proponents "dispute the idea that natural selection, the force Darwin suggested drove evolution, is enough to explain the complexity of the earth's plants and animals. That complexity, they say, must be the work of an intelligent designer."[46] Moreover, "this designer may be much like the biblical God, proponents say, but they are open to other explanations."[47]

Conferences on intelligent design were held at Yale and Baylor, and a student organization, Intelligent Design and Evolution Awareness (IDEA) has been formed. Dembski organized what turned out to be a highly successful—though much resisted and sabotaged—academic conference at Baylor, attended by mathematicians and scientists, two of whom had won the Nobel Prize. "The most striking thing about the intelligent design folks," said the concerned Eugenie Scott, "is their potential to really make anti-evolutionism intellectually respectable."[48] Moreover, Scott struck a verbal match. "They're really saying God does it, but they're not as honest as the Biblical creationists," she charged. The intelligence is really spelled in three letters: G-O-D."[49]

Not so, claims Dembski. Though a Christian, he states that intelligent design "is not creationism. There's not a commitment to Genesis literalism."[50] Dembski makes a distinction between a creator and a designer. "If you examine a piece of furniture, you can identify that it is designed, but you can't identify who or what is responsible for the wood in the first place," he counters. "Intelligent design just gets you to an intelligent cause that works with pre-existing materials, but not the source of those materials."[51]

"Though few of the opposing faculty had the training or knowledge even to understand Dembski's mathematical formula," according to Heeren, Baylor faculty roared their disapproval of the scholar's work.[52] Neuroscientist Lewis Barker, who left the university in protest over the school's "religious policies," saw Dembski's intelligent design as "a form of stealth creationism."[53]

"I would use the words 'devilishly clever,'" remarked Barker, a professor of ecology and evolution at the University of Chicago. Intelligent design "has an appeal to intellectuals who don't know anything about evolutionary biology, first of all because the proponents have Ph.D.s and second of all because it's not written in the sort of populist, folksy, anti-intellectual style. It's written in the argot of academia."[54] Dr. Leonard Krishtalka of the University of Kansas echoed Barker's "stealth creationism" charge: "Intelligent design is nothing more than creationism dressed in a cheap tuxedo."[55]

The near-fanatical reactions to opponents of naturalism is of note. "Belief in evolution is heavily associated with the scientific approach to knowledge," says Finley, "and it is pervasively implied that people who doubt evolution are either superstitious or willfully ignorant."[56] That committed evolutionists disagree with the intelligent design group is neither surprising nor illegitimate. What stands out is the virulent nature of their attacks. Science journalist Fred Heeren found the assault on Dembski astonishing. "Scientists from distant universities wrote letters to the editors of his university newspaper, and biologists spoke up through the surrounding city papers," reported Heeren, "telling the public why this man must be stopped."[57] As for the conference, one angry "professor from another state sent long e-mails to the scheduled speakers, seeking to discredit Dembski and convincing one famed philosopher to cancel."[58]

"The faculty of his own Baylor University voted 26 to 2 to recommend that his research center be dismantled. Eight members of Baylor's science department wrote Congress about the dangers of Dembski's project, and several briefings on the issues were made before a bi-partisan group of congressional members and staff," related Heeren.[59]

The success of the conference provoked the critics all the more. The faculty senate voted to close the center. Baylor president Robert Sloan attempted to mediate the furor. Dembski was pressured not to attend a meeting in Washington where design advocates interacted with members of Congress. He was censored in what he could put on the center's website and in how he could respond to his critics. "Freedom of speech at Baylor, it seems, only works one way," wrote Heeren sardonically.[60]

Amid all this, Sloan had appointed an "independent committee" to evaluate Dembski's work. Despite finding no errors in his writings, and even validating the legitimacy of intelligent design research, the group attacked the research as "too restrictive" and ordered that more "room should be made for a variety of approaches and topics."[61] Furthermore, a university committee would determine what Dembski could research at the center.

The controversy continued, and Sloan, a decent man caught in the crosshairs of a vicious controversy, opted to remove Dembski from his directorship of the center, leaving him to complete his four-year appointment at Baylor as associate research professor in the Institute of Faith and Learning. Heeren concluded his report by stating, "President Sloan achieved peace for his time at the expense of academic freedom." As for the Baylor faculty, "They have ensured that their university will be remembered as the place where the rule of the mob trumps free scientific inquiry. Congratulations."[62]

Clearly, Sloan and Baylor got plenty of bad press over a thorny and complex issue, rung out in emotional terms. Given its dramatic, highly publicized nature, it is tempting to regard Dembski's experience as somehow aberrant or as peculiar to the physical sciences and the white-hot issue of evolutionism versus creationism. As such, it can be attributed to some hysterical exception to a general rule of fairness. That is simply not the case. This is a high stakes political game over ideological turf. Glenn Tinder, a four-decade professor of political science at the University of Massachusetts, said, "In the time I spent as a graduate student [at Berkeley] and professor before becoming a Christian—a period of about twenty years—I never had a single professor, or a single friend or colleague, who expressed any definite interest in Christianity." This was not, however, because no believers were present. "Two or three friends were Christians, but, obedient to the reigning code, they were very quiet Christians, and I knew of their faith only from chance remarks and not from anything we seriously discussed."[63]

The general tendency among Christians, Tinder observed, was to stay beneath the radar, living compartmentalized lives characterized by a dualism in which they seek to comprehend (and often teach) the prevailing views in their field of endeavor, while retaining (all very privately) their theistic, Christian view of life—even if it lay in opposition to the dominant paradigms in their respective fields. "There were Christians in the political science departments of secular colleges and universities. But they were very quiet about faith, and for the sake of professional survival and advancement, they had to be." Tinder goes on to describe the secular view of people of faith. "The reigning assumption was that a respectable intellectual not only had no belief in God, but had not interest even in the possibility of such a belief.... No one said this; the assumption was so dominant and unquestioned that no one had to."[64]

Tinder's observations square with my own experience in secular institutions. When a student in one of my graduate classes referred to her "heavenly Father," I could all but feel the temperature in the room drop ten degrees. Students were either angry at her or embarrassed for her. Throughout my experience, expressing notions of theism openly in such academic settings was to move well beyond being politically incorrect. It was the intellectual equivalent of advocating the beliefs of the Flat Earth Society. The idea of God was at best irrelevant and at worst preposterous.

Ashby Camp also notes that the clash over the matter of origins (and in my experience, any notion of theism) lacks the usual cool, reasoned, evidence-based detachment typical of most intellectual discourse because the conflict is not over "true science." It is far, far larger than that. It is a political struggle between two diametrically opposed worldviews: one atheistic, the other theistic. Any serious challenge to naturalism, more than a matter of scientific inquiry, is an attack on the very creed of atheism. For a committed atheist to entertain the possibility of divine causes is to induce a religious crisis every bit as troubling as the one theists have struggled with since the entrance of Darwin.[65] Thomas Nagel, professor of philosophy at New York University, betrays the bias of mainstream academe. "I want atheism to be true and am made uneasy by the fact that some of the most intelligent and well-informed people I know are religious believers," states Nagel. "It isn't just that I don't believe in God and naturally, hope there is no God! I don't want there to be a God; I don't want the universe to be like that."[66]

In short, the issue is not science, but scientism. Not evolution-related changes in organic development over time, but evolutionism. Not natural, physical laws, but naturalism. Not secular, scientific inquiry, but secularism. Not biology, physics, and geology, but philosophy turned political.

▸▸ The Slaughterhouse

Against the backdrop of such Byzantine politics, my friend Charles becomes a virtual poster child for what seems to happen over and over spiritually to many unwitting sheeplike youth entering the secular slaughterhouse. Reared in Christian environments and evidencing convincing signs of a genuine faith, they leave the spiritual safety of their communities for a mainstream university. There, facing the forces of naturalism and postmodernism, they find their faith inadequate to answer the kind of primal questions with which they are confronted in secular higher education. That education is secular is not in and of itself the problem. Secular, in general, denotes temporal, rather than eternal. The issue, as Walter Hearn points out in *Being a Christian in Science,* is secularism, the view that denies or makes irrelevant the existence of anything beyond the temporal.[67]

It is not fair to attribute apostasy like that of Charles to inadequate discipleship at home. The issue I suspect is more a matter of "turf." Many students come to higher education from an unintellectual, highly emotional (rather than cognitive) Christian tradition. At college age they become more curious, a key characteristic of a vital mind. One of the purposes of education is to expand one's base of reality, and so students adopt new ways of thinking. They discover that their parents' views are not the only reasonable views and bases for judgment, that their social class, race, and culture are not the only vantage points from which to view the world.[68] Indeed, if the educative process does not accomplish at least that, it is defective. Christian parents expect their children to engage new intellectual experiences and perspectives, which are essential to the process of intellectual growth. Thus, the degree to which parents, from any background, can prepare their children for these intellectual adventures is severely limited.

Many students, particularly the ones who grew up in rather narrow, simplistic communities of faith in which they experienced little in the way of an

early challenge to their belief systems, are heading for a spiritually violent collision. The students' faith, after all, is that of their fathers and mothers, believing
friends, and church family. It has been propagated, reinforced, if not indoctri-
nated, but neither examined nor questioned. In fact, these traditions often discourage questioning and attempt to isolate their young from early exposure to
the world at large. Both Roman Catholic and Protestant traditions are replete
with institutions designed to brand, in infancy, their offspring with the mark of
faith before they are old enough to question its truth.

Not only do people reared on such spiritually friendly turf rarely encounter
a faith challenge for the better part of the first two decades of their lives, but
that faith, reinforced by consistent worship and teaching, is regarded as no less
valid or reliable than the multiplication tables. In many communities, religious
belief becomes as basic to life as one's belief in family and country. Hence, young
people are unaware of how strongly that faith is rejected in other circles. Once
they reach early adulthood, their unsuspecting world is suddenly rocked when
the secular onslaught arrives. Educated as they have already been to rely on the
scientific method to learn physics and chemistry, they now find that very
method facing off with faith.

On the turf of the skeptics, they are at a profound disadvantage amid adult
skeptics well prepared to do battle with the ideology of faith, having fought
many such previous skirmishes. Moreover, because the young believers have
come to faith in a nonintellectual setting, yet one that generally accepts the value
of science, they can easily conclude that there is no intellectual basis for Christian beliefs. At the very least, an encounter with a scientific secularism that
respects only concrete forms of truth can engender a genuine crisis of faith. Confronting these alternative modes of thinking without any tools of analysis to
weigh out prevailing bodies of knowledge from a Christian perspective, many
are left permanently conflicted. They become intellectual agnostics, yet affec-
tive believers. In short, they are believers, but they don't really know why, and
so they live in an unresolved cognitive dissonance.

"The modern university with its emphasis on the rationality of the sciences
has launched a veritable assault on Christian doctrine," says Yale graduate Mark
Chenoweth. "Unspoken faith is now the practice of ghettoized Christians."[69]
This is not at all new. In the 1960s, the editors of Harvard's student newspaper,
The Crimson, conducted an extensive survey indicating that one of every two
Protestants who went to the Ivy League school lost his or her faith.[70]

To underplay the gravity of this crisis is to reveal one's own naïveté. Nothing
is being exaggerated here. It is profound. It can have identity-shaking, life-
altering effects for many. When the very tenets of reality, taught by the people

in whom one has the greatest human faith, are in question, identity is in question. At an age when one is seeking certainty amid constant change—running from adolescent glandular development to one's placement in society—uncertainty of a fundamental nature is confronted. Furthermore, however cunningly, this uncertainty means a most agonizing choice may have to be made: a choice between accepting the worldview of those one loves or the worldview of one's education.

It is tempting to use the example of Charles as an endorsement of the Christian college. At the very least, such education is rarely hostile to theistic views. Nonetheless, whenever the Christian college places faith apart from learning rather than making it the context in which that learning occurs, it creates a Christian/secular dichotomy—a schizoid rather than Christian mind. In fact, such an education leaves students like Charles without the intellectual armor to deal with the fiery darts of naturalism and postmodernism as they are encountered in textbooks, in conversations with fellow students, or eventually in graduate school. A compartmentalized view of education—biological science here, sociology there, and art somewhere else, with faith confined to classes in religion and philosophy—neither lives in the light nor redeems the times. It separates the Author of truth from the very truth it examines. That is neither Christian nor ultimately educational.

Notes

1. Darel Rex Finley, "Why I Disbelieve Evolution," http://freeweb.pdq.net/smokin/evolution (accessed January 10, 2001).
2. "50 Reasons to Leave Your Faith (evolution)," http://evolutionlie.faithweb.com (accessed January 10, 2001).
3. Tom Bethell, "No Time for Science," *American Spectator*, December 2000–January 2001, 27.
4. Ibid.
5. Henry James Creechan, "A Brief Analysis of the Scientific/Natural Laws and Phenomena Undermining Current Theories of Evolution and the Origins of Life," http://home.primus.com.au/bonno/evolution1.htm (accessed January 8, 2001), chap. 1.
6. Jonathan Wells, "Survival of the Fakest," *American Spectator*, January 1, 2001, 19–27.
7. Ibid., 20.
8. Ibid.
9. Ibid., 21.
10. Ibid.
11. Ibid., 19.
12. Bethell, "No Time for Science," 27.

13. Wells, "Survival of the Fakest,"19.
14. Gould, quoted in ibid., 21.
15. Ibid., 26.
16. Ibid., 19.
17. Ibid., 23.
18. Ibid.
19. Bethell, "No Time for Science," 27.
20. Wells, "Survival of the Fakest," 23.
21. Ibid., 23–24.
22. Ibid., 24.
23. Ibid.
24. "50 Reasons to Leave Your Faith (evolution)."
25. Finley, "Why I Disbelieve Evolution."
26. Wells, "Survival of the Fakest," 24.
27. Ibid.
28. Ibid.
29. Ibid., 26. The books Wells reviewed included Alton Biggs, Chris Kapicka, and Linda Lundgren, *The Dynamics of Life* (New York: McGraw-Hill, 1998); Neil A. Campbell, Jane B. Reece, and Lawrence G. Mitchell, *Biology* (Menlo Park, CA: Benjamin/Cummings, 1999); Douglas J. Futuyma, *Evolutionary Biology* (Sunderland, MA: Sinauer Associates, 1998); Cecie Starr and Ralph Taggart, *Biology: The Unity and Diversity of Life* (Belmont, CA: Wadsworth, 1998); Sylvia Mader, *Biology* (Boston: WBC/McGraw-Hill, 1998); Peter H. Raven and George B. Johnson, *Biology* (Boston: WBC/McGraw-Hill, 1999); Burton S. Guttman, *Biology* (Boston: WBC/McGraw-Hill, 1999); George B. Johnson, *Biology: Visualizing Life, Annotated Teacher's Edition* (Austin: Holt, Rinehart, and Winston, 1998); Kenneth R. Miller and Joseph Levine, *Biology* (Upper Saddle River, NJ: Prentice Hall, 2000); William D. Schrader and Herbert J. Stoltze, *Biology: The Study of Life* (Upper Saddle River, NJ: Prentice Hall, 1999).
30. Bethell, "No Time for Science," 27.
31. "50 Reasons to Leave Your Faith (evolution)."
32. "How Apes Became Human," *Time*, July 23, 2001, cover.
33. Ibid., 54.
34. Ibid., 60.
35. Sharon Begley, "Bickering over Old Bones," *Newsweek*, July 23, 2001, 40.
36. Wells, "Survival of the Fakest," 26.
37. Ibid.
38. James Glanz, "Darwin vs. Design: Evolutionists' New Battle," *New York Times*, April 8, 2001, 32; Wells, "Survival of the Fakest," 26.
39. Wells, "Survival of the Fakest," 26.
40. Ibid.
41. Ibid.
42. Glanz, "Darwin vs. Design," 32.
43. Ibid.
44. Fred Heeren, "The Deed Is Done," *American Spectator*, December 2000–January 2001, 29.

45. Fred Heeren, "The Lynching of Bill Dembski," *American Spectator*, November 2000, 45.
46. Glanz, "Darwin vs. Design," 1.
47. Ibid.
48. Ibid., 32.
49. Heeren, "The Lynching of Bill Dembski," 45.
50. Glanz, "Darwin vs. Design," 32.
51. Heeren, "The Lynching of Bill Dembski," 45.
52. Heeren, "The Deed Is Done," 29.
53. Heeren, "The Lynching of Bill Dembski," 45.
54. Glanz, "Darwin vs. Design," 32.
55. Ibid.
56. Finley, "Why I Disbelieve Evolution."
57. Heeren, "The Lynching of Bill Dembski," 44.
58. Ibid.
59. Ibid.
60. Heeren, "The Deed Is Done," 29.
61. Ibid.
62. Ibid.
63. Glenn Tinder, "From the Ends of the Earth," in *Professors Who Believe,* ed. Paul M. Anderson (Downers Grove, IL: InterVarsity, 1998), 145.
64. Ibid.
65. Ashby L. Camp, introduction to *The Myth of Natural Origins* (Tempe, AZ: Ktsis, 1994).
66. Ravi Zacharias, *Jesus among Other Gods* (Nashville: Word, 2000), 50.
67. Walter R. Hearn, *Being a Christian in Science* (Downers Grove, IL: InterVarsity, 1997), 12.
68. Harry Blamires, *Where Do We Stand?* (Ann Arbor, MI: Servant, 1980), 130.
69. William F. Buckley Jr., *Nearer, My God* (San Diego: Harvest, 1998), 31.
70. William F. Buckley Jr., *Let Us Talk of Many Things* (Roseville, CA: Prima, 2000), 106.

6

HOW DOES CHRISTIAN SCHOLARSHIP
FIT INTO THE ACADEMIC MAINSTREAM?

To understand the case for the placement of Christian perspectives in the academic mainstream, it may be helpful to use the concepts employed in the study of majority-minority relations.[1]

▸▸ Assimilation

In majority-minority relations, the majority is defined in terms of power rather than number. Power and number are usually synonymous, but the issue is always who is in charge. Whenever a majority group and a minority group encounter one another, their interaction may take one of several forms. The form usually favored by the more powerful majority is assimilation. Assimilation is a process by which all members of a population are socially shaped to fit into the culture of the dominant group. In the case of ethnic minorities in American history, assimilation was the method by which the various nonwhite minority groups conformed to the white, northern European–oriented culture of the United States. Assimilation extinguishes the "objectionable" traits of minorities. They are dissolved in the world of the dominant group. Whether forced or permitted, this "be like us" assimilation strategy is usually the one the majority advocates, because it means the majority sacrifices little or nothing.

The academic mainstream, having adopted the paradigm of naturalism as the dominant explanation of why things are the way they are, wants to assimilate all members of the intellectual community into this paradigm. In many cases, the assimilation is forced to the extent that one resists it at one's own peril. Recall the words of Richard Dawkins: "It is absolutely safe to say that if you meet someone who claims not to believe in evolution, that person is ignorant, stupid, or insane (wicked, but I'd rather not consider that)." Dawkins's position provides precious little running room for those who do not buy into the religion of naturalism. Duane Litfin, president of Wheaton College, noted that the true danger of naturalism is not that it is presented as an intellectual option but

77

that "it declares its way of knowing to be the only legitimate one and then seeks to disenfranchise other voices."[2]

If one does not truly buy into the prevailing paradigm, there is pressure to appear as if one does; hence, the flying-under-the-radar behavior of so many Christians in the academic mainstream. They are undesignated believers seeking to maintain their precarious status in the mainstream. To "go public" is to invite political annihilation. The vocal Christian, unless she is a luminary in her field, may find that she is denied tenure, promotions, key committee assignments or that she must simply endure social and professional ostracism. Academics are very good at imposing rejection.

▸▸ Pluralism

The form of majority-minority interaction commonly favored by minorities is cultural pluralism. Pluralism is a much tossed about but rarely defined word. For our purposes, pluralism is a condition in which minorities are permitted to express—live out—their distinctive subcultural identities while conforming in areas affecting the larger society. For example, by the dictates of pluralism, black communities in major cities should be permitted to advance a truly African American subcultural existence replete with African American art, religious practices, literature, and fashion, provided the members of these communities observe the laws of the state and the nation. Not surprisingly, pluralism was the form most strongly favored by ethnic minority groups in the 1960s, because it involved the minimum amount of cultural repression. It is this pluralist notion to which Christian thinkers appeal when making the case for Christian scholarship in the secular university. In brief, Christians desire to be free to offer distinctly Christian perspectives in the classroom provided they meet the larger academic standards of the university.

George Marsden, in his book *The Outrageous Idea of Christian Scholarship*, bases his case for the presence of Christian perspectives in the research-university community on this very notion of pluralism. Marsden ran afoul of the more strident elements of the "Christian right" for his advocacy of pluralism over "conquest," or ideologically taking over the university community. Not only does he point out that Christians may very well not succeed in Christianizing the university with their ideas, but that by the standards of pluralism, no power play in that direction should be under consideration. Rather, he suggests that Christian scholars take a Golden Rule position when advancing their cause for inclusion within the university community. "How would we want scholars holding other strongly ideological convictions to act in the mainstream academy?" he asks rather rhetorically.[3] "Christians should be models of what it means to love and respect those with whom one differs, even as they may debate their differences."[4]

In fact, it is the fear of just such an imperialistic attempt by Christians that has generated a great deal of resistance to believers in the pluralistic setting of the secular university. This fear has a historical basis. Because conservative Christians were key in founding and directing the early American university, believers are regarded as the historic oppressors. Referring to this resistance to Christianity, Marsden writes, "This is what may be called the multiculturalist reaction to the appeal for more openly Christian scholarship. Not only gays and lesbians, but also many feminists and Marxist scholars may react in this way. So do some ex-fundamentalists. Many Jewish scholars likewise are understandably wary of any suggestion of resurgent Christian influence."[5] It is more a matter of power and politics than it is ideology. Jewish scholars may advocate Jewish studies and support the separation of church and state while continuing to oppose the admission of Christian perspectives. "The difference in their minds is that Christians have been the oppressors and, as the majority in this country, are not to be trusted." There is a double standard operative in the mainline university. Secularists regularly affirm tolerance for the various publics in their community but become ideologically genocidal toward Christians. Nevertheless, it is the fear of oppression that operates as a justification for that political hypocrisy.[6]

The majority concern merits attention. Every other (non-Christian) special interest group vying for a place at the academic table is regarded as a minority, at least in terms of power. Moreover, these groups rightfully trade on that label as a basis for their inclusion. Taking the case of African Americans, for example, the argument goes like this: We blacks are a valid minority group, with a distinct perspective—an ideology, if you will. As it is, that perspective is muted under the homogenizing force of the white majority culture. We request—even demand—that the university remove the oppressive yoke of white, northern European majoritarianism and empower us to express our own identity within the democratic structure of the academic community. Further, for this expression to be genuine, it must transcend the bounds of the student and residential community culture. African American studies must be part of the academic life of the institution. Therefore, our minority perspective must be factored into the classroom experience.

This does not work for Christianity because for many in the mainstream, the belief persists that the United States is a Christian country. This makes Christianity a majoritarian force and therefore viewed as all the more potentially oppressive. The attitude is that Christianity may hold sway in the larger society, but the university will fight to keep Christianity's dominating tentacles out of the academic mainstream. Indeed, a strong case can be made that the United States is far from being a Christian country, but perception is everything here. As long as this nation, with its Christian symbolism—crosses as jewelry, nativity imagery, and Christian holidays—appears Christian to the skeptics, they will feel that oppression by a religious majority, one that was historically in command, remains a risk. For this reason, statements such as "reclaiming our country for Christ" are not always helpful in making the Christian case for inclusion. It is also why secularists react to such comments with near venom. Whereas for the Christian such remarks may signal a recommitment to evangelism, to the skeptic they suggest the suspension of one's right not to believe.

Some vocal believers do most definitely advocate the conquest strategy. They do want to Christianize, or perhaps re-Christianize, the mainstream university by seizing the trump cards of power, rather than by communicating the gospel of God's love. This issue of conquest versus pluralism is a thorny and much debated one, arousing strong passions among believers. As noted earlier, Marsden took some rather mean-spirited blows from parts of the evangelical community for not siding with those who wanted to reannex the mainstream university as a bastion of faith-based education. My vote is with Marsden here. The separation of church and state, although employed as a permission-giver by many agnostic groups to drive all vestiges of religion out of public institutions, is a precious protective doctrine. To the extent that American culture is not truly Christian, it acts as a security device for the practice of the Christian faith. Better, it seems to me, is the argument that Christianity is a valid worldview, one that in its biblically based, transcendent form is now a minority perspective and so merits the same rights and protections afforded other minority and special interest views.

Flowing from that logic, there needs to be a place within the university structure for specific classes in Christian thinking, if not an actual department of Christian studies. Stated another way, if the university is to be true to its commitment to pluralism, then Christians, regardless of historically based concerns, should have a place with the other interest groups in the mainstream university. To do otherwise, says Marsden, "would be to endorse the concerted imperialism of groups who wish to exclude traditional Christianity from public expression." The issue is not whether Christian scholarship should be excluded, but "how to balance fairly the interests of the various sides in an era when basic cultural values are often sharply debated."[7]

As it stands, there is little accommodation made for religion—much less Christianity—in mainstream academe. As noted earlier, sociology departments commonly toss religion in with magic in their textbooks. Psychology departments largely ignore the very existence of religion, other than to account for its existence in purely nontranscendent terms, employing "psychologism" or isolating unrepresentative instances of deviant behavior performed in the name of religion as examples of the pernicious nature of faith. Prominent as religion has been in the shaping of the American democracy, even the most prestigious history departments do not offer courses in religious history. "It is not that leading historians who control such things think that religion is historically unimportant," says Marsden. Although they would acknowledge its import, "they have been so shaped by a culture which accounts for 'the good' without reference to religion that they do not notice religion's absence."[8]

Postmodernism, particularly its emphasis on cultural relativism and subjective interpretations of truth, gives added impetus to the Christian case for inclusion. The pluralist argument is coherent and convincing. It challenges the university to live up to its own publicly trumpeted values of diversity and inclusiveness. According to this notion, if the university is truly what it claims to be—a multiverse of cultures and perspectives—it should welcome Christian scholarship along with other faith-based perspectives. Moreover, as certainly as there is a place for African American, feminist, Marxist, gay, postmodern, and liberationist schools of thought, provided the courses in question meet the basic academic requirements of the university, so also there ought to be room for Christian approaches to the various disciplines.

▸▸ Making the Case

The Christian case for inclusion needs to be made in an unabashed fashion. Feminists make no apology in asserting their right to advance their worldviews in the classroom. One of the most striking examples of this occurred in the case of Lynn Weber, director of the women's studies program at the University of South Carolina, Columbia.[9] Weber instituted a set of guidelines "to create open and civil dialogue in her classroom." Weber's guidelines ask students to "acknowledge that racism, classism, sexism, heterosexism, and other institutional forms of oppression exist, and to agree to combat actively the myths and stereotypes about our own groups and other groups." In other words, Weber all but asks for a collective confession of politically incorrect sin from the students and follows it with a thinly disguised academic altar call to address these wrongs.

As amazing as these "guidelines" are, Weber had used them for almost two decades. Perhaps even more astonishing, they were all but officially endorsed by her professional colleagues in the women's studies field, with her guidelines being published in *Women's Studies Quarterly*.[10] They were also published in the resource collection of the American Sociological Association (ASA) titled *Teaching Sociological Concepts and the Sociology of Gender*. Finally, in 2002, the Foundation for Individual Rights in Education, Inc. (FIRE) raised its voice in protest, claiming that Weber's guidelines constituted "a threat to freedom of both speech and conscience" and that students should not be required to "hold certain arguments as unquestionable truth in order to participate in a class without penalty."

FIRE nailed the issue accurately. The guidelines clearly infringe on the students' rights to freedom of speech and conscience, requiring them to hold certain arguments as unquestionable truth. Yet Weber had used those guidelines for almost twenty years without engendering undue protest. Amazingly, in the face of the FIRE protest, Weber's status seems secure. Rather than censure her violation of students' rights, the ASA Council spun the issue so as to make Weber, not her students, the victim. The council approved a resolution supporting *Weber's* academic freedom. In fact, council member Barbara Risman stated, "Weber's guidelines are used quite widely," and advocated "a public stand for faculty rights to created guidelines for classroom discussion." Imagine if Weber were a professor of Christian studies and required her students to acknowledge that human nature is flawed, that humanity is alienated from God, that it is through a relationship with his divine son, Christ, that humanity is reconciled to God, and that they should agree to combat any and all misrepresentations of the gospel in their own and other groups. What would the ASA Council's position have been? What would the council motion have been? In Weber's case it was this: "The ASA Council wishes to affirm the academic freedom of all faculty to develop strategies or guidelines to encourage open and civil discussion and dialogue of controversial issues that are inherent to the study of inequality and other core subjects." The motion passed unanimously.

The Weber fiasco aside, the academic community now accords feminist perspectives substantial respect, due in part to the growing number of self-proclaimed feminists and their assertiveness. And the ascendancy of feminism in the mainstream has been rapid. Whereas in the early 1970s feminism was regarded as representing rather radical and political formulations by a fringe group of dissidents, today courses in gender identity can be found among sociology offerings. When one compares the two-millennia tradition of Christian philosophy and literature to the relatively recent tradition of feminism, that Christian thinking is all but banished in the mainstream while feminism continues to gain momentum bends the contours of logic.

In any case, Christians need to follow the feminists' lead of advocating their position without reservation. Indeed, Christian perspectives merit the same multicultural regard as African American, Marxist, and feminist views. Such regard will not be gained by humble, self-effacing, ashamed-of-Jesus requests. Not unlike the case of feminism, African American issues were first given a serious hearing when in the 1960s blacks abandoned their traditional hat-in-hand approaches for more direct, even confrontational, stances. Black activism, even militance, gained attention and respect. I don't suggest that Christians need to be setting science buildings ablaze in quest of a place at the intellectual table or that they in any other way abandon the fruits of the Spirit. I do feel, however, that Christian thinkers need to stop taking tentative stances toward the inclusion of their philosophical views in the higher educational community. Christians need not apologize for asserting that Christian subcultures belong within as well as outside the secular university world.

The Christian case for inclusion is further strengthened by the very history of the American university.[11] The university system that now all but overtly excludes Christian values and perspectives owes its very existence to the commitment of Christians to higher education. The university was founded on the belief that education is good and that God has ordained that humanity develop its intellectual capacities to master creation. Although the rule of the church may have at times been heavy-handed, occasionally stifling free inquiry, the Christian faith and the institutional church are more than friends of the modern research university; they are its parents.

The issue does not end there. When given a forum for presentation, other special interest groups rarely dilute, soften, or in any other way compromise their ideologies depending on the audience. Christians, however, too often try to package their notions in secular containers to make them acceptable to nonbelievers. "We have accepted secularism's challenge to fight on secularist ground, with secularist weapons and secularist umpire, before a secularist audience and according to the secularist book of rules," contends Blamires. As a result, Christians have few ideological converts and are misunderstood, as they keep trying to present their views in the context of the secularist mentality.[12]

Indeed, there is a need to appeal to reason and to apply the rules of sound scholarship in presenting Christian views in the academic mainstream. The same should be required of other special interest perspectives. This, however, need not include seeking the secularist's approval by neatly fitting Christianity into a secular framework. Gaining the secularist's intellectual approval is not possible, because at their cores, Christianity and secularism are incompatible. Basic to a Christian worldview are the beliefs that God determines truth, that humankind is his spiritual creation, and that all of reality must be viewed from an eternal rather than a temporal perspective. In brief, Christianity, due to its transcendent perspective, is much larger than secularism.

Consider how greatly Christian notions contrast with secularist thinking. Secularism asserts that the opinionated self is the sole determiner of what is truth, with God and theology as mere "playthings for the mind." It also regards Christianity as a human construction, consisting of little more than a collection of interesting musings about truth and moral behavior.[13] Although the secularist may find Christian morality and its fellowship and spiritual culture admirable, that is where it ends. She regards its central teachings as simply not credible, its theology a tangled mess of outmoded and obscure metaphysics, and its view of humanity's situation and destiny totally incompatible with modern knowledge.[14]

Given this contrast, Blamires calls Christians to a new strategy—one of shifting their ground and moving to the offense. Beginning by accepting the authoritative nature of the Christian faith and the objective nature of Christian truth, such a crawling out from under the secular camouflage would, he feels, not only energize the Christian, but it also would be refreshing to Christianity's intellectual opponents. When secularists attack what they see as a fantastical Christian belief, we need to make clear that we are not operating on secular assumptions and, more important, that we neither invented nor designed Christianity. In fact, we may not like Christianity's entire design, but we cannot alter it at will as if it were a human product.[15]

Furthermore, we need to abandon attempts to gain secular approval by reducing Christian notions to temporal phenomena that serve secular ends. Blamires contends that Christian thinking allows itself to be subtly secularized by offering a purely *chronological* status to the eternal. By making eternal life simply the life that follows this one, rather than the context in which all of life is conducted, its meaning is being twisted to come to terms with the secular mind on a false basis. "The basis is that here and now Christians and secularists can share the same conceptions, attitudes, and modes of action within the temporal sphere, since the essential difference between them—i.e. the dispute whether or not there is God's eternity beyond this world—is one which begins to be applicable only when this life is ended."[16] This is not to say that believers and nonbelievers cannot get along. It is to say that once they move past the general common denominators of the scholarship, their worldviews do not coincide.

The issue of temporality is central, because this life is what the essence of the faith is founded upon. Faith is grounded in the supernatural. To paraphrase T. S. Eliot, Christian education is education with a certain kind of *telos* or goal. "We must derive our theory of education from our philosophy of life. The problem turns out to be a religious problem."[17] To that end, Christian education prepares students for their role in God's universe in both this life and in their ultimate *telos*.[18] The chief aim of humanity is not merely to create a more pleasing temporal environment, as compatible with Christianity as that goal may be. It is larger. It is to serve God in a fallen world. No false accommodation with prevailing secularist thinking need be made. For Blamires, Christian thinking may not be accepted as the pathway to truth, but at least it "should be recognized for what it is: something different, something distinctive, something with special depth, hardness, solidity; a pleasure to fight with and a joy to be beaten by."[19]

▸▸ The Christian Community and Compartmentalization

The problem, however, also lies within the community of Christian scholars. As discussed earlier, many Christian scholars have been functionally assimilated into the naturalism of the university, averting potential science-versus-religion clashes by employing a compartmentalized mind-set. Such scholars rationalize this behavior by claiming that science generates empirical facts, while Christian commitment, writes Wolterstorff, "pertains to—well, *something else*. Accordingly, science cannot possibly put commitment on the defensive."[20] On the face of it, this common approach allows the believer to hold faith in one hand and secularism in the other. In reality, it does no such thing. Such a view places science outside the boundaries of a Christian worldview, not subject to critique. This amounts to a conformism to science. Wolterstorff rightly points out that this approach makes such thinkers "brothers beneath the skin" with the naturalists.[21]

The notion that faith and learning will generate no ideological skirmishes is folly. Their often-jarring interaction is a constant for the Christian scholar. It is rooted in the supernatural-versus-natural orientation. Blamires points out that the Christian views the natural order as grounded within the supernatural order, and time as contained within eternity.[22] This perspective is foundational to Christian thinking. Nevertheless, while one's faith is the basis for a critique of secular notions, so also the nature of scientific discoveries will necessitate revisions in Christian thinking. Such was the case when the Copernican theory—that the sun rather than the earth was the center of the universe—was confirmed. Similar rethinking took place when it was demonstrated that certain life forms do evolve over time. In any case, the faith-and-learning dialogue never ends, and compartmentalization is not a valid option for the genuine Christian thinker.

When the Christian suspends the faith-and-learning dialogue, she becomes an ideological gymnast who jumps in and out of a Christian mind-set as the subject changes from theology to sociology, from faith to physics.[23]

▸▸ Secessionism

In many instances, however, secessionism rather than assimilation is the primary problem among believers. When Christian scholars reject assimilation because it means bowing the knee to a godless ideology, and pluralism is not pursued—either due to an unwillingness to press the matter or to intellectual intimidation—there is but one strategy left: secessionism. Secessionism means the voluntary withdrawal of the minority from contact with the dominant group. That many Christians, not unlike black separatist groups of the 1960s, have employed a secessionist strategy is evident when one observes the rather distinct academic subcultures they have developed.

Alan Wolfe of the Boisi Center for Religion and American Public Life at Boston College weighs in heavily on this issue. Wolfe is particularly tough on evangelical Protestantism, claiming that among religious traditions, it ranks dead last in intellectual stature.[24] He attributes this to its fundamentalist heritage. Historically, as high-church universities abandoned their orthodox roots, revivalism took an increasingly reactionary stance. Scholarship was squashed under the soles of biblical literalism. Viewed as a threat to Christian orthodoxy, disinterested scholarly inquiry was stifled. Particularly in the early part of the twentieth century, simplistic biblical interpretations passed for serious education. Statements like that of Billy Sunday exemplify this genre: "When the word of God says one thing and scholarship says another, scholarship can go to hell."[25]

Evangelical David Lyle Jeffrey, senior vice provost at Baylor, notes the anti-intellectual edge of evangelical Protestantism. His parents disapproved of his decision to attend even a Christian college—Wheaton. "My dad said, 'David, you show me an educated Baptist, and I'll show you a backslider,'" relates Jeffrey.[26] Learning, believed to threaten faith, was to be eradicated.

For Nathan Hatch, Notre Dame provost, the story of evangelicalism is "how ordinary folk came to distrust leaders of genius and talent and to defend the right of common people to shape their own faith and submit to leaders of their own choosing."[27] It can be argued, however, that those "leaders of genius and talent" veered away from Scripture as a source of divine revelation and authority as they worshiped at the altar of reason and science. Nonetheless, an anti-intellectual bias did develop and the term *academic quality* elicited more distrust than enthusiasm.

Wheaton College philosopher Mark Noll describes this fundamentalist tradition as one of "treating the verses of the Bible as pieces in a jigsaw puzzle that needed only to be sorted and then fit together to possess a finished picture of divine truth."[28] The mind-set of "God says it. I believe it. That settles it . . ." has its place, but it dismisses the dynamic nature of historical and cultural forces that shape the thinking and issues of any given era. This is where learning comes in. Were there a finished picture of divine truth, traditions and lifestyles would not change. But they do, and so do the issues of debate. For example, nearly a half century ago a seminary professor at a Christian college faced heresy charges for suggesting that God loves all of humanity, rather than only believers. Today such a position would go unnoticed, most assuredly uncensored. Similarly, matters such as divorce, homosexuality, and the ordination of women were hardly public agenda items in the first half of the twentieth century. In the second half of the century, they all but cried out for careful thinking and study.

Wolfe contends that partly as a result of this "intellectual somnambulism" many evangelical colleges have lost their best and brightest scholars to larger mainstream universities.[29] Nicholas Wolterstorff, Jeroslav Pelikan, Richard Mouw, Alvin Plantinga, and George Marsden are cited among this group. (The first two went on to Yale, Mouw took over the presidency of Fuller Seminary, while Marsden and Plantinga joined the faculty at Notre Dame.) With faculties drawn from a pool of scholars limited to those willing to sign conservative faith statements, and lacking the tight meritocracy of the larger, research university— with its rigorous peer review and lofty requirements for tenure—the exodus of such topflight scholars is thought to have left the evangelical community in a sea of academic mediocrity.

Moreover, Wolfe views evangelical scholars as "democratic to a fault. They see good in nearly everyone. . . . Wanting to ensure that everyone succeeds, they spawn a multiplicity of journals and publishing houses so that anyone can publish anything."[30] Media-savvy Bob Briner agrees: "Christian literature, both fiction and non-fiction, is one of the most ghettoized of all the activities of the church." Christian writers can segregate themselves, he points out. "They can appear on Christian radio stations, be reviewed in Christian magazines, and win prestigious awards without ever getting off the island, without ever leaving the ghetto, but also without taking and applying any of the penetrating salt where it is most needed."[31] In the academic world, the price is mediocrity, for Wolfe. The absence of stringent standards has evangelicals sometimes finding themselves "with no adequate way of distinguishing between ideas that are path breaking and those that are gibberish."[32]

Wolfe's attack is not altogether fair, for several reasons. First, the five scholars cited above hardly constitute a random sample of Christian scholars—all but Pelikan taught initially at Calvin College, a school long considered among the academic elite of Christian colleges. In addition, it is far more likely that most of these people left in part because the research universities that recruited them offered lighter teaching loads and more money, coupled with greater support for their publishing efforts than the teaching institutions at which they began.

Searing the brand of academic inferiority on evangelical institutions is manifestly unfair. Though perhaps light on the research front, there are some first-rate minds doing some genuinely excellent teaching in these institutions. Wolfe himself was impressed with the academic quality of the teaching to which he was exposed when visiting several Christian colleges.[33] Furthermore, when a tenure-track faculty position opens at one of these schools, there is no shortage of quality applicants. Restrictive hiring practices notwithstanding, there is more than sufficient intellectual horsepower within the Christian academic population.

Nevertheless, there is clear evidence of a strain of secessionism among many Christian scholars. Too many Christian academics either do not publish or restrict their contributions to publishing concerns that perpetuate the separatist subcultures of which they are a part. In short, they preach to the converted and do not advance their views in the mainstream academic world. This is not to say that there is no place for the Christian college or Christian academic associations. Rather, it is to suggest that Christian thinkers need to offer their perspectives not only within, but also beyond, the Christian academic community.

There is great value even in publishing mainstream material in one's respective field, because such "credentializing" gives the Christian scholar a more authoritative voice when she offers Christian notions. In short, Christian scholars need to hold dual academic citizenship—that of being members of the larger mainstream intellectual community as well as of the faculties on which they serve. This is currently not sufficiently the case. There were years when I was one of the only faculty members at my college to attend an academic conference in my discipline and surely the only one to present a paper. Not to move in wider circles is merely to reinforce and calcify the separatist nature and repatriations of these Christian academic subcultures.

Christian scholars need to interact with, rather than seal themselves off from, the academic mainstream. Intellectual secessionism results in a closed circuit of communication—an ideological sterility—with members of such communities endlessly quoting one another. Moreover, academic quality suffers when scholars marginalize themselves, retreating from the modern academy, rather than demanding a hearing within it by making quality contributions in their respective disciplines. Further, the Christian college needs a venue in which faith-and-learning approaches are developed, tested for academic respectability among Christian scholars, and prepared for introduction into the intellectual mainstream. In short, faith-and-learning notions may well begin in the Christian community but ought not to reside there permanently.

⇥ Both/And

There has been much lament over the absence of a Protestant Christian research university. This grieving may not be permanent. In 2002, *Christianity Today* reported that the previously cited, Baptist-oriented Baylor University had produced a forty-two-page document titled "Baylor 2012," articulating a vision of becoming a first-rate Christian research university by 2012. "Within the course of a decade, Baylor intends to enter the top tier of American universities while reaffirming and deepening its distinctive Christian mission," notes the plan.[34]

This dream of a "Protestant Notre Dame" (a school that has corralled three of the most celebrated evangelical scholars in Marsden, Hatch, and Plantinga) is a bold and exciting one. Michael Beaty, a philosopher at Baylor, echoes the words of many in saying, "There are a lot of Protestants who want to see a university take its religious identity seriously."[35] What makes the Baylor concept particularly attractive is its assertion that commitment to the Christian tradition and intellectual excellence—faith and learning, if you will—are not mutually exclusive, despite the difficulties in remaining faithful to both. This will most certainly take some careful fleshing out to avoid either academic mediocrity or baptized paganism. To the extent that Baylor succeeds in making the faith-and-learning marriage work, it can offer a both/and solution: solid, mainline research scholarship carried on within a genuinely Christian context.

Though moving from a Christian college culture to a university culture is daunting, Baylor's goal, however, is absolutely consistent with the New Testament call. Baylor "wants to permeate the intellectual culture through high-quality training for people who then can be teachers," says the aforementioned David Lyle Jeffrey, "not just for Christian liberal arts schools, but for people who can move into state schools or top-tier schools." Baylor's aim is "a much more vigorous representation of the Christian mind in the larger intellectual world."[36]

Indeed, the aim is high and the risks are great. For Baylor to make the vision a reality will require much prayer, plenty of money, and the ability to attract topflight graduate faculty and gifted students, in addition to performing successfully the faith-and-learning balancing act that many Christian colleges have not yet mastered. It is, in the words of Notre Dame's Hatch, an "intriguing, impressive experiment."[37] Regardless of its success, the very attempt to develop such an institution is a major step forward in making the faith-and-learning nexus incarnate.

With or without a Protestant Christian research university, the matter of the placement of Christian scholarship within the academic mainstream is a both/and issue. Christians should constitute an intellectually respectable presence on the faculties at the research universities of the mainstream academic world just as Paul was a powerful and respected presence among the intellectuals in pagan Rome and Corinth. Serious work on faith-and-learning syntheses, however, should also be done on Christian college campuses.

To be spiritually invisible at the research university, compartmentalizing one's life such that the third rail of faith never intersects with one's discipline, is not acceptable. Perhaps worse, however, is to engage in baptized paganism at the Christian college. To redeem the times is to redeem the thinking of the times. "In the world of academia," says Chiareli, "this means to take to the intellectual battlefield and confront the very disciplines that in the past three centuries have either emerged out of, or gradually but steadily declined into, strongholds of materialism, humanism, moral and cultural relativism, and secularism."[38] Because the church is not an academic institution, and because the mainstream university is at best pluralistic, the only place this faith-and-learning endeavor can thrive is in the Christian college. Even there, pressures other than the temptations of baptized paganism militate against a true integration of faith and learning. The need to expand enrollment, heighten institutional visibility, generate additional funding from a larger pool of sources, and gain more advanced program accreditation exert a near-gravitational pull on a Christian institution toward compromising its spiritual commitment.[39] Tempting as this accommodation may be, however, it is done at the expense of the institution's identity.

Whether in the mainstream or in the Christian college, to bring all things under the direction of Christ includes the life of the mind. For the Christian scholar, according to Chiareli, "There is no such thing as a neutral educational process."[40] If we are to have the mind of Christ, we must activate both the faith and the learning dimensions when doing scholarship, regardless of our venue.

Notes

1. Taken from David Claerbaut, *Social Problems,* vol. 2 (Scottsdale, AZ: Christian Academic Publications, 1977), 18–23. Based on George Eaton Simpson and J. Milton Yinger, *Racial and Cultural Minorities* (New York: Harper, 1958), 25–36.
2. Alan Wolfe, "The Opening of the Evangelical Mind," pt. 4 of The Loyalty-Oath Problem, http://www.theatlantic.com/issues/2000/10/wolfe4.htm (accessed July 17, 2002).
3. George M. Marsden, *The Outrageous Idea of Christian Scholarship* (New York: Oxford University Press, 1997), 53.
4. Ibid., 54.

5. Ibid., 32.
6. Ibid.; John Eaves, director of Hephzibah House, conversation with author, New York City, February 23, 2003.
7. Marsden, *The Outrageous Idea of Christian Scholarship*, 33.
8. Ibid, 74.
9. The Weber controversy was reported in the official newsletter of the American Sociological Association: "ASA Council Supports Sociologist Weber," *Footnotes* (March 2003): 3, 11. It was also reported in *Chronicle of Higher Education* (September 27, 2002).
10. *Women's Studies Quarterly* 18 (Spring–Summer 1990).
11. George M. Marsden, *The Soul of the American University* (New York: Oxford University Press, 1994).
12. Harry Blamires, *The Christian Mind* (Ann Arbor, MI: Servant, 1997), 117.
13. Ibid., 110–11.
14. Ibid., 79.
15. Ibid., 117–18.
16. Ibid., 69.
17. T. S. Eliot, "Modern Education and the Classics," *Selected Essays* (New York: Harcourt, Brace, 1950), 452, quoted in Brad Green, "Theological and Philosophical Foundations," in *Shaping a Christian Worldview*, ed. David S. Dockery and Gregory Alan Thornbury (Nashville: Broadman and Holman, 2002), 88.
18. Green, "Theological and Philosophical Foundations," in Dockery and Thornbury, *Shaping a Christian Worldview*, 89.
19. Blamires, *The Christian Mind*, 79–80.
20. Nicholas Wolterstorff, *Reason within the Bounds of Religion* (Grand Rapids: Eerdmans, 1984), 23.
21. Ibid., 24.
22. Blamires, *The Christian Mind*, 67.
23. Ibid., 70.
24. Wolfe, "The Opening of the Evangelical Mind," pt. 1, p. 3.
25. Ibid., 4–6.
26. Randall Balmer, "2012: A School Odyssey," *Christianity Today*, November 18, 2002, 65.
27. Wolfe, "The Opening of the Evangelical Mind," pt. 3, p. 5.
28. Ibid., pt. 1, p. 7.
29. Ibid., 9–10.
30. Ibid., pt. 2, p. 5.
31. Bob Briner, *Roaring Lambs* (Grand Rapids: Zondervan, 1993), 120.
32. Wolfe, "The Opening of the Evangelical Mind," pt. 2, p. 5.
33. Ibid., pt. 1, pp. 1–3.
34. Balmer, "2012: A School Odyssey," 64.
35. Ibid.
36. Ibid., 65.
37. Ibid., 69.
38. Antonio A. Chiareli, "Christian Worldview and the Social Sciences," in Dockery and Thornbury, *Shaping a Christian Worldview*, 261–62.
39. Ibid., 262–63.
40. Ibid., 263.

7

WHAT IS FAITH
AND LEARNING?

e have referred throughout these pages to faith and learning, along with Christian scholarship. Nonetheless, there remain those who ask, Can faith and learning truly meet? Moreover, apart from catechism and religious indoctrination, is there really such a thing as Christian *education?*

Despite the often-cynical bias of those who provide instruction in the secular mainstream, the Bible offers an unequivocal yes to both questions. Psalm 36:9 states that we see light in God's light, and Proverbs 9:10 asserts, "The fear of the LORD is the beginning of wisdom." These verses indicate that the essence of learning involves humility before God, a prerequisite to being teachable. This is the antithesis of arrogance, a willful spirit that closes the mind to learning and is invested in impressing others with what one has learned rather than in learning more. Paul's words in Ephesians 4:18 are applicable to this willfulness: "They are darkened in their understanding and separated from the life of God because of the ignorance that is in them due to the hardening of their hearts." Again, the issue is an unwillingness to believe, rather than a struggle with intellectual doubt. This choice is unwise and a movement away from truth. Psalm 14:1 says, "The fool says in his heart, 'There is no God.'" It is one thing to be agnostic. It is another thing to assert that humans are the supreme organisms of the universe and, hence, to rule out the possibility of the supernatural. It is, in the words of the psalmist, the opposite of wisdom.

Although Christianity is not a philosophy, and Jesus is far more than a great teacher, the Scriptures are steeped in wisdom. Not only are the New Testament words of Jesus both brilliant and radical, but the Old Testament book of Proverbs is a cornerstone of wisdom literature, containing over nine hundred verses dedicated to wisdom. Proverbs has much to say about prosperity and success. Although coldly realistic concerning the temporary effectiveness of evil and fraudulent schemes, it never endorses unethical actions. Throughout its thirty-one chapters is found a theme of acknowledging human flaws and humanity's absolute dependence on God.

Wisdom has nothing to do with intelligence or level of education. There is little correlation. Intelligence and credential often breed an arrogance that blinds one to input that is in conflict with one's own biases. The writer of Proverbs alludes to this trait, stating, "Whoever corrects a mocker invites insult; whoever rebukes a wicked man incurs abuse" (9:7). He then points out how the arrogant resist correction as a personal affront, contrasting them to the truly wise: "Do not rebuke a mocker or he will hate you; rebuke a wise man and he will love you" (9:8). He then affirms openness, noting, "Instruct a wise man and he will be wiser still; teach a righteous man and he will add to his learning" (9:9).

To assert that the integration of faith and learning is possible is not the same as defining it. What, then, do we mean by faith and learning? What is a Christian perspective? What do we mean by Christian education? Although questions this broad have no simple answers, we can look to Genesis for a place to start. The Bible opens with, "In the beginning God . . ." Just as an architect designs a building, just as an artist is the originator of a work, and just as a book begins with an author, a Christian worldview of education starts with the Creator of the universe. To be truly Christian, to find truth, learning must start with God in every discipline. That is precisely what the writer of Proverbs meant in saying, "The fear of the LORD is the beginning of knowledge, but fools despise wisdom and discipline" (1:7). Naturalist philosopher David Hume is reported to have said that where one begins is where he ends. To begin our learning endeavors in the wrong place, then, is to end without knowledge, truth, and what the Bible calls wisdom.

▸▸ Putting God in the Equation

When Hume's notion is applied to Christian higher education, we would do well to ask, Suppose we believed in God, how differently would the assumptions or conclusions of our discipline look?[1] In other words, putting God into the equation, how differently would we interpret the body of knowledge in our discipline? What effect would it have on what we are looking for?

For example, would one look at the physical sciences differently if he began with an awe-filled attitude toward God and the complexity of his infinite universe? Would a Christian scholar engage in art and literature differently if he were driven by the notion that a loving God is ever extending grace to a fallen race? Would a philosopher look at truth differently if he believed that ultimate truth does exist but that it has transcendent qualities beyond human comprehension? How might one study economic systems differently if he began with the belief that humans are self-interested and are by nature predisposed to gain wealth at the expense of others? Would one study psychology and personality theory differently if he believed humans are moral agents ever navigating a moral tension of right and wrong? How might a historian interpret past events were he to believe that an eternal, spiritual, and defining force is behind those occurrences?

Learning must have a God-consciousness for education to be truly Christian. If a scholar checks his faith at the door of a discipline in order to be "scientific" and "value-free," that scholar may be a Christian, but he is not a Christian scholar. To delete one's faith from one's academic enterprise is tantamount to studying art without the artist, to read literature while ignoring the author, or to analyze a series of mechanical principles independent of the engineer's role.

The very notion of Christian scholarship, however, evokes rather viscerally negative reactions from members of the mainstream academic community. Some, like a historian quoted in the *Chronicle of Higher Education,* assert that "the notion that scholars' personal beliefs are compatible with their academic interests is 'loony' and reflects a 'self-indulgent professorate.'" Moreover, by his logic, "an important distinction needs to be made between supernatural and non-supernatural ideas. Gender and race are empirical constructs: one's faith is not."[2] Rather than being intimidated by such an attack, the Christian scholar needs to see that such "thinking" is itself loony. Gender and race enter the academic equation not at all because of their empirical aspects but because they have *social, psychological,* and *political significance.* In other words, these empirical constructs are meaningful solely because of their nonempirical impact. Even when used as mere statistical categories, they serve a nonempirical function because their very selection as categories is made on the grounds of their social significance.

This antifaith bias has become extreme. A professor of religion at a large university contended that a person who practiced a given religion should not be allowed to teach about that religion in an academic setting because it would violate the standards of detached scholarship. This notion reaches new heights of faulty reasoning. Imagine the response this person would receive were he to apply this to those instructing in feminist, gay, or minority studies.[3] There is simply an incredible blindness going on here, one that is reminiscent of Paul's earlier cited statements about ignorance coming from the hardening of one's heart.

Again, the naturalist and the postmodernist most certainly do not engage their areas of inquiry in a value-free, fully empirical fashion. Basic to the naturalist's very outlook is the *belief*—the conviction, if you will—that the universe consists solely of natural elements driven randomly by entirely mechanistic processes. Were God to intervene and make the sun stand still, the naturalist would still feel compelled to explain even that phenomenon in wholly natural, mechanistic terms, even if the explanation was untenable. Similarly, the postmodern scholar enters the academy with the lenses of multiculturalism, political correctness, and subjectivity serving as a shiny, clean prism through which he interprets the data in his discipline.

The intensity of the naturalist's and postmodernist's commitments to their respective worldviews must be kept in mind to prevent the Christian thinker from falling prey to the silly but cunning notion that his scholarship is somehow deficient owing to some value-laden bias. Faith is everywhere, even in science. The student heading for the lab has faith that the class will be held in a given room, that the building is basically safe, that the test tubes are indeed test tubes and are reliable instruments in experimentation, that his eyes are seeing real numbers and letters, and that his mind is interpreting them accurately. All of this is taken on faith as a part of the science student's worldview before he engages in step one of the scientific method.[4]

The simple, indisputable reality is that we all have worldviews, or biases. Though some are more obvious than others, they exist and predetermine much of what we "see." The distinction for the Christian is that he works consciously within a worldview, rather than laboring in the illusion of utter objectivity. He operates within the context of what is called special revelation, the belief that God has revealed himself in a particular and special fashion through Scripture and that through this special revelation the scholar is guided in his understanding of the universe.

▸▸ Quality Scholarship

The view that Christians approach their scholarship with a worldview does not, however, render Christian scholarship and sound research mutually exclusive—an ugly canard foisted against Christian academics and exemplified by a letter to the *Chronicle*. All but labeling the term *Christian scholar* as an oxymoron, the writer charged: "If they'd research even the religious philosophies they've accepted, then they could actually call themselves 'scholars.' But they won't."[5] This charge is simply preposterous. The history of scholarship is teeming with Christian contributors. C. S. Lewis, for example, used faith to understand and enrich his work in literature and philosophy. Moreover, the very existence of the likes of Wolterstorff and Marsden refutes this uninformed allegation.[6]

The charges, however, continue unabated. One secularist scholar recommended that one who presents his religious worldviews in the classroom should "inform" the students that the beliefs expressed "are beyond what we have accepted as standards for scholarly proof in modern universities." Still another believed that religious matters are "by definition not amenable to logic."[7] Note what is going on here. It is intellectual self-nullification. The Christian scholar is allowed to state his "biases," provided he admits these are nothing more than unverifiable and unscholarly notions and therefore worthless. Yet were that same scholar to render an explanation of the reasons for an economic downturn, his ideas might constitute a reasoned "theory."

Such jaded views of faith and learning are simply variations of a single theme: that Christian scholarship lacks objectivity and is therefore devoid of academic respectability. If, as philosopher Arthur Holmes suggests, objectivity is defined as being free of presuppositions or guiding principles of thought, then objectivity is nowhere in existence. People—scholars included—are simply not neutral in areas of values and belief. Holmes states, "Objectivity consists rather in acknowledging and scrutinizing one's point of view and testing presuppositions."[8] Objectivity is about the process by which one makes commitments, not the absence of such commitments.

For Marsden, the issue is not scholarship but rather the previously discussed issue of pluralism. He is uncompromising on this point: "Traditional religious viewpoints, I am saying, can be just as hospitable to scientifically sound investigation as many other viewpoints, all of which are ultimately grounded in some faith or other. Hence religious perspectives ought to be recognized as legitimate in the mainstream academy so long as their proponents are willing to support the rules necessary for constructive exchange of ideas in a pluralistic setting."[9]

Seeing the "objectivity process" as does Holmes, Marsden asserts that, far from being aberrant in their methods of seeking truth, Christian scholars use essentially the same standards of evidence as nonbelievers. "These standards work in separating good arguments from bad, and on many topics they can establish a sort of 'public knowledge' that persons from any ideological subcommunities can agree on and which are not simply matters of opinion," says Marsden. "Christians and non-Christians likely will use precisely the same methods in determining the date when George Washington crossed the Delaware to attack the Hessians at Trenton."[10] Similarly, Christians in the behavioral sciences use the same concepts and research designs as secularists, often interpreting the data identically. Were that not so, graduates of Christian colleges would not perform as competently as they currently do in mainstream graduate schools.

Christian commitments, Marsden says, "do not very often have substantial impact on the techniques used in . . . academic inquiry." Despite their zeal, Christians "must be duly dispassionate in order to think clearly and to present their results effectively, without tendentiousness."[11] Moreover, the academic main-stream simply does not exclude all nonempirical "background beliefs" among its scholars. Beliefs in racial justice and gender equality, for example, are passionately supported. In many cases, Christian notions constitute background beliefs much as other interest groups have background beliefs out of which they do their scholarship. Though these beliefs are central to a scholar's worldview and are even his very reason for engaging in scholarship, they are termed *background* because they rarely bear directly on how research is conducted or presented.[12]

The Christian scholar, according to celebrated law professor Michael McConnell, need not retreat in the face of the intellectual skeptic. Once, after McConnell informally related a Christian view on euthanasia, one of his colleagues—in the rich tradition of intellectual secularism—ragingly stated there was no place for "superstition and dogma" in a serious exchange. Another well-intentioned colleague urged the secularist to calm down and realize that it was McConnell's religion he was attacking. Relieved at the time, McConnell was later disappointed in himself. He felt he had acquiesced to the postmodern notion that religious faith is a purely personal matter, and off-limits to challenge, rather than a claim of truth. He felt he should have told the secularist to bring it on, saying, "No, friend, let me respond. My position should be subjected to the same searching inquiry that any philosophy or worldview receives. I am not telling you about my religion. I am telling you what I think is true. I have an obligation to explain why."[13]

In short, one's perspective, or worldview, need not obviate intellectual openness and academic discourse. According to Marsden, although a person may operate from a religious or cultural belief system, one need only be certain to "argue for one's scholarly interpretations on the same sorts of publicly accessible grounds that are widely accepted in the academy."[14]

Much of the difference between Christian and non-Christian scholarship resides in areas that move beyond the provably factual, necessitating interpretation and perception. Just as one person may differ from another as to which is the figure and which is the background in a black-and-white pattern (often used in psychology books to illustrate the nature of perception), a Christian may perceive and interpret a given phenomenon differently from a nonbeliever. Just as a Republican will read history with a different set of "lenses" than a Democrat, and a minority person will view a public issue differently than a member of a society's dominant group will, so a Christian will interpret the world differently than the secularist.[15]

Students often accept this difference in perception when operating within a truly pluralistic setting. Marsden put this to the test as a visiting professor of history at the University of California at Berkeley. Early in the term he informed his students of his "religiously informed viewpoint, presenting this disclosure as analogous to truth in advertising."[16] He stated that he would likely make interpretative statements out of that context but would not require anyone necessarily to agree. Despite this esteemed professor's failure to discredit himself as a scholar or to present himself as one whose beliefs were "not amenable to logic," no objections to his teaching were registered. In fact, a number of students appreciated his candor.

▸▸ The Independent Variable

With the rules of quality scholarship intact, we turn to a key issue: making God the independent rather than the dependent variable. Certainly there is value in looking for evidences (once called proofs) for God in one's discipline. Not only do these exist, but they have a faith-strengthening as well as an intellectually satisfying effect. This is not, however, the only avenue through which God enters the scholarly enterprise. God does not have to validate his existence by popping up serendipitously in our secular studies. Limiting him to this port of entry is secular, because it subordinates him to the body of knowledge under study, making the material, rather than God, the authority. Such an approach repudiates his sovereignty in a *de facto* sense. Yet this is exactly what happens in so many would-be Christian academic settings. If God does not emerge rather routinely in the study of the material, he may as well not exist. Moreover, that approach—God as the dependent variable—all but assures that God is unlikely to make a compelling appearance in courses the likes of advanced algebra or trigonometry.

That God is not, on the surface, the dependent variable is no assurance that he is the independent variable. According to Wolterstorff, when matters of faith and learning collide, Christian scholars often attempt to reduce the dissonance by harmonizing in one of three ways. They may rework their belief commitments, as many did when the heliocentric theory of planetary motion replaced the earth-as-the-center-of-the-universe notion. In other cases, they stretch the boundaries of the Christian context to accommodate seemingly conflicting scientific theories and discoveries, as in the case of certain instances of evolution. In still other instances, they look for ways to "Christianize" scientific theorizing by applying it to the solving of human problems.[17]

Looking at these three responses, there most certainly is a place to think and rethink the relationship between faith and learning, science and religion. The interaction is constant and often exciting. There are times, as in the case of heliocentrism, when one is wise to revise the content of his Christian thinking. When people make the Bible—God's special revelation of himself in history and human existence—an astronomy book, they are likely to run into trouble. Moreover, the boundaries of our worldviews are often rather constricted and require expansion. There is, for example, much adaptation in the universe. There is also much value in finding ways to make scientific notions serve redeeming ends. Justice-in-shalom must be our goal. Nonetheless, without God as the independent variable, this harmonizing is nothing more than a subtle conformity to science. "They all take for granted that science is OK as it is," notes Wolterstorff. "In none of them is there any *internal* relation between Christian commitment and what goes on within the sciences. In none of them does Christian commitment enter the devising and weighing of theories within the sciences."[18]

Faith and learning must begin with God and what we know about the universe from basic Christian doctrine. Thus, we can factor into the learning process certain basic tenets.

- God is eternal. Though personal, he is an infinite, all-powerful, and perfect spiritual being, beyond the capacity of any human's total comprehension.
- This God is the creator of an orderly, patterned, and infinite natural universe, in which he continues to be active.
- All things, animate and inanimate, were made to please and glorify him.
- Humans are the highest level of creation because they are made in God's eternal image. As such, they have distinctive, God-like capacities. Among them are self-consciousness (identity), a sense of morality, a desire for ultimate truth, and a longing for intimacy.
- Humans are the trustees of the earth but are flawed by an inherent imperfection called sin. This flaw manifests itself in rebellion, pride, self-interest, and conflict.
- Despite human imperfection, God desires a personal relationship with each human. This relationship is made possible by the work of his son, Jesus, who atoned for the imperfections of humankind by his death and resurrection.
- Jesus is the human essence of God and is the standard by which all humans are to measure themselves and their conduct.
- God has revealed himself generally through the awe-inspiring means of nature and more specifically through the special revelation of Scripture.
- God infuses those who believe in him with a part of his personality called the Holy Spirit, who guides our thinking toward truth.

- There is but one singular strand of truth. It is God's truth. Hence, our knowledge of God guides our search for truth, and what we find to be verifiable reality in our academic pursuits merely introduces us to more of God's truth.

The challenge for the Christian scholar is to make these basic tenets of historical Christianity deliberate and conscious givens in his area of study and to look for ways in which they do not merely inform but also illuminate the learning process within that discipline. These tenets need to be an intellectual beginning point for the Christian learner, just as the multiplication tables are for the math student and the elemental chart is for the chemist. They are the beginning points because the Christian believes they are true. Whatever the faith happens to achieve in oneself or others, Blamires points out, is secondary to it being true.[19]

▸▸ Truth

The issue of truth often slips through the cracks in faith-and-learning dialogues. For the believer, Christianity is not merely a philosophy, a set of systemic beliefs, or a subjective way of viewing the world. It is the truth. He would have little or no interest in melding faith with learning if he saw Christianity as no more objectively valid than an approach to positive thinking. Under such conditions, the faith may have value, but it would not be a necessary ingredient of the scholarly process. Faith is foundational for the believer because he believes Christianity is true. Therefore, to whatever extent the Christian scholar is committed to discovering truth, he will look at the phenomena of his discipline through the eyes of faith.

"In my estimation," says Chiareli, "what makes the Christian worldview so robust and time-tested is that, quite to the contrary of other worldviews, it is not interested in convincing argumentation, but rather in convicting by proclaiming truth. It is objective because it is truth based." It does not require unthinking adherence. It calls for a careful study of human nature, the character of the world, and the attributes of God.[20]

The believer accepts the basic tenets of the faith as true for specific reasons.[21] The most important of these reasons, according to Blamires, is that the faith is grounded in the supernatural. It is not developed within nature. As such, it is received through revelation from God. It is not a theoretical construction of a group of scholars or theologians. Because it is supernatural in origin, it is objective rather than subjective in nature. Like gravity, Christianity is regarded as an objective reality whether or not one chooses to accept it. That one does not believe in the existence of gravity does not make it any less true for everyone. "Arguing about God's existence, I hold," writes Cornelius Van Til, "is like arguing about air. You may affirm that air exists, and I that it does not. But as we debate the point, we are both breathing air the whole time."[22]

Creation, for example, is a Christian fact. Believing in creation is not a more-or-less matter. Scholars may argue over the degree of evolutionary development in the universe, but in the end, each has to decide whether the universe is the product of a creating God or merely the residue of natural forces. One either believes or doesn't. "It is either the bowed head or the turned back," says Blamires.[23] Christianity's supernatural nature means truth is discovered through inquiry, not determined by majority vote. Therefore, the truths of the faith are authoritative—valid for all—not matters of personal choice. And it is more than faith. "Christianity is a religion rooted in historical reality and historical documentation." There is corroborating evidence concerning people, places, and events in Christendom.[24] Put another way, Christianity is a matter of acts and facts, recorded in the Bible, not a series of speculations. It is about truth.[25]

Clearly this is not the prevailing view in the mainstream. The popular notion is that "the world is divided into two groups: scientists who face the facts, and true believers who shut their eyes to them. The implication is that a real scientist cannot be a true believer," according to Bennett.[26] Yet archaeological digs regularly corroborate the historicity of the biblical record. For example, in 1868 a German traveler named Klein visited Jordan (formerly Moab). He discovered a monument on which were inscribed thirty-four lines by Mesha, King of Moab, lines in memory of his battle against Israel. The names Omri and Ahab appear in 1 Kings 16 and in the inscriptions. In both cases, these kings were described as oppressors of Moab.[27]

Archaeology is about the past. Prophecy, however, is about the future. The Old Testament is brimming with detailed prophecies of the coming Messiah. Contrast this with Islam, for example. There is not a single Islamic prophecy about the coming of Muhammad hundreds of years before his birth. In fact, no cult can point to even one prophecy that foretells its appearance. There are certain "prophecies"—election outcomes, for example—requiring no real inspiration to be accurate. "However," writes Bennett, "try asking any news reporter to identify the candidates who will be running for election twenty or fifty years from now. Ask him who will win, and then ask him for details about where the winners will be born, their future lifestyles, and even the circumstances that will surround their deaths."[28] One of the most striking of such prophecies concerns the birth of Jesus. Micah (5:2) not only prophesied the birth of Christ but stated that the town of his birth would be Bethlehem, not the town from which Jesus' family came.[29]

"Go beyond that and ask the news reporter for reliable information about what will happen in the Middle East 1,000 years from now," says Bennett, pressing further. "Also ask him to specify cities that will be annihilated during that long period of time." As the demands for predictions mount, so do the odds against their being accurate, unless the prognosticator can rely upon God for the inside story. Yet the occurrences mentioned above, along with many more, have been prophesied in the Bible.[30] There is no better example of biblical accuracy than the history of the city of Tyre. Ezekiel 26:3–21 presents the prophecy. The account in the *Encyclopedia Britannica* offers the history. The story is identical. Peter Stoner compared the seven prophecies concerning Tyre in Ezekiel against the historical record, calculating the probability of their accuracy. "If Ezekiel had looked at Tyre in his day," says Stoner, "and made these seven predictions in human wisdom, these estimates mean that there would have been one chance in 75,000,000 of their all coming true. They all came true in the minutest detail."[31]

▸▸ Christian Lenses

Basic Christian beliefs—rooted in acts and facts—form the structure, the context, and the perspective in which we engage our areas of inquiry. Although these tenets will be more overtly applicable to some subjects than to others, they need to be the lenses through which we search for truth in any discipline. And we do so because we agree with the writer of Proverbs when he stated in 2:6, "For the LORD gives wisdom, and from his mouth come knowledge and understanding." We want accurate insight, and we believe that accuracy has a divine origin.

Moreover, the more comfortable we become in using these lenses, the more distinctly we will see truth through them. Wolterstorff states that too few Christian scholars "see the world as Christians. Our indigenous patterns of thought are not those of Christianity, but those induced by the scientific worldview."[32] Viewing our disciplines through Christian lenses must move to the level of perception, rather than being a matter of occasional though conscious decision.

It is my contention that this matter of perceiving the world as a Christian is exactly what is missing in so much of what we call Christian higher education. Rather than putting on the lenses of the faith as we work in our academic disciplines, we set them aside as one does a book or an article that does not seem to be pertinent to the matter being studied. Faith becomes ancillary to learning. We may react when we encounter belief systems that directly contradict Christian faith, but short of that, we ignore the import and relevance of our Christian worldview. Looking at our areas of study through a Christian prism is a form of self-discipline—one I wish I had been more diligent in—and must move to perception. Again, there is no need to compromise the quality of one's scholarship to do this, any more than does the naturalist or postmodernist. What is at stake here are not the principles of scholarship, but a more profound understanding of God's truth. It is about what David said in Psalm 36:9: "In your [God's] light we see light."

Here is what Christians regularly profess: that in the beginning the Word (Christ) existed and that all light and life, wisdom and knowledge, is found exclusively in him (God); that it is in God's light that we are able to see light; and that for us, the fear of the Lord is the beginning of gaining wisdom. Even a cursory reading of these assertions suggests one simple notion: that truth is found with God at the center of inquiry. As Greg Bahnsen notes, "From beginning to end, man's reasoning about anything whatsoever (even reasoning about reasoning itself) is unintelligible or incoherent unless the truth of the Christian scripture is presupposed."[33] Calvinist theologian Van Til pushes it to the limit, stating, "I understand no fact aright unless I see it in its proper relation to Christ as Creator-Redeemer of me and my world."[34]

In short, to engage learning from any other than a God-centered direction is to begin and end in the wrong place. To the extent that one believes any of the aforementioned basic Christian premises, the challenge is to implement those beliefs into one's scholarship. It is to put muscle into one's commitments and so accelerate the process of discovering and communicating truth.

There is yet an additional need. Though one does not need to become a theologian or philosopher to be a Christian scholar, one does need to be familiar with basic Christian theology and its biblical foundations. John Suppe, professor of geology at Princeton, remembers a chapel speaker confronting her Ivy League listeners by saying, "You students have made it to the college of your choice, a top university, and you professors know more about your fields than anyone else in the world, except for maybe ten other people. You people know your business very well. But you have a kindergarten knowledge of Christianity."[35]

Unfortunately, such remedial knowledge is not limited to those in mainstream universities. One Christian who holds a powerful academic position at a major research institution told me of his surprise that many professors at Christian colleges had only a "Sunday school familiarity with Scripture." The better our knowledge of Scripture, the better "we see the *pattern* of our authentic commitment and its wide ramifications." Without it, "our scholarship becomes eccentric."[36] Bits and pieces emerge, but without a systemic whole, distortions become the rule.

If nothing else, putting God at the center of the universe and of one's discipline will have an impact on the temperament of the scholar. For the Christian, the learner is less a creator than a part of creation. He is not subject (a god), but object (part of God's universe). Learning then becomes an act of worship. It venerates God by learning more of his truth within our discipline—truth that in turn transforms the learner. Struck by all that we do not know or have yet to know, the Christian scholar becomes truly scholarly. Rather than being lost in the vanity associated with the possession of knowledge, he becomes teachable.

Notes

1. "Discussion Questions for George M. Marsden, *The Positive Contributions of Theological Context*," http://members.aol.com/jonatboyd/mpctcdq.html (accessed July 16, 2002).
2. George M. Marsden, *The Outrageous Idea of Christian Scholarship* (New York: Oxford University Press, 1997), 5.
3. Ibid., 13.
4. Brad Green, "Theological and Philosophical Foundations," in *Shaping a Christian Worldview*, ed. David S. Dockery and Gregory Alan Thornbury (Nashville: Broadman and Holman, 2002), 82.
5. Marsden, *The Outrageous Idea of Christian Scholarship*, 5.
6. Harry L. Poe, "The Influence of C. S. Lewis," in Dockery and Thornbury, *Shaping a Christian Worldview*, 108.
7. Marsden, *The Outrageous Idea of Christian Scholarship*, 5.
8. Arthur F. Holmes, *The Idea of a Christian College* (Grand Rapids: Eerdmans, 1987), 71.
9. Marsden, *The Outrageous Idea of Christian Scholarship*, 45.
10. Ibid., 47.
11. Ibid.
12. Ibid., 49.
13. Michael W. McConnell, "We Worship the Same God You Do," in *Professors Who Believe*, ed. Paul M. Anderson (Downers Grove, IL: InterVarsity, 1998), 202.
14. Marsden, *The Outrageous Idea of Christian Scholarship*, 52.
15. Marsden's discussion in ibid., 61–62, is helpful on this point.
16. Ibid., 42.
17. Nicholas Wolterstorff, *Reason within the Bounds of Religion* (Grand Rapids: Eerdmans, 1984), 81.
18. Ibid., 82.
19. Harry Blamires, *The Christian Mind* (Ann Arbor, MI: Servant, 1997), 110.
20. Antonio A. Chiareli, "Christian Worldview and the Social Sciences," in Dockery and Thornbury, *Shaping a Christian Worldview*, 257.
21. Blamires, *The Christian Mind*, 107.
22. Cornelius Van Til, *Why I Believe in God*, ed. Jonathan Barlow (Center for Reformed Theology and Apologetics, 1996), quoted in Glenn A. Marsch, "Christian Worldview and Natural Science," in Dockery and Thornbury, *Shaping a Christian Worldview*, 177.
23. Blamires, *The Christian Mind*, 132.

24. Glenn A. Marsch, "Christian Worldview and Natural Science," in Dockery and Thornbury, *Shaping a Christian Worldview,* 164.

25. Blamires, *The Christian Mind,* 111.

26. Richard A. Bennett, *Your Quest for God* (Franklin, TN: Providence, 1998), 27.

27. Ibid.

28. Ibid., 30.

29. Ibid., 33–34.

30. Ibid., 30–31.

31. Ibid., 32–33.

32. Wolterstorff, *Reason within the Bounds of Religion,* 107–8.

33. Greg L. Bahnsen, *Van Til's Apologetic: Reading and Analysis* (Philipsburg, NJ: P & R Publishing, 1998), 22, quoted in Green, "Theological and Philosophical Foundations," in Dockery and Thornbury, *Shaping a Christian Worldview,* 82.

34. Cornelius Van Til, "My Credo," in *Jerusalem and Athens: Critical Discussions on the Theology and Apologetics of Cornelius Van Til,* ed. E. R. Greehan (Philadelphia: Presbyterian and Reformed, 1971), 4–5, quoted in Green, "Theological and Philosophical Foundations," in Dockery and Thornbury, *Shaping a Christian Worldview,* 82.

35. John Suppe, "Ordinary Memoir," in Anderson, *Professors Who Believe,* 70.

36. Wolterstorff, *Reason within the Bounds of Religion,* 107–8.

8

HOW CAN WE BE TRUE
TO THE ROLE OF LEARNING
IN CHRISTIAN SCHOLARSHIP?

t is important to focus on the learning side of the faith-and-learning ledger. In fact, much of the resistance to Christian scholarship within the Christian community is reactionary—a response to the anti-intellectual roots of fundamentalism, cited by Mark Noll and others in chapter 6. To be a Christian is not necessarily to be a fundamentalist. Nevertheless, many Christian groups trace their heritage to fundamentalism, and these fundamentalist roots—with their focus on the heart and the soul rather than the mind—have much to do with the difficulty many Christians have with the role of the cognitive component in the educational process.

▸▸ Fundamentalism

Randall Balmer, in *Blessed Assurance,* ties much of the history of American fundamentalism to the revolutionary spirit.[1] The early Protestant colonists chafed at all European political domination, including control of religious structures. British immigrants, for example, wanted freedom from the Church of England, the official state church. Similarly, other denominational groups rebelled against control from European-controlled religious institutions. Religion in the New World took a pietistic rather than a formal ecclesiastical turn, focusing on the inner spiritual life rather than on doctrinal statements rooted in the bonds of denominationalism, the origins of which were a continent away. This emphasis on intrinsic faith greatly enlivened the spiritual experience of many of the immigrants, making religiosity a matter of spirit rather than native ethnic and denominational culture.

A cyclical force fed the quest for religious independence. The more the various European denominations—Lutheran, Calvinist, and Anglican, among others—attempted to control the religious practices and church structures of the colonists, the more these residents of the New World distanced themselves from such control. Out of this political and religious cauldron grew fundamentalism, the belief that the essence of the Christian faith lay in its basic message of salvation. Evangelism was in. Theology was out. What was important was a conversion *experience* coupled with a literal belief in the Bible as the inerrant Word of God. What followed was a dismissal, and often outright rejection, of structured theological training, formal religious education, and adherence to denominational requirements for ordination. For many in the New World, these smacked of dead orthodoxy and European control. Lay and itinerant pastors, often rather short on doctrinal knowledge, gained great followings, preaching the biblical gospel with charisma at tent meetings and revivals and filling the air with calls to repentance and passionate commitment to Christ. Speaking to the heart rather than the mind, statements such as "No creed but Christ, no law but love" resonated with the spiritually hungry immigrants.

The fundamentalists' rejection of formal European control and the importance of theological education brought a diminution in the respect for scholarship. Education came to be viewed as a cunning tool of the devil, encouraging skepticism rather than faith and substituting human intellectual judgment for the Word of God as the final arbiter of truth. The statement of baseball player-turned-evangelist Billy Sunday, "When the word of God says one thing and scholarship says another, scholarship can go to hell," and that of the father of Baylor's David Lyle Jeffrey, "You show me an educated Baptist, and I'll show you a backslider," were typical. Amid this back-to-God revivalism, a near-paranoiac extremism set in. The only book worth studying was the Bible, and the only education was not really education at all. It was training masquerading as education, Bible-based preparation for a career in the church.

While the American university was in large part the product of nonfundamentalist mainline Protestantism, many of today's Christian colleges have their roots in the anti-intellectual soil of fundamentalism; hence, the rather large cultural, historical, and ideological gap between them. Moreover, it is little wonder that there remains an academically cautionary strain among scholars—those who focus on the mind—in many Christian communities with at least some discernible fundamentalist roots. The near-stereotypical fear that genuine education will be sacrificed on the altar of religious indoctrination has historical precedent. This concern has given rise to ensuring that students in their charge will be educated competently by secular standards. Hence, to avert an unthinking religious indoctrination, baptized paganism is practiced.

I believe that those still mired in this fear simply do not understand the nature of Christian scholarship; neither, however, do those who wish to reduce Christian education to biblical training. Much of the difficulty has to do with a proper understanding of the role of the *learning* side of the faith-and-learning ledger.

▸▸ Learning

Given the focus on Scripture and the basic tenets of the Christian faith, it is imperative to ask, How does a Christian approach to higher education differ from that of a Bible college?

A primary difference lies in the field and intent of study. Whereas the Bible college experience is largely one of understanding Scripture, with the aim of preparing the student vocationally for a career in church and parachurch work, Christian liberal arts higher education involves melding the basics of one's faith with traditional fields of inquiry and modes of analysis.

Furthermore, the Bible college (and even the seminary experience) is conjunctive rather than integrative in nature.[2] It involves the obvious necessity of *adding* an intense grounding in one's faith to the preparation for professional Christian service. At least in theory, then, one's faith can be separated from one's professional preparation. In genuinely Christian higher education, such compartmentalization does not exist. This kind of education attempts to perceive the various disciplines from a Christian perspective, within a Christian worldview. In Christian education, one's faith is ideologically *integrated*—melded with—the discipline in question.

"The Christian regards the Biblical revelation as the final rule of faith and conduct, but he does not think of it as an exhaustive source of all truth," states philosopher Holmes.[3] The Bible is not an astronomy, physics, or biology textbook. It does not speak of atoms, elements, or molecular energy. Nor does it treat the matter of disease in terms of toxins and microorganisms. Despite its numerology, the Bible does not delve into advanced mathematical constructions. The Bible is the special means by which God reveals himself to humans. Therefore, although we can "study" the universe solely through Scripture, such a study is an incomplete study of God's revealed truth on the matter. With all truth being God's truth and all creation God's creation, we would do well to study God's general revelation (nature) revealed extensively in the physical sciences, using the scientific method and other precise tools of analysis.

Similarly, human behavior, though a major focus in the Bible, is not Scripture's primary theme. The Bible does speak to the fallen condition of human nature, the centrality of love, and the importance of Spirit-controlled temperaments, but we can gain an added understanding of human behavior by using the principles of the social or behavioral sciences. The Bible does not speak of cultures and organizational behavior, the components of personality, or economic forces, all of which drive human behavior. The disciplines of sociology, psychology, and economics are just that—specifically defined and structured ways of studying and understanding human conduct more fully. Their perspectives offer rich insights into the mysteries of human behavior.

In addition, as certainly as Scripture illuminates one's understanding in these academic disciplines, these disciplines can deepen our understanding of Scripture. An economist, for example, will likely have an elevated appreciation for the Bible's warnings as to the attractiveness of money. A political scientist most probably would comprehend the arrest and prosecution of Jesus differently than a layperson would. A sociologist may view the challenges facing Paul in the urban cultures of Corinth and Rome differently than the sociologically uninitiated would, and a psychologist will likely understand more acutely the importance of Christian childrearing. This reciprocal effect extends even to the physical sciences. A research professor told me that the logic of his discipline clearly influenced his study and appreciation of Scripture. These are examples of integration, a process that grows almost naturally for those thinking believers who are always looking for truth in their disciplines.

"The Biblical concept of creation imparts sanctity to all realms of nature and to human history and culture," notes Holmes.[4] Thus, the Christian is called to study all of creation boldly and confidently, with the certainty that whatever the Christian is studying will ultimately strengthen rather than undermine her faith. Moreover, because her study is aimed at glorifying the creator of all that is learned, whenever possible she is to use her knowledge to further justice-in-shalom. Holmes states the issue powerfully: "To neglect the kind of education that helps us understand and appreciate God's world betrays either shallow thinking or fearful disbelief."[5] He offers some sage warnings here. Christians cannot afford to engage in shallow thinking in an era of geometrically increasing information and technological complexity. To lag behind the secular culture in the cognitive realm is to make the faith irrelevant to the curious nonbeliever. Fearful disbelief is perhaps worse. Not only is it evangelically suicidal—no one is attracted to a faith in fear of being debunked—it reveals a condition of spiritual immobilization.

Truth is expressed in different forms. The arts and the humanities, in contrast to the physical and behavioral sciences, offer nonmaterial, nonempirical insights into reality. As such, they illuminate truth by presenting it in highly subjective forms that can have profound emotional impact. The novelist offers a parable of life, the painter stimulates thoughts and sensations through his impressions, and the musician brings an indefinable energy to life. Every one of these people will read Scripture somewhat differently, just as certainly as Scripture will guide their art in varied directions.

The case for "learning" is reinforced by realizing that both the believer and the nonbeliever are used by God to accomplish his purposes. Given the disinclination among Christians to look at the animal side of human nature, it is doubtful that valid elements in behaviorism—response to stimuli and reaction to operant conditioning, for example—would have been discovered by Christian scholars. Similarly, it is unlikely that certain aspects of evolution that do harmonize with Christian thinking would have been uncovered by Christian scholars, given the Christian community's general resistance to evolutionism.[6]

The believer in search of Christian perspectives must be willing to investigate all approaches through the lens of Christian tenets—open to any and all knowledge and willing to listen to even the most virulent of naturalistic theories. There are two reasons for this. First, if something is true, it is of God. If it is not true, it will be disproven. Rejecting fearful disbelief, we need to adopt the outlook of Gamaliel, Paul's famous professor, cited in Acts 5. When witnessing the murderous anger of the religious authorities toward Peter and the apostles, this first-century bard cautioned the Sanhedrin against impulsive mob action. "Men of Israel, consider carefully what you intend to do to these men," he reasoned. "Leave these men alone! Let them go! For if their purpose or activity is of human origin, it will fail. But if it is from God, you will not be able to stop these men; you will only find yourselves fighting against God" (vv. 35, 38–39). Because even the most preposterous and atheistic of theories may have grains of truth in them, consideration needs to be given to any genuine attempt at communicating knowledge.

The second reason a Christian needs to be open to knowledge is because a Christian thinker's ideas are of little value if they come from one who has not made herself conversant with a broad range of knowledge. How does the marginally educated person present the Christian faith to a Buddhist or an agnostic without being familiar with the basic beliefs of those traditions? Similarly, how does one present a respectable Christian theory of personality if that same person chooses to know nothing of the various theories known to be hostile to Christian thinking?

Academic inquiry and tools of analysis are also important because they are the products of centuries of thought and study by the best of human minds. Hence, as certainly as we respect the genuine excellence in the athletic performance of the Olympian, we must also regard highly the similar excellence in the work of the finest scholars and thinkers. Their work has immense value. Such scholars are unearthing more of God's truth, whether or not they regard it as such. This matter extends also to the arts that express the finest of human creativity, an extension of the Creator himself. The artist can communicate the human condition in ways that reach the very soul of those that appreciate her efforts.

Moreover, all of this—the physical and behavioral sciences, the humanities and arts—take place in a historical context. Not to understand the historical context of any subject under examination, including Scripture, is not to understand or appreciate it fully. Knowledge of historical context illuminates any theory, discovery, or creation (as well as many passages of Scripture) by helping us understand the setting in which it originated. It clarifies meaning and intent knowing in what environment a matter arose. Conversely, the forces and knowledge existing at a given time influence and even shape the theories, discoveries, and creations that occur.

Take the subject of racism in the United States as it is rooted in slavery. Understanding the history of slavery in this country illuminates the pernicious nature of this social venom. It sheds light on how white supremacist notions were subtly but indelibly sewn into virtually every institution of our nation's life. Conversely, knowledge of the slave era reveals as much ignorance as evil. It helps us understand how otherwise moral citizens could engage in such an unthinkable practice, justifying it with twisted theologies and superstitious notions.

There are powerful, compelling reasons to affirm the learning side of the faith-and-learning ledger. We can return to the first great commandment: to love God with all of one's heart, soul, and *mind.* The more we develop our minds, the greater is our capacity to love God intellectually. And to love God with our intellectual powers is to strengthen them in every available fashion while walking in his light (1 John 1:7).

Further, to commit ourselves to learning is to take seriously the cultural mandate in Genesis 1:28 that we, as the King James translation puts it, *subdue* and gain *dominion* over creation. We are to master creation—not by conquering, subverting, manipulating, and destroying it—but by knowing, comprehending, and understanding its wonders so our mastery will be competent. Such mastery can only occur if we learn absolutely everything we have the capacity to learn about the creation of which we are in placed in charge. Therefore, we are interested in mastering mathematics and psychology just as we are to attempt to master church history and Christian doctrine. Again, whatever truth we learn is God's truth. Applying that logic, the truth that two plus two equals four is God's truth just as certainly as is the truth of his love for humanity through his son, Jesus. It is God's truth because God defines himself as light, life, and truth. Jesus, in stressing his oneness with the Father, claimed in John 14:6 that he was the way, the truth, and the life. He did not merely say he knew the truth, that he was committed to the truth, or that he spoke the truth. He defined himself as *the* truth. Truth, then, lies within a person. It resides within one who created all of reality, including every field of academic inquiry.

▸▸ Sacred/Secular

This matter of all truth being God's truth—a cornerstone of Holmes's Christian philosophy—raises a central issue. Philosophy professor Nicholas Wolterstorff reportedly used to draw a large rectangle on the blackboard in his classroom. He would then divide the rectangle in half horizontally, writing the word *sacred* in the top half and the word *secular* in the bottom half. He would then place a huge *X* through the entire construction and state, "False dichotomy." Though a religion or philosophy of secularism may exist, nothing in itself is secular. From mathematics to the ministry, from cooking to cate-chism, from baseball to baptism, all of creation is from God and belongs to God. "Through him," says John at the outset of his gospel, "all things were made; without him nothing was made that has been made" (1:3). It is as simple as that. The entire universe, all of reality, is part of God's work. Nothing—not astrophysics, anthropology, or architecture—is to be conceded to secularism. To place anything outside the purview of God is to limit him. It is to make him less than almighty.

In that spirit, we want to educate the finest chemists, sociologists, historians, and physicists—from a Christian perspective. The goal is not to achieve cultural respectability in the eyes of the secularist. It is to move the faith off the margins of society, away from secessionism, and into the centers of power and cultural influence. Tertullian once asked, "What has Jerusalem to do with Athens?" It has to do with bringing light and salt to all sectors of a society. It has to do with erasing the sacred/secular dichotomy.[7]

More than two centuries ago, the apostle Paul set out to abolish the sacred/secular dichotomy in several ways. First, he took the gospel into the major cities and into their centers of influence. The intellectually brilliant Paul proclaimed Christ in the synagogues among the learned, on the streets, and in the market square. He did not necessarily call his converts to leave their occupations for the ministry, but rather to serve God in their communities and to build the church. In addition, though he was a Jew at a time when most believers were Jewish Christians, Paul was committed to evangelizing Gentiles, imploring the senior leaders of the powerful Jerusalem church to regard Gentile believers as their equals. To that end, he worked tirelessly at dissolving the barriers of race, gender, economic status, and cultural patterns as hindrances to believers' unity and their collective ability to honor God.

Just as in Christ and the Christian community there was to be no distinction between Jew and Gentile, male or female, slave or free, in Paul's eyes, nothing—not even the most mundane—was inherently secular. Nothing existed outside the kingdom of God. Accordingly, Paul asserted that whatever a person does, no matter how seemingly meaningless, such as simply eating or drinking, the Christian is to do it to the glory of God.

Martin Luther stated that the shoemaker should work on the shoe of the pope as religiously as the pontiff prays for the shoemaker's soul. "There should be no less support or attention for an earnest Christian young person who has been accepted to the Julliard School of Music than for one going off to seminary," remarks Briner.[8] The sociologist is every bit as called to glorify God as is the clergyperson; whether one is in the pulpit or in the presidency, whether at seminary or at quarterback, every believer is in "full-time Christian service."

The Christian life is not a segmented existence. It is all encompassing. The Christian worldview covers just that, the entire world. Christian thinking is no more confined to religious studies than the Christian life is confined to a single day of the week. To the believer, all activities are religious activities. They are acts of worship because they are to glorify God. To think as a Christian—*Christianly*—is to think about all things, from the virgin birth to invertebrate biology, from a Christian perspective. Faith and learning, then, can only be separated for analytical purposes. They are two sides of a single coin, ever in interaction, ever glorifying God. While the learning in higher education presents the student with a wide-angle view of reality, it neither replaces nor competes with faith. It meshes with faith to uncover more of God's truth.

▸▸ Scholar or Thinker

Although we use the words *scholar* and *scholarship* rather liberally in these pages, Blamires calls Christians to move beyond scholarship to thinking. "Occasionally, very occasionally, a man may be both a first-rate scholar and a first-rate thinker," he says, lamenting the dearth of thinkers. "But the nature of our modern educational system is such that this happy combination arises ever more rarely. Potential thinkers are being turned into mere scholars by the pressures of conformity so strong both in the educational world and in society at large."[9]

Blamires is making the same case we are making here. He uses the word *scholar* to describe one who simply researches and masters the prevailing bodies of secular knowledge, rather than thinking them through in a Christian fashion.

The Christian must move beyond learning in the narrow sense to thinking in the spiritual sense. The secular world—with political correctness militating against value-based analyses, and postmodernism removing criteria for critical discernment—tends to submerge thought under learning, prophecy under scholarship, and wisdom under know-how.[10]

To be a scholar in the limited scope is to risk being pushed by the world into its secular mold, rather than having one's mind transformed in the image of Christ (Rom. 12:2). This factor is not to be dismissed. Even for the believer, truly to master prevailing thought systems encourages a conditioning of the mind—however subtle—to think in a limited naturalistic framework. "Indeed," notes Blamires, "the Christian *trains* his mind, *forces* it, to think secularly—so as to help the job at hand to be done efficiently. In this way, by gradual stages, the Christian loses the habit of thinking christianly over the field of practical affairs in which he is actively involved."[11] To think in the Christian sense, however, is to remove indecision and confusion, while distinguishing between correct and incorrect, right and wrong, good and evil.[12] It is to think confidently and coherently. It is to place all learning in a divine and eternal context. It is also to think critically, to use our control beliefs to test the validity of whatever we are studying.

That quite rightly is the challenge for the *Christian* scholar. While the secular scholar learns, the Christian scholar ever synthesizes that learning with faith in search of God's truth.

Notes

1. Randall Balmer, *Blessed Assurance* (Boston: Beacon, 1999). Balmer's treatment of this subject, though dismissing the transcendent basis of fundamentalist faith, offers the reader a thorough journey into the history and nature of fundamentalism. The brief historical capsule in this chapter is much based on Balmer's book.
2. Arthur F. Holmes, *The Idea of a Christian College* (Grand Rapids: Eerdmans, 1987), 7–8.
3. Ibid., 18.
4. Ibid., 15.
5. Ibid.
6. Nicholas Wolterstorff, *Reason within the Bounds of Religion* (Grand Rapids: Eerdmans, 1984), 100.
7. Balmer raises this matter in his "2012: A School Odyssey," *Christianity Today*, November 18, 2002, 68.
8. Bob Briner, *Roaring Lambs* (Grand Rapids: Zondervan, 1993), 175.
9. Harry Blamires, *The Christian Mind* (Ann Arbor, MI: Servant, 1997), 50.
10. Ibid., 51.
11. Ibid., 70.
12. Ibid., 51.

WHERE DOES REASON END
AND FAITH BEGIN?

Faith, according to the writer of Hebrews, is about things not seen. Although it has an intellectual and emotional component, faith is in large part an act of the will. So much of the learning in higher education is about reason and logic, much of which is based on empiricism and the scientific method. When faith begins interacting with reason, though healthy and real for the Christian scholar, there is always tension and potential, if not actual, conflict.

Pope John Paul II, one of the more evangelical popes in history, weighed in on this issue in a brilliant encyclical titled, *Fides et Ratio.* His thoughts, and the very favorable review they received by Wolterstorff in *Christianity Today,* form the contours of this chapter.[1]

▸▸ The Value of Philosophy

In his encyclical, the pope urges a return to a search for truth, slowed considerably in recent times much due to postmodern thinking. Postmodernism has moved philosophy to "accentuate the ways in which this capacity [to know truth] is limited and conditioned."[2] This decentralized approach to philosophy (called deconstructionism) impairs humankind from discovering all that can be discovered about God and his universe. The pope calls for a resumption in philosophy's search for God's truth, the quest for a reality that transcends the boundaries of human existence. To do this, philosophy must break the tape of postmodern barriers—its emphasis on subjectivity, focus on the self, and concern for the immediate.

Christians themselves, however, have too often thwarted the endeavor to seek truth with their mistrust of rational knowledge, philosophical pondering, and speculative theology. Much of this owes to the reactionary nature of fundamentalism, discussed earlier. Indeed, there were "unaskable questions" in the community of my youth. Questions such as why bad things happen to good people, why God permits seemingly random, natural disasters to wipe out entire populations, or simply why he does not seem to answer prayer more consistently often elicited censure for an apparent absence of faith rather than generating empathy and open-ended discussion. These types of questions have plagued believers for centuries and invite, if not beg for, philosophical consideration. To ignore them is to fold the intellectual tent, turn one's thinking apparatus off, and abandon one's search for important truth.

In many religious locales, appearing as if one has the answers and closing the discussion is safer than engaging the probing questions. I recall a pastor once being asked to reconcile predestination with free will in a catechism class. Faced with the human/divine dichotomy, this deeply imbued doctrinalist, rather than acknowledging that these doctrines simply cannot be fully reconciled from a human standpoint, put the powers of logic through Procrustean tortures in a near-frantic attempt to bring about some form of happy equilibrium. When he finished, all but insisting that he had brought the problem to full resolution, I was unsatisfied. Not only was his logic far from waterproof; he seemed more invested in providing an answer than in affirming the mystery. And it was done at a cost. His passionate attempt to cram these transcendent doctrines into the geometry of the catechism stifled further thought and discussion by forcing a symmetry that simply does not exist from a human vantage point.

The matter of faith and reason is relevant outside the boundaries of philosophy. Those in the humanities and the behavioral sciences are every bit as engaged in truth seeking as is the philosopher. Theologically speculative questions arise in the study of literature and psychology, just as they do in philosophy. One is invited by Hemingway's writings to ask, Why does death seem to overtake the best and bravest first? The mysteries of nature (heredity) and nurture (environment) are debated and researched but are unsolved by psychologists. The true scholar—regardless of his academic discipline—invites inquiry, joins the discussion, and permeates old boundaries in the quest to uncover transcendent realities. It is the intellect, the reasoning capacity—a specifically human gift—that makes that quest possible, hence its value.

▸▸ The Search for Truth

Faith, as absolutely essential as it is, simply does not provide every desired answer. It is not meant to. Faith is an act of the will, a leap into the light (rather than darkness). Nonetheless, faith's focus is not on the visible and provable. There is value, then, in venturing beyond even faith itself, to exercise and stretch our divinely ordained powers to reason in a search for a transcendent reality. This is what reason is for—to search out God's truth. Therefore, there need be no unaskable questions, no off-limits speculation, as the believer plumbs the depths of truth in a limited human way, ever confident that whatever truth is to be found is of God.

Not only is this search for truth necessary; it is, according to Wolterstorff, a defining characteristic of humans. From childhood on, people ask questions. They want to know why. This is a major mark of separation between the human and the animal world. Animals, lacking the higher cortical functions necessary for abstract thinking, cannot envision reality in the abstract, or possess a sense of the past or the future. Hence, they do not search for reasons, significance, or meaning. Life in the animal world is truly naturalistic, driven largely by biologically programmed responses to tangible stimuli. Animals, no matter their level of complexity, do not plan or reason, but react to their biological needs for survival, reproduction, and safety.

Life in the subhuman context is one without meaning or significance. It is about staying alive and reproducing, with no thought of tomorrow or of an existence beyond the temporal. The balance-of-nature and food-chain concepts affirm this. It is also a life without rules or morality, symbolism, or even identity. In addition, there are no real relationships in animal "society," because communication is nonsymbolic. In fact, there is no real animal society at all, because the absence of symbolic communication obviates the development of a truly socially constructed reality. To refer to groups of ants with the terms *societies* or *communities* is a misnomer, because these collectives are not societies or communities at all. They are the simple expressions of biologically programmed activities among ants. Clearly, there is no need for faith or reason in a wholly nonspiritual world of biological programming. Truth, meaning, significance — even relationships in the intimate, communicative sense — are uniquely human elements.

But they are powerful human elements. From the earliest of civilizations, there is evidence of humanity's quest for "universal and ultimate truth." The presence of religions in the most underdeveloped of societies is testimony to the human desire to find an absolute truth, one that "might serve as the ground of all things." There are perhaps few culture universals more in evidence than this quest. From that standpoint, the pope makes a powerful statement: "It is unthinkable that a search so deeply rooted in human nature would be completely vain and useless."[3] Indeed, virtually every other conceptual possibility — material or nonmaterial — generated by the human mind, from electricity to love, from alpha waves to self-esteem, has been proven to exist in the real world. It is most certainly inconceivable, then, that humankind has spent its entire existence looking for a transcendent truth that does not exist.

Again, this truth is spiritual. It is not bounded by temporal, finite, and cultural limits. Postmodernism, with its deconstructionist orientation, along with its related tendency to make truth and goodness relative, misses the point of this historical search. The pope holds that humanity's quest must be about transcendent truth, one that surrounds us and defines our very existence on this planet. Traditional philosophy, then, most assuredly has its place. According to the pope, "The autonomy that philosophy enjoys is rooted in the fact that reason is by its nature oriented to truth and is equipped moreover with the means necessary to arrive at truth."[4]

▸▸ Limits

The search for truth is not, however, as simple as the proper application of philosophical inquiry. There are real limits. First, we are limited by the finite nature of humankind to comprehend an infinite, transcendent reality. "Those of us who are awed by the authority of Revelation but cannot by the use of our own reason move our minds to make peace with all of its disclosures," writes Buckley in his spiritual memoir, *Nearer, My God,* "have no alternative than to conclude that our reason is not refined enough to take in divine perspectives."[5] Human reason at its very best can discover and acknowledge the Creator, but it cannot explain him. "We do not abandon reason," says Buckley, "we merely recognize its limitations."[6] Recognizing this limitation is key to sustaining one's faith amid the mysteries of life. If in fact the mysteries of God were fully knowable to humankind, God would lose his transcendent quality. In a word, God would not be God. That we see through the glass of life darkly, that our faith is never perfectly integrated with our learning, is an affirmation of our Christian faith rather than a challenge to it.

There is more. The search for truth is far more profoundly limited by the fallen nature of humanity. Our philosophical exercises "are shaped by history and produced by human reason wounded and weakened by sin."[7] The pope holds that God designed reason as the means by which humans can leap the hurdles of the sensory, material, and tangible, toward the Creator, who is spiritual. Sin, however, introduces a fundamental flaw. It places humanity rather than God at the center of the universe, and in doing so, diminishes our access to God and his truth.

Sin is a much misunderstood concept in contemporary society. It is often viewed in behavioral terms, leaving cynics to deride believers for their judgmental attitudes about activities regarded as sinful. The Christian doctrine of sin, of course, is not at all defined in behavioral terms. It is a pervasive condition, an inborn spiritual disease of imperfection that afflicts every person. The key to understanding sin is that it is a human condition, not a series of behaviors. Sin is as inherent a part of the human spiritual condition as the presence of germs is to the human physical state. As such, we sin because we are sinners, as the Reverend Carl Reitsma, a pastor of my youth, often said; we are not sinners because we sin. Behaviors, then, are not the essence of sin; they are the symptoms of this universal condition.

Dating to the Fall, sin affects and infects everything. "Every cemetery, every hospital, every army and every prison that the world has ever known is the result of man's wrong choice at the beginning of creation," writes Bennett. Sin alienates humans from God and from one another.[8] To be human is to be linked by this alienated condition. "The real reason that we see so much hostility and division between people," says Bennett, "is that sin is the common denominator. Sin ties the atheist to a believer, and an Arab to a Jew."[9] There are no exceptions. In fact, sin is the only universal human condition. "Whether people are prostitutes or preachers, whether they live in the height of luxury or the depth of poverty, whether they are educated or illiterate *all have sinned, and fall short of the glory of God* (Romans 3:23)."[10] Perhaps the most powerful manifestation of sin is that it places the interests of self above those of others, even those of the Creator.

The centrality of self is a huge barrier in fallen human reason, because it crowds out God in human consciousness. That is the problem with secularism. By placing the self at the center of the universe, the secularist attempts to place the Christian faith in his grip, evaluating it as one might the teachings of Plato, Socrates, or Martin Luther King, rather than realizing that all of reality lays in God's grip.[11]

▸▸ Revelation

For the Christian, imperfect human reason is balanced by revelation. Basic to Christian thinking is that truth is the revelation of God's redeeming love. This revelation of acts and facts in Scripture is received through faith. Moreover, revelation, then, is the perfection of reason. It is ultimate truth. Revelation is reason in perfect form, not fully attainable by the flawed reasoning powers of finite, mortal humanity. This concept is absolutely critical to any understanding of Christian scholarship. Revelation is not merely additive—God's way of filling in the blanks of reality for the intellectual. The Bible is more than a book of answers for the curious. To reduce revelation to that temporal level is secularist in spirit and motive. What revelation does is turn the lights on, illuminating reality and truth.[12]

Basic to the Incarnation is the illumination of truth and reality. According to Scripture, Christ's mission was in part to bridge the gap between our finite understanding and the metaphysical (or spiritual) reality that envelops us.[13] We know God and his wisdom by knowing his divine yet human son. "If you want to know what God is like," legendary urban pastor Bill Leslie often said, "look at Christ." We could rephrase that by saying that if you want to know the genuine spiritual or metaphysical truth of reality, look at Christ, the human expression of that truth.

From the Incarnation, it is a short step to the doctrine of the Holy Spirit— that part of the Trinity and of God's own personality that enters the life of the believer, freeing him from seeing the world solely through the confines of the self. It is only through the eyes and ears of God that we can move beyond our selfishness and see God's love and activity in the human drama. Far from making the believer omniscient or superhuman, the Holy Spirit creates within the Christian an openness to things transcendent. It adds a dimension of understanding, functioning as a sixth sense that looks for relationships between the finite and the transcendent dimensions of reality.[14] Through the Holy Spirit, the Christian "sees" her field of inquiry as a necessary but by no means sufficient explanation of reality. The Christian scholar is never a reductionist. In fact, even interdisciplinary perspectives are not complete in her view. The goal in finding truth is always to have what Paul calls "the mind of Christ."

Fallen reason, no matter how highly developed, simply cannot discover real truth, because such reason cannot "recognize God as Creator of all . . . not because [it lacks] the means to do so, [but] because . . . sinfulness [places] an impediment in the way."[15] Fallen reason cannot discern relationships between humanity and the God of grace, because the self-centered nature of sin stands in fallen reason's way. Paul realized this. After confronting powerful Jews, intellectual Greeks, and other cosmopolitan Gentiles, he asks in 1 Corinthians 1:20, "Where is the wise man? Where is the scholar? Where is the philosopher of this age?" He then goes on to assert his case directly, noting it was "in the wisdom of God [that] the world through its wisdom did not know him. . . . For the foolishness of God is wiser than man's wisdom" (1:21, 25).

Clearly, unguided reason inevitably takes wrong turns and collides with, rather than discovers, truth. "None of the rulers of this age understood it," says Paul in 1 Corinthians 2:8, "for if they had, they would not have crucified the Lord of glory." No different from today, the reason the best and the brightest of Paul's day did not understand the revelation of God is that "the man without the Spirit [or the unbeliever] does not accept the things that come from the Spirit of God, for they are foolishness to him, and he cannot understand them, because they are spiritually discerned" (2:14). That Spirit of God—the Holy Spirit—becomes key to the discovery of truth. Naturalistic scholarship has value, but it is incomplete. By refusing to subordinate itself to the source of all truth, it is disconnected from ultimate, spiritually discerned reality. Spiritually blind eyes cannot comprehend the transcendent realities that shed light on all knowledge.

Revelation is a form of grace. It is a gift and does not flow from reason. It comes from God, is received in faith, and is to be studied with humility and gratitude. In 1 Corinthians 2, Paul emphasizes the transcendent nature of truth, stating, "We do, however, speak a message of wisdom among the mature, but not the wisdom of this age or of the rulers of this age, who are coming to nothing" (v. 6). Paul is talking about *special* revelation, "God's secret wisdom, a wisdom that has been hidden and that God destined for our glory before time began" (v. 7). This revelation, not accessible on a purely human plane, comes from "the Spirit who is from God, that we may understand what God has freely given us. This is what we speak, not in words taught us by human wisdom but in words taught by the Spirit, expressing spiritual truths in spiritual words" (vv. 12–13).

Because revelation is a gift from God—totally independent of any human endeavor—believers regard it with reverence. It is a package from God opened only with faith. That faith empowers reason, injecting the illuminating impact of revelation into its reasoning efforts.

St. Augustine writes, "I believe in order to understand; and I understand, the better to believe." Faith and reason are inseparable. Reason is a God-given gift to the intellect by which we learn. Revelation, received in faith, illuminates that capacity.[16] "Faith ultimately is a type of understanding or knowledge (i.e. it is not simply a subjective feeling)," says Brad Green. "At the same time . . . faith is an essential part of *all* knowing. That is, knowledge or understanding *never* occurs without faith."[17] Faith plus reason equals understanding.

Revelation and faith do a number of things. They direct human reason to areas of knowledge that it would not otherwise conceive of—like that of the Trinity. The concept of the Trinity provides elements of philosophical thinking that are incompatible with human reason. Faith-injected reason of this nature uncovers spiritual truth. Although there are always immense expanses of impenetrable mystery in our understanding of truth, revelation and faith stir thought and energize rather than thwart the search for truth. They also serve as correctives to reason. They guide our philosophical activities. While segregating revelation such that it does not conflict with notions generated by philosophy or other disciplines is a common strategy, it is one that is built on fear, driven by a concern to protect the faith against being discredited by academic findings. This strategy is a false road. Both revelation and human reason concern truth. Revelation and faith bring critical discernment, especially necessary when revelation clashes with academic learning.

Wolterstorff's notion of "control beliefs" is helpful to the exercise of critical discernment. Christian beliefs are to function as control beliefs against which the Christian thinker can critique prevailing systems of thought. They assist the Christian scholar in isolating ideas that cannot be reconciled with Christian thinking. Paradoxically, by abandoning an ideological false road, the Christian scholar may actually be taking the first step toward finding truth within an area of inquiry. At this point, by examining and reexamining a theory, the scholar may arrive at a new formulation, one that is sound both academically and from a Christian vantage point.[18]

In the last analysis, faith and learning, religion and science, are not independent of one another. They cannot be so for truth to emerge. Instead, the faith-and-learning venture is one of adventure and constant interaction. To place learning and science above faith is to worship a false God. Nevertheless, to allow simplistic interpretations of Scripture to function as restrictive censors to academic inquiry is to short-circuit the learning process. Clearly, faith must guide the learning process. Learning, however, may also bring the Christian to reexamine the elements of his or her faith commitment (as noted in the case of the heliocentric nature of planetary movement). Thus, there is simply no definable boundary between faith and learning, no precise timberline at which one ends and the other begins.

The absence of a certain boundary creates considerable discomfort for people regardless of their placement on the theological spectrum. Those to the left are concerned that religious doctrines may be used by those in power (in the church or the Christian college) to close down the intellectual search for truth—censoring thought and word and so abridging academic freedom. Those on the right are concerned that matters of faith will ultimately be subjugated to human judgment—the creature becoming more powerful than the Creator.

These concerns have a historical basis. Copernicus, Galileo, and other believing scientists were not only thwarted in their scholarly efforts by the church but were persecuted for presenting their discoveries—findings that today are accepted as scientific fact by the most ardent of believers. More recently, scholars that posit a link between street crime and poverty or other social and psychologically oppressive conditions have been met with charges of near heresy, because they do not simply label this behavior as sin. Those who view alcoholism as a disease or regard certain behaviors as sick or unhealthy rather than evil face similar censure. The unaskable-question syndrome is yet another example of this curtailing of the search for truth.

Some conservative Christians are troubled by the propensity of scholars to marginalize Scripture and basic Christian doctrines, yet these same Christians make secular scholarship central to the learning process. When God becomes the dependent variable, scholarship is headed in a secular direction. These believers wish to safeguard Christian institutions from drifting away from the orthodoxy of their birth into secularist unbelief. They need only point to the history of the American university to offer disturbing and tragic historical precedent for their concern.

Amid the twin dangers of anti-intellectualism on one side and spiritual and theological complacency on the other, the faith-and-learning enterprise remains in dynamic interplay. Scholarship and inquiry need to be affirmed, or there will be no real development of the Christian mind. Scripture, faith, and control beliefs, however, need to serve as correctives to the fallen and limited nature of human reason. Faith and learning, then, are not always happy companions to us who see through a glass darkly. So it must be, given our limited and faulty human vantage point. Nevertheless, faith and learning both are means by which we learn God's truth. As such, they must remain forever in dialogue until we see face-to-face.

Notes

1. Nicholas Wolterstorff, "Faith and Reason: Philosophers Respond to Pope John Paul II's Encyclical Letter, *Fides et Ratio*," http://www.christianitytoday.com/bc/9b4/9b4028b.html (accessed July 16, 2002). Unless stated otherwise, quotes in this chapter are from Wolterstorff's published review, *Christianity Today*.
2. Ibid., 2.
3. Ibid., 4.
4. Ibid., 3.
5. William F. Buckley Jr., *Nearer, My God* (San Diego: Harvest, 1998), 74.
6. Ibid., 171.
7. Wolterstorff, "Faith and Reason."
8. Richard A. Bennett, *Your Quest for God* (Franklin, TN: Providence, 1998), 70.
9. Ibid., 70–71.
10. Ibid., 71.
11. Harry Blamires, *The Christian Mind* (Ann Arbor, MI: Servant, 1997), 146–47.
12. Ibid., 145–46.
13. George M. Marsden, *The Outrageous Idea of Christian Scholarship* (New York: Oxford University Press, 1997), 90–91.
14. Ibid., 94–95.
15. Wolterstorff, "Faith and Reason."

16. Augustine, *Sermons* 43, 7, 9 (*Patrologia Latina* 38, 257–58), quoted in Brad Green, "Theological and Philosophical Foundations," in *Shaping a Christian Worldview,* ed. David S. Dockery and Gregory Alan Thornbury (Nashville: Broadman and Holman, 2002), 81.

17. Green, "Theological and Philosophical Foundations," in Dockery and Thornbury, *Shaping a Christian Worldview,* 81.

18. Nicholas Wolterstorff, *Reason within the Bounds of Religion* (Grand Rapids: Eerdmans, 1984), 76.

10

WHAT ARE THE COMPONENTS
OF FAITH AND LEARNING?

S   o what are the components of the faith-and-learning enterprise? Of what
     does it consist? How are Christians proceeding on this issue? What is its
     current state?

▸▸ Philosophical Component

There are three basic components, or stages, to the faith-and-learning dialogue. The first, essentially preparatory, component is philosophical. There needs to be a philosophical justification for its practice. The philosophical component is rather theoretical, but that is the turf on which philosophers do their very necessary work. Without a coherent, intellectually defensible case for its existence, not only will there be no place for Christian perspectives in the academic mainstream, but Christians themselves become more vulnerable to compartmentalized thinking and therefore to secularist notions. A basis for a clear alternative to mainstream thinking must be spelled out and established. Much of that work has been done, as noted and reviewed in chapter 6. Moreover, Wolterstorff, Marsden, and others have not merely preached to the converted but have made their cases and published their ideas on the main stage of the academic mainstream.

▸▸ Critiquing

The case having been made, we move to the second stage, critiquing. Critiquing means examining prevailing paradigms, accepted theories, and schools of thought from a Christian perspective. Virtually every school of thought, even those in the physical sciences, is founded on several basic, unquestioned premises. What are these doctrines? What is the catechism of these belief systems? What happens when one of the basic premises is questioned or removed?

To assert that there may not be a uniquely Christian political science, economics, or even philosophy is not to say, however, that there are no intellectually defensible Christian perspectives through which one can view various academic disciplines and their theories. Nor is it to say there are no major lines of thinking that yield some valuable insights into the human condition—insights that are symmetrical with Christian beliefs. There are basic elements within many widely held theories that square with a Christian (or at least theistic) view of the universe, and these elements are effective in the pursuit of knowledge. When encountering those that do not square with a Christian view, we need to look at what revisions, if any, can be made to make them fit better before dismissing or even demonizing them.

We must look for the elements of truth in any approach and preserve the healthy baby as the secularist bathwater is drained away. Hence, we need to determine what theories and subtheories comport best with Christian notions of reality and of the nature of human beings. This is the process by which much of feminist, African American, and gay thinking was developed. These groups took prevailing views in history, political science, and other social sciences and critiqued them severely, all the while offering alternative modes of interpretations and revisions. The very existence of gender-neutral and gender-inclusive language is testimony to the critiquing impact of feminist thinkers. Indeed, these groups have published their polemic manifestos, but after intensely reviewing, critiquing, and reformulating what is already out there.

Moreover, simply to lambaste obvious secular ideas as not acceptable is not a very daunting intellectual exercise. Much of that goes on, particularly among Christian political activists, and often these piling-on efforts polarize more than enlighten. Indeed, many of the mainstream notions are anti-Christian, if not anti-theistic, on their face. Others, however, are not. Examining and reexamining, adjusting and readjusting, revising and refining, are activities that have real value, because they move the needle out of the purely theoretical zone and into the arena of developing current Christian thought.

Though notable efforts have been made in assessing current notions from a Christian perspective, it seems Christian scholars and instructors have generally come up rather short in the area of critiquing prevailing paradigms—positively and negatively. Whether because they find the task daunting or fear ridicule from the agnostic community, Christians have not weighed in sufficiently on the intellectual front according to Dr. Willie Jennings of Duke. He feels that the desire of Christian scholars to be well regarded by their secular counterparts has often been at the cost of Christian contributions to the continuing pursuit of knowledge.

This is regrettable. Such critiques of research and theory make strong contributions in the classroom and as a part of the body of knowledge, accomplishing four objectives. The first was noted above—moving the faith/learning needle by getting Christians actively involved in the enterprise of developing Christian thought. Second, the very existence of this activity affirms the intellectual legitimacy of Christian thinking as a substantive exercise. This can be of great value, particularly for those experiencing a crisis of faith. Third, such reviews guide students intellectually in thinking through the validity of the ideas with which they are confronted. When teaching at Christian institutions, few presentations were better received than those in which I outlined some basic points of agreement between major sociological theories and the Christian faith. I concluded that Christian students are genuinely interested in ways in which Christianity and major academic thinking intersect, if only to reestablish a connection to their faith. Finally, a consistent body of such thinking can eventually form the foundation for Christian theories that have intellectual respectability.

This approach stands in sharp contrast to baptized paganism—compartmentalizing religious belief away from learning. Assessment and revision is difficult, exacting work, but without it, Christian scholarship does not really exist, remaining an ideological fetus that does not come to term.

Critiquing need not be confined to the prevailing belief systems in the academic mainstream. If the ideal is to conform every thought to Christ, as Paul informs the Corinthians (2 Cor. 10:5), the Christian scholar should examine all her intellectual work in light of faith.[1] More specifically, Christian scholars need, as Marsden and others would encourage, to apply these critiques to their own pet theories in terms of how they fit a Christian view of the universe. It is human nature to pick the beam out of the adversary's eye (Matt. 7:1–5)—critically reviewing material outside one's own immediate academic sphere. This may even be done in a gifted, insightful fashion, making a major contribution to Christian thought. It is often more difficult to look at one's own academic biases—based perhaps on graduate training, favorite books, or entrenched habits—and examine them with similar rigor. But if we are to be intellectually honest, that is part of the challenge.

▸▸ Theory Building

Growing out of the critiquing stage is a final and ideal component, theory building. Marsden asks rhetorically why there are no identifiable Christian schools of thought in mainstream academe, comparable to Marxist, feminist, gay, postmodern, and African American systems.[2] He suggests that while science may have replaced superstition in the minds of the Enlightenment advocates, prejudice seems to have triumphed over reason. In the secular mainstream's plunge into scientific objectivity, it has dismissed religious perspectives as unreasonable, without a hearing.

There are also other reasons for the lack of Christian schools of thought in the mainstream. One is that Christians have not been as politically active in lobbying the mainstream for inclusion while other special interest groups have been beating the drum loudly enough to gain inclusion, however provisional. As mentioned before, Christian scholars need not be as strident as other, more confrontational groups. The purpose is not to define ourselves simply by what we are against and so accumulate ideological adversaries principally due to our verbal militance. Nevertheless, Christians need to abandon permission-asking approaches and make their case with confidence in its validity. That is what the apostle Paul would do.

There is also the matter of secessionism. By remaining in evangelical enclaves, characterized in part by a fortress mentality, the smoke signals of Christian thought are unlikely to be picked up by the mainstream. And yet another reason is the simple absence of solid Christian models of thought. The mainstream does seem willing to hear from Marsden, Wolterstorff, and others of their ilk as they make the case for faith and learning. Such scholars have been granted prestigious appointments in research universities, their books have been published by quality mainstream university presses, and their ideas are visible on academic websites. What seems to be missing is a body of work by Christian scholars that moves beyond philosophical justifications for faith-and-learning syntheses to actual examples of this type of scholarship.

Again, this is what other special interest groups have done in building a literature much based on the foundation of critiques. Feminist consciousness now abounds. African American perspectives have been present since the 1960s, and Marxist thinking and analyses are widely available. These groups have moved beyond philosophically justifying their right to present different perspectives. They have offered them and are continuing to do so. They have constructed, if not fully developed theoretical models, at least scintillating critiques of what they deem to be unacceptable but prevailing notions in the mainstream, along with alternative perspectives and analyses. And they make no secret of it. They boldly proclaim these views as valid and respectable intellectual alternatives to current thinking.

Some years ago I was invited to Wheaton College to participate in a conference for "Christians in sociology." A welter of somewhat meandering, unpublished papers was presented. (Typical was a British rendering titled, "Toward a Christian Sociologie." The key word in the title was the first: *toward*. The effort was well intentioned and thoughtful, but clearly in an embryonic stage of development.) Discussion and courteous debate flowed freely, all without any real conclusion on just how Christianity and sociology could find marital happiness in academe. The lone public consensus was that the conference was a good exercise and that it should be repeated. To my knowledge, it never was. The reason, I suspect, is that the (unstated) goal of the event was rather ambitious: the development of a Christian sociology.

In reality, there is not—nor will there likely ever be—a genuinely Christian sociology or Christian psychology, any more than there is a Christian mathematics or Christian economics. Any attempt at genuine Christian thinking, however, should be welcomed with excitement, no matter how embryonic. Such work will engender sufficient resistance from adversaries in the mainstream without adding other discouraging responses from the Christian academics. In fact, to revile such attempts is not only to be small, but it is antagonistic to the very mission to which we are called. Writing is difficult; theory construction is even more so. Christians engaging in this component of the faith-and-learning dialogue make a major contribution, at the very least by breaking ground on the theory-building component. No matter how convoluted their initial constructions, they have begun the necessary task of developing within their disciplines models of thought that square with a Christian worldview.

⤻ Paradigms

Thomas Kuhn, in his landmark book, *The Structure of Scientific Revolutions* (1962), explains that the scientific community is dominated by paradigms—foundational belief systems or cornerstones—on which all subsequent research and theory is built. The multiplication tables in mathematics and the elemental chart in chemistry are examples of such paradigms.

These paradigms are often strongly in place prior to being fully validated scientifically. Once founded, they hold sway, even in the face of contrary notions. Rather than being easily rejected—like major political parties—these paradigms are ever revised and embellished, all the while becoming more dominant. Once stubbornly entrenched, a paradigm will remain so unless it is (a) found to be fundamentally erroneous and (b) overturned by another more accurate paradigm. Such was the case in chemistry when Lavoisier's approach to combustion overthrew the phlogiston theory and in astronomy when the heliocentric notion of planetary movement invalidated the earth-as-center-of-the-universe notion.

The social or behavioral sciences (sociology, psychology, political science, and economics, for example) are said to be pre-paradigmatic in that there is no single belief system on which all subsequent theory and research is founded.

There are, nonetheless, a series of competing yet cardinal theoretical models that dominate these fields of inquiry. Functionalism and conflict theory are strong in sociology, whereas behaviorism and cognitive developmental models are among a variety of influential belief systems in psychology.

Extrapolating from Kuhn's notion, the Christian community would benefit greatly from the development of some foundational theories in various disciplines, particularly the pre-paradigmatic humanities and behavioral sciences. Almost any serious attempt at theory building has at least some redeeming value, because it is a seed that can germinate into quality Christian scholarship examination and research. And these, like the paradigms of which Kuhn wrote, could stimulate ongoing research and theorizing, all the while building a body of knowledge that coheres with basic Christian notions. Much of the thinking that presently exists in these disciplines in no way repudiates a Christian worldview, even though it may well have emanated from the scholarship of nonbelievers. Christians can use this work, ever sifting, researching, and theorizing as they build academically competent yet Christian modes of thinking.

This is the trail Christian scholars must blaze more effectively. Stages two and three are the turf on which the game must now be played. The two are linked in that Christian models, not unlike those of other interest groups, will almost certainly be refinements of current secular models that have been carefully critiqued. In any case, quality work needs to be done in these stages. I am not talking about those occasionally esoteric philosophical treatises that no one of sound mind can understand. These are near-zero-impact efforts for all but a select few technical insiders. I am also not talking about special courses highlighting Christian approaches to learning in general. As helpful as these classes are, they still have that "separate category" effect and become permission-givers for other faculty members to abandon faith-and-learning endeavors, leaving the task to the philosophy and theology departments. I am talking about head-on analyses of current models *within the various disciplines,* and the theory building that can flow from it—efforts that are intelligent and intelligible to scholars from any belief tradition.

These models need to go beyond what researchers call "armchair theorizing" and suggest research programs within the various disciplines. "It may be that scientists in fact expend more time and energy pursuing research programs suggested by theories than in devising and weighing theories," states Wolterstorff.[3] Christianity should generate research programs just as feminist perspectives and institutes for minority studies do. Too often solid critiques or a suggested theoretical revision of a current theory "goes nowhere. It suggests no lines of inquiry. . . . It leads to no research program."[4]

Wolterstorff's call for research merits comment. In 1982, John Naisbitt noted that about 7,000 scientific articles were written each day, with scientific and technical information doubling every 5.5 years.[5] From 1990 to 1996, the number of periodicals published in the United States increased by 3 percent, while book publication rose by 46 percent.[6] In the information age, and with the Internet, the amount of research information available to the public is simply incalculable. Christians cannot abandon this intellectual waterfront.

▸▸ Collective Inferiority Complex

All of this is not to say that some excellent work has not been done. Moreover, I suspect many Christian scholars have some very insightful notions about faith and learning in their disciplines that they need only to commit to paper. This raises a sensitive, though hidden concern. It should hardly come as a surprise that I have observed what can only be called a collective inferiority complex among many Christian scholars, given their out-of-the-mainstream status in addition to being rather consistently labeled as second-rate by the likes of Alan Wolfe.

For example, Briner observes this as well, stating, "I'm afraid too many of our Christian colleges have developed an inferiority complex."[7] A symptom of this psychological state is the tendency of Christian institutions and the faculty within them to measure themselves negatively using mainstream standards of research and publishing, forgetting that Christian colleges are teaching institutions. It goes beyond that, however. "It seemed the highest sense of achievement came when one of their students was accepted into a topflight graduate program," said one professor from a research university, in observing Christian college academics engaging in a form of baptized paganism by holding the secular mainstream up as the standard of educational excellence.

This collectively negative self-image is contagious. It spreads to students. "Christian college graduates typically have commitment, but not confidence," says Briner. "They have ideals but not vision. Except for those going into the professional ministry, no one has laid out for most of them either the possibilities or the responsibilities of penetrating every area of society with the message of Christ."[8] For Briner, combating this sense of inferiority among such students is critical. "Too often they feel that as graduates of a small Christian college, they are not adequate to go head to head with the world in important arenas of ministry.... If we are not preparing the next governor, novelist, TV anchor, or filmmaker, we can never expect to find a Christian influence in those culture-shaping professions."[9]

As certainly as I have detected this state, there is no good reason for it. "Obviously, relatively small Christian colleges cannot compete with giant research institutions in terms of facilities and equipment. There will probably never be any atom smashers or giant radio telescopes on Christian college campuses. So what?" Briner asks rhetorically.[10] So what, indeed. Not only are there many first-rate scholars at work on these campuses, but—consistent with our belief in the truth of the gospel—we must view Christian education as superior to all other such enterprises. That is the case among our Jewish counterparts. Those at Hebrew Union in Cincinnati do not covet the endorsement of secular academic institutions. On the contrary, they weigh the quality of secular universities on the scale of Jewish academic standards. Moreover, Scripture provides a basis for a confident outlook. Jesus, the ultimate teacher, made no apology for the quality of his instruction. Paul entered the various intellectual arenas of his time boldly, and Daniel moved assertively to the top of the most powerful secular government of his day. The confident air of the latter two did not have its genesis in personal arrogance, but rather in their awareness that they were doing the work of the Creator of the very cultures in which they moved.

Clearly, the academic mainstream does not have all the answers, and to allow it to have an intimidating, immobilizing effect is a form of intellectual idolatry. "Openness and diversity, we have discovered," notes Marsden, "have their own orthodoxies and their own intolerance. . . . No longer is it widely compelling to say if only people were educated into the more progressive ideals, the world would be a better place."[11] The cynicism of the postmodernists is testimony to the limitations of secular academe, with basic problems such as racism, violence, and poverty unsolved and without readily apparent solutions.

According to Buckley, the mainstream is now tied in intellectual knots. "I am saying, very simply, that the educated elite are not agreed as to what are the central problems which education aims to settle, let alone what is their solution."[12] Buckley's assertions are reminiscent of Paul's observation that the spiritually rebellious are "always learning but never able to acknowledge the truth" (2 Tim. 3:7). Amid this intolerance, loss of direction, and practical ineffectiveness, Christian scholarship offers a refreshing change from the staleness of the secular mainstream. "It is time to recognize that scholars and institutions who take the intellectual dimensions of their faith seriously can be responsible and creative participants in the highest levels of academic discourse," states Marsden.[13] Unfortunately, a major barrier to this participation is a misplaced sense of inadequacy.

Paul left no doubt as to his outlook, calling the gospel of Christ nothing less than divine dynamite (Rom. 1:16). It is time to move out of punt formation.

There are first-rate minds in the faith community that are fully capable of doing first-rate work. And there is a channel for it. Christians have a tremendous advantage, what with the presence of quality Christian publishers willing to examine their ideas. No other special interest group has such an incredible advantage.

The theory-building work of Christian thinkers can go on in the mainstream university or at the Christian college. In any case, there is a need to develop ever stronger Christian academic communities to engage the effort.[14] Some do exist in the form of professional associations. The Society of Christian Philosophers, the Institute for the Study of American Evangelicals, the Conference on Christianity and Literature, the Conference on Faith and History, and the American Scientific Affiliation are examples. Despite the current absence of a major Protestant research university, there are alternatives. Marsden sagely suggests an economic alternative: the founding of a series of research institutes that would stimulate first-rate scholarship by bringing together first-rate Christian thinkers to examine a problem.

Within Christian colleges, faculty development programs could nurture faith-and-learning integrations. Granting sabbaticals, release time, and other affordable "perks" for those willing to engage in faith-and-learning matters could be helpful. Recent programs such as The Lilly Endowment and The Pew Charitable Trust have been developed to examine the meaning of faith in an academic setting and can serve as models for the nature of such endeavors. Discussion groups, conferences, and email correspondence are excellent ways to stimulate this effort. But, again, it needs to be done with an eye toward presenting solid, Christian perspectives that have an illuminating effect on Christian students in all academic environments, as well as toward making an academically respectable case in the minds of nonbelieving scholars. In short, it must move out of the closed system that Wolfe identified all too accurately.

▸▸ Resistance

Approaching the mainstream university community with Christian alternatives will, of course, bring resistance. Some of it is political. The mainstream university is by nature conservative and traditional—unwilling to share its truth-defining power. Despite a professed commitment to diversity and multiculturalism, it will oppose any belief system that does not comport with the naturalistic worldview that is its secular theology. Other groups have encountered similar resistance but have pressed on. Gays, ethnic minorities, feminists, and others with an uncompromising, interest-based agenda have prevailed and have carved out a place for themselves. Thus, Christians must not abandon the secular waterfront.

There is, however, another reason for secular resistance to Christian thinking. It is spiritual. Many within the Christian academic community need to be awakened. The pressing need persists for scholars to see their calling as spiritual as well as intellectual. Every effort needs to be extended to raise consciousness on the Christian campus as to the import of genuinely Christian scholarship—that one's scholarly vocation is not complete unless it includes an ongoing effort at integrating one's faith with one's academic pursuits. This priority must go beyond the theoretical. It should influence hiring practices, faculty evaluations, and intracampus conferences.

There will always be some tension and conflict in dealings with mainstream academe. We are most certainly confronting what Paul, in his letter to the Ephesians, called powers of a dark world, spiritual forces of evil. Confrontation arises because the truth of the gospel is more than intellectual. The Christian scholar knows that education is not a panacea. It is *a* path to truth, not *the* path. Truth goes beyond the intellect. It is moral. It calls for a decision from the hearer—a decision to abandon one's own claim to godlike status by humbly seeking God's truth. Humility, as we know, is in short supply in the intellectual community. Arrogance is everywhere. Theorists regularly defend their intellectual models in the face of the most compelling contrary evidence. Admission of error is humiliating, the bane of the proud academic.

Any Christian worldview must affirm humility. Rather than glorifying intellectuality, it stresses the finite limits of intellectual endeavor in learning the truths of the infinite. It focuses on how much the creature needs to learn from the Creator, rather than that the creature *is* the creator. Pride blinds and closes the mind. To be teachable is to be humble, an attitude the Christian thinker must adopt as she attempts to learn God's truth.

Prideful resistance most certainly did not stop Paul. In fact, in almost every city, before he approached the Gentiles he went into the temple, where the most educated population congregated. There he made his case for the faith, willing to discuss and debate anyone that might wish to engage him. In Athens, he eagerly sought out the educated pagans in his effort to present the gospel. Paul was not a professor, although he studied under one of the most famous teachers of his time, Gamaliel. Paul was, however, unabashed about meeting the society's most learned on their turf, making a compelling case for the gospel in terms they could understand and appreciate.

A brilliant, self-confessed atheist professor once spoke to me of his philosophy of education. "When I was young I was told that the purpose of education was to teach people to think," he explained, "and I took that seriously." If this professor felt called in the secular sense to shape the thinking capacities of students' minds, there would seem to be an even more powerful calling for the Christian scholar to help students develop the Christian mind. Christian scholarship is not evangelism in the narrow sense of the word. It most certainly is evangelism, however, in a larger sense. To develop a God consciousness, to adopt the mind of Christ, and to search for eternal wisdom are all part of the Great Commission's call to make disciples, as well as a partial fulfillment of the first commandment. It is to teach believers how to love God with all of their minds.

Notes

1. Brad Green, "Theological and Philosophical Foundations," in *Shaping a Christian Worldview*, ed. David S. Dockery and Gregory Alan Thornbury (Nashville: Broadman and Holman, 2002), 83.
2. George M. Marsden, *The Outrageous Idea of Christian Scholarship* (New York: Oxford University Press, 1997), 6.
3. Nicholas Wolterstorff, *Reason within the Bounds of Religion* (Grand Rapids: Eerdmans, 1984), 105.
4. Ibid., 106.
5. John Naisbitt, *Megatrends: Ten New Directions Transforming Our Lives* (New York: Warner, 1982), 24; Jimmy H. Davis, "Faith and Learning," in Dockery and Thornbury, *Shaping a Christian Worldview*, 129.
6. U.S. Bureau of the Census, *Statistical Abstract of the United States: 1998* (Austin, TX: Hoover's Business Press, 1998), 580–81; Davis, "Faith and Learning," in Dockery and Thornbury, *Shaping a Christian Worldview*, 129.
7. Bob Briner, *Roaring Lambs* (Grand Rapids: Zondervan, 1993), 158.
8. Ibid., 155.
9. Ibid., 160.
10. Ibid., 158.
11. Marsden, *The Outrageous Idea of Christian Scholarship*, 110.
12. William F. Buckley Jr., *Let Us Talk of Many Things* (Roseville, CA: Prima, 2000), 103.
13. Marsden, *The Outrageous Idea of Christian Scholarship*, 111.
14. Ibid., 102–3.

PART TWO

APPLYING FAITH AND LEARNING IN THE
CLASSROOM AND IN RESEARCH

INTERPASSAGE:
STIMULATING THE DIALOGUE

The basis for the modern university's unwritten directive that the scholar should lay aside her religious beliefs at the door when doing science lies in the centuries-old belief that one should avert any elementary prejudice when engaging in serious scholarship. Though it is ideologically objectionable to believers to assume that God and faith are fantasy, the intent of this rule—to start from a similar base for purposes of harmony—is in itself not unreasonable. As we discussed earlier, in many scientific endeavors, secularists and believers share the same knowledge. They both engage the scientific method, the rules of logic, and the basic tenets of scholarship in doing research, though they may very well differ in interpretation.

Nevertheless, the lay-aside rule is problematic.[1] First, it simply does not work in the pre-paradigmatic disciplines outside the natural sciences. These are, by their very natures, not entirely empirical. In fact, they are often value-based. For example, the lay-aside rule does not unite scholars in a single way of thinking about matters such as personality theory, human relationships, rational political choice, or social change. Furthermore, naturalism and empiricism do not address the larger questions of significance, meaning, and truth. These matters are battled over by political factions and secular ideologists because they are the foundation stones of much academic theorizing. With many scholars and academic institutions claiming their very mission is to find truth, there is no reason to pursue truth if it is not significant.

In addition, the rule is not applied to many nonacademic concerns in the university community. There is, for example, widespread agreement that equal opportunity should be extended to all, regardless of gender, race, and class, and that the disabled need to be accommodated, although there is absolutely no empirical basis for this consensus. Ironically, were a person to be consistent with the doctrine of naturalism, espousing a survival-of-the-fittest outlook (rooted in the doctrine of natural selection), she would be predisposed to rule out special accommodations for the disadvantaged.

Returning to the academic sector, although the belief in an infinite creator cannot be empirically validated, neither can the opposite position—that the cosmos is an undesigned amalgam of natural forces. Yet it is the latter point of view that functions as the norm—the unassailable doctrine—in the current academic mainstream. Clearly, then, even in the world of the physical sciences, the rule of empirical validation is not followed. In reality, one can no more excise one's religious perspective from the scholarly process than a journalist can remove her point of view in presenting the news. Given that many scholars do have religious beliefs, it is simply inevitable that those beliefs will influence their interpretations of knowledge.

The actual directive, however, is that a person is to conduct herself *as if* her religious beliefs are irrelevant. Yet even that is not possible. One's attitude toward theism—the very existence of God—is foundational to one's view of everything. In political science, for example, it is unreasonable to think that even a nominal believer can conduct herself wholly exclusive of her religious beliefs. Virtually every theist believes that morality—right and wrong—exists. That simple presupposition will influence one's view of war, violence, abuse, racism, and the contribution of historical movements. Nor does admission of religious "bias" curtail teaching effectiveness. I, like Marsden, regularly informed my classes of my academic and spiritual biases, assuring them that I had no intention of penalizing those with different points of view. Beyond merely feeling a larger measure of personal integrity in doing so, I also found that students appreciated my candor and seemed to enjoy a greater freedom in expressing themselves.

Finally, and of greatest import, the lay-aside rule does not accomplish its stated purpose: to level the intellectual playing field. Instead, it tilts the surface decidedly toward a naturalistic worldview, one that is most certainly not empirically verified. As we have seen, naturalism has now spread across the disciplines. This orientation is so indelibly scorched into the scholarly process that scholars often draw conclusions from their research based on this premise rather than on the research itself. Examples are myriad. Note that virtually every psychological and sociological explanation of religiosity ignores even the possibility of a transcendent being. Religious behavior is consistently reduced to a series of correlations with social and psychological factors, suggesting that it is no more significant than one's interest in golf. There is not even a discussion of the impact, say, of prayer on healing, or even of the positive influence of Christian beliefs on the development of Western culture.

▶▶ Faith-and-Learning Levels

Faith and learning can relate in a variety of ways.[2] The lowest level of relationship is the conjunctive relationship in which faith is merely added on to learning or the learning process. Christians in the mainstream university, for example, are often pushed toward taking the conjunctive approach. Like the Old Testament Daniel in Babylon, the Christian student walks the spiritual walk while studying in a non-Christian atmosphere. Compartmentalization among faculty is also conjunctive in nature.

One could argue that the faith-and-learning relationship found in the physical sciences—where questions are raised and issues are joined as matters of faith and academe jostle with one another—is one of interaction. Here the two are in important yet endless and often unresolved dialogue. Side by side, they go back and forth informing and clarifying one another. Basic Christian beliefs guide thinking and research, while discoveries in the physical world can correct false beliefs.

For the truly Christian scholar, however, faith and learning relate most directly in the more theoretical disciplines, which are less amenable to tightly controlled empirical investigation. In such areas, the relationship can be integrative. Indeed, as Marsden asserts, "Philosophers are likely more often to be able to identify the pertinence of religious perspectives for their work than will historians or social scientists, who in turn will be able to point to religious influences more often than will chemists or physicists."[3] Integration is the deepest faith-and-learning level. Here faith does not exist alongside learning or in discussion with it. It permeates it and is inseparable from the material studied. Faith becomes the context, the perspective in which one learns in her discipline.

▶▶ Criteria

I suggest five basic Christian criteria that one may find helpful in assessing prevailing theories and systems of thought. Though rooted in Scripture, they are sufficiently noncreedal in nature such that Christians from a wide variety of traditions can use them.

▶ God

In the case of the existence of God, we can first ask, Does the given system of thinking assume his existence? If yes, we have a theory that may have potential for faith-and-learning integration, or at least, interaction. If not, we move to the next question: Could one at least assume the existence of God without compromising the integrity of the system? If yes, the theory at least does not repudiate Christian belief. If not, we are left to ask whether the system obviates the very existence of God. Should that be the case, we will have to revise the system by carefully sifting those aspects that fit Christian belief or abandon it entirely.

▸ Creation

We can apply many of the same questions here as we used in the case of God. There is, however, much elasticity here, because there is a wide range of opinion among Christian scholars regarding specific issues involved in creation, particularly the age of the earth.

▸ Human Nature

A number of questions emerge in the case of human nature. The first involves the *essence* of humankind: Does the belief system assume that humans are spiritual in nature? If not, does it allow for that belief? In addition, we need to ask as to the *moral nature* of humankind: Does the theory allow for the sinful, or at least flawed, moral nature of humans? Given the pervasive nature of conflict and evil, many theories will pass this test. If, however, the theory assumes a perfectionist notion—that humans are at the core good rather than sinful or at least flawed—the theory has problems from a Christian perspective.

▸ Truth

Does the thought system assume that ultimate truth exists? If so, is this truth at least partially attainable? If the first two answers are yes, we move forward to determine what truth, if any, the theory affirms. If the belief system does not necessarily affirm the existence of ultimate truth, it may still have potential, provided it can stand without rejecting the possibility of there being ultimate truth.

▸ Values

Values flow from truth. The central issue here is whether there are ethical values that are not entirely relative to culture. There is, however, danger at the other extreme: a tendency of many believers to equate Christianity with middle-class values and therefore to elevate certain Western cultural values to near-divine status.

In any case, the test of any theory is whether it is compatible with a commitment to spiritual truth—a series of acts and facts. To the extent that a belief system at best affirms, and at least does not repudiate, basic Christian truths, it has potential for Christian thinking.

◀ ▶

These five criteria are not directly relevant to every theory. There are many academic notions that simply do not intersect with some or all of these in any obvious way. A Christian scholar is wise, however, not to assume this too quickly. Theories need to be probed and peeled away to determine what basic beliefs about life undergird them. Only after those underlying doctrines are revealed can one move on comfortably.

Perhaps more important, these five criteria are a start. One most certainly could add the matter of time: the eternal (God-based) rather than temporal (secular) perspective.[4] Basic to the Christian perspective is to see all of temporal reality through the wide-angle lens of a larger, supernatural framework.[5] In short, the Christian mind "sees the natural order as dependent upon the supernatural order, time as contained within eternity."[6] Never given to understatement, Blamires raises some worthy points. Too often Christians take the narrow, temporal view. "In this respect the Christian mind has allowed itself to be subtly secularized by giving a purely *chronological* status to the eternal," he says. "That is to say, the Christian has relegated the significance of the eternal to the life that succeeds this one." When this happens, the Christian unwittingly reaches a false point of consensus with the secularist—that in the here and now, Christians and secularists can share the same theories, values, and modes of action, with the only real difference between them being the issues of whether or not there is a God and a life after this one (a matter applicable only when this life is concluded).[7]

There are many more issues to examine. Holmes advocates exploring the Christian concepts of sin and grace, biblical perspectives on history and social justice, and a large range of other doctrines.[8] Although scholars may differ as to what Christian criteria they choose to apply in their faith-and-learning explorations, one point remains: faith and learning meet when this exploring needs to take place in psychology, sociology, history, economics, and political science classes, as well as those in philosophy and theology classes. The effects of working with faith and learning are geometric. The more a scholar searches for intersecting points, the more her eyes will open to myriad additional points of contact. In short, the pursuit of a healthy relationship of faith and learning ultimately becomes an adventure rather than a task.

◄ ►

The final section of the book is devoted to more specific applications of Christian thinking in the various disciplines. There is considerable variation here. Some are rather philosophical in nature, others more practical. Some involve Christian critiques of prevailing theories, and others offer the rudiments of Christian theorizing along with suggestions for Christian scholarship. No claim to universal scholarship is being made. Rather, I stand on the shoulders of giants, to use a common phrase. Indeed, these formulations come from a variety of sources.

After the chapter on creation, the remainder of the book is divided into three sections and fourteen chapters for purposes of organization. The placement of some of the disciplines noted is understandably open to debate. For example, some scholars may place education among the social sciences rather than the humanities. Colleges and universities themselves differ on such placements. In any case, positioning is of little matter here. The purpose of the final section is to put faith and learning into action. It is to provide examples of how Christians can move beyond compartmentalization and work their faith effectively into a given discipline in a more than superficial or contrived fashion.

►► Stimulating the Dialogue

A major disclaimer is in order here. These faith-and-learning explorations are meant to be *suggestive* rather than exhaustive. They are in some instances provocative, ripe for debate and additional critique. Most are deliberately brief, serving as intellectual appetizers. In every case, they are open to much further development. Rather than providing a set of finished models, my aim is to stimulate the dialogue. Indeed, to the extent that ideas presented here generate debate, discussion, and further research among Christian scholars, they will have served their purpose: to encourage those who are serious about the matter of faith and learning to critique academic systems and work at constructing models of Christian thought.

Notes

1. George M. Marsden, *The Outrageous Idea of Christian Scholarship* (New York: Oxford University Press, 1997), 28–29.
2. Arthur F. Holmes develops these levels throughout his excellent book, *The Idea of a Christian College* (Grand Rapids: Eerdmans, 1987).

3. Marsden, *The Outrageous Idea of Christian Scholarship,* 63.
4. Harry Blamires, *The Christian Mind* (Ann Arbor, MI: Servant, 1997), 67.
5. Ibid., 69.
6. Ibid., 67.
7. Ibid., 69.
8. Holmes, *The Idea of a Christian College,* 56.

12

WHY IS CREATION CENTRAL TO THE FAITH-AND-LEARNING ENTERPRISE?

T here is nothing in our experience, however trivial, worldly, or even evil, which cannot be thought about Christianly," says Blamires.[1] True though that may be, integrating faith concepts, particularly in the physical sciences, has always proved problematic in Christian institutions. In fact, Christian colleges are often hard-pressed to justify to their physical sciences faculty members a requirement that they be present at retreats focused on faith and learning.

►► Paradigmatic Disciplines

The main reason instituting a faith-and-learning dialogue in the physical sciences is a daunting task is because they contain a certain degree of unalterable truth. They are, in a word, paradigmatic. Christians and non-Christians alike operate with the same multiplication tables, the same elemental chart, and the same invertebrate biology. These are not a matter of interpretation. There is no postmodernism in physics, no naturalistic mathematics, no sin-weakened reasoning in biology. There are right and wrong answers. Although mathematical designs vary in elegance and matrices are structured in differing ways, there is objectivity—final truth—in the physical sciences.

The physical or "hard" sciences are simply not conducive to the faith-and-learning integrations achieved in the more theoretical disciplines. In fact, their paradigmatic nature has often proven to be an impossible speed bump for some advocates of faith and learning to negotiate. Even Christians in these disciplines often wonder how their faith can play a central role in their scholarship, given the limited space available for values and theoretical constructs in these areas of inquiry.

With this definitive physical certitude—one that moves beyond one's theological commitments—it is tempting to yield the floor to the sneering cynics who rhetorically and derisively ask whether there is a "Christian math." Obviously, Christian carpenters do not make Christian doors, nor does a door become Christian because it opens to a church sanctuary rather than a bar full of exotic dancers. Clearly, the character and quality of the bodies of knowledge in the physical sciences do not differ for the believer as compared to the agnostic.[2]

The solution to this dilemma, if there is one, must lie elsewhere. I propose that it is found at the beginning of all things: creation.

▶▶ Creation

Not one shred of Christian thought has any validity apart from creation. Creation is the ball game. It establishes theism and leads to the Christian concept of God. Belief in creation does not obviate evolution—gradual developments within and among species. It does, however, rule out evolutionism, a subdivision of naturalism. Although Christian scholars stretch across the spectrum on degrees of evolution and the age of the earth, there is no running room on the basic doctrine of creation. It remains the watershed issue—the central context in which all Christian thinking is placed. Creation is an either/or matter. It is *the* Christian perspective of the origin of the universe and its species. As such, it is important to examine some academic defenses for it, as well as the implications creation has for the Christian scholar.

▶ Origins

Creation is about origins, not the evolving of origins. Evolutionism skips past first causes. In short, evolution is about the development of something already in existence, not the beginning of that existence itself. Using the metaphor of the human fetus, evolution is about the prenatal development of the fetus, not about the fertilization of the egg—the creation of the zygote.

"In the beginning, what?" asks John Patrick, a biochemist from the University of Ottawa. "Certainly not our cosmos. But something was there before us. How did our cosmos come to be? Chance, say many. But the cosmos knows of nothing that is made by chance." Even a flip of a coin is actually not a matter of chance. "[A coin] comes down as it does because of a complex array of interacting forces that are sufficiently random as to allow the use of probability theory." Evolutionary processes themselves do not occur by chance, but involve "a series of discrete chemical changes that we can only describe in statistical terms."[3] For Patrick, there are only two possibilities when it comes to origins: (a) God or (b) a self-creating universe. A self-creating universe is a logical impossibility, because to be self-creating, the universe would need to exist even before creation. Therefore, because science is built on logic, one is left only with God.[4]

James Keener also finds no logical explanation for origins outside of creation and therefore theism. "I find it impossible to believe that there is no creator," states the professor of mathematics at the University of Utah. "In all of my experience, in all of science, I have never heard of an effect that had no cause. I have never seen a design that had no designer, a law that had no lawgiver, an order that had not been ordered, information that had no informer." Keener also engages the issue of chance. "Chance produces nothing. Saying that something happened by chance merely begs the question of the causes that produced the effect. 'It just happened' is simply not an acceptable answer. It is an open admission of ignorance."[5]

Paul M. Anderson, professor of biochemistry and molecular biology at the University of Minnesota-Duluth, School of Medicine, searched for origins early in his career. He was driven to faith by looking for a point at which life was injected into the cosmos. Anderson quotes theoretical physicist Stephen Hawking from *A Brief History of Time*, "Even if there is only one possible unified theory [explaining the physical laws of the universe], it is just a set of rules and equations. What is it that breathes fire into the equations and makes a universe for them to describe?"[6] Again, theism becomes the logical explanation.

Even Saint Thomas Aquinas focused on origins and ultimate causes in his well-known five "proofs" for the existence of God. His first proof held that for something to move, it must be moved by something else, a process that logically ends with a first mover—God. His second dealt with cause-effect relationships, stating there must necessarily be an ultimate first cause in any cause-effect chain, and that first cause is God. The third proof asserts that anything in existence has to emerge from something previous to it, leading to an ultimate first existence—God. The fourth involves "gradation." Using goodness as an example, some things are better (more good) than others. This must lead eventually to a maximum or ultimate good—God. His final postulate, governance, holds that things in nature act in a direction, toward a certain end. To do this, they have to be directed by some intelligent being that directs all things—God. Aquinas used simple "if-then" chains of logic to get at ultimate causes, yet naturalists, whose basic premise resides in causality and determinism, oppose this logic. Wanting it both ways, they affirm an if-then causality (determinism) in the scientific world, but at the same time, rule out that logic when applied as a philosophical argument for the existence of God. In brief, causality works in science but cannot apply to philosophy.

▶ "Designfulness"

According to Blamires, if we dismiss every element of the Christian faith—Scripture, the life of Christ, evidence for the power of prayer, the witness of centuries of believers and martyrs—a simple look at nature, natural revelation, leaves us with the sense that it was "consciously and purposely designed. Things in it belong together."[7] All living creatures have specific and basic needs, and these are harmoniously provided for. "There is water to drink, food to eat, fuel to keep us warm, materials from which to make shelter, clothing, and all refinements of civilized life. Either the whole thing is a mighty accident, or else it fulfills some overall purpose."[8] Bennett, in considering the complexity and precision of the universe, puts the issue in the form of a succinct, thought-provoking question: "If you threw a handful of iron filings into the air, would you expect to catch a Swiss watch on the way down?"[9]

Stated another way, if we remove chance as a force of origin, then the incredible intricacy and coordination of the myriad structures of the universe suggest the activity of an intelligent designer. This view, called intelligent design theory ("designfulness"), is the one held by a number of scholars, including Michael Behe and William Dembski (discussed in chapter 5). Designfulness, a powerful counterpoint to naturalism, is based on the belief that Darwin's theory of natural selection is simply not sufficient to explain the degree of complexity in the universe, particularly among plants and animals. At the expense of being excessively technical, what follows are some examples that give credence to intelligent design theory.

Designfulness is apparent in something as basic as water, a simple combination of oxygen and hydrogen (H_2O). Just two swallows of water (18 milliliters) contain 6×10^{23} of H_2O. Putting that amount in perspective, a sound computer is capable of making 10 million (10,000,000) counts per second. At that rate, it would require 2 billion years to finish the molecular count (6×10^{23}) in just those two swallows of water.[10] The wonder of water becomes perhaps more mind-numbingly incomprehensible if stacks of paper are used as a measure (with 500 sheets reaching a height of 2–3 inches). A paper stack of 6×10^{23} in height would reach from the earth to the sun (93 billion miles away) more than a million times.[11]

The universe itself suggests a very tight design. That it has such a high degree of uniformity is accounted for by an allegedly brief period of inflationary expansion around the time of its origin. Had this smoothing not occurred, the universe would have consisted of a series of black holes separated by near-empty space. If, however, the universe had been smoothed even a bit more, stars, star clusters, and galaxies would not have formed. Just a bit too little or just a bit too much smoothing would have made the universe unable to support life.[12] In a similar vein, if the constant that is associated with the velocity of light were to have changed even the slightest bit, there would be no life at all in the universe.[13]

There is also the stability of protons, affecting the quantity of matter as well as the radiation level relating to higher forms of life. Each proton contains three quarks, which decay through the activity of other particles. This decaying process occurs at the rate of once per proton per 10^{32} years. If that rate were greater, large animals would be extinguished through radiation. If the proton were more stable, however, there would be an insufficient amount of matter in the universe for life to be possible. Such is the precision of the necessary balance.[14]

To attribute the precision of the universe to a function of chance factors stretches the tissues of reason. For example, if the neutrons and protons of an atom were separated by just 1/12 trillion of an inch, matter in solid mass form would not exist. Instead, the world would blow apart in a cosmic nuclear explosion.[15] Similarly, researchers have studied a list of "designed for life" indicators. Measuring the outer reaches of the universe, they have isolated a number of physical characteristics that had to be incredibly exact for life to be possible, giving rise to the anthropic principle, which says that the features of the solar system are "just right" to sustain life.[16]

Designfulness is also evident within the organs of species. The human eye is capable of performing 100,000 separate functions each day, while doing maintenance work during sleep. Considering the complexity and the synchronized nature of its functions, it is difficult to imagine that the human eye evolved over time through a trial-and-error process of natural selection. Furthermore, the eye is useless unless fully developed, so it could not have functioned in basal form and increased its complexity over an evolutionary period.[17]

J. Gary Eden, professor of electrical and computer engineering at the University of Illinois, coheres with intelligent design thinking. "I am persuaded by two truths. First, the physical world—which displays a level of complexity and beauty that we can only begin to fathom (much less duplicate)—bears the unmistakable signature of a superior intellect. Second, Christianity provides a rational explanation for life on this planet as it really is, not as we would wish it to be."[18]

The notion of order and intelligent design are not new. The Christian worldview contributed to the development of modern science. Basic scientific principles emerged from faith that the universe was orderly and able to be understood by the rational mind. Everything, from logical observation to the experimental method, emerged from a belief in an orderly, creating God. "It is surely one of the curious paradoxes of history that science, which professionally has little to do with faith, owes it origins to an act of faith that the universe can be rationally interpreted, and that science today is sustained by that assumption," notes Loren Eisley.[19]

Sir Isaac Newton, a believer, wrote, "This most beautiful system of the sun, planets, and comets could only proceed from the counsel and dominion of an intelligent and powerful Being."[20] Roger Coles wrote in the preface of Newton's *Principia*, "Without all doubt this world, so diversified with that variety of forms and motions we find in it, could arise from nothing but the perfectly free will of God directing and presiding over all."[21] Even Albert Einstein said that for the scientist, "his religious feeling takes the form of a rapturous amazement at the harmony of natural law, which reveals an intelligence of such superiority that, compared with it, all the systematic thinking and acting of human beings is an utterly insignificant reflection."[22]

It is as if we have come full circle. Christianity has historically been a friend of science, with scientists professing their faith in print. In 1859, however, the seeds of naturalism were harvested with Darwin's *On the Origin of Species*. This major detour out of faith, however, was never complete. Belief in creation persisted because the doctrine of naturalism, compelling as it may be, did not provide a sufficient and complete explanation for the origin and operation of the universe. Further scientific exploration has revealed additional problems with naturalism and has emboldened its critics to reject the naturalist paradigm. As a result, the movement toward creationism is fueled by more than evangelical politics. It is also motivated by scientific thinking.

▸▸ Creation Logic

Patricia H. Reiff, chair of the Department of Space Physics and Astronomy at Rice University, offers "creation logic," intriguingly showing how the order in the Genesis account of the six days of creation, at least in general, parallels current scientific understanding.[23] She begins by equating the scientific logic undergirding the big bang theory with the simple directive: "Let there be light!" (Gen. 1:3). Reiff suggests that there was a time when all of the energy of the universe probably existed in the form of a small bit of light energy, making light the logical beginning. From there, condensation had to occur, out of which came the solar system and the planets on day two. "In essence, day one was the big bang and the laws of physics; day two says that the fundamental constraints and local conditions were just right so that galaxies, and specifically the solar system and its earth, could form."[24]

On day three, the land and water were separated and the first forms of life created. "I really don't care whether this took an eye blink or a billion years—

the creation of life from nonlife, even in a single-celled bacterium, is so complicated and unlikely that it has been compared to an explosion in a junkyard resulting in a Boeing 747 jumbo jet," asserts Reiff.[25] The plant life created on day three altered the earth markedly by shifting carbon dioxide from the atmosphere into the soils and sediment. This was necessary to generate food and oxygen for the advanced life to follow.

With the extraction of the carbon dioxide cooling the atmosphere, the clouds were parted and the sun appeared on the fourth day. This did not happen on day one, because we now know the sun is a second-generation star that emerged from the atmospheric debris of a neighboring supernova (a large, exploding star), necessary for the presence of carbon and other life-sustaining elements.[26] "A transparent yet sheltering atmosphere is unique in our solar system," notes Reiff in describing the orderly logic of creation. "Only earthlings can stand on the ground and observe the wonders of the heavens without being scorched by the sun, blasted by cosmic rays or shrouded by thick layers of clouds. Only earthlings have perfect solar eclipses that allow the sun's gorgeous, ghostly corona to be seen."[27] Although naturalists commonly scoff at Christianity's focus on the importance of earth, emphasizing its relatively tiny placement in the solar system, its inhabitants enjoy a uniqueness found nowhere else in the universe. "Alone in the solar system we have a clear, safe view of the wonder-full second heaven," says Reiff.[28]

On day five, animal life abounds, first in the ocean and then in the air. The description of the ocean's leviathans is immediately followed by a reference to birds. Interestingly enough, we now know that dinosaurs were more closely related to birds than to lizards. On day six, humankind is created. That God breathed his very Spirit into humankind is most significant in that it is the genesis of our spiritual and eternal nature.[29]

The issue of intelligent design (and Reiff's scientific logic) returns the matter of origins really to just two possibilities: "Either the whole thing is a mighty accident, or else it fulfills some overall purpose. There is no third alternative," states Blamires.[30]

Often secularists cheat on this matter, taking the form of half-believing. They may accept the idea of God but not accept a God with a purpose for his creation, one who is to be worshiped. People holding this view often reject "organized religion," theological doctrines, and Scripture as divine revelation, while still clinging to some semblance of theism.[31] This postmodern position enables a person to have what one of my more cynical intellectual friends would call "a warm, fuzzy feeling about God" without really submitting to what makes him God, his sovereignty. In reality, this position is really no position at all, because it attempts to stake out an artificial third alternative, one affirming neither naturalism nor Christianity.

Blamires suggests using reasoning at the most basic level to challenge such thinking effectively. One could take, he says, the hypothetical position that all of Christianity is merely "a pack of lies," with God, Christ, the afterlife, prayer, saintly living, and all the rest simply delusional notions. What, then, is life about? Why does anything exist? Why do you and I exist? Faced with a total demolition of the very existence of anything divine, many people will dissent quickly and forcefully. "Hold on. I didn't say that. I didn't mean that. I wouldn't go as far as that. I do believe in God, as a matter of fact," they will say. Once the person is back on the road of "natural theology," says Blamires, he is soon to encounter the matter of purpose, plan, and the validity of Jesus as the Son of God, as well as an orderly theology flowing from it.[32]

▶▶ Implications for Epistemology

The impact of creation moves beyond establishing the existence of God, as important as that is. Creation is the notion of something—the very cosmos—made out of nothing. It is the divine counterpart of the human notion of magic, and it is basic to all things. Among them, something in which all disciplines are interested—the understanding of knowledge itself, what we call epistemology. Naturalism, like aspects of postmodernism, becomes an intellectual cul de sac here. With human perception ever evolving, yet severely limited, there is simply no fixed point at which the naturalist can state that anything is truly and finally known. The postmodern view asserting that nothing ultimately knowable actually exists compounds the matter. Epistemology, then, is dead, or at least curtailed. One cannot truly pursue truth with any confidence if, as a naturalist, one believes there is no fixed point of certainty in the ever-changing evolutionary cycle, or as a postmodernist, that no ultimate certainty is present in the universe.[33]

These views all but force us to ask why one pursues any knowledge other than for the cognitively stimulating value of doing so, much the same reason one does a crossword puzzle. The reason is simply this: We members of the human species want to know. And we want to know with certainty—whether the matter concerns our favorite player's batting average or involves the question of human nature itself. But with naturalism and postmodernism, we simply cannot know; all this despite the presence of famous scholars who claim to have certain knowledge regarding matters on which they have done research.[34]

This is reminiscent of the Berkeley student's lament: "Then I took a philosophy course which sent me spinning. How can one learn the Truth about something when he cannot know for sure if what he is told is the truth unless he knew beforehand what it is, in which case there would be no reason to ask questions?" In short, there is no "In the beginning …" with naturalism or postmodernism. Therefore, there is no beginning of knowledge. Moreover, with naturalism bent toward reductionism able to pass the litmus test of empiricism, the emphasis is not on origins and certainly not on holistic perspectives. With no real order to knowledge, it becomes all but impossible to develop any sensible epistemology.[35]

Christians set creation as the beginning of knowledge. "In the beginning God …" is more than doctrine. It is an epistemological statement. Right there is the beginning point for humanity to learn all that needs to be learned. It is also the end of knowledge. Although history—the story of God's revelation—continues to flow, God is eternal. With God as the alpha and the omega, a being with neither a beginning nor an end, creation is merely the point at which humankind enters the divinely designed stage and can begin to learn through revelation. Everything we can learn now—whether it is of geological layering of ages past or of the latest economic models—is merely a derivative of the eternal Creator. "For in him we live and move and have our being" (Acts 17:28).

The various forms of revelation become understandable to humankind, given the creation of the human brain with its ability to understand and communicate using symbols. It is through that complex brain that we alone among all living organisms can receive and decode the various forms of revelation. There is the life-changing special revelation of Scripture, written records that only humans among all living species can decipher. Guided by Scripture, there is the power of reason, the mechanism by which we humans can discern truth from error, despite our fallible nature and finite limitations. There is also prayer, another capacity based on humankind's ability to communicate in verbal symbols. Still further, there is what Scripture calls fellowship—relationships among humans through which God acts. Most important, however, there is Christ—God in human form such that we can have a relationship with him. Christ is the ultimate medium of communication. Jesus claims so in John 14:6, stating, "I am the way and the truth and the life."

Again, by Christian logic, it is not "I think, therefore I am," but rather, "I am (in the image of God), therefore I think." That "I am (in the image of God)" is the epistemological starting point of true knowledge. Submission to God becomes the true beginning of all wisdom, and only by God's light do we see real light.[36]

▶ Meaning and Purpose

Simply to make God some sort of deistic "First Cause" falls far short of the mark. Creation shows that God made all things with a purpose. In the Genesis account, creation occurs in phases grounded in design and purpose.[37] From here, we can extrapolate that Christianity itself is a faith characterized by order, objectivity, meaning, and purpose.[38] Every aspect of the universe—from the placement of the stars to the balance of nature, from the rotation of the earth to the food chain, affirms the notions of order, objectivity, meaning, and purpose.

Meaning and purpose cannot be separated from the doctrine of creation. Foundational to the notion of a designer is a purpose for what he designed. Scripture provides a ready answer to the question of meaning and purpose for humanity. They are to honor and venerate their Maker, enjoy their relationship with him, and further justice-in-shalom in a flawed world. It is from this belief that Christians gain solace and comfort. Their lives count for something, they have meaning and purpose—value—in the eyes of the Creator. The passage in Romans (8:28) stating that all things work in concert for good in the lives of those who love God reinforces human value.

A sense of security is derived from the Christian notion that things do not happen by accident. There is a reason behind events, a reason that coheres with the will of God. The story of Joseph, recorded in chapters 37–50 of Genesis, illustrates vividly the hand of God behind seemingly random and tragic events. After being ambushed by his jealous brothers and sold into slavery as a teenager, Joseph landed in Egypt. From there, things only got worse. He was imprisoned after falsely being implicated for sexual assault by the wife of his master, Potiphar. After a number of years in prison, during which he interpreted a dream for a temporarily incarcerated member of the pharaoh's staff, he was recommended by that restored member to interpret a puzzling dream the pharaoh had. Pharaoh was so impressed with Joseph's character and skills that he elevated this now nearly forty-year-old man to a chief of staff position. When a severe famine hit the land, Joseph's brothers had to go to Egypt to get food for survival. There their banished brother, who was now in charge of food distribution, confronted them. A marvelous reconciliation took place, and in Genesis 50:19–20 Joseph puts his take on the whole matter in this statement to his terrified brothers: "Don't be afraid. Am I in the place of God? You intended to harm me, but God intended it for good to accomplish what is now being done, the saving of many lives."

Consider the alternative to Joseph's creationist outlook. There is only randomness. According to Oxford's Richard Dawkins, "In a universe of blind physical forces and genetic replication, some people are going to get hurt, other people are going to get lucky, and you won't find any rhyme or reason in it, nor any justice."[39] Dawkins presents an uncharted, undesigned universe—an aimless, empty entity containing living organisms merely passing meaningless time until they expire. As for any master plan? "Nothing but blind, pitiless indiffer-ence," states this atheist. "DNA neither knows nor cares. DNA just is. And we dance to its music."[40]

The believer, the one who believes in a designing creator, says, "Everything happens for a reason." The naturalist says, "Nothing does, because there can be no genuine reason in a universe of meaningless, patternless, absurdity." Clearly, however, the implications of meaninglessness lead everywhere and obviously nowhere. Zacharias raises a seminal question: "If DNA neither knows nor cares, what is it that prompts our knowing and our caring?"[41] To be able to know and care suggests that these sentiments do exist in the universe. If so, how can they exist in a meaningless universe, operating mindlessly according to chance factors?

Once you give up integrity, the rest is easy, said the fictional J. R. Ewing on the popular series *Dallas*. Caring suggests a set of ethics. Why not abandon them in a chance-driven world in which they really don't exist anyway? Think about it carefully. What, for example, would make my ethics any less worthy than yours or anyone else's in a chance-driven universe? There can be no core ethics in a meaningless universe. Ethics imply meaning, and there is no meaning in a world driven only by natural laws.

All that is left, then, is the notion that meaning is what is called a "social construct"—a nonmaterial creation by a society of thinkers. But why should anyone respect any "meaning" based solely on the thoughts of a given collec-tion of meaningless humans living in a certain time and place? Without gen-uine meaning, the exercise itself is oxymoronic. People regularly speak of wanting "a meaningful relationship," but that is something that cannot exist in a world of absurdities. Using the social-construct notion, a relationship is simply a social contract based on that construct. Why, however, should anyone abide by any social contract if it is not in his self-interest to do so? In the animal world, order is determined by predatory power. In general, animals farther up the phylogenetic scale prey on those that are lower. That is the "social order." In a meaningless universe, why should humans be any different?

Without meaning, there is no morality. When people witness one animal viciously attack another, they may be sickened, but they do not react with any moral outrage, because such an attack has no moral significance in an organic order based on power. If, indeed, there is no God and there is no meaning, then any similar attack of one human upon another should not be met with any greater moral outrage. It should not be condemned at all, because it is not an immoral act. It cannot be in a social order devoid of meaning. The often-used "senseless act of violence" phrase may as well be deleted from the naturalist's vocabulary, because all acts are senseless for a naturalist.

Any action, from sexual unfaithfulness to fraud, is permissible by the meaninglessness code. Why have vows at all in a system in which self-denial is no virtue, because virtue does not exist? Hurting another person, in any way and by any means, carries no moral import in an amoral world. Murder is not murder in such a setting. It is merely killing. And because human life is without significance, and hence without value, the taking of human life—prenatally, in infancy, in adolescence, in adulthood, or in senescence—is of no greater gravity than the squashing of a bug. There are no "rights," because nothing is either right or not right. It just is.

When value judgments are entirely subjective, by what standard does one refer to a society as civilized? And what difference does civilization make? In a meaningless, and hence amoral, society, conventional forms of civility inevitably deteriorate. Wanton violence, sexual license, and other seeming excesses are the inescapable emergents in a social order that is driven by power and self-interest. Notions of restraint do not exist in a meaningless social order. Order itself has no essential worth in such a human collective. One would anticipate a coarsening and decivilizing of such an entity, as people have no reason to exercise self-sacrifice. There can be no sinner and there can be no saint; the rules of the imbecile have no less inherent worth than those of the ethicist, because the social order is no more intrinsically meaningful than the congregation of crawling organisms one observes on an anthill. In such a social arrangement, one would do well to eat, drink, and be as merry as possible, for that logically would be the most pleasant and desirable existence for the brief time he resides on this planet.

And while we are at it, how can logic itself exist in a world without meaning? If humans can speak of logical and reasoned positions, does it not follow that reason and logic do in fact exist in the universe? "How did reason come into the world?" asked Nietzsche. "As is fitting, in an irrational manner, by accident. One will have to guess at it as at a riddle."[42] That is the best Nietzsche could do. It is difficult to imagine how our minds could justify the propensity for reason if there were no ultimate reason and no ultimate mind behind the mind of our own.

If, as Dawkins puts it, "the universe we observe has precisely the properties we should expect if there is, at the bottom, no design, no purpose, no evil and no other good,"[43] then there is absolutely no purpose to our existence. There is no significance, no value, nothing. Our very pursuits could be called into question as being baseless—mere means of stimulation.

In August of 2001, C-Span presented the funeral of Maureen Reagan, the daughter of former president Ronald Reagan. I found it a moving event, psychologically and spiritually. One after another, Ms. Reagan's eulogists testified to how, after her father had been diagnosed with Alzheimer's disease, she selflessly invested her energies in the cause of eradicating it. She touched many others' lives profoundly. Though only sixty when she died of cancer, she was regarded as a person who had truly lived a full and meaningful life.

But had she? By the standards of naturalism, there is no such thing as meaning, and therefore no such thing as a meaningful life. In fact, if the purpose of life is the Albert Ellis notion of making it an absolute ball—having as much fun as possible—one could argue that Maureen Reagan may have had a rather unsuccessful earthly sojourn. Clearly a woman of some privilege, there would be no rational reason for Ms. Reagan to deny herself opportunities for self-indulgence or to give to others, in a world in which humans are no more important than flies. The words of the cynical philosopher Jean-Paul Sartre, then, ring with power: "Everything has been figured out except how to live." Meaning is what sustains life. Without it, people become suicidal. Indeed, Sartre's statement—that the only question he could not answer was why he hadn't committed suicide—is a most sensible statement in an undesigned world that makes no ultimate sense.

All of science, physical and otherwise, needs to be seen in the perspective of creation. With creation central to his thinking, the physical scientist cannot lock God out of his academic experience. On the contrary, as he studies his discipline, he will learn more about God's purpose, pattern, and power.

Notes

1. Harry Blamires, *The Christian Mind* (Ann Arbor, MI: Servant, 1997), 45.
2. Harry Blamires, *Where Do We Stand?* (Ann Arbor, MI: Servant, 1980), 7–9.
3. John Patrick, "The Necessity of Trust," in *Professors Who Believe*, ed. Paul M. Anderson (Downers Grove, IL: InterVarsity, 1998), 30.
4. Ibid., 30–31.
5. James P. Keener, "Confessions of a 'Weird Mathematician,'" in Anderson, *Professors Who Believe*, 91.
6. Paul M. Anderson, "A Common Thread," in Anderson, *Professors Who Believe*, 22.
7. Blamires, *Where Do We Stand?* 148.
8. Ibid., 149.
9. Richard A. Bennett, *Your Quest for God* (Franklin, TN: Providence, 1998), 23.
10. Ravi Zacharias, *Jesus among Other Gods* (Nashville: Word, 2000), 80–81.
11. Ibid., 81.
12. "50 Reasons to Leave Your Faith (evolution)," http://evolutionlie.faithweb.com (accessed January 10, 2001).
13. Ibid.
14. Ibid.
15. Bennett, *Your Quest for God*, 22.
16. "50 Reasons to Leave Your Faith (evolution)."

17. Ibid.

18. J. Gary Eden, "Unseen Realities," in Anderson, *Professors Who Believe*, 79.

19. Loren Eisley, *Darwin's Century: Evolution and the Men Who Discovered It* (Garden City, NY: Anchor, 1961), 62, quoted in Eden, "Unseen Realities," in Anderson, *Professors Who Believe*, 75.

20. Isaac Newton, *Principia*, book 3. Quoted in *Newton's Philosophy of Nature*, ed. H. S. Thayer (New York: Haffner, 1963), quoted in Eden, "Unseen Realities," in Anderson, *Professors Who Believe*, 75.

21. Roger Coles, preface to *Principia*, 2nd ed. (1713), quoted in Eden "Unseen Realities," in Anderson, *Professors Who Believe*, 76.

22. Albert Einstein, *Mein Weltbild* (Amsterdam: Querido Verlag, 1934); also Albert Einstein, *Ideas and Opinions*, ed. Carl Seelig, trans. Sonja Bargmann (New York: Crown, 1954), 40, quoted in Eden, "Unseen Realities," in Anderson, *Professors Who Believe*, 77.

23. Patricia H. Reiff, "Three Heavens—Our Home," in Anderson, *Professors Who Believe*, 58–61.

24. Ibid., 59.

25. Ibid., 59–60.

26. Ibid., 60.

27. Ibid.

28. Ibid.

29. Ibid., 60–61.

30. Blamires, *Where Do We Stand?* 149.

31. Ibid., 147.

32. Ibid., 147–48.

33. George M. Marsden offers an excellent treatment of creation and epistemology in *The Outrageous Idea of Christian Scholarship* (New York: Oxford University Press, 1997), 88.

34. Ibid.

35. Ibid.

36. Ibid.

37. Blamires, *Where Do We Stand?* 144.

38. Ibid., 145.

39. Richard Dawkins, *Out of Eden* (New York: Basic, 1992), 133, quoted in Zacharias, *Jesus among Other Gods*, 114.

40. Ibid.

41. Zacharias, *Jesus among Other Gods*, 114.

42. Friedrich Nietzsche, http://users.aol.com/Irdetrigan/bottomframe.html (accessed January 8, 2001).

43. Dawkins, *Out of Eden*, quoted in Zacharias, *Jesus among Other Gods*, 114.

THE PHYSICAL SCIENCES

13

WHAT IS THE MIND-SET
OF THE CHRISTIAN
IN THE PHYSICAL SCIENCES?

The central distinction for the Christian in the physical sciences lies less in specifically Christian theorizing, given the paradigmatic nature in many of the disciplines, than in the mind-set or attitude with which she does her work.

⇥ Attitude

Mathematician James Keener has made this his focus. "The Christian learns the tools of studying math and takes these tools to learn God's universe with a built-in excitement," he explains. "I am awestruck by what I learn in science," says Keener, "and science is an extension of my Christian worldview, part of my religion."[1] It is easy for a person, even in the physical sciences, to lose her sense of awe. Even a sunrise can become mundane if a person studies it long enough and dispassionately enough. It is a matter of habituation. The first time I drove a car, I was overwhelmed. But soon traveling by car was no more special than walking, just quicker.

Another aspect of attitude relates to the popular phrase "You will see it when you believe it." If all a scientist looks for are known, predictable, and mechanical laws, it is likely that she, like Dawkins, will only see "blind, physical forces and genetic replication." Conversely, if God is at the center of her worldview she is far more likely to perceive the majestic nature of his handiwork.

⇥ The Mystery of Life

Nowhere is there a greater basis for being awestruck than in the physical sciences. There is a tendency in evolutionism to simplify the very nature of life and to reduce the universe to a series of physical equations.[2] Although such reductionism

163

may make the universe more intellectually manageable, it offers an unrealistic view of life.

A living human cell contains a complexity beyond comprehension. There are millions, billions, even trillions, of bits and pieces interacting synergistically with one another. Within the hundred trillion (100,000,000,000) cells in the human body, there is DNA. This tape of coded, person-specific information, now widely known due to its use in criminal cases, is so complex that each strand of DNA contains enough information to fill 600,000 pages.[3] If all the coded information contained in the cells of a person's body were transcribed, its typewritten form would fill the Grand Canyon fifty times. Moreover, if all the DNA in a person's body were placed end to end, it would stretch from the earth to the moon over half a million times.

Yet even if we add RNA, a rider cell, amino acids, and protein cells, we still do not have living matter. All those interacting bits and pieces are not alive. Life does not exist in bits and pieces, any more than a fuel injector, a piston, or an engine ring constitutes an automobile. Life resides in the total, functioning cell. If we were to remove any item of the total cell—some DNA, RNA, a rider cell, or a protein, for example—we would be left with a lifeless molecule.

Some famous attempts have been made to generate life in a laboratory through the formation of amino acids. Even the successful formation of amino acids is but a microstep in the manufacture of protein. For example, were one to shake and mix materials over time to maximize the possibilities of interaction and chemical combining, the odds against even one protein being formed are 1 in 10^{160}. Tap that number out in longhand, putting all the zeroes behind that single one, it becomes obvious that this is simply far beyond any imaginable chance factor.

Pushing the bar higher, to reach even these essentially zero odds, "there would have to be sextillion universes to supply enough material to mix in its formation."[4] The time necessary for the mixing would be 10^{143} years. Again, this is outside the bounds of even intellectual manageability. And should even one protein emerge, it would simply be an organic molecule. It would not be life.

Zacharias points out that the statistical probability of forming even a single enzyme, the building block of the gene, is 1 in $10^{40,000}$. It would require more attempts to construct just one enzyme than there are atoms in all the stars and galaxies in the known universe. This again is a statistical "probability" that is simply beyond any real probability.[5]

What remains is the conclusion that only life begets life. As stated by one scientist, "Proteins are dead things, and it is only when the spirit of life breathes on them that these dry bones live."[6] By 1970, laboratory efforts had produced some organic molecules, several small proteins, and a gene. Against that scientific backdrop, Sir Ernest Chain—who won a Nobel Peace Prize with Ambrose Fleming (another scientist who rejected evolution) for his work with penicillin—said, "The laboratory synthesis of even the simplest cell is just not on, and the notion that man is about to compete with God is absurd, and not to be taken seriously."[7]

▸▸ Worship

Given the incomprehensible realties of the physical universe, scholarship in the physical sciences is approached with a worshipful attitude for people like Keener. "A decision of what to study is a way of ascribing value," he claims, "and worship is really an act of ascribing value to something. By regarding the science one studies as a part of God's infinite and wondrous universe, and delighting in the mysteries of that universe, the scholar makes the enterprise of science an act of worship." Such scholarly worship trains the learner's eyes to see God and his majesty in her discipline. Moreover, the Christian approaches the science she studies as a means to an end—to understand and glorify God, and to serve him all the more—rather than as an end in itself. "Everyone needs a reason to get up in the morning, to have a purpose, to do something intrinsically good. That is a person's religion," asserts Keener. For the Christian in the physical sciences, that purpose does not lie ultimately in biology, astronomy, mathematics, or chemistry. It lies in discovering God's universe through the lens of her discipline.

Attitude is everything here. According to Keener, the Christian needs to be constantly aware of how little she knows of the infinite universe, not on what she may be an authority. Such a point of view is proportional to reality. What we know in the physical sciences constitutes but a microcosm mystery of the universe. In that spirit, a good exercise for the Christian scholar in the physical sciences might be to focus on, even identify, what is not known and what apparently cannot be known by human research. This represents a reverse approach, given that most scholars search for "knowns" with near-adolescent enthusiasm. Such a reverse approach is, however, truly Christian in its capacity to help us appreciate the infinite and therefore divine nature of the cosmos.

This approach also rules out arrogance, something that regrettably is not solely the province of the nonbeliever. One need only sit in on discussions among professors at Christian colleges and universities to realize that such institutions are not without academics with airs of superiority. Although there is something about being intelligent that seems to breed a sense of superiority, I have found some of the genuine giants to be among the least arrogant, perhaps because they were more invested in their intellectual task than in self-aggrandizement.

Arrogance cannot characterize genuinely Christian scholarship, because such scholarship is aimed at honoring the Creator, not the creature. Submitting one's intellect to the supremacy and light of God is an absolute intellectual starting point in assessing and developing Christian academic approaches. Any thinking that does not flow from such a point of origin is, of necessity, error-ridden. This is simply logical. If indeed there is a creator of the universe, then to omit that creator as a starting point is to lose all perspective on the knowledge contained in that created universe.

For some Christian scholars, the attitude of humility permeates their teaching as well as their research. "Becoming a follower of Jesus profoundly affected my view of work," says Ken Elzinga, professor of economics at the University of Virginia. Using Jesus' example of leader-as-servant, Elzinga sees his role as a teacher to be one of serving the students by preparing, being accessible, and being certain his students succeed.[8] This is truly Christianizing the role of teacher/mentor. I recall one of my favorite undergraduate professors, nationally renown in his field, taking the Elzinga approach. He always treated me with care and undeserved respect, right down to the nature of his comments on my less-than-brilliant papers and bluebooks.

Keener bases his pedagogy on John 15:15 (in which Christ says, "I no longer call you servants, because a servant does not know his master's business. Instead, I have called you friends, for everything that I learned from my Father I have made known to you."), seeing himself as the mentor of people who will become his colleagues. His teaching style emphasizes group decision making, peer learning, and collective projects. As a teacher, he is merely the leader of a group of which he is a member. He takes his students along to conferences, and includes them in research efforts, all with an eye toward their becoming colleagues. "I want them to be able to represent me at professional meetings," says Keener. "We become friends."

How different this collegial, facilitating approach is from so much of graduate education. The experience of a friend of mine, seeking a doctorate in sociology and studying under a well-published author who had taught in an Ivy League university, is typical. The professor continually frustrated him with pedantic exercises and casual dismissals. Once when visiting the professor in his office to review a paper butchered with corrections, the professor ended the brief conversation abruptly, saying, "I believe our conference is over." He then unceremoniously turned around in his chair and began typing, leaving my friend immobilized with embarrassment.

▸▸ A Paradoxical Apologetic

Naturalism often tries to dismiss the concept of God by focusing on the evolving nature of humankind and its ever-greater capacity to dominate the earth. This seems to reinforce the naturalist's certainty that, indeed, humans are the most highly evolved species of the natural world. William Temple, author of *Nature, Man, and God,* provides a thought-provoking twist to this humanity-over-all mind-set. Believing that the most striking aspect of the universe is not the suns, stars, or the planets—not even human beings with their incredible physiology and brain development—what affirms his faith is the *interaction* of humankind with the environment. Human beings, made in the image of God, are the keys that unlock the wonders of nature and produce wondrous things from it. Clearly, humans were created to subdue God's earth. As Blamires says, "How extraordinary! The key fits the lock. It must have been purposely designed for it."[9]

From this vantage point, science and technology can just as well support faith as challenge it. "Why on earth should anybody's faith be disturbed by the discoveries of the space age?" asks Blamires. "What kind of faith is it that receives a knock when an astronaut lands on the moon?... As a rational being, I am baffled by the claim that anyone's faith can be diminished by new advances in rocketry. Surely new advances in technology should have the very opposite effect, each one making the Christian's faith more secure."[10] As things become more and more technologically complex, the less likely they are to be the product of accidental forces. Blamires gives an example by saying that the more advanced a given car model becomes, the greater is his faith in the designing expertise of the manufacturer.[11]

If a world contained nothing more than several trees and plants, one could imagine it was the result of random forces. When that world contains men and women with capacities to produce satellites, computers, and other wonders, however, it appears to flow from a master plan. Here again, design reenters the discussion. Humans are intentional beings. They have motivations; they are creatures with plans and designs. The logic is internally consistent: the designing Creator has plans for his creation, and the creatures made in his image bear that stamp in part by their designing function. Keener believes that it is logical that creatures would bear the marks of their Creator. Such is the case with human rationality, and more important, with our spirituality.[12]

Blamires urges us to dismiss the "illogical notion" that scientific advances ought to function as challenges to one's faith. "Every development and invention that shows afresh how complex is the connection between what we human beings can do and the sort of world we inhabit," he says, "is further evidence the whole scheme was devised by a mighty Intelligence which makes man's own understanding and skill look slight by comparison."[13]

▶▶ Purpose

Faith-based perspectives are appropriate in even technical areas of inquiry.[14] Faith, of course, can be the motivating force in why a Christian scholar does her work conscientiously, wanting to glorify God by giving him her best. Although the desire for excellence is not the sole province of Christian scholarship, the basis for that desire—to honor the Creator with excellence—is. A more defining difference for a Christian scholar in the physical sciences may involve focus. Whereas those in the arts, humanities, and behavioral sciences are awash with designs and theories to critique, there is, as Keener says, no postmodernism in the physical sciences. "There are variations in elegance in the line of reasoning in mathematics, but it is still a matter of objectivity—a final reality." Faced with final finite truth, the Christian may use her value system to determine *which* questions and mysteries to investigate scientifically.

From there, of course, religious commitments may influence how a person *applies* that scholarship. Technical work in areas running from bacteriology to biofeedback, when done with the intent of furthering justice-in-shalom, becomes Christian scholarship. Such work may in turn generate new specialty areas or value-oriented subfields (such as geopolitics or holistic medicine) or simply isolate and define problems requiring research-driven solutions. Faith becomes relevant to any topic—even in the physical sciences—the instant the matter is associated with issues of wider significance. We can study something as seemingly value-free as air composition in a controlled setting, but the topic invites faith-injected thinking the moment it is examined in the context of humankind's stewardship of the environment.

Of course, there are limits to what science can do, from a Christian perspective. One limitation involves humankind's limited finite capacity to master the infinite universe. We might call that the objective limitation. By Enlightenment standards, if problems cannot be solved by human means, they are beyond resolution. Though falling short of acknowledging the existence of an infinite, creating God, such a position refers to the objective limitation. There is, however, another limitation, which is moral or spiritual. The spiritual limitation expresses itself in the failure of humankind's fallen nature to implement available solutions with a justice-in-shalom intent. Expert technology, used to improve the health and living conditions of millions, is also used to develop weapons of mass destruction and methods of biological warfare. Well-conceived economic and industrial systems can generate sudden upward thrusts in a society's standard of living while contributing to environmental pollution at the same time. Political institutions can be vehicles of freedom and common good, but they can also be instruments of imperialism and mass oppression.[15]

These limitations, moral and spiritual rather than technological in nature, make the physical sciences anything but value-neutral. When viewed more holistically, the physical sciences can no more be separated from values than the sacred can be separated from the secular. An awareness of this spiritual dimension can only heighten the motivation of the Christian scholar to apply her research for the betterment of the human condition.

One becomes a Christian scholar at the point that she "contextualizes" her field of study, viewing it as a subdivision of God's creation, according to Keener. "Knowledge is not to be pursued in the abstract," says Keener, "scripture indicates that God wants us to learn." This is not to say that pure (as opposed to applied) science is without value. Pure science is the foundation on which science becomes applied. As noted above, science will sooner or later be used for some purposeful end. It is to say that as enjoyable as learning itself is, looking at science as a subdivision of God's creation can motivate scientists to study certain questions.

And there are questions. One of Keener's favorites is, How does a God-seeking person enjoy mathematics? How does she glorify God with it? In what mathematical questions might a Christian take particular interest? While these questions are unanswerable on the surface, it is the mind-set underlying them that drives the believer in a different direction from the agnostic in the physical sciences.

In this same spirit, when the technical scholar reflects on the over-all significance of her work—its meaning—the framework of faith in which her work fits may be a major factor in how she views its significance. Faith—the desire to learn about, glorify, and serve God—becomes the central reason for her endeavors, the element that brings meaning and significance to her life as a scholar.

Moreover, results may be less important than faithful scholarship. Whenever major breakthroughs in disease prevention and cure occur, they are often the results of decades of research. The seeds were planted by one set of scholars and harvested by another set. So it may also be for the Christian in the physical sciences. While Christian critiquing and even theory building may occur in some other disciplines, things may not move as rapidly in the physical sciences. A career of research and teaching may be invested without groundbreaking contributions to human welfare or to faith-and-learning insights, but no service is without reward. As certainly as the universe is not a series of accidents for the Christian, she believes her efforts will contribute to God's design.

Notes

1. James P. Keener, conversation with author, Chicago, spring 2002. Other undocumented references to Keener are also from this conversation.
2. Much of this section on life is from Henry James Creechan, "A Brief Analysis of the Scientific/Natural Laws and Phenomena Undermining Current Theories of Evolution and the Origins of Life," http://home.primus.com.au/bonno/evolution1.htm (accessed January 8, 2001).
3. Ravi Zacharias, *Jesus among Other Gods* (Nashville: Word, 2000), 66.
4. Creechan, "A Brief Analysis," chap. 14.
5. Ibid., 65.
6. Creechan, "A Brief Analysis," chap. 14.
7. Ibid.
8. Kenneth B. Elzinga, "Christ the Anchor, Christ the Servant," in *Professors Who Believe,* ed. Paul M. Anderson (Downers Grove, IL: InterVarsity, 1998), 108.
9. Harry Blamires, *Where Do We Stand?* (Ann Arbor, MI: Servant, 1980), 150.
10. Ibid.
11. Ibid., 150–51.
12. James P. Keener, "Confessions of a 'Weird Mathematician,'" in Anderson, *Professors Who Believe,* 91–92.
13. Blamires, *Where Do We Stand?* 151.
14. This discussion is adapted from George M. Marsden, *The Outrageous Idea of Christian Scholarship* (New York: Oxford University Press, 1997), 63–64.
15. Ibid., 97.

14

CHRISTIAN IMPLICATIONS
IN THE PHYSICAL SCIENCES

God is everywhere. Christ promises that if you seek him, you will find him. Indeed, you can find evidences of God in the physical universe, but study in the physical sciences—albeit often rather technical—can also point to spiritual truths.

►► Physics as Theory

We have discussed at length in these pages the intersection of theory and science. The injection of theory, however, reduces whatever it is mixed with to a level below absolute certainty. In some instances, however, theory cannot be separated from the scientific exercise and can reinforce spiritual truths. Most people, for example, would place any discussion of physics in a scientific rather than a philosophical category. Prior to Einstein, that would have been the case. Stanford physicist Richard Bube notes that the ability to define reality by fixed physical laws was "the final argument against the existence or at least the necessity of God."[1] In lay terms, this amounted to an attitude of "Who needs God? We have it all figured out."

Until Einstein came along, physics was almost entirely deterministic, implying that all aspects of physical reality were predictable, owing to cause-effect sequences. As nature was investigated at a subatomic level, however, certain problems arose that were unable to be resolved by the prevailing paradigm of classical physics. Called "Einsteinian," a new physics emerged, one that introduced the concept of theory into physics and, in effect, blew the doors off the confined nature of this previously deterministic discipline. Simply put, Einstein viewed physics as more than merely a series of tightly defined laws of measurement.[2]

The theoretical dimension became necessary when the study of quanta (units smaller than atoms) necessitated a completely new explanation for their activity. In 1927, quantum research led Werner Heisenberg to conclude that it was impossible to determine precisely both the momentum and position of a particle. If the exact value of one (momentum or position) is known, the other will be uncertain. That simple discovery was revolutionary. Physics was no longer fixed. After 250 years of paradigmatic rule, Newton's precise physics could not account for certain experimental data. This gave rise to quantum theory, a system that simply could not be confined within the classical concepts of physical law.[3]

Though not an argument for creationism, this new physics and its uncertainty principle delivered a jolt to determinism, from which philosophers are still recovering. In short, quantum theory indicates that the universe may be far more "open" to both physics and philosophical considerations than naturalists had thought.[4] The reason is that the universe could not be *reduced* to simple deterministic laws of classical physics and chemistry. In fact, sewn into the nature of the universe was "an intrinsic indeterminism present in principle at every level of physical structure."[5]

Quantum theory is philosophical—a theory. Rather than consisting of a set of specific mathematical operations, quantum theory is general, descriptive, and predictive in nature. Short of offering solid explanations, it offers new ways of thinking about matter and energy. It is not specific and certain. Subatomic particles, for example, do not have defined locations, speeds, and directions, as do objects examined by classical physics. Quantum theory uses terms like *chances* or *likelihood*.

The contributions of quantum theory are difficult to overestimate. Without it, scientists could not have developed nuclear energy or constructed the electric circuits basic to the functioning of computers. As discussed earlier, no scientific construct is necessarily total, absolutely certain, or final. "The real world," wrote Bube, "is usually too complicated for the scientist to tackle directly. . . . To treat any problem theoretically, therefore, he must simplify the problem greatly."[6] Any conceptual model is a partial standard of "scientific truth." To assert that all material reality is definable in terms of the mechanical laws of physics is a faith, for which there is no absolute proof, rather than a factual statement.[7]

In any case, this more recent form of physics breaks physical boundaries such that we can no longer isolate the exact point at which the physical ends and the metaphysical begins. Obviously, this is a problem for naturalists, one that raises the issue of intellectual consistency. Ravi Zacharias, in a dinner discussion with a group of scientific scholars, confronted this issue.[8]

Realizing that most physicists subscribed to the big bang theory of origins, Zacharias asked the group what preceded the big bang and the complexity that resulted from this cosmic explosion. As he suspected, their answer was that the universe was a shrunken, singular entity.

Knowing that the existence of multiple forces is basic to physics, Zacharias pressed the obvious question: "But isn't it correct," he asked, "that a singularity as defined by science is a point at which all the laws of physics break down?"

They agreed.

"Then," concluded Zacharias with if-then logic, "your starting point is not scientific either."

After an uncomfortable silence, Zacharias weaved in the issue of quantum physics. First, he asked if the group agreed with David Hume's position that the principle of causality in science could not be applied to a philosophical argument for the existence of God.

"'Now,' he said, "when quantum theory holds sway, randomness in the subatomic world is made a basis for randomness in life. Are you not making the very same [philosophical] extrapolation that you warned us against?"

Finally one man replied with a self-deprecating smile, "We scientists do seem to retain selective sovereignty over what we allow to be transferred to philosophy and what we don't."

"There," according to Zacharias, "is the truth in cold, hard terms."

▸▸ Faith-and-Learning Adventures in the Physical Sciences

John F. Walkup, professor of electrical engineering at Texas Tech, looks inside his field to find implications for Christian thought. Studying the physical properties of light and vision, he points out the spiritual truth of seeing when believing.

Light is basic to life. Humans need natural light from the sun to live and grow physically. Absence of sunlight has devastating effects for animal, human, and vegetable life. Walkup sees a spiritual parallel here. According to Scripture, spiritual light is as necessary for our spiritual health as sunlight is for our physical well-being. Furthermore, although to live without sufficient spiritual light may not bring physical or even spiritual death, it causes certain retardation in spiritual development.[9] As Paul points out in Colossians 1:9, those without spiritual light will lack the wisdom and spiritual understanding necessary to understand the will of God.

The analogy has strong apologetic value. Spiritual light is not necessarily central to our physical and mental lives. Thus, those who walk outside of God's light may still function in those dimensions, because they do have the requisite physical light to function. They cannot, however, function well spiritually. Lack of spiritual light, according to 1 Corinthians 2:14, can wipe out basic spiritual sensitivity and awareness: "The man without the Spirit does not accept the things that come from the Spirit of God, for they are foolishness to him, and he cannot understand them, because they are spiritually discerned." Healthy spiritual living requires divine photosynthesis, along with the living bread and living water. Those living without this divine energy will show the symptoms of spiritual malnourishment, although their physical and basic intellectual faculties may remain sound.

Using the field of optics, in which we find that the lower the light level, the more difficult become tasks such as basic vision, Walkup states that in a parallel fashion, the lack of spiritual light affects discernment and can result in outright spiritual blindness—the darkened understanding and ignorance referred to in Ephesians 4:18. As with physical reality, spiritual blindness does not make the spiritual dimension any less real. It merely makes the "visually impaired" unable to live fully within that dimension.[10] Walkup has used these analogies widely, including with scientists in Russia. They have been received very favorably, in part because they show metaphorically why brilliant secular scholars are so unwilling and perhaps unable to entertain a transcendent reality.

C. S. Lewis also used scientific analogies to illustrate spiritual truth. He suggested that just as in the physical realm there is vast complexity, the spiritual realm is also incredibly multifaceted and not what we anticipate it to be. In the scientific sense, for example, a table is really not just a table but is also a collection of atoms, electrons, and so forth, and the universe is much more than the sum of its parts. Similarly, the physical world as we see it is not all there is in the spiritual sense. As certainly as the physical sciences look past the visible for more profound realties, the spiritual worldview also sees things beyond what they appear to be.[11]

▸▸ Time

Time is a key concept in Christian thinking. Blamires points out with great zeal that the eternal perspective is absolutely foundational to Christian thinking. Far more is at stake in the temporal-versus-eternal issue than whether the universe is the product of supernatural origins. The issue permeates to the very core of each person's existence, even separating meaning from non-meaning for humankind. Basic to the temporal view of reality is the belief that actions are devoid of enduring significance and time is running out. All one has is the here and now. This affects the totality of one's life. Sex, for example, then becomes a matter of either pleasure or procreation. It has little if any relational meaning, much less long-term significance. It symbolizes nothing. To see life only in terms of the passage of time with no final judgment, no evaluation, and no accountability creates a consciousness that favors youth-retention, life-extension, and pleasure-obsession, rather than committed relationships, moral development, and care for others. Moreover, life itself being solely temporal, it is no longer sacred or in need of protection. It is merely moving matter.

The temporal view, and the consciousness that it generates, works to the deterioration and destruction of civilizations. Temporality does provide a direction to life, a selfish one. It implies that it is every person for himself, that each of us should get the biggest "gulp" we can out of life, and that we should let no one stand in our way during our limited time on planet Earth. The temporal view can only posit a humanistic morality, a behavioral code that deems acceptable any action that does not interfere with the freedom of another. The temporal view affirms the concept of victimless crimes, because it sees each person as having the right to do anything he chooses to do, provided his actions do not infringe on the rights of others. Moreover, any action engaged in by consenting adults is acceptable, because all we have is the here and now. Unfortunately, the morality of the temporal view is not really moral, because the code is not rooted in ultimate rights and wrongs. Therefore, it disaffirms a genuine sense of conscience that comes from the Creator of all things.

Such an agnostic "morality" cannot hold people to self-denial for the greater good. It is truly Darwinian in that it creates discord, violence, and endless battles over the scarcity of resources and means. It therefore runs counter to cooperative group living, relational harmony, and emotional health. What inevitably emerges from this regressive "animalizing" of humanity is a society continuously filled with violence, anger, and mad pursuits of pleasure.

The temporal view does not encourage self-examination in terms of how honorably one lives his life. And if the unexamined life is not worth living, then there are certainly a lot of worthless lives out there. I have a friend in his fifties who lives at a near-adrenaline level every day of his life. He all but refuses to reflect on larger values. He is also afraid of death. "I have nowhere to put that. I can't relate to death," he says. When a famous, seemingly bigger-than-life person he and I both admired died at age seventy-two, my friend was angry. The very concept of death seemed to him unfair. For the temporalist, death is the ultimate tragedy.

My friend has plenty of company in his lifestyle and non-thoughts of death. Ever more people well into adulthood are in too much of a hurry to stop and realize that more than half their lives are over by any actuarial standard. That, perhaps, is why they are in such a hurry. Like the youngster who shuts his eyes tightly and makes his body rigid before jumping into the cold swimming pool, these adults similarly shut their eyes and try to keep busy until suddenly they are no more. One octogenarian television producer said he would never retire. He would work until one day his head hit his desk and he would be gone. To live the unexamined life was better than to ponder the other side of the human divide. This thinking flows from a temporal perspective.

If history is merely cyclical, and all of life is temporal rather than progressing toward an ultimate end, then the seemingly basic human tendency to be goal oriented makes no sense. It is at odds with temporal views of reality. Further, the natural human tendency to think in terms of past, present, and future suggests an unrealistic orientation toward life. This tripartite concept is valueless other than as a basis upon which each individual can choose a happier course in the days he has left.

Yet humans do think in terms of goals and do look at time from all three angles, past, present, and future. One could argue that this suggests not only that we are intellectually designed for an existence that is progressive and climactic but also that such is the essence of life. Were it not so, one would have to conclude that humans are living outside the boundaries of the laws of the universe.

But this does not fully answer the skeptic. Even if, for the sake of argument, one accepts the concept of God and eternity, you need not debate very long with a skeptic conversant about basic Christian doctrine before you lock horns on the other aspect of the time issue: free will versus predestination. On the face of it, this seeming polarity poses a major conundrum. How can human beings truly have free will—the power of choice and volitional autonomy—if God is sovereign and almighty, especially if he has created the universe and already has a plan for the lives of each human before that person is born? The essence of the problem is the belief that God has foreordained human activity eons before the existence of the very humans presumed to be acting with free will. In short, how can there be a divine script, with actors remaining free to choose their own lines? For the thinking Christian, these doctrines are hard to mesh. With simple logic suggesting that planning precedes and, therefore, determines an activity, the free will-versus-predestination issue is one of time.

There are Christians who weigh in on both sides of this seeming dichotomy. Calvinists highlight the sovereignty of God, making the matter of predestination central, while Armenians have become well-known for their emphasis on the freedom of the human will. Still others do not bother to engage this issue at all, subsuming the matter under the rubric of divine mystery. In fact, there is a tradition within Judaism that encourages one, when facing a seeming paradox, simply to embrace both extremes in faith rather than attempting to reconcile them. There is wisdom and humility in this tradition. Certainly we are far less capable of understanding the seeming contradictions in Christianity than even a child is capable of harmonizing apparent paradoxes observed in the adult world.

Notwithstanding, Patricia Reiff, with her "creation logic," provides a fascinating perspective on the human limitation in understanding time. She credits Edwin Abbott's *Flatland* for helping her visualize a higher-dimensional God. Abbott describes how life appears to two-dimensional beings on a plane. It is one of triangles, squares, and similar configurations. Such creatures can see one another's perimeters but are unable to look inside one another. Therefore, they cannot imagine a three-dimensional entity. They can only observe a three-dimensional object when it intersects their world. "If a three-dimensional person sticks three fingers into their plane, the fingers look like three separate circles to them," explains Reiff. "The 3-D being can see inside them and can even flip them over and turn them inside out, things they cannot do for themselves."[12] From here, Reiff extrapolates to time; God is outside of time. She suggests that were we to imagine being on a plane with two dimensions—time and space—God could look left to the past or right to the future, yet all of it would remain *now* to him.[13] Hence, time is a human conception.

Tony Campolo offers another approach to this doctrinal dilemma. He takes us back to the physics of Einstein, which views time as relative to motion. In brief, the faster person A travels in relation to person B, the slower time will pass for person A. "If I were to get into a rocket ship," says Campolo, "and travel into space at the speed of 130,000 miles per second relative to the people on this planet, with instructions to travel for ten years before returning, I would, upon coming back to earth, find that I had aged 10 years while everyone else had aged 20 years." In brief, ten years of his time at the accelerated speed would equate to twenty years of time for those who were earthbound. Pushing the speed to 150,000 miles per second, a day in the space traveler's time would equate to a thousand years for earthbound humans. At the speed of light, 186,000 miles per second, time—as we conceive of it—all but disappears. All of human history is then compressed into a moment, and all that is left is an eternal "now."[14]

In the Old Testament (Ex. 3:14), Yahweh calls himself the great "I Am." Not "I Was," or "I Will Be." Just "I Am." God is always in the present, because to God there is only a timeless presence. Thus, from the perspective of the physical sciences, it can be said that time is a human concept relative to speed. As Peter points out, to the eternal God, to whom "a day is like a thousand years, and a thousand years are like a day," everything is now (2 Peter 3:8).

▸▸ The Challenge

God reveals himself in many ways. When Christians speak of natural and special revelation, they are referring to general categories of divine revelation. Believers worldwide know that one can study Scripture (special revelation) daily for a lifetime and never run out of new insights into the nature of God and his divine reality. That it is never mastered, never completely understood, is so much of the beauty and mystery of Scripture. The same, however, can be said about natural revelation. The more we study it with spiritual eyes, searching for the truth, the more God reveals himself to us.

The challenge for the Christian in the physical sciences is this: to seek and find God's wisdom and truth in nature, and to impart it to others.

Notes

1. Richard Bube, "Physics," in *Christ and the Modern Mind,* ed. Robert W. Smith (Downers Grove, IL: InterVarsity, 1972), 300.

2. Walter R. Hearn, *Being a Christian in Science* (Downers Grove, IL: InterVarsity, 1997), 66.

3. Hearn, *Being a Christian in Science,* 66–67; Charles E. Hummel, "The Natural Sciences," in Smith, *Christ and the Modern Mind,* 240. Hummel cites two valuable supporting references on the matter: Lincoln Barnett, *Universe and Dr. Einstein* (New York: Morrow, 1957), a lucid account for the layperson of Einstein's work with quantum physics and relativity; and Eric L. Mascall, *Christian Theology and Natural Science* (London: Longman, 1956), chap. 2.

4. Hearn, *Being a Christian in Science,* 66–67.

5. Bube, "Physics," in Smith, *Christ and the Modern Mind,* 300.

6. Ibid., 297.

7. Ibid., 298.

8. Ravi Zacharias, *Jesus among Other Gods* (Nashville: Word, 2000), 64.

9. John F. Walkup, "From Religion to Relationship," in *Professors Who Believe,* ed. Paul M. Anderson (Downers Grove, IL: InterVarsity, 1998), 84.

10. Ibid.

11. Armand M. Nicholi Jr., *The Question of God* (New York: Free Press, 2002), 54.

12. Patricia H. Reiff, "Three Heavens—Our Home," in Anderson, *Professors Who Believe,* 58.

13. Ibid.

14. Anthony Campolo, *A Reasonable Faith* (Waco, TX: Word, 1983), 129. Campolo cites James A. Coleman, *Relativity for the Layman* (New York: New American Library, 1959), 65–73, as additionally helpful in viewing the concept of time relative to motion.

THE ARTS AND HUMANITIES

15

HOW DO WE LOOK AT ART
THROUGH CHRISTIAN EYES?

C hristianity has never seemed to know exactly what to do with art. The freedom of expression essential to art does not rest well within the confines of systematic theologies. The artist has therefore often resided rather uncomfortably within the Christian community. I suspect much of this difficulty has to do with the artist's open expression and uncensored freedom. Christianity, of course, comes with limits. With the word *disciple* emanating from the word *discipline,* many feel there ought to be *discipline* in the form of limits, especially for the Christian artist. In fact, some Christians believe limitless open expression is merely license to express one's sinful state in raw form. For them, art, like life, needs to be censored.

Art, however, is about creativity, a capacity that reflects our being made in the image of the Creator. Christian writer Dorothy Sayers stated that the idea of creation is the most vital contribution Christianity makes to aesthetics. Moreover, art belongs in learning because it is a major component of virtually every culture. It is everywhere in contemporary society, which is awash in music, visual art, literature, and film. There is no escaping the presence or impact of art. To suppress it is to go beyond healthy discipleship to suppressing a fundamental feature of human life.

▸▸ The Critical Viewer

Many people argue that the artist merely holds up a mirror to reality—that the art depicts culture. Others, however, argue that it shapes culture. This issue has become part of the "culture wars." According to William Bennett, "The battle for culture refers to the struggle over the principles, sentiments, ideas, and political attitudes that define the permissible and the impermissible, the acceptable and the unacceptable, the preferred and the disdained, in speech, expression, attitude, conduct, and politics."[1] Again, much of it is fought in the arts. "This battle," writes Bennett, "is about music, art, poetry, literature, television programming, and movies; the modes of expression and conversation, official and unofficial that express who and what we are, what we believe and how we act."[2]

And art has awesome impact. A kindergarten knowledge of social psychology and its research findings on the shaping effect of the environment on the personality would alert any discerning believer to the seductive and powerful impact of film. In the case of violence, for example, the findings indicate that viewed violence, rather than having a cathartic effect by providing an imaginary channel through which the viewer can rid himself of excessively violent tendencies, actually stimulates violence. In short, humans are a highly suggestible species. In a conference titled "The Impact of the Media on Children and the Family," researchers from major universities presented studies and conducted workshops on the impact of the mass media. "Given the diversity of participants," remarked one conference organizer, "they reached a surprising consensus that values in much of the mass media, especially in violent and sexually explicit materials, are on the collision course with traditional family values and the protection of children. This review found harmful effects in 86 percent of the studies and ends the debate about whether or not there is harm."[3]

There is perhaps no concept more distorted in music, film, and literature than love, a distortion acted out daily by millions of youth. "The cult of the pop singer is a plain instance of perverted romanticism," writes Blamires. It is a powerful amalgam of music and sexuality, coupled with appearance—physique, style, and dress—aimed at maximizing sensate impact.[4]

A false image of love is presented in magazines, popular literature, and film, an image driven by eroticism and psychosexual stimulation rather than meaning and commitment.[5] Such a representation of love is a form of emotional heresy. It educates people to look for something that is actually not there; at least it is not love. Scripture states that God *is* love. First Corinthians 13 describes love as kind, humble, well-mannered, truthful, trusting, and enduring. This certainly bears no resemblance to the concept of love presented in much of popular culture. That "love" (which is really passion, stimulation, and ego-inflation) is transitory and lodged in superficial forms of attraction. It results in a serial and cyclical process of attraction, followed by bonding, and ending in disappointment. Often the cycle ends in bitterness and the suspicion that genuine love does not exist. This heretical concept has generated a population of emotional nomads.

Love, however, will always be a central theme in art, because love, or at least humanity's search for it, is basic to emotional life. In a Christian frame, love is timeless and immortal. "More than that, love *needs* immortality. Death is incompatible with love," says Blamires.[6] It is in this sense that genuine love is spiritual.

Blamires sees love as otherworldly, a glimpse of the divine and eternal. "The works and lives of the great Romantic artists, if they testify to nothing else," he writes, "certainly testify to the Christian belief that man is tortured and delighted by dreams and longings which earthly experience can never realize or set at rest."[7]

Love involves a quest to complete that which is incomplete, to make intimate that which is broken. It mirrors the human desire to be in a healthy relationship with God, something that C. S. Lewis emphasized. Blamires cites Coventry Patmore's theme that "the lover's desire for the beloved reflects the desire of God for the human soul. The husband's union with his wife is, in some mysterious way, related to God's union of himself with humanity in the act of incarnation."[8] He also suggests that romantic love gives the lover a vision of glory based in human form—incarnate.[9]

Love is divine in that the lover, as novelist Charles Williams points out, sees his beloved not as she is, but in an idealized form. He sees her as innocent and thoroughly good, as all people would see one another were humanity not in a fallen state. He sees his beloved as all humankind ought to see their fellow beings in the context of God's creation. The joyful relationship of giving and receiving in which lovers engage is the relationship that should join all humanity together.

What Blamires offers is more than a Christian view of love. "In short," he says, "there is nothing in our experience which will not look different to the Christian mind than to the secular mind."[10] He thus gives the Christian artist and the viewer of art, Christian lenses through which to view, reflect upon, and assess how love is portrayed in the arts. It is through the use of lenses like these that the Christian can redeem the times rather than become a victim of them.

▸▸ Film

There is perhaps no more powerful popular artistic medium than film. Christians differ greatly in their attitudes and conduct with regard to this medium. Many Christians practice self-censorship. Some do not view certain films; others abstain totally from this medium. There is much to be said for this self-regulating approach. Film—at least in the movie theater—is an especially potent art form. The larger-than-life screen and the highly developed, wrap-around sound system all but place the viewer in the film psychologically. From a sensory standpoint, the viewer is very nearly a participant in the film. The impact of this is not to be underestimated.

For that reason, many Christians are concerned about exposure to films that subtly communicate non-Christian values and lifestyles. Routine vulgarity and profanity; sex without boundaries, meaning, or emotional impact on the participants, provided they are consenting partners; violence as a form of conflict resolution; and marginalizing and trivializing religion and those who take it seriously, while the self-sufficient, irreverent character is glamorized, are all presented as natural, realistic, and morally acceptable. It has been said that the R-rated film may be more pernicious than its X-rated counterpart. In the latter case, sin is not disguised or rationalized. It is presented as sin. In the former, however, evil is presented as normative and respectable. Language is cleverly constructed to glorify wrongdoing and carries cunning and misleading moral connotations. As certainly as the story of the Fall suggests that sin is a subtle perversion of the truth, much of popular film subtly encourages the unwitting viewer to relax the moral and spiritual boundaries of his mind and venture more deeply into a secular mind-set.

Against the backdrop of this spiritual tension, self-censorship for many Christians is not an act of spiritual pride or self-righteousness. It is rather one of holiness, in the sense of consecrating oneself to God by setting oneself apart from the evil of the world. For the Christian viewer of film as well as for the Christian artist, this medium provides a unique challenge for the Christian mind. Blamires contributes valuably here. In the context of his statement that nothing in life will fail to look different to the Christian mind as opposed to the secular mind, he adds: "And many of the issues and activities which will be most vitally transformed by being regarded Christianly are precisely those that are with us now as constant topics of public controversy—war, crime, delinquency, disease, divorce, insanity, vice."[11] In that spirit, what follows is an attempt to apply a Christian perspective to the works of a controversial artist, Paul Schrader.

Writer/producer/director Paul Schrader, a 1968 graduate of Calvin College who did not see his first movie until he was eighteen, is a major figure in the film industry. *Taxi Driver, Hardcore, Cat People, The Last Temptation of Christ, Affliction,* and *Auto-Focus* are among his credits. An envelope-pushing rebel, his films are often raw, hard, and disturbing. Yet they are also morality plays, almost invariably with a detectable Christian theme.

There is no shortage of sin in Schrader's work, and he presents it in its crudest, most unvarnished form. He does not, however, glamorize sin. Instead, he rides sin to its ultimate end such that it often has a sickening effect on the viewer. He shows, though not in a preachy way, that often the wages of sin are indeed death. Schrader does this with violence and prostitution in *Taxi Driver,* pornography in *Hardcore,* and adulterous promiscuity in *Auto-Focus.* In addition, however briefly, the gospel is often presented, yet without life-changing impact.

The viewer gets the impression that Schrader believes the Christian world is simply not willing to do what Calvin urged Christians to do: to take its message to where the nonbeliever really lives his life.

Schrader seems to imply that Christ can have a transforming effect on any situation, but the Christian community has less than sufficient impact. The church is irrelevant because it simply is not willing to get its hands dirty in caring for a lost world. Whether or not these are Schrader's intended messages, they do provide grist for Christian thought, moving the viewing experience beyond a mere submersion in sin toward one of looking at spiritual realities.

▸▸ Basis for Assessment

The Christian mind must be in the "on" position when engaging film and literature. Often the words *serious, realistic, sincere,* or *authentic* are used to establish the moral legitimacy of a film or a piece of literature. As appealing as these adjectives may sound, they are actually irrelevant from a Christian perspective. The moral quality of a play, novel, or piece of literature does not depend on its seriousness, realism, or sincerity, but on whether or not it recommends moral rather than immoral behavior. When adultery, rampant violence, addictive behavior, and other such matters are presented in way that leads the viewer or reader to feel that those involved in these activities are right in doing so, the art's message is not moral.[12] As Bennett would have it, the issue involves what is permissible and impermissible, acceptable and unacceptable.

Art does not have to be message-heavy or unsophisticated to be moral. "A comic treatment of adultery may be moral," says Blamires, "because it points out the incongruity between what people should do and what they in fact do."[13] In short, the issue is not what *subject* the artist treats, or even what *style* he uses in treating it, but from what *moral perspective* it is presented.

There is, however, another subtle twist requiring vigilance. Much film and literature reflects a postmodern drift away from substantive insights into truth, toward subjective, sensationalized immersions into the world of experience. Experience becomes reality as rationally grounded thinking is abandoned in favor of spontaneous and emotional excursions to nowhere.[14] Moreover, this experiential immersion is often without boundaries. Satanism, the occult, and the spirit world become legitimate arenas of experience to explore without discernment. The artist may claim that such experiential forays carry no message, if for no other reason than that postmodernism does not advance grounded perspectives. They do carry a message, however, by implying that any experience, provided it is not overtly damaging, is good. It can only expand one's engagement with life. It is harmless and no different from a roller coaster ride at the amusement park; one always returns safely from the trip.

Such art is often reinforced by what Blamires calls the critics' "approval noises" rather than sober evaluation. Instead of comments explaining *why* a work proves effective or is relevant, one is more likely to hear that it "really worked" or that it "ticked." It may also be approved for being disturbing, shocking, or riveting. These approval noises are no more grounded in any rational basis of assessment than are the adjectives "serious," "realistic," or "sincere," referred to earlier. Approval noises, like so much of contemporary film and literature, focus on sensation rather than evaluation and on experience rather than significance.[15]

Again, there *is* a powerful message in this kind of art, one that many artists have lived personally. "There is," writes Blamires, "the artistic cult of uninhibited personal creativeness, spontaneity, and originality, which breeds amoral 'religious' devotion to intemperate neurotic personalities. It was an idolatry of this kind which destroyed Dylan Thomas; and many others, artists and idolaters alike, have suffered from the spuriously sanctified cultivation of eccentricity and excess."[16] He may have added Elvis Presley, Jim Morrison, and a host of other pop figures in music and film. The cult gives rise to unhealthy excesses, reckless experimentation, and bingeing—things that waste, alter, and even end lives.

Despite the resistance to art from so many in the Christian community, there is no need for the Christian to shun art media. To assume a position on the negative side of the culture wars is simply another way of abandoning turf to secularism. Secularism in the arts is no more subtle or pernicious than it is in the other sectors of the academic world. It merely takes different forms. Art is powerful and is a wonderful medium for Christian impact. The challenge for the Christian is to step into the vacuum and engage art constructively in a way that brings light and direction to artists and to those who appreciate art.

Notes

1. William Bennett, *The Devaluing of America* (New York: Simon and Schuster, 1992), 10, quoted in Kina Millard, "Christian Worldview and the Media," in *Shaping a Christian Worldview*, ed. David S. Dockery and Gregory Alan Thornbury (Nashville: Broadman and Holman, 2002), 264.
2. Ibid.
3. Michael Medved, *Hollywood vs. America* (New York: HarperCollins, 1992), 125, quoted in Millard, "Christian Worldview and the Media," in Dockery and Thornbury, *Shaping a Christian Worldview*, 270.

4. Harry Blamires, *The Christian Mind* (Ann Arbor, MI: Servant, 1997), 180.
5. Ibid.
6. Ibid., 186.
7. Ibid., 178.
8. Ibid., 186.
9. Ibid., 185.
10. Ibid., 83.
11. Ibid.
12. Ibid., 98–100.
13. Ibid., 99.
14. Blamires, *Where Do We Stand?* (Ann Arbor, MI: Servant, 1980), 110.
15. Ibid., 142–43.
16. Blamires, *The Christian Mind,* 180.

SOME GUIDELINES
FOR THE CHRISTIAN ARTIST

A rt—whether it be film, painting, or literature—is no different from any other enterprise within the community of learning; it is about truth. An artist friend of mine once said, "The artist is the most objective of all people."[1] By that he meant that the true artist does not try to shape, structure, or manipulate truth. She merely reveals it honestly, as she sees it. It is truth uncensored.

Art, however, is never the original reality. It is a depiction, a rendering, a representation, of reality. In that sense, art is an illusion, a "lie." "Of all lies," said Gustave Flaubert, of *Madame Bovary* fame, "art is the least untrue." Or as Picasso put it, "Art is the lie that helps us see the truth."

It is in this raw truth, often presented with disturbing unrestraint, that so much of art's potency resides. Because of its sensate nature, art can communicate the lessons of truth (or messages of error) often more powerfully than any other medium. This is not only why Christians should not dismiss art but also why they need to participate in it.

▸▸ The Christian Artist

A traditional definition of the visual arts would term it an intentional design aimed at appealing to one's sense of beauty. In view of the expansion of art forms, Karen Mulder states that an artist will no longer be taken seriously with such a narrow definition. She offers this definition: "Art is a form of deliberate, intentional human expression. Make no mistake," she says, "this is a bridge-building definition. It allows artists of any belief to speak to one another about the potential of art, and Christians to enter the arena of high art."[2] Furthermore, postmodernism, with its subjectivism, has actually opened the door to Christian content in the arts, according to Mulder. With the no-boundaries approach extant in postmodernism, there is a willingness to receive all forms of artistic expression, giving believers the opportunity to have an impact, something of which many Christian artists are taking advantage.[3]

Contrary to those who only decry the fallen state of art in contemporary society, Mulder adopts no such hand-wringing posture. She contends that the Christian artist has every reason to be optimistic. Chief among them is that the Christian artist, made in the image of the Creator, is connected to an infinite, divine source of creativity, something that needs to be much more in evidence among Christians. "We don't always act as if we have access to an infinite and free source of endless creativity, because the obvious, the trite, and the cliché are safer than mystery and open-ended assertions," writes Mulder. These pedestrian expressions repudiate the spiritual identity of the Christian. They may be safe, "but Christians ought to exhibit an innate creativity if they are truly expressing the creative image of the Creator."[4] Furthermore, Mulder believes Christians have much to offer, particularly in an age celebrating the expression of self, because God is very much a part of the believer's self. "Artists of faith," she says, "who are wittingly gaining perfected knowledge in the nature of God, in whose image they are made, will express part of this knowledge as their 'self' gained expression through art."[5]

For Mulder, a staid and conventional approach need not typify Christian art. Jesus was a "pattern-breaker," she claims. "The Lord's example is one of bold innovations, response instead of visceral reaction, and nonconformity that fly in the face of superficial word games or pharisaical traps." She also suggests that a bit of edginess is appropriate for the Christian artist. "If art is truly emulating Christ, it ought to have elements of the creatively nonconventional, the healthily subversive, and the surprising."[6]

This point is critical for the Christian who wishes to move beyond critiquing art to creating art. Too often Christian discussions of art focus exclusively on such matters as "how far a Christian will go" in the arts, the appropriate use of the human body, or whether shock value can be defended.[7] In short, some believers want to restrict the artist to tame material. Responsibility in the handling of material is important, but that is not what is at stake. The breaking of every commandment is part of the human condition, and no single commandment is any more important than any other. James (2:10) tells us that stumbling at even one seemingly minor point of God's law renders us guilty of breaking the entire law. Thus, the elevation of some commandments above others and the labeling of some sins as being more serious than others are not Christian. No subject should be off-limits to the Christian artist. Nor need there be any limit on how realistically a subject is presented. More than sensationalism is involved here. Some subjects necessitate highly realistic presentation for the impact of the artist's message to take hold. What is at issue is not style but substance and responsibility—the moral message the artist conveys.

Wolterstorff has written extensively on art and aesthetics. In *Art in Action,* he discusses the institution of high art (those works recognized by the cultural elite—lovers of great art) and the role of the artist within it. Wolterstorff points out that this institution reflects its fallen state in a variety of ways. Among them is its insatiable appetite for new work, which "drives its agents into acts of plunder and rapacity."[8] Moreover, the way recognition is accorded encourages the artist to forget quality expression in quest of validation as an artist. The artist then abandons a healthy expression of self and begins producing for the good opinion of others. Moreover, in its push for innovation and total commitment, the art world damages lives and spirits. Many sensitive artists are victimized and judged to be failures simply because they are out of touch with prevailing stylistic innovation or are not accorded critical success.

This issue is made even more serious for the artist because of the self-contained nature of the institution of art. The entirety of the artist's identity—her ego—is often defined by her status within the art world.[9] Not unlike the world of professional sports, the art world becomes life itself for many of its inhabitants. To elevate a sphere of life beyond its proper limits is not only unchristian; it is idolatrous. A professional athlete once told me he longed to be referred to by his name only, rather than by his name and the appendage "of the Chicago White Sox." For him, the appendage both defined and limited his identity. Moreover, a lack of success in his professional role can too easily degrade his value as a human being. So also, the artist is regularly in peril of having her very worth determined by her status in this subjective yet closed world.

Currently, the institution of art, as Briner points out, is almost totally secularized. There is a worship of the renowned artist within the art community, with the artist rising to near-deity status. In this ascribing of value, God is challenged rather than worshiped. Nonetheless, the institution does yield great work, productions that enrich our lives. Indeed, all truth and beauty remain God's truth and beauty. To lose awareness of this is not only to lose much of the essence of art; it is to ensure that only secularists will contribute to the world of art.[10]

▶▶ Issues for the Christian Artist

In Wolterstorff's opinion, there are several matters that ought to concern the Christian artist.[11] The first involves being responsible and continuing to assess values and priorities. The Christian artist need not move with trends and fads, but rather should look for ways of making significant contributions, because she serves God rather than her own raw desire for self-expression. As for assessment, Wolterstorff acknowledges that artists become uncomfortable when having to take a stand on the value of a given work, not wanting to pass judgment on movements that are trivial or important. "Yet in spite of their skittishness," writes Wolterstorff, "artists themselves, when sitting on evaluation panels for, say, the National Endowment of Arts, do in fact make such judgments of relative importance."[12] Therefore, the Christian artist need not be reluctant to assess the contributory value of her endeavors.

For Wolterstorff there is no escaping the issue of priorities and values. The Christian artist has a responsibility to God, her neighbor, herself, and nature; therefore, she must weigh priorities in terms of the direction she invests her efforts. It is irresponsible for the believer to leave the priorities to popular demand, in effect, pandering to the public. Occasionally, the artist's decision to resist the public's axis may only bring greater enrichment to her fellow human beings. She serves their needs rather than their wants.

The Christian artist should also strive for wholeness and integrity in life. This is a call away from compartmentalization and toward a Christian worldview, one that most certainly includes her art. There are goals and aims that give shape and direction to the images, harmonies, and situations that arise so spontaneously. Although the raw materials of a production may have come from a mysterious blizzard of creativity, the final product is a deliberate action. Similar to Mulder's position, Wolterstorff believes the Christian artist's work will incorporate her Christian commitment. Often one will hear artists say they are responsible only to their own selves and the art they produce. This is incompatible with the Christian in art and is not necessary, as witnessed in the number of Christians who have produced great art.

Finally, the Christian must keep the role of art in context, given the self-contained nature of the art world. "Art does not provide us with the meaning of human existence. The gospel of Jesus Christ does that. Art is not a way of rising toward God. It is meant instead to be in service of God. Art is not man's glory. It displays man's degradation as well as his dignity."[13] Art is not the Savior, but needs to be in service of him.

Art—as Mulder, Briner, Wolterstorff, and others advocate—need not be the institution of the secularist. The gospel can be proclaimed as powerfully in the institution of art as in any other field. If anything, the Christian community would do well to recommit itself enthusiastically to infusing the art world with its message of hope. Briner argues loudly for the Christian to get involved. "What I'm calling for," he writes, "is a radically different way of thinking about our world. Instead of running from it, we need to rush into it."[14] Briner, an Emmy Award–winning television producer, sees no reason why the top Hollywood film director could not be a Christian, or why the works of a Christian artist could not be on display at the Museum of Modern Art, or why the principle dancer in the Joffrey Ballet could not be an active believer. Why hasn't this happened? For Briner, it is because of a fortress mentality within parts of the Christian community. "In fact, I believe it has been the pessimistic vision of the church that has prevented generations of young people from venturing out into the culture-shaping professions of the world," he notes.[15]

The world of art needs believers. Renowned film critic, Michael Medved has cited many instances of an antireligious bias in Hollywood, with moviemakers going out of their way to attack religious values. "It's easy for most movie makers to assume a patronizing attitude toward religiously committed people," says Medved, "because they know so few of them personally."[16] "We've left the interpretation of our faith, our church, and our Savior up to non-Christians," echoes Briner.[17]

And it isn't as if there are no opportunities for Christian involvement in the film industry. Briner tracked down the producer of the acclaimed film *Chariots of Fire*, David Puttnam, in London and asked him why there were so few quality films following it. "He said there were just no good scripts being brought to him," writes Briner. "He had shown an affinity for producing quality, uplifting, affirming, even Christian-oriented movies, but no one was bringing him scripts of quality. I couldn't help wonder where the Christian screenwriters were."[18]

The lack of a Christian presence in the arts extends beyond the film industry. "Christians seem to have forgotten the power of the visual arts," notes Briner. "We are so verbal, so language-oriented that we have neglected painting, sculpture, photography, and architecture to the point where there is now almost no evidence of the gospel message, and no image of Christ in modern art. This is a tragedy, a disaster."[19]

Elton Trueblood, in his book *The Company of the Committed,* stated that "the test of the vitality of a religion is to be seen in its effect upon culture."[20] That is the call for the Christian in the arts. Moreover, C. S. Lewis's words about education apply equally to the arts. "If all the world were Christian," he says, "it might not matter if all the world were uneducated, but as it is, a cultural life will exist outside the church."[21] But because that cultural life does exist, the able Christian must step forward. "To be ignorant and simple now," he continues, "not be able to meet the enemies on their own ground, would be to throw down our weapons and to betray our uneducated brethren who have, under God, no defense but us against the intellectual attacks of the heathen."[22] As Anthony Ugolnik stated at a conference of Christians in the Visual Arts (CIVA): "The wasteland of twentieth-century secularism—the desert to which Christ or the monk goes—is alive with possibilities. . . . Refuse to be marginalized. Render holy the process of image-making."[23]

Notes

1. Gregory Athnos, conversation with author, Chicago.
2. Karen L. Mulder, "Christian Worldview and the Arts," in *Shaping a Christian Worldview*, ed. David S. Dockery and Gregory Alan Thornbury (Nashville: Broadman and Holman, 2002), 204.
3. Ibid., 213–14.
4. Ibid., 214.
5. Ibid., 215.
6. Ibid., 216.
7. Ibid., 208.
8. Nicholas Wolterstorff, *Art in Action* (Grand Rapids: Eerdmans, 1980), 192.
9. Ibid., 192–93.
10. Ibid., 192.
11. Ibid., 193–96.
12. Ibid., 194.
13. Ibid., 196.
14. Bob Briner, *Roaring Lambs* (Grand Rapids: Zondervan, 1993), 31.
15. Ibid., 79–80.
16. Michael Medved, quoted in ibid, 80.
17. Briner, *Roaring Lambs*, 80.
18. Ibid., 83.
19. Ibid., 138.
20. Elton Trueblood, *The Company of the Committed* (New York: Harper & Row, 1961), quoted in Briner, *Roaring Lambs*, 165.
21. C. S. Lewis, quoted in Briner, *Roaring Lambs*, 160.
22. Ibid., 160–61.
23. Anthony Ugolnik, CIVA Conference, Messiah College, Pennsylvania, 1993, quoted in Mulder, "Christian Worldview and the Arts," in Dockery and Thornbury, *Shaping a Christian Worldview*, 217. Ugolnik is the author of *The Illuminating Icon* (Grand Rapids: Eerdmans, 1989).

17

HOW DO WE TEACH LITERATURE IN A POSTMODERN WORLD?

D espite art's general quest for truth, postmodernism, with its subjective view of the universe, has had its way in the arts. Its effects are particularly disturbing to lovers of literature. Whereas good literature was often so labeled because of its expression of universal truths, the postmodern rejection of ultimate truth has made an evaluation of literature much more difficult.

Timothy Beals, in his essay "Some Explorations of Milton's *Lycidas:* Toward a Normative Theory of Literary Criticism," engages this issue cogently. Beals, whose work is certainly applicable to film as well as to literature, begins by citing the fragmentary nature of modern literature and criticism—a postmodern morass that leaves one merely to describe and attempt to interpret what a given work, by a given author, means at a given time, all through the eyes of the beholder. He reminds us that this was not always the case. In the early part of the twentieth century and on into the 1960s, the focus was on literature's moral and didactic value. The serious reader learned lessons of life, truth, and reality from good literature. Good literature, an English scholar once told me, conveys universal truth. By 1970, and the onset of postmodernism, literature lost its very definition, as the quest for morality and truth all but dissolved in an ocean of subjectivity, fragmentation, and literature for literature's sake. When the meaning of literature is reduced to the lowest common denominator of "the meaning of literature means whatever it means to you," subjectivity reigns and there is little room for the Christian teacher to navigate.

▶▶ Limitless Subjectivity

The matter of subjectivity extends to the use of language. The subjectivist's view of language—something that can be both fascinating and subtle—is by no means a recent skill. C. S. Lewis's students pointed him to Alec King and Martin Ketley's book *The Control of Language,* which showed how a subjectivist expresses his view of language and morality.[1] The book stated that when one says "the waterfall is sublime," he really means, "I have sublime feelings."[2] In other words, the writer is not making a declarative statement about the nature of the waterfall, but rather he is expressing a subjective feeling. Harry Poe notes that this approach to literature made its way into educational thinking by way of A. J. Ayer's theory of emotivism: "The contention that when one says, 'X is good' he is saying only 'I like X,'" merely making a statement with an emotional overtone.[3]

Lewis nails the essence of this thinking: "Firstly, that all sentences containing a predicate of value are statements about the emotional state of the speaker, and secondly, that all such statements are unimportant."[4] They are unimportant because, by the standards of the subjectivist (or postmodernist), there is no real truth. Without real truth, we are left floating on an ocean of subjective reactions, with literature losing much of what Beals refers to as its moral and didactic value, a characteristic that has made it so appealing to Christians over the centuries.

▸▸ Literature: A Definition

In dealing with the challenge of postmodern thinking, Beals begins by offering an intelligent definition of literature and follows that with a basis for its evaluation. "In short," he writes, "literature can be defined as a repetitively selective series of concretions revealing a value scale."[5] He then breaks this down by stating that literature uses concrete rather than abstract language. "The primary factor in literature," says Beals, "and the factor that separates literature from philosophy, is literature's attempt to use concrete language. It can be asserted that the aim of literature and philosophy is the same: general truth."[6] Whereas philosophy uses abstract language, literature uses "sensate evidence," tangible images that are often more intellectually manageable and have greater impact than more abstract constructions. Because literature is concrete, it is also selective rather than inclusive. "Out of the near infinite number of possible concrete images, writers can select only a few."[7] This limitation forces the writer to offer a more discernible product than does the more theoretically oriented philosopher. Finally, literature is repetitive. "Any study of literature," notes Beals, "especially the study of individual authors, will reveal that within a single work and between all of the works by the same author, there are identifiable, limited, and repeated themes."[8] In other words, the author's worldview is repeatedly expressed and can therefore be discerned by the student.

The Christian scholar inevitably perks up with the subject of values. Beals contends that an author, by repeating a given set of concretions, reveals a scale of values that are his own, independent of the subjective notions of the reader. In fact, literature is simply unable to be read outside a context of values. Values are the very structure in which an author communicates a message, the boundaries within which a message has meaning. This, then, leads to the question of finding competent criteria for the evaluation of quality literature—a basis for literary criticism.

▸▸ A Basis for Evaluation

Beals offers two criteria, the first being that literature must deal with the world of reality. The work must comport with what is probable. Art, as Aristotle pointed out, must imitate life. It is right here that so much film and literature fail. For example, for most men and women, irrespective of religiosity, sexual intercourse generates some form of emotional vulnerability. The intense physical bonding usually carries an emotional residue. Yet in much popular literature (and film), one is led to believe that sexual unions have no more psychological impact than sharing a cup of coffee. Moreover, unless it is central to the plot, people in such popular art do not encounter unwanted pregnancies or contract the AIDS virus or any other sexually transmitted disease. Similarly, we know that in the real world, violence—also prevalent in film and literature—generates a host of psychological reactions. Loss, fear, shock, post-traumatic stress disorder, and insomnia are among its products. Again, this is almost totally absent in the depictions of violence in much popular film and literature. Such depictions fail the test of realism.

Buckley made a similar argument in discussing historical novels on C-Span. He stated that a historical novel must depict things that either happened or could logically have happened, given the historical context of the story. A historical novel presenting, say, Robert E. Lee as a union sympathizer would fail the test of realism.

When art is effective in imitating life, it has immense impact. R. L. Brett, in *Reason and Imagination,* stated, "Poetry is an idealization of actuality: it reveals the truth of things through sensory images which possess a vividness that the abstractions of the intellect lack."[9] For Beals, "lessons of any kind are better taught by literature than history."[10]

The second criterion involves honesty or ethical generalization. "This principle says in essence that characters in literary works should act as they wish to be acted upon. If the characters fail to act with probity, then their deeds can be condemned and they become negative examples of ethical generalization. If a work or many works by the same author fail to generalize ethically, we can say that they are 'bad.'"[11] The insertion of the Golden Rule as a basis of ethical generalization is particularly helpful. Though Christian—it is a derivative of the second great commandment of loving one's neighbor as oneself—it is acceptable to many other philosophical traditions, making Beals's second criterion more than a narrow, religious construct.

In addition, C. S. Lewis, in *The Abolition of Man*, shows how this law operates in many cultures and, in *Mere Christianity*, treats it as a basis for rational living. Social psychologist Michael Kohlberg implies the importance of ethical generalization in *Essays on Moral Development*, while Jewish scholar Marcus Singer deals with this principle in *Generalization of Ethics*. "When applied to literature," notes Beals, "this principle makes it possible to establish right and wrong, good and bad, as these terms pertain to the characters' actions and to the author's interaction with his subject matter."[12] Ethical generalization gives literature direction.

Beals, a Christian, makes a substantial contribution here. Short of offering an explicit Christian approach to literature or criticism, he blazes a trail out of the fog of postmodernism in offering a "systematic approach to the meaning and evaluation of literature."[13]

It is one thing for the literary scholar to read literature with healthy spiritual lenses. It is another for the student to do so. This poses a singular challenge to the Christian teacher of literature.

▸▸ Guidelines for the Teaching of Literature

Barbara McMillin offers guidelines for handling literature that crashes against a Christian worldview.[14] She suggests that the instructor begin by anticipating these collisions and reducing the shock value by readying his students for these confrontations. From there, dialogue needs to be stimulated that can illuminate a Christian approach to the material as well as help students appreciate grains of truth that emerge from secular thinking.[15] This latter point is important. As surely as secularists dismiss and marginalize Christian insights, Christians are often guilty of similar misdeed, rejecting truth when it comes from anyone other than fellow believers. The works of Hemingway and Camus may come from rankly secular worldviews, but writers such as these make powerful statements as to the human condition.

McMillin goes on to advocate a reader-response method.[16] In this method, the reader asks, "How do I feel about this work?" This is an intriguing, mind-opening exercise. Despite the postmodern danger of elevating the reader's subjective response above the truth value of the literature, by acknowledging feeling, the student is admitting a personal involvement in the work. The student is also confessing an injection of personal bias in her interaction with the material. It is at this point that discussion with other students can help the student assess the work from a Christian point of view, with the instructor ensuring that truth rather than mere sensation is engaged.

Biographical critique is another effective device advocated by McMillin.[17] This raises the question, What is the writer's worldview and how does he or she reveal it in the work? McMillin uses Katherine Anne Porter's short story "Noon Wine" as an example of the biographical critique method. Porter's spiritual stance is not obvious in the work, but once one realizes Porter's commitment to Catholicism, the spiritual messages become evident. (Certainly the same can be done in reviewing the films of Calvinist-reared Schrader.)

Given the postmodern emphasis is on the reader's interpretation, what does one make of the notion that meaning resides solely within a work? Called the New Criticism, it all but invalidates the reader-response and biographical critiques, leaving the only door through which Christianity can travel is one inherent in the work. Fortunately, suggests McMillin, English literature is replete with biblical references and Christian worldviews. She cites David Lyle Jeffrey's *A Dictionary of Biblical Tradition in English Literature* and Roland Bartel's *Biblical Images in Literature* as especially helpful here. Moreover, including literature with Christian messages enables the Christian instructor in literature to be faithful to the discipline as well as to the creator of the work.

Postmodernism, with its ever-moving targets, does indeed pose a daunting challenge to the Christian teacher of literature. The very existence of postmodern literature, however, gives the teacher the opportunity to explain what postmodernism is and how it negates truth. From there, the call is for careful analyses and creative approaches. Those reviewed here will, I hope, stimulate other excellent teachers to create new methods and chart new directions as they seek to lead their literature students out of the darkness of postmodernism toward the light of truth.

Notes

1. George Sayers, *Jack: C. S. Lewis and His Times* (San Francisco: Harper & Row, 1988), 179, quoted in Harry L. Poe, "The Influence of C. S. Lewis," in *Shaping a Christian Worldview*, ed. David S. Dockery and Gregory Alan Thornbury (Nashville: Broadman and Holman, 2002), 98.

2. C. S. Lewis, *The Abolition of Man* (New York: Macmillan, 1955), 14, quoted in Poe, "The Influence of C. S. Lewis," in Dockery and Thornbury, *Shaping a Christian Worldview*, 98.

3. Poe, "The Influence of C. S. Lewis," in Dockery and Thornbury, *Shaping a Christian Worldview*, 98.

4. Lewis, *The Abolition of Man,* 15, quoted in Poe, "The Influence of C. S. Lewis," in Dockery and Thornbury, *Shaping a Christian Worldview,* 98.

5. Timothy Beals, "Toward a Normative Theory of Literary Criticism" (graduate research essay, Western Michigan University, 1985), 2.

6. Ibid.

7. Ibid., 3.

8. Ibid., 4.

9. R. L. Brett, *Reason and Imagination* (New York: Oxford, 1960), 22.

10. Beals, "Toward a Normative Theory," 4.

11. Ibid., 8.

12. Ibid., 9.

13. Ibid., 10.

14. Barbara McMillin, "Christian Worldview and Literature," in Dockery and Thornbury, *Shaping a Christian Worldview,* 149–54.

15. Ibid., 150.

16. Ibid., 150–51. Paul Munson employs a similar method in determining how one relates to music. Munson suggests five questions: Why does one listen to or make music? How does one select the songs? Does it matter? What does music mean? What is its moral significance? See Paul Munson, "Christian Worldview and Music," in Dockery and Thornbury, *Shaping Christian Worldview,* 220.

17. McMillin, "Christian Worldview and Literature," in Dockery and Thornbury, *Shaping a Christian Worldview,* 151–53.

18

PHILOSOPHY UNDER A CHRISTIAN LENS

P hilosophy is an inquiry into the meaning of life, and perhaps more than any other, this discipline is ripe for Christian analysis. Sometimes the intersection of Christianity and philosophy reaches an unhealthy extreme, as Christianity becomes known as simply one of many philosophies, rather than as a one-to-one relationship with Christ. That notwithstanding, many scholars have come to faith in part through reading the works of Christian theological philosophers.

▸▸ Leading toward Light

Glenn Tinder, an accomplished political scientist who received his Ph.D. from the University of California, Berkeley, and followed that with postdoctoral work at Harvard, is one thinker who came to faith through the work of Christian philosophers. Tinder searched intensely for truth. "It would be accurate to say," he writes, "that for about twenty years I stumbled along in the dark but caught occasional glimpses of light far ahead; gradually the light grew brighter."[1] Although Tinder read Plato, he found the Christian thinkers more attractive in leading him toward light.

"Standing slightly taller than any of the others in my memory is that great, but now largely forgotten, Christian philosopher Nicolas Berdyaev."[2] Berdyaev was a Russian aristocrat with a set of views that were not entirely orthodox. For example, he affirmed a cosmic freedom that put limits on God's sovereignty, bringing about tragedy for God himself. In addition, Berdyaev did not address in detail the central Christian doctrines of sin and forgiveness. What attracted Tinder was Berdyaev's bold, wide-ranging system of thinking, rooted in Christian perspectives. Berdyaev allowed Tinder to take the mystery of human freedom very seriously. He also made the subject of eschatology—the Second Coming—a real and dramatic focus.[3]

The works of novelist-philosopher Fyodor Dostoyevsky, however, had even greater impact on Tinder. Dostoyevsky reinforced Tinder's awareness of the expansiveness of human freedom.[4] Unlike Berdyaev, however, Dostoyevsky showed Tinder that this very freedom can become a bottomless reservoir of evil. Perhaps more important, Dostoyevsky focused on God's incredible mercy and its power over human sin. Through Dostoyevsky, Tinder saw that sin is not overcome by human interventions but only through suffering and grace. Moreover, Dostoyevsky pointed to the tragic and devastating consequences associated with a fading of Christianity in a culture, something he saw coming, and dramatized these consequences in *Crime and Punishment, The Possessed,* and *The Brothers Karamazov.*[5]

Indeed, Tinder's story is but one example of the value of Christian philosophy in its capacity to have life-changing impact on those searching for truth. There is, however, a danger when a philosophical system rather than orthodox faith becomes central. Sometimes believers, attempting to make the faith more intellectually palatable, will try to "assist" Christianity by incorporating secular notions into Christian thinking. Rather than critiquing prevailing philosophies in the context of faith, they bend faith to fit the philosophical constructions.

Keith Yandell, professor of philosophy and South Asian studies at the University of Wisconsin, makes a strong argument for remaining faithful to the basics of Christianity when doing philosophy. Yandell pored through the spectrum of secularized hybrids of Christianity, running from Rudolf Bultmann's demythologizing notions to some of Paul Tillich's ideas and even to "death of God" theories. "After this extensive reading," Yandell states, "I drew a moral that I continue to accept: *Secularized versions of mere Christianity are uniformly very less reasonable to accept than is mere Christianity itself.*" Even atheism seemed more reasonable to Yandell than the diluted versions of Christianity. "Atheism I can respect; it has some impressive representatives and formulations. Christianity filtered through some sort of secularism is not something that I, as a philosopher, can take seriously."[6]

If nothing else, Yandell reminds the Christian scholar that he is to critique philosophies from a Christian perspective rather than allow philosophies to critique the central tenets of his faith. In that spirit, we will look at some of the basic concepts of some well-known philosophers. Indeed, any chapter on faith and learning in philosophy could give the reader a taste of eternal life—it could go on forever—so we will limit ourselves to four existentialist philosophers, looking especially at how their ideas, albeit often far from being Christian, can contribute to Christian thinking.

▸▸ Existentialism

Existentialist philosophy is especially amenable to Christian analysis. Even the most ardent of secularist existentialists offer ideas that parallel Christian thought. Rather than a philosophy, existentialism is a way of determining truth through commitment. If at conversion, and therefore at the time of commitment, one becomes a new person in Christ (2 Cor. 5:17)—seeing truth with spiritually opened eyes—then indeed the Christian life affirms an existentialist experience.

▶ Jean-Paul Sartre

No philosophical friend of theists, Jean-Paul Sartre affirmed the power of commitment. He contended that meaning, identity, and personhood could be found only at the point at which one makes a commitment to what he believes to be ultimate truth. This is not a postmodern, subjective, whatever-gets-you-through-the-night truth. Rather, it must be a truth that the person deems objectively true for all of humanity. Such a commitment provides a direction for life.[7]

Sartre would certainly not have affirmed an existentialism of dropping out, common to Western youth in the 1960s. Many in that era abandoned their college careers, claiming they needed time to reflect and to "find themselves." According to Sartre, employing such a method is impossible. Looking within oneself, there is nothing to find. The self only becomes real at the point at which a person attaches that self to a universal truth larger than his own being. Stated another way, meaning and truth are to be found in the external universe, and the individual becomes a substantive entity only at the point at which he attaches himself fully to such a truth.

Christians have no difficulty with the outside-the-self aspect of Sartre's thinking. Life becomes real at the point of a commitment to Christ. If indeed Jesus is real, it can be no other way. Ten verses into Ephesians, Paul states that God's purpose is "to bring all things in heaven and on earth together under one head, even Christ." In short, all things in the universe point their way to Christ. As such, it is the only correct direction to take. To look to any other source for truth would be tantamount to looking at the earth to understand the sky. This reinforces the belief that no knowledge, no education, is truly complete apart from Christ.

Campolo quotes Paul's words in Philippians 1:21, "For to me, to live is Christ and to die is gain." The implications of this "to live is Christ" notion are immense. It indicates that one's ego is not to be vested within the individual; it is to orbit around Christ, the center of identity. Moreover, it defines the purpose of one's life by providing a mission statement for his very existence. Beyond that, it implies that there is no reality apart from Christ. This is why Christianity is not a philosophy. It is not about searching for truth. It is truth. Two plus two are not really four outside of Christ, who created all of reality, including mathematics.

If a primary purpose of humanity is to glorify—worship, praise, venerate, esteem—and enjoy God, not to do so is to live a purposeless life. Thus, commitment to the work of God, loving him and loving our neighbor as our own self, is the path to meaning. It is to be grounded in reality. The latter part of our purpose—to enjoy God—is alien to many believers' experience. For many, following God is suffused with guilt, obligation, and struggle. Clearly, that humans are imperfect makes adhering to a life of God-glorification less than effort-free. Nonetheless, that a sizable slice of psychological research connects emotional well-being to one's effectively serving others supports the notion that joy and satisfaction result from such a quest. The reason for this is that whenever one glorifies God, he is in harmony with the very purpose of his existence.

Investing one's energy in the glorification of God rather than in personal fulfillment squares with Christ's assertion, "Whoever finds his life will lose it, and whoever loses his life for my sake will find it" (Matt. 10:39). Although this statement has a paradoxical, counterintuitive ring, it again indicates that commitment to the ultimate, supernatural truth that moves us beyond the limits of our fallen nature is the way life—and, therefore, enjoyment—is found.

To the skeptic, none of this makes sense. I once heard noted psychologist Albert Ellis, founder of rational-emotive therapy, conduct a symposium at a university in Chicago. He stated that the purpose of life is to have a raging ball. By this standard, life is about self-indulgence and egocentrism, and the successful life is measured by the degree to which one has experienced the maximum amount of pleasure and moment-to-moment happiness. It is "me first." Moreover, Ellis all but rejected the validity of guilt. Taking sexual advantage of an emotionally vulnerable person, for example, is easily dismissed when one considers that had he not done so, someone else would have.

The validity of the raging ball–driven life is easily tested in several ways. First, one could use generalized application: What would happen if everyone operated in this pleasure-without-moral-rules fashion? The answer is that we would not have society as we know it. A society functions in part on the basis of internalized norms—rules that become part of one's moral compass. Without the moral boundaries these rules define, a near-totalitarian external force would be necessary to control conduct, or all would be chaos. From another less extreme vantage point, if Ellis's belief really constituted ultimate truth, suicide rates would be the lowest, and reported levels of well-being would be the highest, among the affluent and most pleasure-laden population groups. Rather than the psychiatric depressions and intense meaningless feelings often reported by the most materially privileged in Western society, there would be mass evidence of raging happiness.

That such is not the case is as powerful an argument as any for the doctrine that human beings are spiritual in nature. Nothing that is natural to this earth ever satisfies continually. Nothing. A child begs his parents for a bicycle for Christmas, with the sincere expectation that he will want nothing else if the two-wheeler shows up under the tree. Once the precious gift is ridden, the priorities regarding happiness and want change. By the New Year, that same child is wondering how far away the next Christmas is, because there is now a new item on the list.

Among the more grown-up, sex—at the outset—can be so very exciting, so intensely enjoyable, and so incredibly satisfying, that one can imagine nothing but fulfillment if only he had open access to it. Soon that same indescribably delightful activity can become boring. Similarly, those who develop dependencies on alcohol or controlled substances report an initial heaven-on-earth attachment to indulging. The ecstasy is brief, however, as they soon report that the highs are not as high and the lows are lower than ever as dependency takes hold.

Enter Christ as the living bread and water, eternally satisfying for those who eat and drink of them. Central to these concepts is that humans are spiritual, and as such, connection with something larger (God) than one's human self is absolutely essential to genuine life satisfaction. No physical substances or pleasures will completely scratch the inner itch, because that sensation is spiritual. Conversely, a harmonious relationship with God brings a wholeness and an inner joy that is larger than one's temporal circumstances. Indeed, the spiritually alive public-aid recipient is often happier than the spiritually starving millionaire.

▸ Søren Kierkegaard

Another existentialist, Søren Kierkegaard, offers an approach to meaning with a more spiritual twist.[8] It was his contention that the modern person, in the face of excessive autonomy and an overwhelming array of life choices, would experience anxiety and immobilization rather than genuine freedom. Finding this excessive freedom burdensome, a person would fill his life space with hyperactive ventures into senseless stimulation and entertainment. It would be easier, thought Kierkegaard, for a person to conform to the trends of the culture than to endure the loneliness and difficulty incurred in taking the road to meaning.

It is hard to argue with Kierkegaard's ideas. The contemporary pace is ever more rapid, and the level of incoming stimulation from the various media increasingly intense, such that there is little time for reflection. A businesswoman told me of a remark she heard a speaker make at her church. Commenting on the maddening pace of life, the speaker said that the only time people in earlier eras lived with such stress and tension was when they were in combat. At Western civilization's current tempo, life goes unexamined as one tries to get to Friday. Once there, weekends become pleasure-seeking safaris, if only to avoid facing one's sense of emptiness. If meaning is not found, distraction will do.

Christians are not immune to this. A skilled therapist initiated a series of sessions focusing on Phillip McGraw's *Life Strategies* at an urban church.[9] As the weeks passed and the people delved more deeply into the purpose of their lives, the group got smaller and smaller, until not one remained. The therapist told me he was not surprised, that the more real and vivid the examined lives of the participants became to them, the more difficult it was for them to persist.

Kierkegaard posited three stages through which people go to resolve the "angst" of meaninglessness. The first he called aesthetic, a stage in which there is a quest for passionate experience—an immersion into music, art, or painting, for example. This search is for peak experiences, however, and is temporary. Once one realizes that true and consistent inner fulfillment are not acquired in this fashion, he moves to the ethical stage.

The ethical stage—engaging in good works and charitable acts—seeks to bring the kingdom of God to earth. Again, disillusionment awaits. Once one becomes aware that all the hungry are not fed, all the illiterate are not reading, and all the social maladies are not expunged, a sense of futility develops. It becomes evident that perfection even within one's own life is simply not attainable.

At this point, the person is ready for the final stage—the leap of faith. Here the person plunges into a radical and personal commitment to God. It is this highly personal commitment that is the essence of true religion, according to Kierkegaard, not an embracing of doctrines or church involvement. Indeed, such a thrust may well put the person at odds with the prevailing religious structures, but that is really irrelevant. What counts is the purity and totality of the person's commitment. For Kierkegaard, this stage carries no assurance that one's life is truly moving in God's direction. All that one can do is submit himself to the leading of God's Spirit as he understands it. This lack of certainty brings fear and discomfort, but these unpleasant states must be accepted as part of being truly religious and fully human.

Kierkegaard tells of being taught to swim by his father. He would thrash about in the pool, hollering, "Look at me; look at me. I'm swimming!" all the while with one foot safely anchored to the bottom of the pool. He had taken no real leap. The true leap of faith means plunging into the unknown waters of serving God as we come to understand him, rather than following the "safe" cues of culturally approved morality. The leap is lonely and uncertain but made with abandon.

There is much for the Christian to embrace in Kierkegaard's sage observation that the modern person is not as free as life on the surface would indicate. Seeing humans as essentially spiritual, he notes that excessive freedom is not liberating but a form of bondage, particularly when life is explored materially, with God factored out of it. In addition, Kierkegaard felt that the sinful condition of humanity rendered it impossible for anyone to find fulfillment apart from God. The aesthetic stage falls short in large part because of its self-absorbed, Ellis-like outlook.

The ethical stage, though superficially more noble than the aesthetic stage, is doomed largely because it does not emanate from a deep-set spiritual base. It is the individual counterpart of the failure of many humanistic attempts at urban reform in the turbulent 1960s. Dr. William Leslie of Chicago's LaSalle Street Church summed up the plight of these efforts. "I remember that in the 1960s the only ministries in this [low-income Chicago] community, other than ours, were carried on by very liberal churches—churches who thought the key to salvation and meaning was social action. Now they are all gone. They burned out. Realizing they were never going to solve all the problems, and that the human standards of success they believed in would not be attained, they became depressed and gave up."[10] When a spiritual commitment is present in this stage, it is all too often attached to a self-justifying, self-validating salvation by works. Without a sense of grace and a desire to serve in gratitude, the ethical stage is just hard work that is less than fully satisfying.

Kierkegaard's overall belief that the angst of excessive freedom pushes the meaning-seeking person toward God has much merit.[11] Moreover, he offers us a version of losing one's life in order to find it. Letting go of the handrails and diving toward God becomes the path to true life. Regrettably, however, Kierkegaard's intense bias toward a truly individual pilgrimage obviates any sense of community. His spirituality is basically nonrelational, and it is here that his thinking misses the mark. Although the essence of Christianity is a personal relationship with Christ, this is buttressed by the spiritual nurture provided by a community of faith. In brief, the Christian life is about a vertical relationship with God and a horizontal one with other believers. Jesus was intensely relational, as evidenced in his life with the twelve apostles, particularly Peter, James, and John. Moreover, after Jesus' resurrection, the bonding among the disciples became much fuller, as they, along with Paul, dedicated their lives to founding relational Christian communities called churches. Without a community to nurture and guide those who take the leap of faith, there is only ambiguity. Kierkegaard leaves us with the specter of a host of spiritually unattached individuals leaping into the metaphysical unknown.

Another flaw in Kierkegaard's concepts is his notion of the unknown. The Bible—in promising peace to the true disciple of Christ, rather than the uncertainty and discomfort of the world—offers much more assurance than does Kierkegaard. Without the guidance of Scripture (and fellow believers), there can be none of the inner peace the Bible offers, but only a blind leap into dark uncertainty.

▸ Martin Buber

According to Martin Buber, there are two general areas that a person can know of another person. One area includes the objective traits that can be observed or related verbally. The other, however, is outside the scope of that which is objective and easily explainable. It is what Buber would term a transcendental zone of selfhood, a sacred essence of another, called the "Thou." When in a truly intimate relationship with another, my "I" (my own transcendent dimension of self) experiences the "Thou" of the other person, and through that connection, alienation and estrangement evaporate as a mystical intimacy is formed. The I-Thou relationship is contrasted with the more common I-It alliances, in which we relate to others as objects—as people in occupational roles, for example—rather than as sacred creations of God.[12]

The I-Thou relationship involves mutual surrender, a pulling down of walls enabling two spirits to find oneness. It is an in-the-moment experience. Once reflected upon, it is over. It becomes objectified, placed in the past and part of one's "me." The I-Thou encounter is experienced as special, transcendent, which is qualitatively different from the relational norm. It is Buber's contention that in every such experience, a person senses that the "Eternal Thou," Yahweh, is present. People truly become discernibly spiritual and eternal in these moments. God, then, is present in every I-Thou encounter.

Believers can find much of value in Buber's existential model. First, it affirms humans as spiritual, transcendent beings—truly persons—more than as psychological or rational entities. They are truly persons, spiritual in nature. No theory goes anywhere for the Christian thinker if it rules out the spiritual essence of humanity. Buber integrates the horizontal (relationships with other humans) with the vertical (relationship with God). There is much scriptural support for this. Christ underlined the importance of human reconciliation, stating that a person cannot even worship God honorably if anything is abridging his relationship with a fellow believer (Matt. 5:22–24). The apostle John put it rather boldly, stating that a person who claims to love God and has hate for another brother or sister is a liar (1 John 4:20). Moreover, all the emphasis on fellowship in the New Testament further reinforces this interpersonal synergy.

In addition, the I-Thou surrender, reconciliation, and wholeness is a model of the believer's relationship with God. It is perhaps as good a description as any of what heaven—eternal oneness with God—is. Even in our finite being, God is totally and perfectly connected to our Thou. The only way for one to relate authentically to God, then, is in the I-Thou dimension. As Creator, he is never an It. When people try to objectify God, they abandon the only valid relationship they can have with him. It is this intensely personal relationship that makes Christianity more than a philosophy, more than a set of doctrines.

One might question Buber's assertion that God is experienced in every I-Thou alliance. Many human linkages of ecstasy are better marked by the momentary absence of alienation and loneliness than by the unique presence of God. Nonetheless, there may well be a divine quality to any experience in which the ravages of alienation and estrangement that separate people evaporate in a Garden of Eden emotional experience. When souls touch in true emotional intimacy, spiritual in-the-image-of-God beings, however imperfect, connect.

▸ Paul Tillich

Philosopher-theologian Paul Tillich emphasized the personal nature of God, applying the I-Thou principal directly to the relationship the believer has with God. To Tillich, God cannot be described in objective terms but is to be encountered in the here and now of the I-Thou relationship. From this perspective, one can know all the right theology, immersing oneself in the best of systematic catechism, but be in the wrong relationship. In sum, salvation ceases to be driven by an intellectual commitment to doctrine and instead is driven by one's becoming one with God.[13]

Tillich defined sin as estrangement. He pointed out that humankind was originally at one with even the physical environment, described in the first two chapters of Genesis. Jesus modeled this same relationship in the New Testament, speaking to the winds and the waves, which then obeyed him. For Tillich, sin broke this harmony. Now, as science holds human consciousness in its grip, elements of nature—mountains, trees, and animals, for example—begin being perceived as objects. They are no longer a part of the humanness of humanity but are forces to be conquered in humanity's material quest of progress.[14]

Nature (natural revelation) is spiritual as well as physical. When nature is merely a set of physical forces to be manipulated by humans, there is a loss of relationship with God. Much of this manipulation has been justified by using God's words to Adam in Genesis 1:28, "Be fruitful and increase in number; fill the earth and subdue it. Rule over the fish of the sea and the birds of the air and over every living creature that moves on the ground." Instead of interpreting these words as humankind holding a responsible trusteeship, they have been used to legitimize exploitation, even destruction, of nature in pursuit of material convenience.

Indeed, the price of gouging nature has been steep. Belching, toxic smoke emerges from factories and vehicles, bodies of water have become marine cemeteries to the very fish created to swim in them, expansive acreage has been damaged by chemical treatments, all driven by a quest for materialism. The result is potential eco-catastrophe, in which humanity, once the seeming master of nature, is in peril of becoming the slave of its manipulation and exploitation.

For Tillich, this desire to control and manipulate—to engage in I-It alliances—does not end with nature; it extends to human relationships. Instead of intimacy, there is manipulation, control, and dehumanization. Tillich views this condition as one in which people are physically close, yet psychically and relationally estranged, creating a hellish circumstance.[15]

Tillich is fairly criticized for being soft on basic Christian doctrine. Nonetheless, his emphasis on an intimate relationship with God and the alienating nature of sin provides much insight into what is missing in contemporary life. Thus, the Christian scholar can do much with Tillich's concepts. They are applicable to sociology, psychology, economics, and political science, as well as philosophy and theology, providing a framework for understanding the root of the problems with which behavioral scientists deal. It is alienation and estrangement and the desire to control that is at the core of much racism, sexism, and classism. It is what pits husbands against wives, unions against management, and nations against nations. Although Tillich may not offer specific prescriptions for these social dilemmas, his thinking helps the scholar look in the right places when examining the problems.

▸▸ Contemporary Postmodern Philosophy

As with the other disciplines, philosophy is ever moving. We will therefore look at postmodern philosophy through the works of Michel Foucault.[16] (Another postmodernist, Jacques Derrida, will be discussed in the chapter on education.)

Foucault believes that what people accept as permanent truths about human nature changes over time. Influenced by Friedrich Nietzsche's belief that human behavior is driven by a desire for power and control and that the force of traditional values have eroded, Foucault looks at how changing societal rules alter what is believed to be true or false at different points in history.

Foucault takes the non-Enlightenment position that reason can be oppressive rather than liberating. In *Madness and Civilization,* the incarceration of the insane in asylums is viewed as a stigmatizing treatment of nonconformists, reminiscent of the treatment of lepers.[17] In short, madness was deemed a form of social failure and an object of condemnation, because it was regarded as the opposite of reason. The result was a triumph of conformity over the unusual, and the group over individual selfhood. In a similar vein, in *Discipline and Punish,* Foucault describes the prison system as moving away from physical torture toward mind control through the watchful activity of wardens.[18] Knowledge through surveillance becomes a form of social control and dehumanization. Foucault sees evidence of this prison perspective in modern society in the aggressive observation by police, psychiatrists, teachers, and others as they classify nonconforming individuals as dangerous, therefore robbing them of a sense of self.

Foucault applies this same thinking to sexuality, seeing a shift away from sex being considered primarily a bodily concern, as in the Middle Ages, to a current focus on the motivations behind sexual behavior. Sex then becomes categorized and controlled. While one may feel free to talk about sex, society is actually removing one's freedom, as it observes and directs sexual behavior.

In general, Foucault considers the search for reason and truth to be futile. He sees these concepts as too often used by the state to exert power over its citizens and by ordering behavior, shaping the self. In short, truth is what those in power can foist on the powerless.

A Christian studying Foucault will note that his postmodern dismissal of reason and truth as grounded realities takes away any central direction or purpose of life. It also removes any genuine morality, leaving humans without ultimate behavioral boundaries. People without purpose and morality can indeed be dangerous. What if they are the ones in power?

Defenders of Foucault might advance the perfectionist view of human nature, that humans—free of institutional controls—evolve into ever more loving creatures. This, of course, obviates the existence of sin, leaving one to wonder from where this "sinful" destructive desire for power comes. Though constraints on sexual behavior have loosened greatly since Foucault's death in 1968, his views of the state cohere well with that era's activism.

Despite his non-Christian premises, Foucault makes several thought-provoking contributions to Christian thought. His description of how the state and other powerful institutions shape the individual self—the identity—is a chilling reminder of the power of often invisible forces as described by Paul in

Ephesians 6:12. Moreover, as a society becomes increasingly secularized and hostile to matters of faith, its control is no longer aimed at restraining destructive behavior, but rather at subtly shaping the minds and identities of its citizens to adopt a worldview that is entirely naturalistic.

For the Christian student of philosophy, the call is to analyze—compare and contrast. Although the existentialists are hardly orthodox Christian philosophers, careful analysis of their work reveals glittering insights and indisputable grains of truth that enlighten the Christian scholar. Isolating these while comparing (and revising) other less Christian notions is both stimulating and effective in one's pursuit of truth. As for Foucault and the postmoderns, the call is more to contrast them with Christian notions. This, however, is also valuable, because the light of truth shines more brightly when seen against a background of darkness.

Notes

1. Glenn Tinder, "From the Ends of the Earth," in *Professors Who Believe,* ed. Paul M. Anderson (Downers Grove, IL: InterVarsity, 1998), 152.
2. Ibid.
3. Ibid., 153–54.
4. Fyodor Dostoyevsky, *The Gospel in Dostoyevsky* (Farmington, PA: Orbis, 1988), vii.
5. Tinder, "From the Ends of the Earth," in Anderson, *Professors Who Believe,* 153–54.
6. Keith El Yandell, "Christianity and a Conceptual Orientation," in Anderson, *Professors Who Believe,* 209.
7. Anthony Campolo, *A Reasonable Faith* (Waco, TX: Word, 1983), 89–92; Campolo cites a biographical sketch of Jean-Paul Sartre by Philip Thody, *Sartre* (New York: Charles Scribner's Sons, 1971).
8. Campolo, *A Reasonable Faith,* 103–7. Campolo refers to Søren Kierkegaard, *The Point of View for My Work as an Author,* trans. Walter Lowrie (New York: Harper Torchbooks, 1962); and Walter Lowrie, *A Short Life of Søren Kierkegaard* (New York: Anchor, 1961). Also note Søren Kierkegaard, *Concluding Unscientific Postscript,* trans. David F. Swenson and Walter Lowrie (Princeton, NJ: Princeton University Press, 1941), 96ff., 262ff.
9. Phillip C. McGraw, *Life Strategies* (New York: Hyperion, 1999).
10. William Leslie, quoted in David Claerbaut, *The Reluctant Defender* (Wheaton, IL: Tyndale, 1978), 222.
11. Campolo, *A Reasonable Faith,* 107.
12. Martin Buber, *I and Thou,* trans. Walter Kauffman (New York: Charles Scribner's Sons, 1970), quoted in Campolo, *A Reasonable Faith,* 172–75.
13. Campolo, *A Reasonable Faith,* 134–35. Campolo points the reader to *The Theology of Paul Tillich,* ed. Charles W. Kegley and Robert W. Bretall (New York: Macmillan, 1961) for an appraisal of Tillich's work.
14. Campolo, *A Reasonable Faith,* 168–69.
15. Ibid., 169.

16. There are a variety of websites that are helpful in summarizing and explicating the philosophy of Foucault. Two that were helpful here are "Michel Foucault," http://www.connect.net/ron/foucault.html (accessed October 29, 2003), and Chris Bates, "Foucault: A Snapshot," http://www.epistemelinks.com/Pers/Fouc/Pers.htm.

17. Michel Foucault, *Madness and Civilization,* trans. Richard Howard (New York: Vintage, 1961, 1988).

18. Foucault, *Discipline and Punish,* trans. A. M. Sheridan Smith (New York: Vintage, 1975, 1995).

19

ATHEIST VS. CHRISTIAN: FREUD AND LEWIS DEBATE THE GREAT PHILOSOPHICAL QUESTIONS

We will take a different twist here. Rather than review the theories of various philosophers, we will look at seminal questions of human existence from various philosophical points of view. That, however, is exactly what Armand Nicholi, Harvard psychiatrist, did in his delightful book *The Question of God*. Based on a class Nicholi taught, it pits the atheism of Sigmund Freud against the faith of C. S. Lewis. Technically, neither Freud nor Lewis is categorized primarily as a philosopher, Freud being viewed as the father of psychology and Lewis an estimable figure in English literature. Both debated and wrote extensively about the great metaphysical questions of human existence, and their points of view are representative of atheist and Christian positions in general.

▸▸ God

The first issue involves the existence of God.[1] Freud was preoccupied with the concept of God, dividing people into two categories: believers and unbelievers. He claimed his worldview was scientific because he believed all knowledge emerged from research and research was his base. There is a crack in Freud's argument, however. The claim that *all* knowledge comes from research is itself philosophical, denying all other sources, including, of course, revelation.[2] Freud held that any belief in the divine was an illusion rooted in deep-seated wishful thinking. In short, the belief in God provides comfort and so turns into faith.[3] God as wish-fulfillment was and is a common view among atheists. Freud believed that an individual's belief in the divine has its roots in childhood, with God being a projection of the grandiose father image. Moreover, because human fathers are often both loved and feared—the protector and the disciplinarian— Freud thought believers were ambivalent toward God.

Freud's notion that humans created God in their own (father) image turns the Genesis message upside down. Freud's own biography provides insight into his thinking. His father, a grandfather before Freud was born, fell on hard financial times such that Freud, an accomplished scholar, considered him a failure. Freud's negative feelings were intensified upon discovering that his father did not defend himself vigorously when confronted with bullying anti-Semitic behavior. (Tragically, Freud himself was a lifelong victim of anti-Semitism, which understandably soured him toward Christianity.) Finally, his father was a religious Jew, one who read Scripture, which led Freud to associate him with religiosity in general.

There were inconsistencies in Freud's approach. Freud may have been protesting too much. His personal letters include many quotations from the Bible, even phrases like "if God so wills," "God's grace," "God's judgment," and "after the resurrection." For someone who believed a slip of the tongue (the Freudian slip) had meaning, this is more than puzzling.[4]

Nevertheless, Freud's public stance was unbending and merciless in its scorn for believers. Freud held that believers lacked intelligence, suffering from a "universal obsessional neurosis." Similar to Auguste Comte's positivist stage, Freud thought that the human race would evolve to a level at which the concept of God would disappear. When a physician friend described his conversion, Freud called it a hallucinatory psychosis. An intelligent believer was an oxymoron, he believed, resolving the dissonance created by his physician friend by labeling such people delusional.

Lewis also had a troubled relationship with his father and spent his early adult life committed to atheism. He addressed Freud's wish-fulfillment charge by stating that the Christian worldview, though comforting, begins in dismay. It begins with the conviction that there is a universal moral law, that we are unable to live up to it fully, and thus are out of relationship with the divine. Moreover, Lewis claimed that one cannot find comfort by searching for it. Instead, one must pursue truth, out of which comfort may come. Lewis also acknowledges there is pain in belief, arising from having to cede our own stubborn wills back to the God who made us. This point is critical. Belief may not be difficult, but committing one's life to faith is.

As for Freud's notion of ambivalence, Lewis strongly desired for God not to exist. In Lewis's days as an atheist, God represented interference, a violation of Lewis's wish to be left alone. To conform his flawed human will to that of a perfect creator was not an attractive thought. Lewis also contended that wishing for something may be evidence for its very existence. "Creatures are not born with desires," he says, "unless satisfaction for those desires exists. A baby feels hunger: well, there is such a thing as food. A duckling wants to swim: well, there is such a thing as water. Men feel sexual desire: well, there is such a thing as sex."[5] In time, Lewis desired what he called "joy," defining it as a desire for a relationship with his Creator. Moreover, Lewis suggests that all humans have a desire for a relationship with their Creator and life beyond the present one.

The orientation to believe—have faith—is not aberrant to human neurological functioning. In the spirit of Lewis, Nicholi states that recent neuroscientific research indicates that the human brain is "hardwired" (genetically programmed) for belief.[6]

Lewis extends his if-you-desire-it-it-must-exist premise, claiming, "If I find in myself a desire which no experience in this world can satisfy, the most probable explanation is that I was made for another world."[7] Accordingly, he stated that life includes a longing for ecstasy that remains just beyond grasp. For the believer, there will come the day of attainment. Freud had a similar desire, and used the word *Sehnsucht,* the same word Lewis used in describing it. He was haunted throughout life by a longing to walk in the woods with his father, as they did when Freud was a child. He said he was never free from the desire for the beautiful woods near his childhood home.

Freud never let go of his preoccupation with the existence of God. His final book was entitled *Moses and Monotheism.* Why could he not put the issue to rest? asks Nicholi rhetorically. Lewis's answer would likely be that God cannot be explained away and the hunger for relationship with him is never quenched. It is basic to human nature. Moreover, as with naturalists who so vehemently oppose believers in academe, Freud's philosophical treatises lack the objective tone of the clinical psychiatrist. "Instead," writes Nicholi, "they exhibit an intense, emotional, argumentative and, at times, desperate and pleading tone."[8]

In addition, Freud's views were contradictory. While scorning believers as lacking intellect, he acknowledged that many of the greatest minds in human history were believers. Among the intellects he most revered were Isaac Newton, Oskar Pfister (a Swiss pastor and fellow psychoanalyst), and St. Paul, who he claimed held a singular place in all of history.

Lewis took a positive view regarding the IQ of believers. Advancing the notion that Christians, like scientists, see past the visible in search of deeper realities, he believed the Christian worldview actually sharpens the intellect. Citing John Bunyan (author of *The Pilgrim's Progress*) as an uneducated believer who wrote "a book that has astonished the world," Lewis's position affirms the activity of the Holy Spirit as a guide to wisdom and insight.[9]

Though disagreeing with Freud's atheism, Lewis did not discount the validity of much of Freud's psychoanalytic thinking, concluding that while he was indeed a clinical specialist in working with neurotics, he was an amateur in philosophy. Pfister, Freud's friendly ideological foe, noted that Freud had seen only the unhealthiest forms of faith in his personal life and as a clinician, which distorted his views. "Our difference," Pfister wrote to Freud, "derives chiefly from the fact that you grew up in proximity to pathological forms of religion and regard these as 'religion.'"[10]

▶▶ Good and Evil—A Universal Moral Law?

Morality is another divisive philosophical issue.[11] Holding to the naturalist position that all knowledge emerged from the scientific method, Freud believed one's sense of right and wrong came from what one's parents taught. He asserted that, beginning at about age five, a child internalizes part of his parents' moral directives. These form the basis of the conscience, and coupled with a system of rewards and punishments cohering with the religion one is taught, they set in a deeper religious orientation. Freud maintains that religion is learned, that there is no inherent *sensus divinitatis* (sense of the divine) within humanity. Religion is merely the cultural transmission of delusional thinking from generation to generation. Therefore, moral law is an entirely human invention and not always healthy. It produces guilt, which Freud frequently associated with neurosis—interference with normal functioning. He supported this assertion with his findings that badly depressed patients often became better after the severity of their superego (which houses the conscience) was relaxed.

Furthermore, Freud contended that a universal moral law is in conflict with reason. Ethics, he believed, are not based on some divine imperative, but rather on what humans find to be the most expedient for living together. Freud believed that social order should be based on an enlightened self-interest. Pushing the matter further, Freud claimed that if a God had provided a moral law, he did a very poor job of it, given the atrocities of human behavior.

Continuing to juxtapose logic and faith, Freud believed the answer to life's human cruelties lay in the imposition of reason. In a letter to Albert Einstein on protecting humanity against war, Freud wrote, "The ideal condition of things would of course be a community of men who had subordinated their intellectual life to the dictatorship of reason."[12] Freud believed that whatever was moral was really only that which is self-evident. Education equaled civilization because education is based on reason. Sadly, Freud discovered that even the knowledge of psychoanalysis did not seem to make his fellow practitioners any more moral than other professionals.

Lewis offered many counters to Freud's views. He accorded science great respect in its capacity to report things as they are but felt science stops at the "why" of things and whether there is any Intelligence behind the "that" of reality. Lewis, who saw the moral law as a force from within, pointed to two sources indicating a creator. The first is the universe itself, what Calvinists call natural revelation. The second is the moral law scorched into our minds. In the case of the latter, Lewis joined forces with the German philosopher Immanuel Kant, who also cited a moral law from within the human spirit. Perhaps both had in mind the words of Jeremiah 31:33: "I will put my law in their minds and write it on their hearts."[13]

Although agreeing that the formative influence of parents is powerful, Lewis felt this does not make morality a human invention, stating that one's parents no more create the moral law they impart than they do the multiplication tables they teach. He conceded that there are cultural conventions but stated that genuine morality is neither cultural nor changing. He notes the similarity in basic moral law, stretching across cultures, citing the prohibitions against running away in battle, deceiving others, and exhibiting selfishness as examples. Pointing to Nazism in Germany, Lewis asks, "What was the sense in saying the enemy were in the wrong, unless Right is a real thing which the Nazis at bottom knew as well as we did and ought to have practiced?"[14] To Lewis, a God-ordained moral law was as reasonable as Freud's claim that it was not.

Lewis noted that almost all human beings not only embrace a morality but also sense that they do not adhere to it consistently. As for varying levels of morality, Lewis believed that although moral law is unchanging, cultural or personal sensitivity to it may differ in degree. For Lewis, Nazi Germany is an example of a lowered cultural sensitivity, his own pre-Christian life a personal one. "When I first came to the University," he writes, "I was as nearly without a moral conscience as a boy could be. Some faint distaste for cruelty and for meanness about money was my utmost reach—of chastity, truthfulness, and self-sacrifice I thought as a baboon thinks of classical music."[15] To the extent that a culture or person has a deadened moral sensitivity, it will reject the need for atonement and redemption, by Lewis's thinking. Hence, cultural and moral relativity are pernicious. "Who will take medicine," he asks, "unless he knows he is in the grip of disease? Moral relativity is the enemy we have to overcome before we tackle Atheism."[16]

As for Freud's argument for reason and the self-evident nature of morality, Lewis agreed, but in an interesting way. He believed that it is the universal moral force from within that makes moral principles rational. It is because of this logical self-evidence that we tell people to "be reasonable" when wishing them to act justly. While Freud, amid his atheism, saw himself as a moral man, for Lewis this was not evidence of a dictatorship of reason but the rule of pride.

Freud witnessed the debilitating aspects of guilt and thus took a negative view of a morally based sense of right and wrong. Lewis looked at the matter in terms of spiritual awareness and sensitivity. "A moderately bad man knows he is not very good: a thoroughly bad man thinks he is all right. . . . Good people know about both good and evil: bad people do not know about either."[17] Moreover, giving in to bad impulses then brings confusion and fog, while even an attempt at virtue brings light.

Despite his protestations, Freud was perplexed by his own sense of morality. Biographer Ernest Jones wrote, "Freud himself was constantly puzzled by this very problem—a moral attitude was so deeply implanted as to seem part of his original nature. He never had any doubt about the right course of conduct."[18] In a letter to Dr. James Jackson Putnam, he admitted that he often did the right thing when it was not in his self-interest to do so, something that might leave the impression that a sense of right and wrong may well be innate.

▸▸ Pain

To live is to suffer, and Freud and Lewis both addressed the problem of pain, a constant companion in each of their lives.[19] Freud lost his nanny to death at three and later lost a daughter and a beloved grandson. Throughout his life, Freud suffered from some of the most severe forms of anti-Semitism, much of which came from Roman Catholics in heavily Catholic Vienna. Beyond that, he suffered from bouts of depression and various phobias and spent the last sixteen years of his life with a painful cancer of the palate. Amid this Job-like existence, Freud implored his pastor friend Pfister to explain how one could reconcile all this pain with a universal moral order. Never resolving the issue, Freud claimed that were he ever to confront God, he would have more with which to charge God than God would for him. His view reminds me of a client I once had in therapy. "If God is my father," she said ruefully, "then he is a child abuser."

Freud was forever in search of the origins of pain and suffering. He placed no credence in a God blessing those who followed his divine will. Such thinking was outside the bounds of credulity for Freud. Natural disasters in particular, he noted, make no distinction between the believer and the nonbeliever; moreover, virtuous people usually came out on the losing end of important situations. His rejection of a loving God led Freud to conclude that the Devil was an invention of humanity on which to blame suffering, taking God off the metaphysical hook.

Of note is that Freud was much taken with the concept of the Devil. On the last day of Freud's life, when he died of euthanasia, Freud read Balzac's *Fatal Skin*, in which the protagonist makes a pact with the Devil. Freud's favorite book was John Milton's *Paradise Lost*. In a letter to his fiancée, he quoted not from God, but from the Devil. He often referred to the Devil allegorically, but also in quotes from other great literature, as he did in a letter to colleague Carl Jung. Nevertheless, he buried his view of the Devil in a psychological explanation, one that attributed the positive side of religious ambivalence to God and the negative side to the Devil.

Lewis lost his mother early in life, a traumatic event matched decades later by the death of his wife. He was injured as a youth of nineteen in World War I and witnessed unspeakable cruelty and violence in the military theater. Depression and loneliness plagued him as it did Freud. Grief for Lewis was so enveloping, it felt as if he were drunk. All of this led him to ask the question, Where is God? He concluded that in happiness one feels little need of God, while in pain one senses only his absence. "But go to Him when your need is desperate," he wrote with great impact, "when all other help is vain, and what do you find? A door slammed in your face and a sound bolting and double bolting on the inside."[20] Knowing that Christ felt forsaken by God on the cross was of little comfort for Lewis.

Looking in many places for meaning, Lewis conceived of God as a surgeon, bringing great pain for a greater good. That could be the only reason a loving God would even permit life's tortures. Eventually, Lewis realized he may have impeded his ability to receive comfort through his intense search for meaning. In time, Lewis experienced God's presence like that of a dawn on a warm day. There was no sudden revelation or relief, merely a gradual sense of healing.

Aware that he had been focusing too much on himself and not enough on God, Lewis did not see suffering as good. "What is good in any painful experience is, for the sufferer, his submission to the will of God, and for the spectators, the compassion aroused and the acts of mercy to which it leads."[21] In short, God in his complex way, made good out of evil and suffering. As for the existence of evil, Lewis saw the universe as being partly under the control of Satan. He noted the frequency with which the New Testament referred to the powers of darkness—the force behind sin, death, and disease—as evidence.

Lewis understood Freud's rage. As an atheist in early adulthood, Lewis also could not square cruelty and injustice with a loving, all-powerful God. Nevertheless, the very notion of justice and injustice presupposed for him an awareness of the existence of an ultimate good—God. That pain does not perfectly fit an intellectual system was something Lewis learned to accept. Still he did not deny the basic intellectual problem of pain, stating that a good God would want his creatures to be happy; an almighty God would be able to do so. That his creatures are not happy raises the question of whether God is either not good or not almighty.

This premise for Lewis is not sensible. God, he believed, could do all things that are *intrinsically* possible. Some things, however, are not intrinsically possible. For example, if humans have free will and nature runs on a fixed, neutral path, it is not possible for there not to be evil or suffering. To exclude those possibilities in the context of nature and free will is to deny life itself. In addition, Lewis did not believe that love and kindness were synonymous. Love involves perfecting that which can at times be painful. Kindness does not. Although kindness may keep one from sending his child to the dentist because of the pain involved, such an act would not be loving. God is about altering the imperfections within us to bring us to a better state—a process that may involve pain. Lewis even reconfigured the definition of happiness. He believed that true unhappiness comes from efforts to find happiness outside of God. "And out of that hopeless attempt," he writes, "has come nearly all that we call human history—money, poverty, ambition, war, prostitution, classes, empires, slavery—the long terrible story of man trying to find something other than God which will make him happy."[22]

Freud and Lewis agreed that the greatest pain and the greatest suffering are inflicted by humans on one another. For Lewis, this was not a mysterious matter. With free will, humans can choose their actions, and given humankind's fallen nature, often those choices are evil and destructive. In any case, he believed that pain must be attended to. For Lewis, God whispers to us in our pleasure but shouts to us in our pain. In pain, he makes clear our need for him.

▸▸ Death

If, as Socrates stated, "The true philosopher is always pursuing death and dying," then Freud and Lewis were true philosophers.[23] Freud dated his awareness of death back to the age of two, when his brother, Julius, died. Freud's mother explained to him that people are made of earth and that upon death they return to earth. In a paper he wrote, Freud offered a striking insight, noting that death does not exist in our unconscious mind. "Our unconscious then does not believe in its own death; it behaves as if it were immortal."[24] As for his public position, Freud stated that the secret to enduring life was to prepare oneself for death. Freud, however, was unprepared. He was obsessive, superstitious, and fearful of death.

At thirty-eight, Freud wrote that he would likely suffer for another four to eight years before dying from a heart attack. At fifty-three, he visited William James in the United States. He was impressed at the fearlessness with which the ill James confronted his own death. Believing that his time was running out, Freud did not enjoy birthdays; he found them depressing. At sixty-six, he wrote to a friend of sixty, "Now you too have reached your sixtieth birthday, while I, six years older, am approaching the limit of life and may soon expect to see the end of the fifth act of this rather incomprehensible and not always amusing comedy."[25]

In short, Freud was constantly preoccupied with life's end and consistently predicted at what age he would die. Biographer Jones wrote: "There were the repeated attacks of what is called 'Todesangst' (dread of death). He hated growing old even as early as his forties, and as he did so, the thoughts of death became increasingly clamorous. He once said he thought of it every day of his life, which is certainly unusual."[26] According to Freud's outlook, people accepted a religious worldview because they feared death and desired permanence.

The deaths of others—his father, his beloved daughter Sophie, and her son—left Freud devastated, helpless, and unable to resolve the matter of death. Full of fear, depression, and physical pain, he told his physician, Max Schnur, "You promised me then not to forsake me when my time comes. Now it's nothing but torture and makes no sense anymore."[27] Wanting to know when he would die, Freud had Schnur inject him with a lethal dose of morphine.

Paradoxically, during Lewis's years as an atheist, death was not a problem. Christianity was worse. "The horror of the Christian universe," he wrote, "was that it had no door marked *Exit*."[28] At least as an atheist, death marked the end of an unhappy existence. It was the exit door. Once becoming a Christian, Lewis viewed death from two angles. It was both the result of the Fall and the only way to overcome the effects of the Fall. Death, then, was a matter of ambivalence—its very existence a victory for Satan, but also the means by which Christ conquered sin. Unlike Freud, Lewis enjoyed getting older.

The most difficult death for Lewis was that of his wife, Joy Davidman, who died from cancer. He wondered if God might be simply "The Cosmic Sadist, the spiteful imbecile."[29] Accepting her loss was incredibly difficult. "I look up at the night sky," he writes. "Is there anything more certain than that in all those vast times and spaces, if I were allowed to search them, I should nowhere find her face, her voice, her touch? She died. She is dead. Is the word so difficult to learn?"[30]

Lewis eventually saw loss as part of the life process. Bereavement would follow marriage, as marriage did courtship. As for one's own death, Lewis believed people handled it in one of three ways. They either desired it, lived in fear of it, or ignored it. The latter, he believed, was the most uncomfortable.

For Lewis, death was a form of deliverance, the dropping off of the weakened body of pain for a spiritual life eternal. He saw better things ahead than one might leave behind. After recovering from a serious heart attack, Lewis wrote this to a friend: "Tho' I am by no means unhappy I can't help feeling it was rather a pity I did revive in July. I mean, having glided so painlessly up to the gate it seems hard to have it shut in one's face and know that the whole process must some day be gone through again.... Poor Lazarus!"[31]

Lewis spent his last days happily rereading his favorite books. The basis of his peace lay in his faith. "If we really believe what we say we believe—if we really think that home is elsewhere and that this life is a 'wandering to find home,' why should we not look forward to the arrival?"[32]

On November 22, 1963, a fateful day in American history, a cheerful Lewis died an hour and a half after his four o'clock tea.

Notes

1. Armand M. Nicholi Jr., *The Question of God* (New York: Free Press, 2002), 36–56.
2. Ibid., 37.
3. Ibid., 41; Sigmund Freud, "The Future of an Illusion," in *The Standard Edition of the Complete Psychological Works,* vol. 21 (London: Hogarth, 1962), 30, 33.
4. Nicholi, *The Question of God,* 51.
5. C. S. Lewis, *Mere Christianity* (San Francisco: HarperSanFranciso, 2001), bk. 3, chap. 10, quoted in Nicholi, *The Question of God,* 46.
6. Nicholi, *The Question of God,* 46.
7. Lewis, *Mere Christianity,* bk. 3, chap. 10, quoted in Nicholi, *The Question of God,* 47.
8. Nicholi, *The Question of God,* 53.
9. Ibid., 54.
10. Freud, *Psychoanalysis and Faith* (New York: Basic, 1963), 122, quoted in Nicholi, *The Question of God,* 56.
11. Nicholi, *The Question of God,* 57–75.
12. Albert Einstein and Sigmund Freud, "Why War," in *The Standard Edition of the Complete Psychological Works,* 22: 213, quoted in Nicholi, *The Question of God,* 64.
13. Nicholi, *The Question of God,* 59.
14. Lewis, *Mere Christianity,* bk. 1, chap. 1, quoted in Nicholi, *The Question of God,* 62.
15. C. S. Lewis, *The Problem of Pain* (San Francisco: HarperSanFrancisco, 2001), 37–40, quoted in Nicholi, *The Question of God,* 62–63.
16. C. S. Lewis, *The Latin Letters of C. S. Lewis* (Chicago: St. Augustine, 1998), 89–91, quoted in Nicholi, *The Question of God,* 73.
17. Lewis, *Mere Christianity,* bk. 3, chap. 5, quoted in Nicholi, *The Question of God,* 74.

18. Ernest Jones, *The Life and Work of Sigmund Freud*, vol. 2 (New York: Basic, 1981), 416, quoted in Nicholi, *The Question of God*, 74–75.

19. Nicholi, *The Question of God*, 187–215.

20. C. S. Lewis, *A Grief Observed* (San Francisco: HarperSanFrancisco, 2001), 4–5, quoted in Nicholi, *The Question of God*, 125.

21. Lewis, *The Problem of Pain*, 110–11, quoted in Nicholi, *The Question of God*, 203.

22. Ibid., 47.

23. Nicholi, *The Question of God*, 216–39.

24. Sigmund Freud, "Thoughts for the Times on War and Death," in *The Standard Edition of the Complete Psychological Works*, 14: 289, quoted in Nicholi, *The Question of God*, 218.

25. Sigmund Freud, *Letters of Sigmund Freud* (New York: Dover, 1992), 339, quoted in Nicholi, *The Question of God*, 219.

26. Jones, *The Life and Work of Sigmund Freud*, vol. 3, 279, quoted in Nicholi, *The Question of God*, 221.

27. Nicholi, *The Question of God*, 229–30.

28. Ibid., 222.

29. Ibid., 234.

30. Ibid., 235.

31. Ibid., 236–37.

32. C. S. Lewis, *Letters to an American Lady* (Grand Rapids: Eerdmans, 1986), 80–81, quoted in Nicholi, *The Question of God*, 239.

20

EDUCATION:
THE BATTLEGROUND

his entire book is about education. It is about faith and *learning*—which, in the believer's view of education, are actually indistinguishable elements. Historical and philosophical foundations of education are woven into nearly every page. We are regularly critiquing the mainline university's educational model while offering Christian alternatives for the reader to consider. Education is the battleground on which the war for the mind is waged.

There are, however, a few additional points to be made with respect to education.

▸▸ Education—Where Secularism and Christianity Collide

The most important statement to be made in discussing education is that true education is Christian. "To be sure," writes Chiareli, "a novel is best explained by its author. Similarly, a painting can best be interpreted by its artist. In the same way, I believe that our human essence is best defined and illumined to us by our Creator."[1] This suggests that there is a far greater gap between secular and Christian education than many people acknowledge.

This difference is often trivialized. For example, many secularists—and unfortunately, some believers—feel there are really only two things that separate them from the Christian scholar. First, is there a God up there? And second, is there life after death? Because there is no certain proof for the existence of God and he is "up there"—out of immediate view—the first question is for them an abstraction. Moreover, because the afterlife is just that, after this life, it is irrelevant to current scholarship. In sum, it appears there really is no practical difference at all.[2]

Although Christianity and secularism collide at almost every point in life, that their clash is especially sharp in the institution of education is hardly surprising. "This is bound to be the case—because education is the nurturing of human beings to fully human living," says Blamires.[3] *Webster's Student Dictionary* states that to *nurture* is to protect and bring up carefully. It defines an *educated person* as one who is cultivated.[4] If we put those two thoughts together, we have the essence of education at every level: it is to cultivate a person in a careful and protective fashion. From a human perspective, there are few endeavors more important than that, and therefore, few over which people of differing life views will do more intense and emotional battle.

▸▸ The Teacher

It is important to return briefly to the role of the teacher, because almost without exception, she is central to the educational process. Rarely will a person not be able to name his or her favorite and least favorite teachers, even if the experience with those teachers are more than a half century past. It is difficult to argue then with Thomas Rosebrough when he writes, "I believe that the process—the *how* of learning—is at least as important as the disciplinary assumptions—the *what* of learning."[5] He encourages the Christian teacher to take seriously the fruits of the Spirit, outlined by Paul (Gal. 5:22–23), as they speak to the process of learning.

Most of us appreciated our favorite teachers more for who they were than for what they taught. Our favorites nurtured us, often in a Christlike way (even if they weren't believers). For years, I believed my favorite professor—a Christian who distinguished himself at an Ivy League university—attained that status in my eyes because of his brilliance, scholarship, and effective communication skills. On further reflection, I must confess it was not his brilliance, scholarship, or communication skills that endear him to me. It was his modeling of the Christian life, his kind, caring, and respectful manner (similar to that advocated by Keener and Elzinga in chapter 13).

Although teachers do vary in their interpersonal skills, failure to teach with what is perceived to be a conscientious, Christlike style can remove the impact of any other professorial effort to impart a Christian perspective. I recall studying under a professor in a Christian institution of higher education who ruled his class with fear. An estimable scholar and ordained minister who went on to teach in a reputable seminary, the professor made it his practice to cite audibly the poorest performers as he handed out the test results. To this day, I can recall nothing of what he taught, but much of how poorly I thought of him. There were others as well, who are better remembered for their pompousness than for the quality of their teaching. Rosebrough urges Christian teachers to examine their worldviews thoroughly. The clearer and more developed the Christian teacher's worldview—one that includes her treatment of and relationship with her students—the more effective she will be, no matter the educational environment.[6]

▸▸ Instrumentalism—A Critique

Among the many educational models, few invite Christian critique more than that of John Dewey's instrumentalism.[7] Dewey believed education should be rooted in experience. By experience, he did not mean a carefully controlled laboratory-like exercise, but rather the basic reality of daily living. Dewey contended that learning takes place in response to problems, because they generate problem-solving hypotheses. Through the application of these hypotheses comes growth. Because one regularly confronts problems, simply by living, Dewey reasoned that the more education immerses the learner in experience, the more she will learn.

He believed that nothing is really permanent or absolute. Learning is ongoing, because it is situational and situations always change. For Dewey, learning is nearly synonymous with adaptation. Although the learner may build up a fund of experience from which to draw in confronting problems, the fund is limited because old applications do not consistently fit new situations and because she cannot draw from any universal values or truths. These do not exist.

Dewey's philosophy is a relative of naturalism. It is natural selection applied to learning. Nonetheless, there is much to be said for reality-based, experience-oriented education. I have taught in several urban institutes that have used this method with great success. A close look at Dewey's thinking, however, should encourage the Christian scholar who values experiential education to examine—as we have urged—her own pet academic theories in terms of their commitment to fixed truths and eternal values.[8]

Philosopher Arthur Holmes challenges "Deweyism," stating that education must be aimed at developing responsible people. Responsible action occurs in the context of reflective thinking and sound values. Experiential education, then, is most effective *after* one is well grounded in a discipline, fully aware of the ethical bases of whatever it is one is studying. Holmes writes, "Experience, to be fully educational, needs historical, theoretical, scientific, and ethical input and scrutiny."[9] To be valuable, experience must occur within a context, one that enables the learner to interpret the experience accurately. Outside of a grounded context, the learner becomes a mere reactor to a series of transitory situations, rather than a developing and responsible person.

There are still other problems with Dewey's philosophy. Once the learner excises theory and values from a learning situation, she is left with little more than empiricism. Even empirical observation is not truly pure. As in the case of phlogiston theory in chemistry, for example, it involves selectivity and is influenced by theoretical assumptions and personal biases. "This," Holmes states, "has become evident in the history of science: and if experience is not enough for science, how can it be enough for education?"[10] Holmes expresses the problem syllogistically.

> Experience alone is not understanding.
> Education requires understanding.
> Therefore, experience alone is not education.[11]

Taking the first premise, Immanuel Kant asserted that experience is not self-interpreting. Here we return to context. Our experience is interpreted—given meaning—in the context of our worldview. Therefore, a Christian will likely interpret interpersonal relationships differently from an atheist. For the Christian, understanding occurs against the backdrop of unchanging truths.[12]

The second premise implies that education is more than training—developing robotic responses to a set of circumstances. It is also not indoctrination—the imposition of information on the will of the learner. In both instances, the learner is being directed rather than taught to make thoughtful choices on the basis of her knowledge. To be taught in the truest sense of the term, she must *understand* truth and value, interpret (understand or comprehend) a situation competently, and apply truth and value to that situation.[13]

▸▸ Summerhill

More radical than Dewey's instrumentalism is A. S. Neill's Summerhill concept. Neill was born in Scotland in 1883, attended Edinburgh University, and was a patient of psychoanalysis. Over time he developed ideas emphasizing freedom for children. In 1921, he founded a school in Hellerau, a suburb of Desden, but eventually became disillusioned with what he felt were excessive rules inhibiting the students' development. With his first wife's assistance, Neill moved the school to a Catholic region in Austria, where his radical, non-Christian ideas received much resistance from the locals. He moved twice more until settling the school in its present location in Leiston, Suffolk County, England, where he ran the school until his death in 1973.

Summerhill's four basic aims remain largely unchanged. These aims could be summarized as:

1. To allow children freedom to grow emotionally;
2. To give children power over their lives;

3. To give children the time to develop naturally;
4. To create a happier childhood by removing fear and coercion by adults.[14]

The philosophical cornerstone of the Summerhill boarding school is freedom from fear. "The absence of fear," said Neill, "is the finest thing that can happen to a child."[15] One gains a clue as to the likely genesis of the founder's belief in discovering that Neill's father was a stern schoolmaster in Scotland, renowned for using corporal punishment as a means of control.

Student-centered to the extreme, everything at Summerhill flows from this doctrine of freedom. Students—age five to seventeen—are allowed to play as much as they wish; class attendance is not compulsory, and lessons are optional. There is ample room for experimentation, mistakes, and second chances. Students create the school's rules and policies, and all members of the community—adults and students—are regarded as equal. Despite the seemingly free-wheeling nature of Summerhill, there are rules—230 of them for the 65 resident students. All rules, however, are voted upon democratically and are not based in any morality, but rather on the premise that one's freedom ends when it interferes with the freedom of a fellow member of the community.

Summerhill is not concerned about learning pace. Students, they believe, will choose to learn as they see its value. Moreover, healthy learning is fun and natural, so it will come in time. Such an approach is thought to foster independence and self-confidence. Summerhill also believes that students can become mature and responsible without being taught moral values. Because the school affirms children's innate goodness, teaching moral values is scoffed at as having no greater effect than teaching one to like the taste of cheese.

Christian students often have little difficulty in critiquing Summerhill's philosophy, particularly as it relates to a perfectionist view of human nature and the totally humanistic dismissal of morality. They run into a major intellectual barricade because of Summerhill's fame and apparent success. The key word here is *apparent*. A 1999 governmental inspection by the Office for Standards in Education found the school failing to provide an adequate education for its students.[16] Moreover, Summerhill's deficiencies had been cited consistently for nearly a decade.

The report's main critique centered on Summerhill's core value, freedom. Finding the students well-behaved but rather foulmouthed, the report noted that while some students advanced acceptably, others were left to drift behind academically. The problem lay in a lack of attendance. The report suggested that school was confusing educational liberty with the right not to be taught, while the students were mistaking idleness for personal liberty.

The problems with Summerhill, from a Christian perspective, are obvious. The challenge for the Christian scholar is not, I believe, in citing these obvious variances from Christian thinking. It is precisely the opposite. It is to rein in one's inclination to dismiss Summerhill in its entirety, failing to see its strengths in the process. For example, Summerhill's focus on individual autonomy not only reinforces the Christian notion of free will but also the concept of personal responsibility. The Summerhill student not only lives with the consequences of her actions, but grace is extended at Summerhill, as mistakes are not magnified and second chances are the norm. In 1 John 4:18 we read that perfect love expunges all fear. Love at Summerhill is not of a divine nature, but its value on freedom from fear has merit. Furthermore, the affirmation of the individual worth of each student comports well with the Christian belief that all humans have value and are created in the image of God. The emphasis on natural growth, freedom from coercion, and the equality of every community member also squares with much Christian thinking.

▸▸ The Postmodern View of Jacques Derrida

Born in 1930, Jacques Derrida has become arguably the most important philosopher of his time.[17] He is best known for his deconstructionist view of language and meaning, and because it is central to the learning process, Derrida is regarded by many as an educational philosopher.

There is no simple way to summarize Derrida's deconstruction thinking. In fact, students have claimed they understand no more than ten percent of the material in his lectures. Deconstruction stands in opposition to structuralism, which has long been the prevailing paradigm in the study of language, holding that underlying all forms of communication are structures — rules and relationships that turn words into language.

To deconstruct is to deny a single meaning as superior and to prove that words can only be known in relation to their opposites. This is what Derrida does with various texts to show how they do not succeed in making the points they appear to be making. Much of Derrida's focus is on language and how, rather than conveying coherent truth, the language of writers invariably contradicts itself. As an example, he points to Hemingway's assertion that bullfighting is not sport but a tragedy, all the while using analogies from American sport to describe the activity. Derrida also takes issue with Plato's claim that oral discourse is superior to writing because speech "is written on the soul of the listener." That Plato used the word *written* as his pivotal metaphor shows, according to Derrida, Plato's failure to make the very distinction he is attempting to make.

In a similar vein, Derrida says, "Oh, my friends, there is no friend," to indicate that one really cannot communicate fully and with total clarity with anyone—even one's own self. Moreover, he points to the contradictions inherent in our concept of friendship—loving within limits, caring yet competitive, connectedness yet separation.

Derrida regularly examines writings, emphasizing the importance of what does not belong—the marginal. He uncovers ambiguities, thought fragments, and contradictions within the footnotes, margins, parentheses, and prefaces of works. Although he regularly asserts that nothing exists outside the text—making the life of the author irrelevant—Derrida's focus on marginality may betray his own life experience, that of growing up as a Jew enduring anti-Semitism in Algeria. Derrida does see himself as marginal. Even as an adult, he is both an esteemed professor and a man who is destroying norms of structuralist thought.

For Derrida, communication is not transparent. Everything is open to interpretation, carrying with it a point of view—a context. Derrida's deconstruction resists the notion that the world is simple, able to be known with certainty. Rather, it is complex and contradictory. For Derrida, there is no one answer, no ultimate truth, no single reality. Rather, the world can be viewed from a variety of different—multicultural—perspectives. He contends that were the world simple, political and ethical decisions would be so obvious as to engender little or no interest.

Derrida has his critics among secular as well as Christian scholars, who affirm the importance of finding truth. Though accused of being a nihilist, he is more of a multiculturalist—one who finds a multiplicity of often irreconcilable meanings depending on the context. In any case, central to his thinking is the postmodern belief that there simply is no truth. Although there is value in looking beyond the obvious and questioning face-value statements, with no "In the beginning God . . . ," there is also danger at the extremes for Derrida and his ilk. Without such a grounded belief, much scholarship moves away from finding simple, immutable truth toward endless, confusing strands of insight that do not inform, much less educate.

Derrida admits to being obsessed with the thought of death, which filled him with anxiety. Perhaps that is because there is an undeniable simplicity about it. We are all destined to die once, says the writer of Hebrews (9:27). For Derrida—and for all of us—this is a reality, a simple truth that cannot be deconstructed.

▸▸ Sharpening the Focus

Despite their merits, the educational philosophies of Dewey, Neill, and Derrida are naturalistic at the core. It is helpful for the Christian student to sharpen her focus by contrasting them with a Christian philosophy of education on three major points.[18]

▸ What Is Reality?

For the naturalist, reality is the material cosmos. It is no more and no less than the physical and material elements and forces that drive the universe. Humans exist in this context and learn to adapt or die within it. The Christian believes that reality begins and ends in God. He is the creator, designer, and author of all that is real. To know God is to know reality. To focus solely on the material and physical is to study part of reality. More important, however, to reject the existence of God is to live in an illusion.

▸ What Is a Human Being?

The naturalist views a human being as the highest of the known life forms—the most complex of living organisms. The human being is an intricate physical machine. Moreover, human life has no purpose other than survival, comfort, and reproduction. One human may be meaningful to another due to the human capacity for relationship, but that meaning is entirely subjective. In objective terms, life is meaningless and ends when the body dies.

The believer also believes humans are the highest life form. Not, however, due to their complexity, but because they are cast in the image of God—the basis of all life and all reality. Humans, then, are to be treated with care, not because of a value of freedom or a right to noninterference, but because human beings are sacred, bearing the stamp of their divine Maker. Affirming humanity's intrinsic dignity, Immanuel Kant said, "Act so that you treat humanity, whether in your own person or in that of another, always as an end and never as a means only."[19] In addition, human life has purpose: to reflect and bring honor to the God that made it. Human relationships are sacred because they both mirror the relational nature of God and are forged in the context of love—the major attribute of God. Furthermore, physical death is not the end of life. Because humans are cast in the image of God, they are spiritual, and the spirit is eternal.

The educational implications in this definition of humanity are profound. The Christian notion affirms ultimate worth as well as freedom. Though imperfect by nature, human worth is a given, grounded in the image of God. We are supremely valuable. As Lewis asserted, in Christian thinking there are no ordinary people. Freedom refers to humans being choice-driven moral agents, responsible stewards of the life and opportunities the Creator has given us. Human life, human choices, and human actions make a difference. Education, then, must aim at developing a sense of worth and responsibility, rooted in the divine and eternal nature of humankind.

▸ What Is the Basis for Morality?

For the naturalist, morality is an entirely subjective social construct. It is developed by humans to regulate conduct so that life on a collective (or group) level can exist with minimum destruction. Morality is subjective, practical, and relative to the group in which it exists. Morality is based on consequences. Actions considered taboo are those that bring about unpleasant or what is consensually believed to be destructive consequences for others. Any action consensually engaged in by two or more humans is not immoral, because mutual consent removes all responsibility for a negative consequence. Given that humans are metaphorically viewed as machines, human behavior is no more morally meaningful than how faithfully one adheres to an automobile owner's manual. Moral rules, like the directives in the car manual, exist primarily to make life more safe and pleasant.

For the believer, morality is objective. There are absolute and fixed moral principles founded in the nature of God. These morals are supracultural—transcendent—as basic to the reality of the universe as are the physical laws.

These three points form a scale on which we can weigh various educational philosophies and approaches. On the surface, various secular approaches may not in practice seem to conflict with Christian thinking. Nevertheless, any substantive educational approach emerges from a philosophy—a set of basic beliefs—the tenets of which will eventually become visible. The mission for the Christian student in developing her own philosophy of education is twofold. It is to grow by remaining open to innovations in thought and practice, while exercising careful Christian discernment in the process.

Notes

1. Antonio A. Chiareli, "Christian Worldview and the Social Sciences," in *Shaping a Christian Worldview*, ed. David S. Dockery and Gregory Alan Thornbury (Nashville: Broadman and Holman, 2002), 245.
2. Harry Blamires, *Where Do We Stand?* (Ann Arbor, MI: Servant, 1980), 56.
3. Ibid., 55.
4. *Webster's Student Dictionary*, ed. P. H. Collin (New York: Barnes and Noble Books, 1999).

5. Thomas R. Rosebrough, "Christian Worldview and Teaching," in Dockery and Thornbury, *Shaping a Christian Worldview,* 296.

6. Ibid., 296–97.

7. Arthur Holmes, "Shaping the Academic Enterprise," in Dockery and Thornbury, *Shaping a Christian Worldview,* 89–92. For those who wish to study Dewey's thinking more fully, see *The Collected Works of John Dewey,* 37 vols., ed. Jo Ann Boydston (Carbondale, IL: Southern Illinois University Press, 1991).

8. Holmes, "Shaping the Academic Enterprise," in Dockery and Thornbury, *Shaping a Christian Worldview,* 89.

9. Ibid.

10. Ibid.

11. Ibid.

12. Ibid., 91.

13. Ibid., 92.

14. These are taken from http://www.summerhillschool.co.uk as is much of the rest of the review.

15. Ibid.

16. Ibid.

17. There is a multiplicity of material explicating the thinking of Derrida. Few do a better job than Mitchell Stephens of the journalism and mass-communication department at New York University. A sample of his work can be found at http://www.nyu.edu/classes/stephens/Jacques%20Derrida%20-%20LAT%20page.htm.

18. Adapted from Rosebrough, "Christian Worldview and Teaching," in Dockery and Thornbury, *Shaping a Christian Worldview,* 285.

19. Immanuel Kant, *Critique of Practical Reason* (Indianapolis: Bobbs-Merrill, 1956), quoted in Rosebrough, "Christian Worldview and Teaching," in Dockery and Thornbury, *Shaping a Christian Worldview,* 293.

21

WHAT IS A CHRISTIAN HISTORIAN?

J ust what is a Christian historian? There are church historians, denominational historians, and biblical historians, but they are not necessarily Christian historians. There are historians who profess an orthodox Christian faith, but that does make them Christian historians. The Christian scholar will almost certainly differ from the nonbeliever in how he reads, analyzes, and interprets history, but where, if anywhere, does the point of injection of his faith come? Although the relationship of Christianity and history has been much written about, if one reviews the literature, he will find comparatively few essays that provide a Christian perspective on teaching history.[1]

So what is a Christian historian? We need to begin by separating a personal Christian perspective on history from the practice of engaging the historical technique within the discipline. History itself is a bit of an academic nomad. Its placement within the academic structure is problematic. "History is not a social science, not a behavioral science, not a humanity, and not an exact science," writes Robert Clouse. "It is partially all of these contained in one integrated package."[2] No matter its placement, there is a high value on objectivity.

►► Cardinal Christian Concepts

Several doctrines are central to the Christian historian.[3] These include progressive revelation, the nature of humankind, universal truth, and ultimate values.

Beginning with progressive revelation, history, in a phrase, is the story of God's revelation to humanity. As such, the Christian historian will look for the fingerprints of God's nature and activity throughout history—in the Dark Ages, the Middle Ages, ancient China, and so forth. Furthermore, how does the study of these periods illuminate scriptural truth? Key to this process is the belief that history is progressive, not cyclical, as the secularist believes. History is linear, moving toward a culmination. It is the unfolding of God's plan for the universe, moving steadily toward the end of time.[4] The progressive view is an antidote to the pessimism and cynicism of believing history is merely an ongoing recording of people's inhumane and brutal treatment of one another. Progressive revelation offers hope and meaning, rather than the randomness and meaninglessness of the naturalist paradigm. About the only practical value history serves for the naturalist is to learn its calamitous events, and perhaps to prevent repeating them. Rather than history being part of a larger, transcendent plan, it has at best only a here-and-now, temporal value, providing information as to how we got to where we are and a series of cautions as to how we should conduct ourselves in the future.

As for human nature, there are two key points for the Christian historian. The first is that we humans are flawed in our very essence, owing to the ravages of original sin. Embracing the doctrine of original sin removes the all-too-human tendency to divide peoples and even civilizations into good guys and bad guys. Although evil regimes have and do exist, no one group has a corner on evil. The doctrine of original sin also obviates any sense of cultural supremacy, which elevates a given nation or race to an inherently superior status. The American tendency to proclaim a civil religion, one that elevates the United States to a level of moral and cultural superiority, is checked by this doctrine.

The second point is that we humans are molded—cast—in the image of a perfect Creator. This side of the coin serves as a counterbalance to the negative, sinful side. It makes humans, despite their flaws, sacred beings worthy of care and preservation. This view prevents a casual attitude toward human atrocity, like that of the warring totalitarian leader who felt the pain he inflicted was no more cruel than nature.[5] The elevated regard for humans makes genocide, massive war with its casualties, colonialism, and racism genuinely evil, because such practices are more than crimes against humans, they are crimes against the God who dwells within them.

Embracing immutable, universal truth is particularly important in the discipline of history. The Christian historian can study nations, civilizations, and eras in the context of how much truth is understood, accepted, and practiced. Genuine enlightenment to the Christian scholar is not synonymous with the rise of science, despite its incredible advances. In fact, the Christian historian who sees science becoming an object of extreme veneration, a religion that quenches the spiritual vitality of generations, may also assess its predominating impact negatively. He may also associate genuine enlightenment with spiritual sensitivity and an awareness of divine truth. The acceptance of truth has far-reaching implications. Although the Puritans and their stern, moralistic theology get bad press from secular historians, Christian historians, aware of their own excesses, are likely to see value in the Puritans' God-centered consciousness.

Believing in ultimate values—the opposite of cultural relativism—is another Christian distinctive. Supracultural values provide a framework for assessing the quality of nations, civilizations, and social movements. Without this framework, history becomes descriptive rather than analytic and evaluative. Evaluative thinking, though anathema to many secularists, gives the study of history a richness and meaning as eras, nations, and civilizations are examined in the context of ultimate rather than relativist criteria.

Behavioral scientists frequently use institutions as tools of analysis, for example, using the PREFER (politics, religion, education, family, economics, and recreation) system to analyze a culture or civilization. American historians, as mentioned by Marsden, have largely omitted religion as a sphere of historical inquiry, despite acknowledging its formative impact on the United States. When a commitment to humanism as the vehicle for human well-being and cultural development exists, it all but blinds secular historians to the positive contributions religion has made to the nation, including education itself.

Within the institution of religion, there needs to be a focus on the church as an institutional form. Too often left to the denominational or seminary-based church historians, the church is the most important of all the institutions, because it is the only institution that belongs uniquely to God. It is the body of Christ. The church is an amazing phenomenon. Founded by a relatively uneducated, unsophisticated, and often dissension-ridden group, it has been in existence for two millennia and is bigger than ever. Moreover, no matter how imperfect its members, no matter how intense the opposition to the church becomes, it will stand until the end of time. The very gates of hell will not prevail against the church, says Christ in Matthew 16:18.

From any vantage point—political, economic, or educational—the church is among the most significant institutions any historian can study in learning about the people and events of which it is a part. The church's relationship with a society is interactive. It shapes and influences a culture or a nation—even an entire civilization—something many secular historians seem to gloss over. Yet the church is also shaped by the social context of which it is a part. If one wants to look for God's interaction with any group of people, at any one time, the church is a good place to start.

▶▶ Expansion and Contraction

The study of history has expanded, particularly in the last third of the twentieth century, to study world civilizations, rather than only Western civilizations. Moreover, efforts to remove Western imperial biases in studying non-Western civilizations (though never completely successful) can prove immensely illuminating, as Elisabeth Elliot, the famous missionary to the Aucas, discovered. "So here are 'heathen' people, I told myself. And here is the Word of truth." It all looked rather simple initially. Then she went on. "What would 'Christian' conduct mean to the Aucas?" she wondered. "I came to see that my own understanding of these subjects was not nearly as clear as I had supposed. I kept balancing the Auca way of life against the American, or against what I had always taken to be Christian. . . . A comparison did not convince me of the superiority of any other group." Although polygamy was not forbidden among the Aucas, a strong sense of faithfulness and responsibility existed among Auca husbands. "I saw the Indians live in a harmony which far surpassed anything I had seen among those who call themselves Christians. I found that even their killing had at least as valid reasons as the wars in which my people engaged."[6]

Elliot makes a powerful case against Western self-righteousness and moral superiority, considering that these Aucas had killed missionaries, one of which was her husband. The missionary often adopts what sociologists call an ethnomethodology approach, one that attempts to study a culture from the inside — from the point of view of its members. Although this can tread dangerously close to cultural relativism, it can help the student to step outside his own, often unconscious, societal values. For the Christian, however, this holds special potential. "Often Christians have identified their faith with social values worked out in the Western world," notes Clouse, "many of these values going back to the emphasis built into Christianity by the late medieval church. A global approach can liberate the student from this dangerous situation."[7] Rather than cultural relativism, the desired outcome is a more pure, gritty, and distilled faith.[8]

History has also contracted. Special interest groups (African, Asian, and Hispanic Americans, for example) have pressed hard for historical perspectives indigenous to their cultures and subcultures. Feminists have also lobbied for courses on gender and the experience of women in a variety of civilizations and eras. A basic argument in favor of these perspectives is that they contribute to the knowledge and understanding of humankind. By making history meaningful in the now, these views become agents of social change.[9] Moreover, that they are sometimes a bit ideologically tilted (always a point of contention among traditional historians) is not surprising. History, as they say, is written by the winners — those in power. Too often the result is the vilification of the vanquished, blaming the victim, rather than a balanced presentation of the interpreted facts.[10] Furthermore, in many cases, the dominant group neither needs to nor attempts to acquaint itself with the subcultures of the minorities.[11] Therefore, similar to efforts at affirmative action, these minority orientations are often viewed as correctives to the white, northern European, blaming-the-victim worldviews that dominate so much of historical literature and analysis.

▶▶ Faith and Learning—Some Issues

So where is the Christian in all of this? It is important for the Christian historian to have integrity when "doing" history. Clearly, the discipline provides a near-engraved invitation for the Christian to attach his interpretation to the events of time. After all, isn't history the story of revelation, with God the author of it all? The problem lies in the unique nature of the discipline, something that raises special issues for the Christian. The instant a believer constructs a Christian model in another discipline, the insertion of spiritual concepts is obvious to all. That it is a "Christian" theory is visible on the surface. History, being so vulnerable to the worldview of the historian, however, is different. Except in the most empirical, fact-based arenas, interpretation is inevitably wedded to history's telling. In a discipline that includes solid, scientific research yet is so devoid of any paradigm, it is relatively easy to tuck in one's biases unintentionally. Indeed, certain Christian revelations are "obvious" to the believer. Inserting one's biases can also be a deliberate attempt to manipulate or "spin" the presentation. That secularists casually or deliberately assert their naturalistic notions is not, I believe, a permission-giver for the Christian to do the same.

Clouse comes down hard on this. "The cry for an interpretation of the human story is not a desire for history, but for 'prophecy,'" he declares. "Those who wish their history written with a rich interweaving of value judgments and moral statements should turn to an application of the insights of holy Scripture to life."[12] Clouse may be protesting a bit much in quelling the desire to offer a philosophy of history here. It is simply impossible for the Christian scholar not to "see" God's hand in the human historical drama. Hence, it would take incredible style-crimping restraint for a believer not to have some of that thinking slip through the net in his teaching and writing. Perhaps that is why Marsden alerted his students at Berkeley as to his point of view. Nevertheless, Clouse's stand is sound. God does work mysteriously, so the Christian is wise to take care to avoid subtly yet deliberately bending his presentation of history to fit his Christian worldview.

This caution is especially pertinent when working with causal relations. Because history is particularly concerned with time and the sequence of events, it is extremely tempting to indulge in rather simplistic if-then, cause-and-effect presentations that square with one's Christian worldview. Clouse uses the Reformation as an example. Certainly a Protestant's view of this event will differ from that of a Roman Catholic. "The search for causal relationships is complex," says Clouse, "for behind every human event is a multitude of forces, some known, and others unknown, and often these are difficult to relate."[13]

History can be studied "objectively," with a scientific focus on facts and tangible findings, and some causality can be gleaned from its study. Clouse's warning at overreaching here is most appropriate. Even facts are never entirely separable from interpretation. The age, race, socioeconomic status, education, and current social environment of the historian will mediate what he "sees" and how he will communicate it. The Christian historian, in the spirit of integrity, needs to take special care here. Unlike the secularist who sees nothing but random events and natural causes as explanatory variables, the Christian historian hails from a tradition containing mountainous literature examining God's hand in the matters of history.

The issue of a philosophy of history has long been explored. In 1952, Herbert Butterfield, a giant in the endeavor of integrating history and Christianity, offered a three-pronged approach that continues to provide an excellent foundation for the study of history. In the first "biographical way," we see humans acting freely and being responsible for those actions. The second "scientific way" approaches history in the realm of law that determines what happens. In the third "theological way," we see God working out his divine plan through personalities and processes. Each way is valid in and of itself, but it is wise to employ all three to gain a truly full view.[14]

The Christian thinker will most definitely agree that the best view of history is one that employs all three ways. A reckless Christian philosophy of history, devoid of careful objective study, is error-prone at best and a form of propaganda at worst. It disserves the discipline as well as Christian thought. Conversely, scientific history—though never purely objective—factors out the creating author of all history and so is incomplete. To dismiss all Christian interpretation is to refuse even to attempt to understand what God is teaching us about himself and us over the millennia. More than offering an insightful typology, Butterfield, by encouraging the historian to combine all three ways, is well on his way to describing what it means to be a Christian historian.

▸▸ Opportunities for Christians

Though ancillary to this discussion, I believe there is an area in history in which Christians could be far more active, even taking the lead. That is in studying, teaching, and writing history with an eye toward adopting a multicultural perspective. Despite its claims of offering diverse perspectives, the history mainstream continues to present a largely Anglo view of the past. Were that not the case, there would be far less clamoring by minorities for universities to offer history courses emanating from their own specific cultural vantage point. This issue of being multicultural is, I feel, a matter of justice and fairness. That in itself makes it Christian.[15]

I am conversant with the protestations of the traditionalists. Their commitment to scholarly care and excellence is admirable. Nonetheless, racism and classism by their very natures have a blinding effect. They are often unconscious phenomena every bit as much as the secular worldview is to the nonbeliever. At best, many mainstream academicians tolerate special interest courses (in a variety of disciplines), viewing them as mere political accommodations with potentially disruptive groups. When backs are turned, however, the courses and the instructors are the butt of mean-spirited witticisms and are roundly demeaned as intellectually inferior. To the extent that there is merit to these dismissals, one could argue that the perceived deficiencies are the result of a self-fulfilling process. The current practice of marginalizing and ghettoizing these group-specific studies into separate departments or divisions creates a separate but equal atmosphere within the university—one that is more separate than equal. It would be far better if those that proclaim the importance of academic respectability took steps to widen the lenses of their own worldviews, something that would certainly lessen the need for special interest historical perspectives. A commitment to cultural and intellectual diversity needs to exist throughout academe. In addition to its being fair, it presents a better, more balanced education.

For the Christian, taking a stand on this matter of multiculturalism may have a secondary benefit. Remembering that Christians are every bit the minority that African Americans are, a multicultural advocacy can be a basis for legitimizing a reintroduction of a much needed respect for the importance of religion and Christianity in mainline history courses.

The caution to avoid asserting causal relationships or to manipulate insertions of Christian interpretation is to be balanced with another caution: that the quest for academic objectivity in history not serve as a comfortable rationalization for compartmentalization. A commitment to a rigorously objective study of history can result in the believer keeping his faith at a safe distance from his scholarship. The principles of sincerely attempted objectivity and tolerance have their place in the traditional practice of history, if only as safeguards against propagandizing and ideological manipulation. The rules change when one enters the turf of special interest history. The presence of special interest–based interpretations of history should legitimize the Christian to offer his faith-based perspectives as well. No integrity need be lost here, provided that he labels his interpretations as such.

In a postmodern era, one in which diversity of opinion is valued, there is great opportunity for the Christian historian to offer his versions of history. The Christian historian needs to be bold here, just as other special-interest scholars have been, looking for ways to present integrations of his faith with his discipline. He need not do it with a political or ideological bent as some special interest advocates do. "Such deliberately distorted history is really not history at all," states Clouse succinctly.[16] Instead, labeling it as such, the Christian historian can include Butterfield's third theological way and thus offer a fuller view of history to all who wish to understand and be guided by the past.

Notes

1. Robert G. Clouse, "History," in *Christ and the Modern Mind*, ed. Robert W. Smith (Downers Grove, IL: InterVarsity, 1972), 172, cites several classic sources relating Christianity to history. These include Hendrikus Berkhof, *Christ, the Meaning of History* (Richmond, VA: John Knox Press, 1966); Herbert Butterfield, *Christianity and History* (London: Bell, 1949); and Alan Richardson, *History, Sacred and Profane* (Philadelphia: Westminster, 1964).
2. Clouse, "History," in Smith, *Christ and the Modern Mind*, 166.
3. David S. Dockery, "Introduction: Shaping a Christian Worldview," in *Shaping a Christian Worldview*, eds. David S. Dockery and Gregory Alan Thornbury (Nashville: Broadman and Holman, 2002), 6.
4. Clouse, "History," in Smith, *Christ and the Modern Mind*, 167.
5. Ibid.
6. Elisabeth Elliot, *The Liberty of Conscience* (Waco, TX: Word, 1968), 15–17, quoted in Clouse, "History," in Smith, *Christ and the Modern Mind*, 169–70.
7. Clouse, "History," in Smith, *Christ and the Modern Mind*, 167.
8. See Robert G. Clouse, Robert D. Linder, and Richard V. Pierard, eds., *Protest and Politics: Christianity and Contemporary Affairs* (Greenwood: Attic, 1968), for an example of historians questioning evangelical social views.
9. Ibid., 170. This approach was used heavily in the 1960s. Clouse cites *Towards a New Past, Dissenting Essays in American History*, ed. Barton J. Bernstein (New York: Pantheon, 1968); and Staughton Lynd, "Historical Past and Existential Present," *The Dissenting Academy*, ed. Theodore Roszak (New York: Random House, 1968).
10. David Claerbaut, "Antidotes to Victim-blaming," in *Metro-Ministry*, ed. David Frenchak and Sharrel Keyes (Elgin, IL: David C. Cook, 1979).
11. David Claerbaut, *Black Jargon in White America* (Grand Rapids: Eerdmans, 1972).
12. Clouse, "History," in Smith, *Christ and the Modern Mind*, 167.
13. Ibid., 167–68.
14. Herbert Butterfield, "God in History," in *God, History, and Historians*, ed. C. T. McIntire (New York: Oxford University Press, 1977). The Butterfield typology is reviewed by McIntire in the Fall 2001 edition of *Christianity Today*.

15. This is a subject of great professional and research interest to me. See David Claerbaut, *Black Student Alienation: A Study* (San Francisco: R&E Research Associates, 1978); Claerbaut, ed., *New Directions in Ethnic Studies* (Saratoga, CA: Century Twenty One Publishing, 1981); Claerbaut, "Minorities in Higher Education: The Forgotten Crisis," in *American Ethnic Revival*, ed. Jack Kinton (Aurora, IL: Social Science and Sociological Resources, 1977); Claerbaut, "Black Students and Christian Colleges," *The Reformed Journal* 26, no. 10 (December 1976): 17–20.

16. Clouse, "History," in Smith, *Christ and the Modern Mind*, 172.

THE BEHAVIORAL SCIENCES

REFLECTIONS FOR THE CHRISTIAN POLITICAL SCIENTIST

olitical science is an interesting name for this discipline, one that is teeming with nonmaterial, moral concepts that are far out of the confines of science. Political science lacks not only a central paradigm but also any semblance of boundaries. Flying to Chicago with a published political science professor, I asked her to define her field. She was unable to render a crisp definition. The Areas of Study section in a popular political science website illustrates the meandering nature of the discipline. It includes such disparate topics as African Studies, Asian Studies, Congress Link, Environmental Studies, International Development, National Election Studies, Political Thought, American Women/Politics, and Western Europe.[1] This chapter therefore consists of a series of topics—reflections—of concern for the Christian political scientist.

Political science is commonly viewed as the study of the forms, practices, and processes by which people organize themselves governmentally. That, however, is not the essence of what politics is. Hans Morgenthau's amorphous and wide-ranging definition is closer to what political science is truly about: "Political science deals with the nature, the accumulation, the distribution, the exercise, and the control of power on all levels of social interaction, with special emphasis on the power of the state."[2]

Politics is about power. And because Christians accept only one ultimate power as fully justifiable, that is reason enough for believers to be interested in this discipline. Christians are always dual citizens. They are citizens of whatever flawed human political locale they inhabit, yet at the same time, citizens of God's invisible church community. Moreover, on one hand, Scripture affirms the necessity of legitimate power structures. On the other hand, these human constructions invariably fall far short of adhering to Christian values.

▶▶ Religion

Political science is based on the notion that humans live in collectivities called tribes, clans, communities, states, and nations. Physical anthropologists attribute this tendency to evolutionary history, cultural anthropologists to cultural adaptation. Christians can point elsewhere. In Genesis (1:27–28; 2:18), Scripture teaches that God ordains humans to live in community.[3] The presence of political entities is found in Genesis (17:4) when God promises Abraham that he will be the father of many nations. In fact, the Old Testament is in part a history of nation-states. Israel, the chosen people of God, was not just a people; it was a nation. God ordained the very existence of political structure. It is not a mere social construction of humankind.

Collective living can be viewed as an expression of humankind being in the image of God, both in his Trinitarian being as well as in his relationship with his creation. Humans mirror that with their relational capacities. They develop common patterns of feeling, thinking, and acting and, through language, shared identities to form collectivities. Additional evidence for humans being in the image of God can be found in the near-universal existence of religion. No matter how underdeveloped or advanced a society is, some form of religion is almost invariably present. That this is consistently overlooked by social scientists in their analyses is at best curious. To study human behavior scientifically would seem to necessitate examining the intrinsic religiosity of the human race.[4] It is particularly relevant to any study of human political behavior because almost every nation-state addresses it. There have been theocracies, secular governments that designate a state church, nations that attempt to separate church and state, and some political regimes that have unsuccessfully attempted to expunge the very existence of religion.

Regardless of a given state's stance toward religion, humans, by intuition, seem to affirm a basic biblical doctrine: that human nature is flawed. They therefore enact laws and develop other modes of social control for their protection. Theologically, we could say that collectivities develop laws to restrain sin. In fact, some or all of the final six of the ten commandments are evident in the laws of myriad societies, suggesting an instinctual awareness that collectivities cannot be driven by raw power alone if they are to survive. That power is legitimated, becoming what we call authority.

Christian thinkers have been chided for not indulging in utopian thinking. They cannot, however, because such musings are grounded in a perfectionist concept of human nature. The universal existence of laws in civilized societies goes far in supporting the Christian view of sin. Political scientist Glenn Tinder found theologian Reinhold Niebuhr particularly helpful. "If Niebuhr had a single guiding idea," writes Tinder, "it was that of original sin—sin as not merely one human trait among others but as an orientation of the soul, distorting and misdirecting all human traits."[5] Niebuhr's work helped Tinder deal realistically with the harsh nature of the contemporary political world. "Much of the tragic folly of our times," says Tinder, "not only on the part of extremists like Lenin but also on the part of middle-of-the-road liberals and conservatives, would never have arisen had we not, in our technological and ideological pride, forgotten original sin."[6]

▸▸ Justice

Members of free societies regularly affirm a basic Christian value: justice. There is a near-universal sense of justice or fairness within humankind. Disenfranchised groups rise up against oppressors with regularity. The atheistic Marx would attribute this to a never-ending dialectic rooted in power differentials. There is evidence for that. But often those out of power revolt because they see their oppressors being *unfair* or *unjust* in the use of that power. Justice is so central a Christian value that over eighty verses in Scripture express God's concern for justice.[7] Although often viewed in terms of rights—giving each person his due in the political system—that is not a complete scriptural view of justice. God loves the poor and equates their protection with justice. "Justice is not cold impartiality but food for the hungry, shelter for the homeless, a fair trial for the poor, a family for the orphan, and liberation for the oppressed."[8] Justice addresses shalom and wholeness for all members of a society.

There remains, however, much "health and wealth" theology in American Christianity. Evangelists often state that God wants his people to prosper, an outgrowth of the Protestant ethic. The Protestant ethic is the notion that material success is a sign of God's blessing one's faithful endeavors. In its simplest form, the Protestant ethic now "suggests that if one works hard, he or she will succeed and 'get ahead.'"[9] The doctrine is not without merit. Few would argue that to succeed, one has to work hard and that hard, honest work honors God.

The problem with the Protestant ethic lies in what one might call the corollary of the doctrine: if a person is not successful, it is probably because she did not work hard.[10] The latter justifies a great deal of antipoverty prejudice, something contrary to Scripture's strong advocacy of the poor. The belief that to be poor is to be deficient and perhaps outside of God's favor is completely unscriptural. There are over four hundred verses in the Bible affirming God's love for the poor.[11] Moreover, Christ claimed it to be easier for a camel to pass through the eye of a needle than for a rich person to enter heaven.[12] Rather than blaming the powerless for having merited their plight through past transgressions, Christians are enjoined to care for "orphans and widows."[13] More than just worshiping from the spirit, believers are instructed "to act justly and to love mercy and to walk humbly with your God."[14] The life of Christ, as recorded in the New Testament, provides one long look at a lifestyle counter to the values of most societies. He enters the world in a stable—a barn area—rather than in Cedars-Sinai Hospital. He associates with the poor constantly and proclaims God's love for them. "Blessed are you who are poor," says Christ in Luke 6:20, "for yours is the kingdom of God." He mixes with the uneducated and crude of society, running from his disciples to Mary, Martha, and Lazarus.

Moreover, there are no outcasts in the eyes of Jesus. His principal followers included women—who were viewed as possessions in the culture of his time—and among them Mary Magdalene, who was formerly ill and demon-possessed.[15] In addition, the lengthy visit of Jesus with the woman at the well is loaded with social voltage. Not only was she a woman, but she was also a minority (a Samaritan, a person of mixed ancestry, despised by the Jews) and was married five times and currently living with another man.[16] Clearly, Christianity is not aimed at the powerful and well established, those who are in the best position to ensure its continuance in human civilization, but rather those who are removed from a society's center of power.

Political science is not a field typified by dispassionate theorizing. Despite its claims to neutrality and nonpartisanship, it is one of advocacy. This is likely due to how central power is to the nature of politics. The capacity for one person or group to impose its will on another is something about which people feel strongly. Christians, as they become a minority in Western societies, are no exception. The Christian political scientist, then, should have much to say about the nation-state power. Moreover, in his assessment of a political society, it is wise to evaluate that nation-state using criteria founded on Christian values. Basic to the application of Christian values in societal analysis is a commitment to a whole-person gospel.

▶▶ Whole-Person Gospel

One of Christianity's hallmarks is its whole-person gospel. One is saved in body, mind, and spirit. Christ modeled this clearly and brilliantly in his ministry. He fed the hungry, healed the sick, and ministered to the emotionally distressed in addition to declaring himself the spiritual Messiah. Christians need also be concerned with how their political systems address temporal matters.

The body is sacred in Christianity. Because we are the work of a supernatural Creator, issues such as abortion, euthanasia, cloning, and stem cell research are important to Christians in the context of the spiritual significance of physical life. We are, according to the psalmist in Psalm 139:14, "fearfully and wonderfully made." The sanctity of life, the sacred nature of marriage, the intimacy and relational meaning of sex, as well as the prohibitions against murder and suicide, all emanate coherently from a gospel that affirms that the body is the "temple of the Holy Spirit," the earthly residence of God.[17] Without this belief, no one and nothing is safe. Not the unborn, not the aged, and no one in between. Moreover, when sex becomes an essentially nonrelational form of pleasure or amusement, unhealthy practices and distortions develop, even including rape, incest, and assault. When in major cities teenagers and small children are "pimped" to eager pedophiles because they bring higher fees than adult prostitutes do, it is the residue of a society that no longer regards the body as sacred and valuable in itself. Christians hold funerals and preserve the bodies of their dead, in part because of this whole-person gospel dimension and the belief in a physical resurrection.

Again, the physical and spiritual are intertwined in Christianity. Christ himself is referred to as the Lamb of God, tying the physical sacrificial system of the Old Testament to the spiritual Messiah of the present age. He also presented himself as the "living bread" and the "living water," suggesting that irrespective of how much tangible food and drink (and other material goods) one has, there remains a spiritual hunger and thirst that must be sated for one to be whole.[18] Putting this spiritual concept into physical terms is yet another example of the integration of body and soul. The most important physical aspect of Christianity, however, is the resurrection of Jesus, which is the centerpiece of the Christian faith. Moreover, the most sacred event in Christian worship is partaking of the Lord's Supper, ingesting physical elements as representatives of the actual body and blood of the Messiah. Furthermore, because believers are said to house the Holy Spirit in their bodies, Christians can worship anywhere.[19]

The elevation of the physical body is excellent evidence of the totality of God. All of creation is his, all of it valuable, all of it to be dealt with according to divine imperatives. Though we humans are the highest of his creation, we are to be stewards of the natural world we inhabit, regarding our lives and the lives of others as sacred. The importance of the state as a guarantor of personal freedom and protection, as well as the protector of the natural resources of creation, is then a matter of great concern to the Christian political scholar.

In Christianity, the mental and emotional life is sacred, though not synonymous with the soul. Christ affirmed this in his compassionate dealings with deranged, demon-possessed people and lepers (quarantined, terminally ill people). In addition, he preached the importance of inner peace through faith.[20] Paul urges against excessive worry, directing us to live a life of thankfulness and prayer.[21] There is more the Scriptures say about the mind in the cognitive sense.

In Proverbs 23:7 we read that we are what we think in our inner selves. The New Testament epistles tell us to adopt the mind of Christ.[22] It is because the mind is sacred that Christianity has advanced the frontiers of education. Unafraid of scientific inquiry and intellectual enlightenment, it continues to foster the development of the mind in Christian institutions of higher learning.

The truly spiritual life is holistic. The bodily "temple" houses a cognitive and emotional component in addition to the will. In short, to be a Christian is to be fully relational with God—a commitment of the whole self to the life of God, with all that includes. Because the life of faith is a journey of body, mind, and spirit, God's concern for us is similarly multidimensional. Hence, we are also concerned about and pray holistically for our own health and that of the nations of the world.

▸▸ Christianity in Action

The Christian's interest in political science is grounded in a whole-person gospel. Political structures do more than restrict or advance the practice of religion. They have a direct impact on the quality of people's physical and mental (as well as spiritual) lives. With human personhood being sacred, there are few temporal forces more important to Christians than political ones.

Although the example and teachings of Jesus are the basis of Christian social activity, Christianity has been charged with turning its back on a whole-person theology. Moreover secularists attack repetitively the social irrelevance of the church and the alleged cash-laden nature of "organized religion." Though not without some merit, such criticism is shortsighted. The history of Christianity is rich with efforts to serve rather than dominate, to attend to the sick, the indigent, and otherwise needy. Almost every Western social institution has its roots in Christianity. Christians have founded hospitals, mental health facilities, shelters for the poor, and programs for the treatment of alcoholism. "Through the ages, Christian saints have chosen the most unDarwinian objects for their love," states celebrated Christian thinker Philip Yancey.[23]

An adversary of the faith, Nietzsche long ago accused the church as having "taken the side of everything weak, base, ill-constituted."[24] He was right. The church, throughout history, has been at the absolute forefront of concern for the poor and oppressed. Although examples of this commitment to society's outsiders would fill volumes, it may be well to cite several.

Few realize that Alcoholics Anonymous was begun as a Christian ministry. One of its twelve steps requires that addicted persons turn their lives over to their higher power. (*Higher power* is the term A.A. uses to make its ministry nonsectarian and available to anyone, though many substitute *God* or *Christ* for it.) Few people in this century are better known than Mother Teresa, whose care for any homeless or rejected soul in India was miraculous. Less known is the work of Jean Vanier, who founded the l'Arche Movement. She employs a seventeen-person staff that works with ten men and women so severely handicapped that they will never be able to speak or perform coordinated hand movements. The founder of the now renowned hospice movement, Dame Cicely Saunders, of London's St. Christopher's Hospice, felt driven by her Christian sensitivities to develop a system of genuine care for the dying. Millard Fuller, a millionaire, feeling God wanted him to build homes for the poor, started the national Habitat for Humanity program. Fresh from his born-again experience, the once-hardened politico, Charles Colson, created Prison Fellowship, a now international holistic ministry to the incarcerated. Bill Magee, a Christian plastic surgeon, started Operation Smile, a ministry that repairs facial deformities among Third World children.[25]

Not only does the whole-person gospel nature of Christianity have strong social and political implications, it also places Christianity in direct contrast to Hindu and Buddhist traditions. In every religion except Christianity, the temple is a physical structure in a geographical place. It exists independently of the human bodies of the people who gather there. That Hindus and Muslims have been involved in deadly bombings over a dispute regarding the birthplace of a Hindu deity, on which a mosque had been constructed, is evidence of this. So also is the Muslim practice of not permitting a church in their country to be built with a steeple higher than a mosque.[26]

Despite the existence of buildings used for worship, in Christianity, the true church is not a nonliving physical structure but the "body" of believers. It is the physical, bodily collective of those who confess Christ as the Son of God and the redeeming agent of humanity. According to the words of Christ, whenever two or three such people are together, his Spirit is present.[27]

The Holy Spirit—who lives in the body, mind, and spirit of believers—is foundational to Christian thinking and to the whole-person gospel notion. Less is known about the Holy Spirit than about the other two members of the Trinity, perhaps because he enters the scriptural scene after the Old Testament activity of the Father and the New Testament life of Jesus. Yet the Bible is very explicit about the existence and work of the Holy Spirit. Jesus told his disciples that a counselor, the Holy Spirit, would come and complete his spiritual work in them. The book of Acts is replete with descriptions of the coming of the Holy Spirit and the incredible impact he had on early believers. The Holy Spirit is credited with giving the often-persecuted apostles the boldness to keep on preaching about Jesus, as well as the capacity to perform miraculous physical healings.

Today Christians throughout the globe talk of, believe in, and pray for the power of the Holy Spirit. I have witnessed incredible outcomes among Christians who pray intensely for the Holy Spirit to act in their lives and in the lives of others. The Holy Spirit is that part of God active today, and the degree to which a believer submits herself to his power directly affects the quality of her spiritual life. The Holy Spirit guides, comforts, convicts, and heals, among other things.

That we can be filled with the Holy Spirit is a differentiating variable of Christian faith. It puts God in the here-and-now temporal life of the believer. "This is unique among the world's religions," writes Jim Cymbala. "Buddhism, Islam, and the rest pay honor and respect to a god, or gods. But the gods remain 'out there' at a safe distance; they don't come and fill up redeemed worshipers in an intimate way, a dynamic way. This is the unique note of Christianity."[28]

▶▶ Christianity as a Social Movement

Political scientists regularly study social movements because they are a means by which people express power. The women's movement, the civil rights movement, and the gay rights movement are examples of politics in the form of social movements. Though not a nation, Christianity is itself a social movement. Antonio Chiareli, at Union University, lectures on the first-century "Jesus movement," comparing it with the civil rights movement in the United States and the landless movement in Brazil. Chiareli shows his students that by human, political criteria, the Jesus movement should have been a total failure.[29] His lecture merits comment because of its potential for the Christian who instructs in political science.

The first-century Christian social movement is devoid of characteristics typifying enduring social movements. Its leader, Jesus, was a minority of humble birth reared in a nondescript town called Nazareth. He did not hold an official position in the society, and his public tenure lasted only three years. Furthermore, he focused his attention on the poor, the sick, and the powerless. He was not an organizer and led no armed revolt. In fact, he advanced a church-state (Caesar/God) separation. Leaving behind no original writings, he was murdered as his followers fled. By human social and political standards, Christ's public career was unsuccessful. In his prime years of ministry, Jesus never had more than perhaps twenty-five faithful followers, fewer than the number of students enrolled in most basic political science courses. Moreover, those followers were socially, temperamentally, and politically disparate. They included a tax collector for the Romans and a political zealot who wished to overthrow the Roman government. They were, for the most part, poor, not well educated, and without political influence. They did not form a social movement—the church—until after the death of their leader. Yet that social movement now has literally billions of members. Indeed, this is reason enough for political scientists in the mainstream to stop marginalizing Christianity and study its claims with care.

▸▸ Western Perversions

A Christian approach to political science needs to go beyond whole-person theology. It also needs to be corrective. Western nations, particularly the United States, advance a heresy called civil religion, in which political institutions blur the boundaries between religion and the state by elevating a sense of political righteousness and righteous citizenship to a religious level.[30] Though encouraging to hear people singing "God Bless America" in packed stadiums in the wake of the September 11, 2001, attack, there exists the danger that people will equate good citizenship with the Christian life. Moreover, the constant infusion of religious language into public discourse is a matter of ambivalence for many Christians. The Bible regularly speaks of the import of a nation's honoring God. This notwithstanding, such language often communicates the notion that the essence of the Christian life is little more than practicing good citizenship that contributes to the fulfillment of a divine vision for a good and lawful society.

Blamires, an Englishman, takes issue with this equation of nationalism with God's will. Believers need to assess the rightness of its nation's acts. Referring to a newspaper's summation of an unsuccessful invasion, he writes: "Now we have the act summed up as a 'great and multiple error of political judgment.' This is not the language of Christendom. Let them believe that the invasion of Egypt was a good act; let them believe it was an evil act. Let them take their stand accordingly. But to call the invasion a mistake is to lift the whole business of vital international action out of the sphere of the truly human activity upon which truly human judgments can be passed. Man is a moral being. His actions are good or evil."[31]

Blamires also comments on the quest for disarmament, so much a part of the cold war era concern with Communism. Often advanced as a Christian cause, the movement was subtly misguided. "Again, Christian thinking seems to play only a very small part in the Campaign for Nuclear Disarmament," notes Blamires. "Study of their publicity suggests that the main C.N.D. platform is

'Better Red than Dead.' This is not a view that a Christian pacifist could sub-scribe to. The Christian cannot possibly accept death as ultimate and final evil to be resisted at all costs. The Christian pacifist objects to killing, not to being killed."[32] A Christian thinker focusing on the C.N.D. issues would have to shift the emphasis of the movement. "Propaganda addressed to particular areas about what would happen to *your* town if an H-bomb were dropped on the nearest big city is not likely to search the Christian's conscience deeply. For propaganda of this kind makes a crude appeal to our love of comfort, of the amenities of life, and of physical existence itself. In short it tries to play upon our basest fears."[33] As for the possibility of nuclear war, Blamires feels the Christian's attention should "be turned to such matters as the uncertainty whether radiation may not permanently, or at least for many generations, damage the human species, impairing numberless unborn human children."[34]

Blamires has his finger on a key issue: the tendency of political behavior to be based on self-interest, rather than on the larger well-being. Politicians gain votes by promising a higher standard of living, and Christians often respond favorably, rather than asking, How about the poor?[35] These appeals communi-cate the notion that what is good for the majority—those on the inside of the political system—is what is good for the nation. The poor and the powerless, those God loves and includes in his definition of justice, are dismissed.

In a similar vein, observers of American political behavior speak of "rational political choice," referring to the tendency to vote on the basis of logical self-interest, rather than in response to charisma, emotion, or nonmaterial values. Nowhere is this more evident than in the predictable voting patterns of differ-ent subgroups in the United States who base their political choices on issues peculiar to their specific group interests. This is so common that state and national political figures go beyond constructing their electoral strategies with this in mind; many base their decisions on this tendency when in office. Though widely accepted, such behavior is not Christian, but rather a reinforcement of the biblical notion that humans are self-centered rather than God-centered.

▸▸ Other Issues

There is no shortage of topics for the Christian political scientist to study, review, and research. Many of these topics have been raised by nonbelievers. Marx's focus on work is one such example. He contended that in a capitalist society, the masses are alienated from their work, with the factory worker left to labor mindlessly at her machine. Marx's critique provides an excellent first step for the Christian thinker. Clearly there is nothing Christian about work that is meaningless and totally devoid of personal investment. The answer, however, is not merely in becoming the capitalist and owning the means of production. For the Christian, work is not political in nature. Ideally, it is an act of worship.[36] We expend ourselves in our work to honor God. Some work is explicitly Christian; the Christian ministry is an example. Other work can have a strong Christian overtone—teaching, medicine, childrearing, and social work. Nevertheless, all work is Christian if it is done to God's glory, if one sees himself as working for a divine, rather than a human, employer.

Here are some other issues needing discussion and research: What constitutes a biblically just war in an age of terrorism? Does a nation have the moral right to invade another nation that poses a major threat to them, as the United States did in Iraq in 2003, or is that a violation of sovereignty? What is a just and moral policy in a nuclear age of terrorism and ideological, rather than national, conflicts? Clearly things have changed as the nations have rearranged themselves and the threats are no longer simple. Christian political scientists have an opportunity to reformulate Christian principles regarding international relations that are grounded in biblical notions of justice.

Change is also extant within the United States, such that old questions need to be re-asked. For example, should Christians agitate for the inclusion of prayer in public schools, realizing that in some areas the Jehovah of the Scriptures may not be the God the majority worships? At what point does the separation of church and state stop protecting the free exercise of religion and begin becoming a permission-giver for nonbelievers to frustrate the advancement of the gospel or even to attempt to replace Christianity with agnosticism as the national religion?

What is a Christian approach to corrections? Christians regularly debate the issue of capital punishment, but rarely do they make a scriptural case for incarceration. What is the proper role of the police in an increasingly urban, pluralistic society? With violence a common form of conflict resolution, along with high levels of addiction and gang activity on one hand, and calls for an end to racial profiling and highly aggressive behavior on the part of law enforcement officers on the other, the role of the police needs definition. There is also the matter of civil disobedience, the importance of wealth generation, the degree and nature of governmental intervention, even the value of capitalism and democracy themselves.

All of these are divisive issues, generating intense debate. The Christian community does not need more white-hot controversy splintering it. These issues need to be studied by political scientists, carefully applying Christian criteria and analyses. Although consensus may never be reached, even among believers, heat must give way to light. Without question, few fields are as ripe as political science for those committed to faith and learning.

Notes

1. "Ultimate Political Science Links," http://www.rvc.cc.il.us/faclink/pruckman/PSLinks.htm (accessed October 29, 2003).
2. Hans Morgenthau, "The University of Oklahoma Department of Political Science," http://www.ou.edu/cas/psc/defpsc.htm (accessed January 23, 2004).
3. Antonio A. Chiareli, "Christian Worldview and the Social Sciences," in *Shaping a Christian Worldview*, ed. David S. Dockery and Gregory Alan Thornbury (Nashville: Broadman and Holman, 2002), 244.
4. Ibid., 243–44.
5. Glenn Tinder, "From the Ends of the Earth," in *Professors Who Believe*, ed. Paul M. Anderson (Downers Grove, IL: InterVarsity, 1998), 155.
6. Ibid.
7. David Claerbaut, *The Reluctant Defender* (Wheaton, IL: Tyndale, 1978), 92.
8. David P. Gushee, "Christian Worldview, Ethics and Culture," in Dockery and Thornbury, *Shaping a Christian Worldview*, 118.
9. David Claerbaut, *Social Problems*, vol. 1 (Scottsdale, AZ: Christian Academic Publications, 1976), 86.
10. Ibid.
11. David Claerbaut, *Urban Ministry* (Grand Rapids: Zondervan, 1983), 18.
12. Matthew 19:24.
13. James 1:27.
14. Micah 6:8.
15. Luke 8:2.
16. John 4:7–26.
17. 1 Corinthians 6:19.
18. John 6:51; 4:10.
19. 1 Corinthians 6:19.
20. John 14:1.
21. Philippians 4:6.
22. 1 Corinthians 2:16.
23. Philip Yancey, *What's So Amazing about Grace?* (Grand Rapids: Zondervan, 1997), 266.
24. Friedrich Nietzsche, *The Anti-Christ* (New York: Penguin, 1968).
25. Yancey, *What's So Amazing about Grace?* 265, 267.
26. Ravi Zacharias, *Jesus among Other Gods* (Nashville: Word, 2000), 72.
27. Matthew 18:20.
28. Jim Cymbala, *Fresh Power* (Grand Rapids: Zondervan, 2000), 60.
29. Chiareli, "Christian Worldview and the Social Sciences," in Dockery and Thornbury, *Shaping a Christian Worldview*, 260.

30. Ibid., 253; Chiareli cites several treatments of the notion of civil religion. These include Robert N. Bellah, "Civil Religion in America," in *Religion in America,* ed. William G. McLoughlin and Robert N. Bellah (Boston: Houghton Mifflin, 1968); and John A. Coleman, "Civil Religion," *Sociological Analysis* 31, no. 2 (1970).

31. Harry Blamires, *The Christian Mind* (Ann Arbor, MI: Servant, 1997), 22.

32. Ibid., 33.

33. Ibid., 33–34.

34. Ibid., 34.

35. Ibid., 87.

36. Colossians 3:23; 1 Corinthians 10:31.

23

PSYCHOLOGY:
NEED THEORY—A PLACE WHERE
FAITH MEETS LEARNING

Psychology is the science of human and animal behavior"; so reads a common textbook definition. The key word in that sentence is *science*. In reality, psychology attempts to study human and animal behavior scientifically. Its claim to being a science resides in its naturalistic tendency to study animal behavior and functions scientifically and then to extrapolate the findings to human existence. Beyond this, the discipline falls far short of being a science. In brief, psychology is a pre-paradigmatic discipline, with the major theories that apply to humans being open to Christian critique and development.

Because the field is so ripe for Christian critique, revision, and even theory building, the psychology section is divided into two chapters. The first will look carefully at need theory, focusing on Abraham Maslow and Erik Erikson. The second will examine personality theory and propose a structure for a Christian mental health model.

▸▸ Maslow's Hierarchy of Needs

Few theories are more amenable to Christian critique and revision than Maslow's hierarchy of needs.[1] Presented in pyramid form, Maslow offers an ascending set of needs requisite for healthy human functioning. Though basically a need theory, one may find Maslow's hierarchy in basic psychology texts as well as in books on personality theory, in courses in mental health (often called mental hygiene), and in educational psychology. Derivations of Maslow are even found in business management classes, as a tool for understanding and improving employee motivation. (In fact, Maslow wrote on psychological aspects associated with business.)

For those unfamiliar with Maslow's pyramid, what follows is a brief review of his hierarchy of needs. Each need level in his five-level structure must be satisfied—in order—before one can move to the next rung. Moreover, according to Maslow, once a need is satisfied, the person will move directly toward satisfying the next level of need.

At the base of the pyramid are the physiological necessities, representing the need to survive. The second level, safety needs, refers to having a sense of security that one's survival needs will be met for the foreseeable future. Once the person is confident that her temporal needs will be satisfied for the long term, Maslow says she will move in an inward direction, turning her attention toward the belongingness needs—the need for quality social and personal relationships.

Once the love and companionship needs are sated, Maslow suggests humans look to develop self-esteem. This involves a sense of identity, significance, purpose, and worth. Much of self-esteem comes through work and achievement. The final level is called self-actualization. Here a person maximizes her potential, doing what she is best suited for. The writer writes, the physician practices medicine, the homemaker takes care of the home. According to Maslow, few people reach this level. Most of us are either stalled at lower levels or simply denied the opportunity to engage in a lifestyle perfectly compatible with our skills and temperament. In fact, the hierarchy is presented as a pyramid to illustrate that fewer people gain satisfaction at each ascending level.

In general, Maslow's construct works reasonably well from a Western, middle-class perspective, particularly in the theory's focus on achievement. For the Christian, however, it has a glaring weakness. The model is completely temporal, offering a heaven-on-earth action plan. But does it offer even that? Only to the extent that the person is largely aspiritual. There is room in the theory for values, belief systems, and meaning, but Maslow gives little or no import to the spiritual dimension of human existence. The theory therefore would not work—at the personal level—for a number of Christian intellectuals who achieve much while living out their professional dreams.

E. C. Ashby is a professor emeritus in chemistry and biochemistry at Georgia Tech. Maslow's model would not work for him, because the fulfillment of basic physical and psychological needs was simply not enough to satisfy Ashby. This, in brief, is his story. Having received an appointment at Georgia Tech with the help of 1979 Nobel Peace Prize winner, H. C. Brown, Ashby was soon directing a research team of ten Ph.D. students. Publications abounded, and Ashby was in heavy demand on the university and international academic lecture circuit.[2]

"But all this success did not bring me satisfaction; in fact, I felt quite empty," notes Ashby. He then joined a Roman Catholic colleague at a three-day spiritual retreat, called a *cursillo*. There he heard the salvation message and the call to a life of commitment to Christ. "I said yes to Jesus in every aspect of my life, and instantly all doubt and lack of faith disappeared. I felt a profound sense of the presence of God in my life, which to this day has not left." From there, the Bible became a living form of revelation for Ashby, and he activated his faith in a non-denominational church.[3]

For decades, John Suppe, Blair Professor of Geology at Princeton University, lived with a curious "combination of success, happiness, and an absence of meaning and purpose." He began attending campus chapel services in search of some answers. There a speaker charged the academically gifted audience with being authorities in their respective fields but having less than an elementary knowledge of Christianity. "Her words shot like an arrow through the Gothic arches right into me," he notes. Realizing that "if there is any truth to Christianity, I had better start looking into it," Suppe began the process.[4]

First he read books *about* Christianity. Then he read the gospel of Mark, the first gospel written. The experience was life changing. Suppe sensed that the book was true and historical, rather than fictional or fanciful. More important, he came face-to-face with Jesus and his claim to be the divine Son of God. As he recalls, "Certainly the idea that the universe was created was not an unreasonable possibility.... The idea that the universe exists by itself is just as remarkable as its being created." That a loving creator might want to communicate and be personally involved with his creation was even more important. "My sudden impression was that if this were true, it would be the most important fact of human existence. To live life without taking part in the implications of this fact would be to miss out on the essence of what it meant to be human."[5]

From there, Suppe moved from spectator to participant in the church and began a life of continual spiritual adventure and fulfillment.

Mark T. Clark, a political scientist in the California State University system, had a similar experience. Prior to teaching, while in the Marine Corps, he felt a gnawing emptiness. "I was acknowledged by our superior officers as a top-notch marine. But I was not happy," he writes. "On the outside, I was successful, but on the inside, I was feeling miserable."[6]

Clark committed his life to Christ, but with reluctance. Soon, however, the new life took hold. "As timid as I was when I turned my life over to Christ, I began to feel more alive than ever," he writes.[7] Although Clark's Christian journey has been one of highs and lows, with many faith-and-learning wrestling matches, meaning and happiness have always been present.

Louisa Hulett, the much-honored chair of the political science department at Knox College, provides yet another example of the need for spiritual nurture. Describing herself as an academic who worshiped the idols of earning a Ph.D., racking up publications, gaining tenure, and relishing success, Hulett was starving on the inside.[8] "Despite this great life, however," she states, "I began to feel that something was missing." She found herself questioning the value of life itself. "What was my purpose in life? Why is there a universe?" she pondered.[9]

Hulett agreed to attend a retreat with a Christian colleague but soon dreaded having committed to go. She literally prayed she would get sick and thus avoid having to attend this time-wasting event. The first two days were nauseating, she says. "People talked about God all day long as they plied me with cookies and conversation," she recalls. On the third day, she engaged in some genuine soul-searching and felt the loving presence of Christ.[10] Born again, Hulett's life changed drastically. Her faith permeated every area of her life with meaning and mission, including her academic work. She developed a course called Christianity and Politics and began leading Christian groups on campus. For Hulett, faith brought balance, meaning, and joy.[11]

Paul Anderson, professor of biochemistry and molecular biology at the University of Minnesota Duluth, felt a spiritual vacuum in his life. "I had a wonderful wife and family, a new home and a successful career," he writes. "I thoroughly enjoyed science and felt fortunate to have a career in that field. Yet, I felt an emptiness, a lack of purpose and meaning." Looking at his material success and career prestige, he asked, "Is that all there was to life?"[12] Years earlier when Anderson was in graduate school at Minnesota, a celebrated biochemist, Fred Smith, had challenged Anderson to consider a relationship with God. Not much had come of that. Though retaining an intellectual belief in the existence of God, Anderson simply went on with his life as if God didn't matter. Things changed when he spent a year in Indiana, where he met a believer who directed Anderson's interest in God toward the person of Christ. Anderson pored through most of the New Testament in a few weeks. "Here was a blueprint for living and a description and explanation of the sense of separation from God that I had been experiencing," enthuses Anderson.[13] Over a period of years, his faith flowered and he began looking at ways to integrate his faith with the physical sciences.[14]

For the psychologist, the lives of these scholars begs the question, Is temporal success, amid a life without ultimate meaning, really enough? And if life truly is meaningless, why study psychology at all, other than to learn to manipulate others for one's personal benefit? From where does the value-laden language of the discipline—and elsewhere in academe—come? Why, for example, does the adjective *manipulative* have a pejorative connotation? Words such as *honorable*, *respectable*, and *of excellent character* have no relevance in a world without meaning or spiritual morality. In such a world, for example, how would one define *honorable, respectable,* or *of excellent character?* What would be the measure? What is a humanitarian in a value-free social order? And more important perhaps, who cares?

►► A Christian Approach to Need Theory

Maslow's structure has value for need theorists. His order is sound, and the overpowering importance of physical and safety needs squares with our finite and mortal natures. Jesus affirmed the importance of physiological needs. He used food and water as metaphors for himself as the spiritual food and drink, and he miraculously fed huge throngs, healed illnesses of every sort—physical and mental—as well as returning people from death.

On the security level, Christ handled matters in a counterintuitive way. Rather than emphasize hoarding for the rainy days, Jesus focused on priorities. In Matthew 6:33, he tells his followers to first seek the kingdom of God—a right relationship with the divine—and God will add the temporal blessings as needed. Moreover, a right relationship with God has practical dimensions. It emphasizes the virtues of honesty, good stewardship, the proper use of one's skills, and a spirit of responsibility among other things. These practical traits are the stuff of which reliable, employable citizens are made. It also mandates caring for the poor and others unable to use their skills to make a living. Going back to God's consistent care for the children of Israel in the Old Testament, the Bible is consistent about the importance of temporal necessities.

A Christian model of need theory would definitely include a relationship with God as a significant factor at the belongingness level. To feel a sense of spiritual belongingness not only provides wholeness in and of itself, but it also offers incredible strength in the case of social rejection or relational failure. Belongingness is central in Christianity. The essence of the Christian life is not found in doctrines, philosophy, or the teachings of Christ. It is in the relationship one has with the living Jesus. Unlike other religious traditions, in which God is either impersonal or distant, Christianity answers what many feel is humanity's greatest need: relationships. The great messengers of the other traditions are dead. What is left are their teachings and writings. Christianity worships a living Christ, one who enters a personal and intimate relationship with believers. Furthermore, on a human level, there are no deliberately rugged-individualist Christians according to the Bible. Rather, Christianity promotes fellowship—a network of positive human relationships with fellow believers—as part of the very spinal column of the faith. Christ not only gathered a dozen close followers; he became particularly close with three of them, Peter, James, and John.

Above all, Maslow's self-esteem level might well be reworked to include one's sense of spiritual worth. From a Christian perspective, human worth is not lodged in the conferring of approval from one human to another. It is in one's identity as a child of God and an object of grace. Internalizing this makes self-worth spiritual, eternal, and invincible. It is at the self-esteem level that Christianity, when understood properly, excels. According to Scripture (Ps. 8:5), we are cast in the image of the divine, made "a little lower than the heavenly beings." In 1 Corinthians 6:19, Paul calls our very bodies temples of God. Moreover, we are worth the very blood of God's son and are regarded as joint heirs with Christ of God's riches (Rom. 8:17). Although the language is sometimes abstract, it conveys a near-royal status for Christians.

Dr. Verna Benner Carson, long-time member of the nursing faculty at the University of Maryland, has taken bold professional steps for the faith. She advocated a Christian component in mental health in her teaching and even in her publishing. After writing *Spiritual Dimensions of Nursing Practice,* she coedited a text titled *Mental Health Nursing.* Noting that current texts omit spiritual issues and their import in mental health, her text has a "theistic worldview" that affirms the existence of a personal God who cares about his creation. Realizing she would engender resistance from many of her colleagues in the university mainstream, Carson stated that she believes she must see her profession as an extension of John's directive (1 John 3:23) "to believe in the name of his Son, Jesus Christ, and to love one another as he commanded us."[15]

There is one caveat for Christians, as it relates to self-esteem and emotional well-being: Christians need to focus on our intrinsic value to God, rather than submerge the gospel in a message of guilt. The gospel is not about guilt and sin. The gospel is good news. *Guilt is not good news.* The gospel message is that guilt and sin no longer need plague the follower of Christ. Repentance for Christian believers does not mean an immersion into guilt, followed by a promise never to make the same mistakes again. Repentance is a daily spirit one adopts, an attitude that God is perfect and we want him both to forgive us of our imperfections and to work within us each day to live in rhythm with his will. There is indeed a struggle in the Christian faith, because believers—carriers of the original sin virus—are every bit as imperfect as those who do not believe. Thus, we are often oriented toward doing things that fall short of God's will. This tension, however, need not generate depression and self-hatred, because we are purged of guilt through Christ and promised changes in the inner self through the power of the Holy Spirit. To the extent that a believer wishes and is willing to have the Holy Spirit work these wonders, change will occur over time. The Christian life, then, is an adventure as one becomes more like Christ.

Beyond self-esteem and using Maslow's standards, we could agree that many Christians do not experience self-actualization in this life. For those that do, however, it would seem impossible to do without a sense of meaning. The Christian is always committed to a cause larger than herself. She is committed to a divine cause, one that will live on long after she is gone. When I was a child, my mother displayed an incredibly simple aphorism: "Only one life 'twill soon be past; only what's done for Christ will last." To have a complete sense of fulfillment, one would need to incorporate that simple truth. Self-actualization is doing what God wants us to do. We are to be his vehicles by which he accomplishes his will in the world. Self-actualization is therefore associated with following the owner's manual for life. This does not come from a job, profession, or relationship, but from being committed to a faithful living-out of God's will as we understand it.

Self-actualization in terms of inner satisfaction and spiritual serenity is possible for the Christian if he or she truly chooses a life of faith. Male or female, a person can be physician, a steamfitter, or a football coach. The incredible beauty—the self-actualizing dimension—of the Christian faith lies in the bridge that connects the mortal and the immortal, the finite and the infinite, humanity and God. These polarities are linked in Christ. Hence, by definition, we are involved in a cause larger than ourselves. What we humans do on this planet has divine implications, while at the same time divine interventions in terms of healing and guidance influence activities on earth. Humankind and God are in partnership. The effects of sin (our basic imperfection) that make us human and separate from God are removed by the ultimate bridge—the God/man, Jesus Christ. In God we "live and move and have our being," says Luke in Acts 17:28.

▸▸ Erik Erikson's Developmental Theory

Erik Erikson's renowned "Eight Stages of Man" cuts the normal life cycle into eight distinct phases.[16] Each stage involves a crisis that a person must negotiate successfully to move forward in a psychologically healthy fashion. As with Maslow, no stage may be skipped. Though labeled a developmental psychologist, Erikson is a major need theorist as well. Although one could critique each of Erikson's eight psychosocial stages, the final three, beginning in young adulthood, are of particular interest because they address the level of well-being in the context of reaping the consequences of one's choices.

Erikson recommends a series of life choices much in keeping with Christian living. The crisis of young adulthood, for example, involves the distinction between intimacy and isolation. Here the decision is between being relational and interactive or closed and self-protective. Erikson weighs in on the side of the former, believing that proper psychological development necessitates intimate personal alliances. So does Scripture. In only the second chapter of the Bible (Gen. 2:18), God speaks the words of relationship, saying, "It is not good for the man to be alone." Scripture presents isolation—except in times of prayer and meditation—as negative.

Isolation often brings loneliness, a condition that kills. "A nine-year study by researchers at the University of California shows loneliness has a greater impact on the death rate than smoking, drinking, eating, or exercise. The study found that people without spouses or friends had a death rate more than twice as high as those with social ties."[17]

People dread loneliness and will expend much energy to escape its pain. The constant buzz of televisions, radios, CD players, and simple conversation—however meaningless—becomes psychologically necessary for people who cannot stand to deal with silence, a reminder of being alone. To stop their distracting, frenetic pace reminds them of how incredibly alone they are in the inner person. It all but forces them to embrace that aloneness and spend time reflecting on the direction of their life. So says Harvard psychiatrist Armand Nicholi: "Perhaps we distract ourselves," he suggests, "because looking at our lives confronts us with our lack of meaning, our unhappiness, and our loneliness."[18] In those moments of silence, people realize that death is at the end of the road. Then what? For many, loneliness reminds them of death, even of hell. The latter is perhaps best described as the ultimate loneliness that comes from complete separation from God. Therefore, constant stimulation, no matter how superficial, serves the purpose of distracting people from feeling the emptiness, guilt, and fear that is just under the surface. Pascal believed that the quest for overstimulation betrays an inner unhappiness. If people's lives were truly happy, they would not attempt to divert themselves from reflecting on their existence.[19]

Loneliness takes many forms. Five have been identified: Loneliness In (a relationship)—the condition of being with, but not psychologically related to, another; Loneliness Out—the isolation one feels in the absence of a rewarding human relationship; Intrapsychic Loneliness, which arises from identity confusion and a sense of not really knowing who one is; Spiritual Loneliness—the awareness of the spiritual nature of life, but a profound emptiness in that area; Situational Loneliness—an apartness that is generated by circumstances such as being away from home or in a new and unfamiliar work environment or residence.[20] No matter the type, each evokes an interior loneliness—loneliness in the inner person that is unsettling to the spirit. Erikson realized this, and in his adult stages placed intimacy at the top of the list for healthy emotional development. Again, so does Scripture, which presents a relationship with God, even more than flawed and temporal relationships with fellow human beings, as basic to a healthy existence.

In Erikson's adult stage, the struggle is between generativity and self-absorption. A person either focuses her energy on the development of a succeeding generation or chooses to live for solely selfish purposes. Here Erikson clashes with Albert Ellis's notion advocating that the goal of life is having a ball. By Erikson's calculation, losing one's life is indeed a way of finding it; selflessly investing one's life in the well-being of future generations becomes a way of finding wholeness. To commit oneself to a life of narcissistic self-indulgence is the opposite of the message found in Scripture and deemed unhealthful by Erikson.

Perhaps the most useful of Erikson's constructs is his description of the crisis of senescence: integrity versus despair. It was the psychologist's contention that successful negotiation of the preceding stages would leave one with a sense of satisfaction and a good feeling at the end of life. The alternative is despair, a realization that relationships were not nurtured and the glorification of self had taken center stage. With that, a bitter depression takes over, as one realizes that the choices have been made and the harvest is not sweet.

There is much to be said for Erikson's eight stages. Implied within them is the concept of choice and the sense that a choice in one direction is made at the expense of another path. He suggests that commitment to a lifestyle of egocentrism and narcissism all but obviates healthy, giving relationships. The payoff for this commitment to what is often temporary pleasure and ease rarely includes a long-term sense of well-being. The troubling incidence of depression and self-destructive behavior in the form of substance abuse and even suicide among the affluent that opt for lives of self-indulgence is testimony to this.

A friend of mine, a former major league baseball all-star, told me that from childhood his father steered him toward baseball. Once in the major leagues, his ultimate professional goal became signing a huge, multiyear contract, something that ensured career and economic security. After coming through the lower ranks, living the bologna-and-cheese life of the minor leagues, and struggling through the early major league years, he finally established himself. He was a cornerstone of his team, and the organization wanted to sign him to a long-term contract. He had reached the summit—what he had dedicated his life to. The magic day came and my friend marched triumphantly into the team office and signed a six-year pact for a veritable fortune.

Similar to the professors cited earlier, however, he wasn't happy.

"When I drove home from the team office," he said slowly, "I began to cry."

For my wildly successful friend, the experience was one of the most painful of his entire life. He had discovered the truth behind the French proverb "Money makes a good servant but a terrible master."

My friend's experience of not knowing what is truly important and so adopting a materialist, in-the-now perspective, is a common theme in literature. Thornton Wilder's play *Our Town* centers on Emily Gibbs, who dies in childbirth and is able to observe from beyond the activities in what was once her home. Given the chance to return to earth for a single day of her choosing, Emily selects the celebration of her twelfth birthday. Amid the food, talk, and scurrying activity, she quickly notes that the entire focus is not on the people and their worth and significance but on activities and things to be done. Sadly, Emily realizes that her loved ones are missing out on the essence of life. As she bids farewell to the party, Emily cries, "Oh earth, you're too wonderful for anyone to realize you!" and then asks the narrator/stage manager, "Do any human beings ever realize life while they live it—every, every moment?"

"No. The saints and poets, maybe—they do some," he replies.

There are many points of agreement between Erikson and Maslow. Despite his focus on individual fulfillment, Maslow affirms the critical import of healthy relationships as a precursor to self-esteem and self-actualization. Although neither contends that humans are spiritual in nature, both move past the determinism of the naturalist and advocate a life involving personal intimacy and self-reflection. Moreover, Erikson's formulation suggests (and Maslow's does not refute) that a life based on Christian values would certainly yield a sense of "integrity" and satisfaction.

Values are associated with moral development, an area many child and adolescent psychologists address. Erikson approaches it in his references to shame and guilt in early life, and later despair, as opposed to more positive emotions. Often Christian scholars get lost here, seeing moral development in terms of doing good things as opposed to bad things, often the same criteria for good and bad behavior that secularists use. Harry Blamires offers a higher order of moral sensibility for believers. In distinguishing oneself from the secular culture, there are two questions the Christian should ask himself or herself: "(1) What should I, as a good man or woman, do or say in this case? and (2) What should I, as a Christian, do or say in this case? The Christian ought always to be a good man or woman, and therefore the answer to 1 will be contained in the answer to 2."[21]

The issue of depth satisfaction, however, offers real possibilities for Christian inquiry. Further research might well be focused on adult emotional well-being as it relates to intrinsic spiritual faith. For example, current medical research does indicate that intrinsic religiosity has a scientifically demonstrable positive effect.[22] In addition, Nicholi determined that college students that underwent evangelical conversion experiences found their new faith enhanced their functioning. "They reported positive changes in their relationships, their image of themselves, their temperament, and their productivity." Moreover, peers who knew them before and after their conversions confirmed the students' view.[23]

There is great potential in studying the secular need theorists in the context of Christian thought. A Christian scholar might attempt to mix some of Maslow's insights with those of Erikson and others and—employing Wolterstorff's control beliefs—construct an academically sound and research-based Christian model of healthy psychological development throughout the life cycle.

Notes

1. Abraham H. Maslow, "A Theory of Motivation," in *Psychology in the World Today,* ed. Robert V. Guthrie (Reading, MA: Addison-Wesley, 1971), 101–19. See also Abraham Maslow, *Motivation and Personality* (New York: Harper, 1954).
2. E. C. "Gene" Ashby, "God Is Faithful," in *Professors Who Believe,* ed. Paul M. Anderson (Downers Grove, IL: InterVarsity, 1998), 50.
3. Ibid., 51.
4. John Suppe, "Ordinary Memoir," in Anderson, *Professors Who Believe,* 69–70.
5. Ibid.
6. Mark T. Clark, "Semper Fidelis," in Anderson, *Professors Who Believe,* 122.
7. Ibid., 124.
8. Louisa (Sue) Hulett, "A Prodigal Child Finds Faith," in Anderson, *Professors Who Believe,* 131–32.
9. Ibid., 132.
10. Ibid.
11. Ibid., 138–39.
12. Paul M. Anderson, "A Common Thread," in Anderson, *Professors Who Believe,* 20.
13. Ibid., 21.
14. Ibid., 22.
15. Verna Benner Carson, "A Life Journey with Jesus," in Anderson, *Professors Who Believe,* 103. Carson's publications include *Spiritual Dimensions of Nursing Practice* (Philadelphia: W. B. Saunders, 1989) and *Mental Health Nursing: The Nurse-Patient Journey* (Philadelphia: W. B. Saunders, 1996).
16. "Erik Erikson's Eight Stages of Man," in David Poponoe, *Sociology* (Englewood Cliffs, NJ: Prentice-Hall, 1974), 124–28. See also Erik Erikson, *Childhood and Society* (New York: Norton, 1950).
17. ABC newscast, 7:00 A.M., December 14, 1983.
18. Armand M. Nicholi Jr., *The Question of God* (New York: Free Press, 2002), 6.
19. Ibid.

20. David Claerbaut, *Liberation from Loneliness* (Wheaton, IL: Tyndale, 1984), 46–47.
21. Harry Blamires, *Where Do We Stand?* (Ann Arbor, MI: Servant, 1980), 37.
22. W. J. Strawbridge, R. D. Cohen, S. J. Shema, and G. A. Kaplan, "Frequent Attendance at Religious Services and Mortality Over 28 Years," *American Journal of Public Health* 87, no. 6 (June 1997): 957–61; H. G. Koenig, L. K. George, and B. L. Peterson, "Religiosity and Remission of Depression in Medically Ill Older Patients," *American Journal of Psychiatry* 155, no. 4 (April 1998): 536–42; M. E. McCullough and D. B. Larson, "Religion and Depression: A Review of the Literature," *Twin Research* 2, no. 2 (June 1999): 126–36; H. G. Koenig, "Religion and Medicine II: Religion, Mental Health, and Related Behaviors," *International Journal of Psychiatry in Medicine* 31, no 1 (2001): 97–109; H. G. Koenig, D. B. Larson, and S. S. Larson, "Religion and Coping with Serious Medical Illness," *Annals of Pharmacotherapy* 35, no. 3 (March 2001): 352–59; H. G. Koenig, "Religion, Spirituality, and Medicine: Application to Clinical Practice," *Journal of the American Medical Association* 284, no. 13 (Oct. 4, 2000): 1708; Nicholi, *The Question of God*, 52.
23. Nicholi, *The Question of God*, 93–94.

24

FAITH MEETS THE
MENTAL HEALTH MODELS

I n addition to being pre-paradigmatic, psychology as applied to humans is at best a hybrid field. It incorporates elements of philosophy, sociology, history, and even political science into its theories. Moreover, most models of human functioning consist of a series of empirical facts and research findings melded with attempts to patch the holes with theoretical constructs offering, at least on the surface, a complete account of some phenomenon. This does not make the models invalid. It does, however, leave them far short of being definitive explanations of human behavior.

Because the human dimensions of psychology deal with thoughts, feelings, and behaviors, matters about which Scripture and Christian doctrine have much to say, they are of particular interest to believers. In addition, the Christian concepts of soul and spirit all but intersect with psychology's study of emotions (or affect). Furthermore, psychotherapists talk of personality changes, while Christians speak of all things being new to the born-again believer.[1] Mental health practitioners focus on value change in the person, while values are central to the Christian life.

Basic to mental health models is personality development. In the behavioral sciences, personality is generally defined as an organized system of values, attitudes, beliefs, and behaviors characteristic of an individual. Because personality development is so heavy with theory and touches many issues the Bible speaks to extensively, it is particularly ripe for Christian comment and analysis. In this chapter, we will review some of the classical personality theories and suggest some directions for a Christian model of mental health.

▶▶ Sigmund Freud

Though critiqued, revised, and even discredited in many academic circles, the work of Sigmund Freud continues to loom large in the field of personality theory. There are still many institutions that proclaim a Freudian orientation, and varying forms of his psychoanalytic method are still widely practiced. Freud is perhaps best known for the id, ego, and superego trinity.[2] According to Freud, the id is the source of all uncensored desire and impulse. There is neither morality nor control in the id, simply desire. The superego (actually a part of the ego) includes the conscience and what Freud called the ego ideal. The superego is a morally inhibiting force that runs counter to the powerful id. The ego is the morally responsible will. It is the place from which commitments come. The ego is the managing, decision-making dimension of the personality. It mediates between the id and the superego in determining behavior.

There is much to be said for this construction. Though a self-confessed atheist, Freud betrays his Jewish roots by presenting a virtual intrapsychic morality play—an ongoing struggle of good versus evil.[3] The unbridled id corresponds with the fallen nature of humanity, the force that covets and lusts, wishes to exploit and murder, and entertains feelings of hate and aggression. The image of God is present in the superego, with its moral focus. Implicit in Freud's thinking is the Christian notion of a lack of complete harmony within the human psyche. The believer would attribute this disequilibrium to the fallen nature of humanity—original sin. The more one moves away from God, the more the id seizes control, generating pleasure but not peace, release but not fulfillment. A healthy rather than guilt-ridden, graceless, distorted superego represents the leading of the Holy Spirit, the spirit of Christ. The ego can choose to follow either God or the desires of his fallen nature in almost any given circumstance. The more closely one follows Christ, however, the more one's ego can internalize the mind of Christ.

The power of the id in its war against the superego is consistent with Paul's personal travails. "I do not understand what I do. For what I want to do I do not do, but what I hate I do," he anguishes. "For I have the desire to do what is good, but I cannot carry it out." Note that Paul feels the answer is in drawing the mind (ego) closer to Christ and his grace. "Who will rescue me from this body of death?" he asks. "Thanks be to God—through Jesus Christ our Lord!"[4]

Implicit in Freud's thinking is the Christian notion that humans have the power to choose. Though every bit the naturalist, Freud views a human being as far more than a conditioned beast. A human being is truly a person, with the capacity to think and direct, making him a responsible, moral agent. Obviously, Freud does not trace the origin of morality to God. In fact, he asserted that God is imaginary, based on one's projection of the father figure. Although his theory as to the origin of the idea of God—arising from the plaguing memory of a murdered father figure—is at best bizarre, it does make the concept of God personal and relational in nature.[5]

There is more of value in Freud. He paints humankind as egocentric and self-serving in nature. Beyond that, he claims that within each human is the presence of Thanatos, the death principle.[6] Freud contends that humans are oriented toward death and destruction. One can see a glimmer of original sin in the Thanatos orientation. Though he did not believe in original sin, he did not have a lofty view of human nature, having reputedly said, "I have found little that is good about human beings. In my experience, most of them are trash." Thanatos is in conflict with Eros, the principle of love and life. Their battle parallels the spiritual struggle between the force of life and love in Christ, and the force of death and destruction in human nature.[7]

Freud was a deep believer in the unconscious as a repository of experiences and sensations. In his psychoanalytic work, he aided his patients in pulling material from the unknown unconscious to the known conscious. His affirmation of the unconscious, if nothing else, gives humans a complexity far beyond that accorded by the empirically driven behaviorists. Moreover, the unconscious can be interpreted as, at least in part, spiritual or soul-like.

►► Carl Jung

Carl Jung, a prolific writer, employs a complex set of concepts in describing the nature and processes involved in the ego and self.[8] Jung was part of the early psychoanalytic movement and a follower of Freud.[9] A clinician, Jung's approach balanced the outer world (events) with a person's inner world, consisting of fantasies, dreams, and symbols.[10]

According to Jung, the ego was not the mere static decider that Freud conceived it to be, but was essentially how one felt about oneself in association with the conscious and unconscious feelings supporting it. A major aim of the ego was the development of the self—the core of the psyche that gives cohesion, meaning, and direction to the person. Outside the ego was what Jung called the shadow, personal attributes and aspects of experience that are kept out of the ego, often because they have been labeled negatively by significant others. There is also the persona or mask one shows to others to protect his or her inner self.

Jung is well known for his concept of the collective unconscious—a reservoir of experience, lying below the conscious, available to all human beings. From the collective unconscious, come archetypes—typical modes of expression common to all human beings.[11]

The goal of Jungian therapy is psychological wholeness and is accomplished in part by establishing a continuing relationship between the ego (conscious) and the unconscious, a dialogue between what is happening daily and what is going on below the surface.

Though not an orthodox Christian, Jung was no atheist. He affirmed a belief in the activity of God, believing he spoke mainly through dreams and visions. In addition, Jung employed many concepts common to the Christian vocabulary. He wrote about good and evil, right and wrong, and in *Psychology and Alchemy,* he stated, "We know of course that without sin there is no repentance and without repentance no redeeming grace, also that without original sin the redemption of the world could never have come about."[12] Moreover, Jung believed that a right kind of conscience moves in the direction of God, while a wrong one can distort one's moral universe, turning good into evil and evil into good. In short, Jung's views comport well with the Christian belief that letting one's conscience be one's guide is only helpful if that conscience is forged in the direction of God.

Clearly, Jung provides valuable material for Christian dialogue. In addition to the foregoing, Jung's notion as to the complexity of the human psyche is in rhythm with the assertion that humans are "fearfully and wonderfully made" (Ps. 139:14). His collective unconscious, though a matter of much debate, transcends the limits of naturalism and approaches a common spiritual essence. Furthermore, his focus on whole-person functioning coheres with much Christian psychotherapy.

▸▸ B. F. Skinner

Burrhus Frederic Skinner was a behaviorist who devoted his time to studying empirical, observable behaviors. He would have scoffed at Freud's claims that his psychoanalytic work was scientific, because for Skinner, science came to a full stop once one began theorizing about internal thinking mechanisms and motivation.[13]

Skinner became famous for his use of operant conditioning. In brief, Skinner's model advocates that people perform behaviors for which they are reinforced, or rewarded. Behaviors become stronger the more they are rewarded, weaker (and possibly extinguished) when not. Central to Skinner's thought is that behavior is a *response* to a reinforcing stimulus and can be shaped simply by manipulating and managing the reinforcing stimuli. Shaping and changing behavior is called behavior modification. Skinner felt so strongly about the principles of behaviorism, he wrote a novel, *Walden II,* describing a utopian existence run entirely by behaviorist principles.[14]

The ultimate naturalist, Skinner states that freedom, dignity, and morality are meaningless, unscientific constructs spread by delusional moralists. For him, humans are no more highly developed than animal respondents to stimuli. In proclaiming behaviorism, Skinner said that while the conventional view of humans might elicit the statement, "'How like a god!'... Pavlov, the behavioral scientist, emphasized, 'How like a dog!'"[15]

There is little of Skinner that squares with Christian thinking. His naturalism rules out God, creation, human nature, truth, and values. If anything, Skinner's approach affirms the Christian notion of original sin in that humans—though reduced to animals in his model—operate totally on the basis of self-interest. There is little room for altruism in his system. That which is done for others, he would argue, is done because some reward, perhaps approval, is the reinforcing stimulus. There is no room in the Skinner Inn for the Christian concepts of grace and forgiveness. They can only be extended if there is a perceived payoff for the giver, which of course makes them not really grace or forgiveness in the pure, biblical sense.

▸▸ Carl Rogers

Carl Rogers believed that people are basically good and that they possess an actualizing tendency.[16] Similar to Maslow's concept of self-actualization, this refers to an innate desire to develop oneself to the fullest extent possible. It is due to this tendency, Rogers advocated, that we want to survive, eat, drink, relate to others, create, and grow. Moreover, Rogers holds that this orientation exists in every creature—human and animal. People, in quest of actualizing, create cultures and societies. Eventually, however, culture becomes a force in its own right and can interfere with the actualizing needs of the society of which it is a part. When that occurs, Rogers believes, the culture dies along with the potential of its members.

Rogers further holds that people value positive regard—love, affection, nurture, and attention. Society, however, often offers conditional positive regard by attaching conditions to its members' standards of worth. This conditional positive regard gives rise to a conditional positive regard among its members. For many, societal standards put their real self out of sync with society's definition of an ideal self. The gap between one's real self and ideal self generates incongruity, which in turn creates neurosis, anxiety, and a set of defenses, similar to Freud's defense mechanisms. Rogers defines psychosis not so much in terms of a disconnection with tangible reality but as a condition in which one's defenses are totally overwhelmed.

Rogers characterizes the healthy person as being open to new experiences, living in the now, trusting one's feelings to do what feels right and natural, engaging the freedom to make choices along with responsibility for their consequences, and being creative in the sense of contributing to the actualizing of others—similar to Erikson's "generativity" in adulthood.

From a Christian standpoint, we can affirm Rogers's actualizing tendency with a twist. We can agree that humans do indeed desire actualization. However, in the spirit of C. S. Lewis, we might suggest that it cannot be reached outside of a relationship with their Creator—that we long for a perfection that cannot be experienced on earth because we are not made for just this life.

We can also applaud Rogers's emphasis on freedom and responsibility with regard to choices. He is not deterministic or fatalistic in his thinking but accords each person the dignity of being a worthwhile and responsible moral agent. Although his urging to live in the now—though aware of the past and the future—has a strongly secular and temporal ring, it is another step away from environmental determinism and inaction.

Rogers was very popular with the "Do your own thing" and "If it feels good, do it" thinking of the 1960s and 1970s. As healthy as his encouragement of coming to terms with one's feelings is, this outlook has proven dangerous and destructive to many who have adopted it. A Christian might say that its downside lies in Rogers's belief that people are basically good and should therefore do what is natural. If one's nature is good, then doing what is natural is good. If, however, one's nature is flawed, then one's "natural" actions may often be unwise.

▸▸ A Christian Mental Health Model

The foregoing theories give the Christian concepts to accept and reject. Even rank atheists like Freud speak versions of the truth. Moreover, whether directly or indirectly, each speaks to the matter of mental health. This, I believe, is extremely important to the Christian interested in human functioning. Given all the accusations of pathology associated with Christian belief, and even simply theistic belief, extant in the mental health field, it would be interesting to see a Christian mental health model. Thus, I suggest consideration be given to several components.

Many years ago I heard Christian psychologist, Lloyd Ahlem, author of *Do I Have to Be Me?* discuss the matter of identity from a Christian perspective. He pointed out that for the Christian, the ego (the self) is not central but orbital. If "to live is Christ" (Phil. 1:21), and if "in him we live and move and have our being" (Acts 17:28), then we are to be theocentric (or Christocentric) rather than egocentric. Basic to the ego-orbital theory is that the believer is to reside *in*

Christ, and believe *in* Christ, rather than merely subscribe to a series of doctrines. Ahlem's ego-orbital theory differs from every other theory of personality in existence and so merits analysis and research.

In addition, a Christian model should have faith and love replacing cynicism and fear. Perfect love, or perhaps the internalization of perfect love, is said (in 1 John 4:18) to eradicate all fear. Fear is an immobilizing emotion. If the believer can reside in faith and the assurance of God's grace-laden love, there should be liberation—emotional freedom. This squares rather nicely with Verna Carson's focus on the spiritual as basic to emotional health. It is totally logical. If God exists, and if humans are spiritual as well as physical and mental beings, then a Christ-centered focus grounded in faith and internalized love is the only way to optimum mental health.

As for those skeptics who point out the various aberrations common to "religious fanatics," there is this to consider. Religion is carried out in human institutions directed by fallen people. Whenever the vessel carrying the truth is made by human hands, it is flawed—a testimony to the inherent imperfection that is sin. The issue in oppression and manipulation of religion is not faith. It is the fallenness of its purveyors.[17] Borrowing an argument from psychologist Gordon Allport, simply because some concept is perverted does not invalidate its reality. In the case of truly powerful notions, the potency of their misuse could be said to reinforce their reality. For example, does anything in human existence generate more human tragedies than misguided notions of love? People regularly do insane things in the name of love. Yet no one suggests that love does not exist. Religion is no different. People regularly pervert and twist religious truth en route to deranged and destructive behavior. That does not mean, however, that God does not exist or that the gospel is untrue. As with dynamite, love and religion are real yet explosive. Dealt with healthily, they are roads to truth and fulfillment. When twisted, they can bring great destruction.

A Christian mental health model should be holistic—including the physical as well as the spiritual. As discussed previously, Christianity affirms the unity of the body, mind, and spirit. This suggests that any Christian model might affirm the value of physical well-being or at least maintenance. Although perhaps a peripheral point, it should stimulate thought.

There is so much more to consider. What does it mean to be in the image of God? Being in the image God affects everything—body, mind, and spirit, thoughts, feelings, and behaviors. It places humans above the animal kingdom, limiting the degree of extrapolation (animal to human) possible. It also implies the Christocentric notion of Ahlem. And what about sin? Sin, a negative strain running through our lives, infects every aspect of human existence. It explains the basis for everything from common character defects to interpersonal conflict.

From the negativity of sin we move to grace. Psychotherapist David Seamands concludes, "The two major causes of most emotional problems among evangelical Christians are these: the failure to understand, receive, and live out God's unconditional grace and forgiveness; and the failure to give out that unconditional love, forgiveness, and grace to other people."[18] Grace enables us to accept forgiveness, expelling lingering guilt and putting our past behind us. It also empowers us to forgive others, liberating us from the emotionally corrosive effects of living with unending hate and bitterness. The issue of grace is central to a Christian mental health model because it is a uniquely Christian notion.

Again, there is much to flesh out here, but the ingredients, the raw materials, are there.

Notes

1. 2 Corinthians 5:17; Galatians 6:15.
2. Sigmund Freud, *The Id and the Ego,* ed. James Strachey, trans. Joan Riviere (New York: W. W. Norton, 1972).
3. For additional material on Freud's view of religion, see Sigmund Freud, *The Future of an Illusion,* ed. and trans. James Strachey (New York: Norton, 1989).
4. Romans 7:15, 18, 24–25.
5. Anthony Campolo, in *A Reasonable Faith* (Waco, TX: Word, 1983), cites Philip Rieff, *Freud: The Mind of the Moralist* (New York: Viking, 1959) as an excellent use of Freudian theories.
6. Sigmund Freud, *Civilization and Its Discontents* (New York: Norton, 1961), 91f., quoted in Campolo, *A Reasonable Faith,* 82.
7. Campolo, *A Reasonable Faith,* 83.
8. For the best compilation of Carl Jung's voluminous writings, see C. G. Jung, *The Collected Works,* 20 vols., ed. Herbert Read, Michael Fordham, and Gerhard Adler, trans. R. F. C. Hull, Bollingen Series XX (Princeton, NJ: Princeton University Press, 1953–79).
9. Marilyn Geist, "A Brief Introduction to Jung and Analytical Psychology," http://www.cgjungpage.org/articles/geist1.html (accessed Oct. 30, 2003). See also *The Freud/Jung Letters: The Correspondence between Sigmund Freud and C. G. Jung,* ed. William McGuire, trans. R. F. C. Hull, Bollingen Series XCIV (Princeton, NJ: Princeton University Press, 1974).
10. C. G. Jung, *Memories, Dreams, Reflections* (New York: Pantheon, 1961).
11. C. G. Jung, *The Concept of the Collective Unconscious,* vol. 9, *The Collected Works;* Jung, *The Archetypes and the Collective Unconscious,* vol. 9, *The Collected Works.*
12. Jung, *Psychology and Alchemy,* in Bollingen Series XX, vol. 12, 29–30.
13. For an excellent presentation of Skinner's behaviorist views, see his *About Behaviorism* (New York: Random House, 1974).
14. B. F. Skinner, *Walden II* (New York: Macmillan, 1978).

15. B. F. Skinner, *Beyond Freedom and Dignity* (New York: Bantam, 1971), 192, quoted in Campolo, *A Reasonable Faith,* 73.

16. "Personality Theories," http://www.ship.edu/~cgboeree/perscontents.html (accessed January 26, 2003). This is an excellent website in which many of the major personality theories are intelligently and understandably summarized. For Carl Rogers, see his *On Becoming a Person* (Boston: Houghton Mifflin, 1951).

17. Antonio A. Chiareli, "Christian Worldview and the Social Sciences," in *Shaping a Christian Worldview,* ed. David S. Dockery and Gregory Alan Thornbury (Nashville: Broadman and Holman, 2002), 257.

18. David Seamands, "Perfectionism: Fraught with Fruits of Self-Destruction," *Christianity Today,* April 10, 1981, 24–25.

25

SOCIOLOGY:
FAITH IN THE EYE OF NATURALISM

ociology is the study of human group behavior. The principal difference between sociology and psychology is that the former focuses on the group, while the latter is centered on the individual. Sociology is also a pre-paradigmatic discipline. Despite the mounds of empirical research ground out each year in the major journals and sociology's ardent claim to scientific status, there is no grand theory subscribed to by a consensus of scholars. Instead, there are a number of social theories, many of which are associated with specific theorists in the field.

Below are several synopses of major sociological theories. None are avowedly Christian, but that should not come as a surprise. The essence of the discipline is naturalistic, such that every group pattern, from marriage to government, is considered a "social construction" rather than a God-ordained entity. Humans are viewed as no more than the most highly evolved members of the animal world, possessing intricate brain functions enabling them to develop complex group structures and functions. No mainstream theory affirms the existence of God or creation. Nor does any adopt a moral view of human nature or assert the existence of universal truth or values.

Despite the thoroughly secular nature of the discipline, there are strands of thought that the Christian can embrace and embellish upon in this eye of naturalism.

▸▸ George Herbert Mead

George Herbert Mead was a social psychologist. Social psychology is a hybrid subdiscipline positioned between psychology and sociology. Mead, coming from the sociological symbolic interactionist branch, offers some valuable insights compatible with Christian thinking. He contributed heavily to the study of human identity, employing the concepts he called the "I and the Me."[1] The I is the essence of who a person truly is in the interior self. It refers to one's inner soul, that aspect of the self that is always in the present throughout life. In the case of you, the reader, it is the essence of your personhood throughout life. If your name is Rita, it is your inner and ongoing Rita, the core of your self that flows from womb to tomb. It is what a person is experiencing, where she is honestly and truly living life at any given moment. The I is ongoing, never changing. It is the permanent flow of an individual from birth to death. Grammatically speaking, it is the subjective (rather than objective) phase of a person's identity.

The Me is the collection of facts, experiences, affiliations, and characteristics that are a part of a person's life history. It is the part of the self that is presented to and viewed by others. Whenever a person describes herself in terms of age, race, family background, educational attainment, employment, interests, or even religion, she is describing the Me. The Me is what one projects to others. It is the part of the identity that is polite, fits in, and functions in society. It is the part that says, "Fine," when asked, "How are you?" even though one's life may be in shambles.

Well in excess of 99 percent of what most people reveal to others is from the Me rather than the I. Only a person's most intimate associates are allowed into one's I, and then only partially. One's parents and siblings may be almost totally ignorant of a family member's I. In fact, even psychotherapists rarely get to the I. When a person says, "I may be older, heavier, and no longer living in your community, but I am still Rita," she is distinguishing her I from her Me.

The I is only cathected with through high-quality intimacy, not unlike Buber's I-Thou dyad. S. Kirson Weinberg's relational typology provides an insight that parallels the I and the Me.[2] He claimed that relationships are personal, impersonal, antipersonal, or nonpersonal. A personal relationship is one involving intimacy, unlimited approachability, and private personal disclosures that provide a glimpse into the I. Most people have very few of these relationships. Impersonal alliances, no matter how friendly, are utilitarian and instrumental in nature. They are founded in practicality rather than intimacy. A relationship with one's psychiatrist is impersonal, because money is exchanged for private services. Even a relationship with a sexual lover may be impersonal, because it is driven more by mutual pleasure than by inner emotional sharing. It is an I-It relationship by Buber's calculation.

Antipersonal relationships are characterized by conflict. Here the participants often attack one another's self-esteem. Personal relationships gone bad can deteriorate into antipersonal ones, because there is emotional ammunition to strike painful blows at the now-adversary's psyche. The nonpersonal alliance refers to how a person relates to the faceless, anonymous masses he or she may encounter in a ticket line or getting on and off a crowded subway. Using Weinberg's typology, the personal relationship is the only one with the potential of involving the I.

A look at bestseller lists, as well as the seminar and workshop market, indicates how much humans long for I-based relationships. The difficulty is that so few ever develop the ego strength and relational skills necessary to satisfy this thirst. The Johari window model of intimacy describes this well. The window is divided into four slots or panes. The "open" pane includes all material known to us as well as to others. A second "hidden" slot refers to what is known to us only. It is what is unshared. A third area is "blind." It houses what is known only by others (about us). Aspects of our reputations are in the blind area. The fourth "locked" pane contains insights not known either to oneself or to others.

Ideally, the largest pane for most relationally healthy people would be the open one. Typically, however, it is the smallest. For most people, there is much more hidden and blind and a good deal locked. I have often tested this, asking a class, "How many of you have really wanted to tell another person something significant about yourself but didn't have the courage to do it?"

Invariably, 90 percent of the students put a hand in the air.

"Why didn't you?" I would ask.

"Because I am afraid of what they will think," one would say.

"I could be rejected," another would add.

"I just don't want to make myself that vulnerable," was another typical comment.

In the last analysis, people do not engage in self-revelation either because they are not accepting of themselves or because they fear others will not accept them.[3] This two-sided psychological coin results in people having far less relational nurture than they seek.

It is difficult to take issue with most of Mead's basic concepts, because they are self-evident to us. We live them each day. His formulations have solid potential for spiritual understanding. For example, we could say the psychological importance of the believer's personal relationship with Christ lies in the reality that human relationships are badly flawed. Many relationships fail entirely. Others are corrupted by selfishness and involve conditional commitments at best. The grace-driven nature of the personal relationship with God moves beyond these limitations. It is both healthy and real. It is healthy because it is entirely safe and unconditional. It is real in its effect on believers. We have noted the research indicating that intrinsic religiosity brings positive change.[4] Metaphorically speaking, human relationships are a form of bread and water, but they are far from being the living bread and water.

We could also suggest that the need for a relationship with God affirms the biblical view of human nature. If human nature were without flaw—sin—our relationships with fellow human beings would be far more nourishing and involve far less hurt. Moreover, the wish for idealized human relationships—without flaw—points to an ultimate truth: that lost humanity longs for a reunion with a perfect God.

▸▸ Emile Durkheim

The concept of alienation has been a prime focus in the works of major social theorists.[5] "Investigations of the 'unattached,' the 'marginal,' the 'obsessive,' the 'normless,' and the 'isolated' individual all testify to the central place occupied by the hypothesis of alienation in contemporary social science," says Robert Nisbet.[6] Their work provides grist for Christian thinking. Among the alienation theorists in sociology was one of its true giants, Emile Durkheim, who developed the concept of anomie. Durkheim defined anomie as a societal rather than an individual state. "It characterizes a condition in which individual desires are no longer regulated by common norms [rules of conduct] and where, as a consequence, individuals are left without moral guidance in the pursuit of their goals."[7]

Robert K. Merton built on Durkheim's concept of anomie, believing anomie arises "when there is an acute disjunction between the cultural norms and goals and the socially structured capacities . . . to act in accordance with them." In other words, anomie occurs when ideals such as wealth and economic security are held out to all members of the society but the means to reach these ideals are not available to everyone. Merton then described certain responses to anomie, which included innovation (crime and deviant activity), ritualism (deriving satisfaction from compulsively keeping the rules instead of advancing in society), retreatism (withdrawing, exemplified by alcoholism, drug addiction), and rebellion (attempts to overthrow the social structure).[8]

The material on anomie relates rather well to Christian thought. First, there is an implied assumption that humans often experience an insatiable hunger for material goods. This can take the form of ingratitude and avarice. The more affluent the larger society becomes, the more elevated the dissatisfaction among those on the outside will be. Merton suggests that humans will break rules, become self-destructive, and even engage in revolutionary conduct when faced with conditions in which they want more than they are receiving. At the core is a sense of estrangement from society, a dimension of sin—often defined theologically as alienation or estrangement from God. One could argue that the Fall, as described in Genesis 3, had the quality of anomie. The fruit available was simply not enough for the curious Adam and Eve. So instead of being grateful for what they had, they used a form of innovation (breaking God's rule) to reduce the anomie.

The work of Durkheim and Merton invites a larger Christian critique. The very notion that humans intensely desire material rewards in the material realm implies the existence of alienation—a condition of sin—between the Creator and his creatures. Humans are God's eternal children. When they participate blindly in a society mindlessly driven by materialism, convenience, and the acquisition of wealth, they are abandoning their spiritual natures in quest of the temporal.[9] They are, in a word, indulging in their flawed, sinful natures. In assessing the spiritual condition of a given society, Blamires says, "No doubt, if exhaustively pursued, the issue would raise such questions as—How far is the widespread use of motor vehicles increasing the slavery of men to machinery and consequently impairing man's delicately balanced status as a spiritual being in a material world? Are the inventions of modern technology being used for the betterment of human life over our planet as a whole, or are they being used as stimulants to covetousness and self-indulgence in the lives of a selfish minority of the world's inhabitants?"[10] In short, are a society's members living wholly in the temporal domain?

The matter goes deeper. A materialist society does more than venerate wealth, communicating that the good life is defined by the degree to which one can live in ease and affluence. It exacts a cost for this, even among the wealthy. It brings a servitude to materialism that is more than a way of living. It becomes an unexamined way of looking at the world.[11] It conditions a temporal, materialist perspective rather than a Christian one. Active *thinking* is replaced by a static *mind-set*. Technology—cars, television, film—reduces humanity to an almost nonhuman, responsive functioning. We are mindlessly directed to action rather than encouraged to choose and decide in a purposeful fashion.[12] The price is steep. While the home has become the center of humanity's worship of materialism, the family inhabiting the home continues to crumble as focus is shifted from familial intimacy to material well-being.[13]

There is more. The materialistic society also suggests that those on the outside in such a society are somehow deficient. Not only are they living a disadvantaged existence, they also wear the badge of inferiority—a lowered self-worth. Inherent in the ideology of materialism, then, is the belief in human superiority and inferiority, with wealth and occupational prestige the measuring devices. Western materialist thinking places much weight on occupation, the means by which one both attains both personal wealth and contributes to society's wealth.

Occupation is usually the primary variable used in determining socioeconomic status. In Christian terms, an identity built on the prestige of one's occupation is wrong. We are not what we do. We are the children of God—persons rather than functioning entities. From an eternal and spiritual perspective, notes Blamires, "the things to be insisted upon when salvation is at issue are things which link you and me with the duke and the tramp, the millionaire and the dustman."[14] A study of anomie, if nothing else, can direct the Christian thinker away from the secular and toward eternal and spiritual values.

▸▸ Karl Marx

For the atheistic Marx, alienation was associated with economic powerlessness. The materialist Marx believed industrialization robbed the worker of individuality and identity. Using the weaver as an example, he stated that the worker is merely "one of the instruments of labour, and being in this respect on a par with the loom, he has no more share in the product (the cloth), or in the price of the product, than the loom itself has."[15] The worker, the loom, and the cloth are all components of a material process driven by the capitalist in the effort to gain wealth.

Similarly, psychologist Paul Tournier believed "science itself depersonalizes man." It attempts to "eliminate the individual factor, the personal coefficient, and to repress everything that stirred up his heart."[16] It was Marx's contention that capitalism separated (alienated) the worker from the product he created. Note the pride of a child when she creates something for which she receives praise. The creation and the link to the adult is part of what makes the child spiritual.[17]

In Marx and Tournier, we again have estrangement: humans lose their freedom—their very identities—due to enslavement to materialist forces. Loss of creativity and meaning generates a profound alienation, a form of psychological death. In brief, when materialism becomes a society's god, humans are torn from their spiritual roots and live empty lives.

Marx is anathema to many Christians, due in large part to his indictments of religion. He claimed religion was used by the power elite to legitimize their authority and as a psychological drug to pacify the masses.[18] Nonetheless, he made some salient contributions for Christian scholars. Among them is that a society's morality is often distorted, if not shaped, by the interests of its ruling class. For example, capitalists promote private property and laissez-faire economic competition and therefore socialize (socially shape) their children to feel strongly about material success and free enterprise itself. Furthermore, those in control of the means of production—wealth—determine "truth" in the postmodern sense. They make the rules and enact the laws in the context of their philosophy, dictating what is moral. That philosophy has had theological over-tones as expressed in the Protestant ethic and latter-day "health-and-wealth" advocates. In addition, an unchecked focus on "getting ahead" (in the form of material advancement) can generate the I-It kind of manipulative relationships to the physical and social environments mentioned by Tillich, as well as the alienation of the person from her work cited by Marx.

Foundational to the Protestant ethic and health-and-wealth thinking is a high valuation of progress and material success. Progress has often been a permission-giver for the manipulation and exploitation of nature and people. I once took a class to a Native American section of a city. During our visit to its community center, an elderly man, known by a tribal name as well as a "Chris-tian" name, addressed the group in Tillich-like tones. "The white man speaks of progress," I recall him saying in a booming voice. "But the Indian sees the land being raped, the water polluted, and the air dirty. 'If that is progress,' says the Indian, 'then I don't want progress.'"

Marx was a conflict theorist. He believed that society was constantly in con-flict or in a state of gurgling tension that leads to conflict. Nothing is ever static. There is an ongoing thesis-antithesis-synthesis dialectic present in Marx's think-ing. Once a system is in place, its dysfunctions begin generating an opposing system (antithesis); out of this conflict comes yet a new system (synthesis). That conflict—imperfection—is inherent in his social theory and coheres with the Christian doctrine of sin in the universe. Nothing here can ever be truly perfect by Christian standards, and Marx's ideas align well with that belief.

▸▸ Structure-Functionalism

Another major school of social theory is called structure-functionalism. Having many intellectual fathers, structure-functionalism views a society as similar to a complex organism, consisting of a harmonious set of structures (designs) with functions (activities) the occupants of the structures perform. Humans, then, are actors who play roles on society's stage, and in these roles they contribute, often unselfconsciously, to the well-being of the society. If one were to become a teacher, for example, she would be serving in the societal institution of edu-cation—one of the society's major structures. Simply by performing her role, she would be executing the functions of the educational structure, that of imparting skills and knowledge to the society's youth so they in turn can also contribute functionally to the society.

Structure-functionalists view religion secularly, in terms of how it con-tributes to social cohesion and order in a society.[19] Religion is no more or less than a social creation that *functions* as a binding force for members of a society. The structure-functionalist may, for example, favorably regard worship services and funerals in the wake of national tragedies like those of Oklahoma City and September 11, 2001, not because they bring divine healing and spiritual comfort, but because they have a socially unifying effect.

By structure-functionalist logic, major social change occurs only when a structure in the society no longer functions. Provided the functions of a given structure (an institution such as education, family, economics, etc.) outweigh its dysfunctions, the structure will endure. Change does occur in this model, but usually rather cooperatively. A structure may change over time, resulting in a related structure picking up additional functions. The family, for example, was once a major educational agent in agrarian America. As the nation grew, however, the public school system arose and expanded to discharge more of what were once family educational functions.

Some structure-functionalists have made it "open season" on the church, claiming it is irrelevant, no longer functional in contemporary society. Christian scholars need to be ready for this. "One has seen it proclaimed that the Church is facing its 'gravest crisis for centuries,'" notes Blamires. "The press delights in these topics. 'Can the Church Survive?' 'Is Religion on the Way Out?' 'Is There a Place for the Church in the Modern World?'"[20] These attacks all regard the church as a human institution with only temporal relevancy, and therefore as something to be judged by humans rather than God. This is reductionist thinking in the extreme. It is one thing to look at the church in terms of its current social relevancy. Even church leaders do that. It is another thing, however, to assume that temporal relevancy is its chief (let alone only) purpose.

"Can the church survive, indeed! Can the *world* survive?" asks Blamires in a typically exclamatory tone.[21] According to him, it is the world, not the church, that is most definitely in crisis. "The world is like a great express train hurtling towards disaster—perhaps towards total destruction. And in this truly desperate situation certain passengers are running up and down the corridors announcing to each other that the Church is in great danger!"[22] He offers an alternative vision of the church, that of a powerful oceanliner riding through a storm. "Safely on deck, one cannot take seriously the cries of those who, having jumped overboard into the perilous sea, scorn the proffered life-belts, and use up their last resources of energy before being engulfed to warn those still aboard that they are in a doomed vessel."[23]

The church can never be destroyed. "It cannot even be gravely damaged," observes Blamires. "It cannot be decimated numerically: too many of the Church's members are already beyond the barrier of death; too much of the

Church is already safe at home."[24] Blamires rightly sees the structure-functionalist criticism of the church for what it is—a critique of God's creation—when he warns, "Above all, we must not transfer from the secular to the religious sphere the fallacious nineteenth-century doctrine of progress."[25]

Structure-functionalism is an inherently logical approach to social analysis. It is more descriptive than analytical. It describes what one can see for oneself when looking at a society. A question the structure-functionalist school of thought raises for Christians involves social determinism. The approach is heavy-handed in suggesting that human behavior is socially prescribed, conceptualizing humans as little more than functioning entities in social systems, all but removing choice and intellectual freedom. This connotes a subhuman level of functioning similar to the critique of Marx. "Purpose is the expression of the living personal will. Function is the activity of the object: purpose the activity of the subject," says Blamires pointedly.[26]

There is little doubt that the social environment, no different from the physical environment, has a shaping effect. The question is, how much? To what extent are we responsible for our thoughts, feelings, and actions? To what extent, if any, is that responsibility mediated by the power of the society of which we are members? It would be easy for evangelicals quickly to suggest that any attribution of responsibility outside the province of the individual person is a form of blasphemy. Are we not all called as individual souls to account for our lives? Yes, but the Bible is replete with examples of nations being righteous or evil, of kings leading their people toward or against God. Paul refers to principalities and powers that are suggestive of institutional determination. In deference to the individual responsibility side, the New Testament epistles regularly inveigh against intense associations with unbelievers, implying that such involvements incur negative influences. The clear implication is that one can choose her relationships. But what of the case of a society at large and its influences? That is not the choice of the individual.

The problem is a thorny one. Perhaps we should yield the floor to the philosophers here. Nevertheless, any attempt at a Christian theory of social functioning needs to make a delineation between individual and societal responsibility. A simple both/and response is not sufficient. The individual and society may be two sides of the same coin, but they remain distinctly separate sides.

▸▸ Max Weber

One of Max Weber's major contributions to the field was his analysis of bureaucracy. Bureaucracy, with its obsessive focus on technical efficiency, has been charged with having a dehumanizing and depersonalizing impact on those within it.[27] Characterized by a cold rationality and objectivity, obedience to impersonal authority is a cornerstone of bureaucracy. Using the example of a civil servant, Weber pointed out that the punctuality of such an employee may be less a matter of custom or self-interest than "the result of his abiding by office regulations ... which he may be loathe to violate, since such conduct would ... [be] abhorrent to his 'sense of duty,' which to a greater or lesser extent, represents for him an absolute value."[28]

That bureaucratically controlled humans mindlessly follow rules, drifting ever further away from their spiritual center, picks up a bit of the alienation of Marx and the unself-conscious activity in structure-functionalism. Weber's bureaucracy derives from rationalization—a commitment to a rational-scientific explanation of reality and direction of life. Part of Enlightenment thinking, rationalization excludes from consideration all things spiritual, and human life becomes one of pursuing material gain in the absence of spiritual and even emotional satisfaction. Weber is also addressing determinism here. He saw rationalization as an irreversible social force and predicted that bureaucracies would ultimately prescribe human behavior with such expansive impact that humanity would be caged by its own bureaucratic rules.[29] And so it has become.

For the Christian, what is at stake in looking at Weber's ideas is the matter of control. As tools of efficiency, bureaucratic structures have great value. The problem arises when the bureaucracy no longer serves the well-being of its creators, but rather makes those who created it its slaves. As with wealth and technology, the issue is inherently spiritual. Blind service to an organization, an all-out pursuit of wealth, or a total commitment to technological wonders becomes a form of worship—an ascribing of great value—such that the object of that worship assumes God-like control of its worshipers.

▶▶ Issues in Christian Theory Building

Although there is no all-encompassing Christian approach to sociology, that need not be a reason to move away from Christian critiques and analyses. To omit sociology from Christian investigation is to leave one of the most rankly secular of disciplines untouched. The task is daunting, however, in part because sociology's focus on human group behavior steps away from the personal, one-soul-at-a-time relationship with God. Psychology, for example, with its emphasis on the individual, is more conducive to the personal ethos of the faith. There is also the virulent anti-Christian bias within the discipline of sociology (mentioned earlier in chapter 3, "Relatives of Naturalism"). That, however, is not unique to sociology. The social or behavioral sciences are "disciplines that emerged and developed—quite intentionally so—virtually outside the boundaries of any biblical framework."[30] What Chiareli calls the "tyranny of scientific rationality" is also widespread. This demand for empirical support for any absolute claim militates against Christianity, because its absolutes are grounded in faith and the supernatural.[31]

▸▸ Cultural Relativism

A major challenge to Christian thinking lies in the commitment of sociology (and other behavioral sciences) to cultural relativism. Chiareli finds this doctrine among the most pernicious of all. As such it deserves treatment. Sociologists treat all worldviews—Christian, gay, feminist, Marxist—as *subjectively* true. Each is regarded as true within the context of the subculture of which it is a part, but only within that context. It is not universally true. The only alternative to this approach of studying what are considered subjective matters is to reduce all sociological examination to empirical conditions. But dismissing all "subjective elements" from analysis would impoverish the discipline greatly, removing too much from analyses of culture and human life to make it worthwhile. The effect of cultural relativism, according to Chiareli, "is not to be understated. It is the negation of the Christian belief in absolute truth because it is presumed—ironically by faith—not to exist on its own, but only through the expression of this particular 'social construction of reality.'"[32] The impact of this notion is to remove any grounding of analysis on the "control beliefs" of the Christian faith, because Christianity is regarded as merely one of a number of interpretations of reality according to the worldview of sociologism.

Cultural relativism is indeed a watershed issue. It pulls God off the throne, reducing him to a label slapped on one of many, often silly, ideologies. Regrettably, however, cultural relativism is rarely critiqued effectively. "It is a logical fallacy," notes Chiareli, "to argue that, because many views of reality exist and because they are therefore considered subjectively true only within their own cultural contexts, that absolute truth does not exist."[33] Look closely at the worldviews of the major religions—Christianity, Hinduism, Buddhism, and Islam—each one of them claims to have an exclusive hold on truth. Each religion has its own definition of who God is—ranging from pantheistic to nontheistic to monotheistic—and what the meaning and purpose of life is.[34] On these and matters of like import, each claims to be the sole path to ultimate truth.

This leaves us with a dilemma. Either none of these views is correct or one of them is right and all the others wrong.[35] That's it. Those are the only reasonable choices. Robert Clark says the entire notion of cultural relativism is based on faulty reasoning. "As Moberg (1962) has pointed out, one cannot legitimately infer from the fact of cultural diversity that there are not any absolute and ultimate values and standards. A difference of opinion among different peoples as to what is true 'in no way proves that the object toward which the opinion refers does not exist.'"[36] In brief, culturally varying views as to what is true can coexist with an absolute and ultimate reality that transcends any relativism.[37]

Upon careful examination, what the secular social sciences are doing is to negate any existence of ultimate truth on an *a priori* notion about the subjective nature of religious belief. "To say that all worldviews contribute subjectively and equally to scientific knowledge," says Chiareli, "is inconsistent with any notion of rationality in the social sciences, which claim to seek objectivity in analysis even when faced with subjective ideas."[38] Such a claim infers that all religious worldviews contribute essentially nothing to the fund of objective knowledge and truth. Those who advance this view in the social sciences are engaging in a combination of intellectual laziness and an ideological militance against the notion of God. It is intellectually lazy simply to categorize all religious views in a postmodern framework of "If it works for them, good!" without examining the essence of these beliefs more carefully. Militance is evident in the steadfast refusal to acknowledge even the possibility of a reality grounded in the transcendent.

Some of this militance may be lodged in the historical dominance of Christianity in the university system. There are traces of this in another obstacle to melding faith and learning, mentioned by Chiareli: "That is, critics believe that if religious knowledge is ideological, then it must possess a hidden political agenda. Consequently, we must be suspicious of it."[39] Critics who study social movements within the discipline tend to view Christian organizations as attempting to push their views on the society at large with the intent of enjoying political gain.[40] Unfortunately, such perversions of the faith continue to occur, making it all the more difficult for Christians to gain any traction among secular scholars.

Chiareli summarizes the faith-and-learning challenge well. "By all secular accounts, therefore," says Chiareli, "the notion of a worldview being superior to all others—and a religious one at that—runs counter to basic axioms of the social sciences, at least in the sense that it precludes all other interpretive frames from also contributing to our understanding of reality."[41] Note that this is by *secular accounts*. Secularists have their own worldview—naturalism—one that is also not wholly verifiable scientifically yet precludes all other interpretive frames of reality.

▸▸ Methodological Challenge

The challenge remains: How one can integrate faith into a discipline so committed to experimentation and empiricism, despite the pre-paradigmatic nature of sociology? Chiareli begins with the assertion of John Stott: At a point in human history, God chose to take on human flesh and speak to the world. Few dispute the historicity of Jesus, and there is substantial extra-scriptural evidence for his life, death, and resurrection. His claims need to be examined.[42]

But there is more. It is not possible to prove empirically the existence of love, guilt, innocence, and justice. Yet these, and other nonempirical elements, are presupposed to exist by many in the scientific world, based on wholly circumstantial evidence. Scripture (special revelation) and creation (natural revelation) are God's circumstantial evidence for his existence. It is reasonable that the matter of God be treated in the same way that other nonmaterial elements based in circumstantial evidence are treated. As noted, genuinely hard evidence is overrated in the social sciences in general. In a world supposedly driven entirely by naturalistic laws, words such as *right, wrong, fair, just, innocent, love,* and *moral* remain much in use. None of these even exists in a completely natural world. By naturalistic logic, they are social constructions and so are devoid of intrinsic meaning. Again, however, they are assumed to exist. If that is the case, it would seem that some space might be made to consider the metaphysical.[43]

The need for Christian insights in sociology is compelling. In fact, that contemporary social life is lived in ever larger, more powerful, and more complex cultural confines all but mandates that Christian scholars look carefully at sociology. Moreover, although the two routes to knowledge—secular and Christian—are ideologically irreconcilable, there is no need to abandon the discipline to the turf of the secularists or to be intellectually intimidated by those skeptics who may sneer at attempts at integrations of faith and learning.

Attempts at integrating faith and learning in sociology date back to 1895. They need to continue.[44] If nothing else Christian sociological thought can illuminate for the believer the impact of the abstract and subtle, yet very powerful, social environment. A heightened consciousness can move the believer away from being a mindless and meaningless actor discharging functions within a social structure. Social change is made possible by social consciousness, which in turn leads to better decision making—whether one is making policy at the highest level, educating future generations, or simply voting.

Sociology, often referred to as social philosophy in its early years, was developed largely to address urban social problems growing out of the French Revolution and the later Industrial Revolution.[45] As such, it was value-based despite an early commitment to science and objectivity. Today students of sociology are still predisposed toward social action. We need, then, a "gospel embedded" sociology that works toward social justice that is not based on class or race.[46] Such a holistic sociology will make us better stewards of the creation turned over to us, and through that stewardship, we can fulfill our earthbound mission of glorifying God.

Notes

1. Anthony Campolo, *A Reasonable Faith* (Waco, TX: Word, 1983), 124–28; Mead's lecture notes were published in George Herbert Mead, *Mind, Self, and Society,* ed. Charles W. Morris (Chicago: University of Chicago Press, 1934).
2. S. Kirson Weinberg, "A Relational Typology," in David Claerbaut, *Liberation from Loneliness* (Wheaton, IL: Tyndale, 1984), 46–47.
3. Claerbaut, *Liberation from Loneliness,* 89.
4. This is noted in chapter 23 and is based on Armand Nicholi's review of research.
5. David Claerbaut, *Black Student Alienation* (San Francisco: R&E Research Associates, 1978), 3.
6. Robert Nisbet, *The Quest of Community* (New York: Oxford University Press, 1953), 15.
7. Claerbaut, *Black Student Alienation,* 3.
8. Robert K. Merton, *Social Theory and Social Structure,* rev. ed. (New York, Free Press, 1964), quoted in Claerbaut, *Social Problems,* vol. 1 (Scottsdale, AZ: Christian Academic Publications, 1976), 108–9.
9. Harry Blamires, *The Christian Mind* (Ann Arbor, MI: Servant, 1997), 162.
10. Ibid., 145.
11. Ibid., 163.
12. Ibid., 159.
13. Ibid., 162.
14. Ibid., 172.
15. Karl Marx, *Wage-Labour and Capital* (New York: International Publishers, 1933), 18–19.
16. Paul Tournier, *Escape from Loneliness,* trans. John S. Gilmour (Philadelphia: Westminster, 1977), 35–36.
17. Campolo, *A Reasonable Faith,* 167–68.
18. Antonio A. Chiareli, "Christian Worldview and the Social Sciences," in *Shaping a Christian Worldview,* ed. David S. Dockery and Gregory Alan Thornbury (Nashville: Broadman and Holman, 2002), 253; Chiareli suggests *Religion in Society* by Ronald L. Johnstone for a thorough yet concise review of the sociological perspective on religion.
19. Chiareli, "Christian Worldview and the Social Sciences," in Dockery and Thornbury, *Shaping a Christian Worldview,* 253.
20. Blamires, *The Christian Mind,* 152.
21. Ibid.
22. Ibid., 153.
23. Ibid., 154.
24. Ibid., 152.

25. Ibid., 155.

26. Ibid., 167.

27. Max Weber, *General Economic History,* trans. Frank H. Knight (Glencoe, IL: The Free Press, 1927), 174–75; *From Max Weber: Essays in Sociology,* trans. and ed. H. H. Gerth and C. Wright Mills (New York: Oxford University Press, 1946), 50.

28. Max Weber, *Basic Concepts in Sociology,* trans. S. P. Secher (New York: Philosophical Library, 1962), 71.

29. Max Weber, *The Theory of Social and Economic Organization,* trans. A. M. Henderson and Talcott Parsons (New York: Free Press, 1947), 363–73, in Campolo, *A Reasonable Faith,* 182. Campolo also cites Weber, *From Max Weber,* chap. 8, in addition to an excellent statement on Weber's concept of rationalization found in Julien Freund, *The Sociology of Max Weber* (New York: Vintage, 1968), 17–24.

30. Chiareli, "Christian Worldview and the Social Sciences," in Dockery and Thornbury, *Shaping a Christian Worldview,* 249.

31. Ibid., 254.

32. Chiareli, "Christian Worldview and the Social Sciences," in Dockery and Thornbury, *Shaping a Christian Worldview,* 251; Chiareli also directs the reader to the relation of social constructions of reality to religion in Peter L. Berger and Thomas Luckmann, *The Social Construction of Reality* (Garden City, NY: Doubleday, 1967) and in Peter L. Berger, *The Sacred Canopy* (Garden City, NY: Doubleday, 1967).

33. Chiareli, "Christian Worldview and the Social Sciences," in Dockery and Thornbury, *Shaping a Christian Worldview,* 255.

34. Ravi Zacharias, *Jesus among Other Gods* (Nashville: Word, 2000), 7.

35. Meredith B. McGuire, *Religion: The Social Context* (Belmont, CA: Wadsworth, 1997); Chiareli, "Christian Worldview and the Social Sciences," in Dockery and Thornbury, *Shaping a Christian Worldview,* 256.

36. Robert Clark, "Thinking about Culture: Theirs and Ours," *The Sociological Perspective,* ed. Michael R. Leming, Raymond G. De Vries, and Brendan F. J. Furnish (Grand Rapids: Zondervan, 1989), 72; David O. Moberg, "Cultural Relativity and Christian Faith, *Journal of the American Scientific Affiliation* 14, no. 2 (June 1962): 34–48; Chiareli, "Christian Worldview and the Social Sciences," in Dockery and Thornbury, *Shaping a Christian Worldview,* 256.

37. Chiareli, "Christian Worldview and the Social Sciences," in Dockery and Thornbury, *Shaping a Christian Worldview,* 256.

38. Ibid., 256–57.

39. Ibid., 251.

40. David A. Snow and Pamela E. Oliver, "Social Movements and Collective Behavior," *Sociological Perspectives on Social Psychology,* ed. K. Cook, G. A. Fine, and J. S. House, (Boston: Allyn and Bacon, 1995), 571–99; Chiareli, "Christian Worldview and the Social Sciences," in Dockery and Thornbury, *Shaping a Christian Worldview,* 251–52.

41. Chiareli, "Christian Worldview and the Social Sciences," in Dockery and Thornbury, *Shaping a Christian Worldview,* 252.

42. Ibid., 258; John R. W. Stott, *Basic Christianity* (Downers Grove, IL: InterVarsity, 1977), 14.

43. Chiareli, "Christian Worldview and the Social Sciences," in Dockery and Thornbury, *Shaping a Christian Worldview,* 258–59.

44. Ibid., 242. Chiareli cites the following efforts at relating Christianity to the discipline: Charles R. Henderson, "Sociology and Theology," *American Journal of Sociology* 1 (1895): 351–83; Shailer Matthews, "Christian Sociology" [series], *American Journal of Sociology* 1 (1895): 182–94, 359–80, 457–72, 604–17, 771–84; 2 (1896), 108–17, 274–87, 416–32; David Lyon, "The Idea of a Christian Sociology," *Sociological Analysis* 44 (3): 227–42; Peter L. Berger, *The Sacred Canopy* (Garden City, NY: Doubleday, 1967); Ronald J. Burwell, "Sleeping with an Elephant," *Christian Scholar's Review* 5: 195–203; Richard Perkins, *Looking Both Ways: Exploring the Interface between Christianity and Sociology* (Grand Rapids: Baker, 1987); William H. Swatos Jr., *Religious Sociology,* eds. (Westport, CT: Greenwood, 1987); Michael R. Lemming, Raymond G. De Vries, and Brendan F. J. Furnish, eds., *The Sociological Perspective* (Grand Rapids: Zondervan, 1989); and David A. Fraser and Tony Campolo, eds., *Sociology through the Eyes of Faith* (San Francisco: HarperSanFrancisco, 1992).

45. Chiareli, "Christian Worldview and the Social Sciences," in Dockery and Thornbury, *Shaping a Christian Worldview,* 260.

46. Ibid.

26

ECONOMICS:
SOME CHRISTIAN VIEWS
ON THE "DISMAL" SCIENCE

Economics examines, analyzes, and advocates the distribution of goods and services within a society. Though paradigmatic—yielding to precise forms of measurement and logic—it is also called the "dismal" science because predicting how these powerful and determinative forces will operate in any given society is difficult. A comment by one of my colleagues is illustrative. "We are like a pilot who lost contact with his radar," he said to the faculty during a volatile economic period. "We are not certain where we are going, but we are getting there very quickly."

▸▸ Lack of Consensus

When we mix this unpredictability with variances in theology, it is obvious why there is no genuinely Christian economics. Theological differences are so severe that Christians cannot even agree on what is the proper economic system for a society. Certainly, the capitalist system is not advanced in Scripture as the God-ordained model for the distribution of goods and services. In fact, the early church lived a rather pure socialism, holding all things in common. If anything, wealth was consistently deemphasized in first-century Christendom.

When Christ sent out the disciples two-by-two to do ministry, they were to pack little more than a figurative toothbrush as they went out to proclaim the good news. In fact, they were to rely on the hospitality of believers for food and lodging, going out in faith as testimony to their message. Christ himself was an itinerant preacher. As he traveled, followers in the various locales took him in. Mary, Martha, and Lazarus, residents of Bethany, were among these providers. All we know of Christ's economic ventures is that he was the stepson of Joseph, a carpenter. Some historians believe Jesus may have labored in that craft until he was thirty, perhaps to care for a widowed Mary (adult males had short life spans) and his younger siblings.

In any case, Jesus did not amass wealth. Neither did many of Christ's followers. The early disciples *left* their places of employment to follow Jesus. Matthew abandoned tax collecting, an unsavory white-collar profession in which collectors charged fellow Jews whatever they could, pocketing the difference between the amount collected and the portion required by Roman government. Peter and others abandoned fisheries to serve Christ. Peter was likely a member of the upper-middle-class of his community, given that he owned a rather high-quality fishing boat. Paul was a tentmaker by vocation, so he did not have to rely on the churches he founded to support him. Many did support him, however, freeing him up to travel and preach. Nonetheless, his missionary career is testimony to his disinterest in gaining wealth. Paul was a highly educated Jew as well as a Roman citizen, rare for a minority. This suggests he either came from wealth or had access to it. For Jesus, Paul, and many other early believers, amassing wealth was either a matter of indifference or viewed as evil. Indeed, the Bible is not very kind on the subject of materialism. Paul called the love of money "a root of all kinds of evil" (1 Tim. 6:10). And in Matthew 6:24, Jesus says we cannot serve both God and our desire for wealth.

There are several reasons to veer away from economic independence as a life strategy. One is that the pursuit of money can lead to finding one's security outside of God. Christ directs his listeners not to concern themselves with worldly possessions but to focus on serving the interests of God, living in faith that he will provide for their needs (Matt. 6). In short, poverty can breed faith; the lesser one's dependence on wealth, the greater his reliance on God.

Another reason is that the acquisition of wealth often makes one a captive of materialism. Wealth brings comfort, ease, and societal prestige. It is alluring, intoxicating, and ego gratifying, such that the pleasures of the temporal can snuff out interest in the spiritual and eternal. Much more can be said here. In present-day Western civilization, few things are prized more highly than wealth. In fact, wars are often discussed in terms of their impact on the national economy every bit as much as their cost in human lives. Television channels are devoted entirely to the stock market and other economic indicators and concerns. This is an extension of secularism—the notion that the earthly tenure is all there is. Money, not unlike one's sex life, is an intensely personal matter. Amid this dominating effect of materialism, giving to Christian causes is truly a statement of identity, an investment of personhood, and a genuinely spiritual act.

All of this clashes with health-and-wealth theology, alluded to earlier, which has permeated certain sectors of Christianity. Much media preaching emphasizes God's desire that his people live healthy and prosperous lives. In a curious parallel to the Protestant ethic, other evangelists all but assert that God will materially bless those who give to his cause, which, not surprisingly, is also *their* specific ministry. "Plant a seed" in faith, some claim, and God will reward you with material wealth. The subtle but heretical message is that one's "seed" is not a contribution but an investment in God's eternal economy that will yield tangible dividends. These appeals are cast in the context of believers' royal status as children of the Almighty—sons and daughters of the creator of all wealth. Again, the notion is that God wants the earthly best for his heirs.

The theology of healing ministries is lodged in the belief that disease is not part of God's will for his people. Founded on the healing model of Christ, the Great Physician, millions are urged to pray in faith that their maladies are to be healed and to take a step of faith. Not unlike the disabled masses of Christ's time, thousands line up to be touched by a famous media faith healer.

The matter is confusing. Indeed, believers are to focus on eternal treasures of a spiritual nature. Yet Christ's acts of healing and God's material blessings on his followers such as Abraham, Solomon, David, and—when faithful—the children of Israel suggest material gain is not antithetical to a life of faith. Several matters are beyond dispute, however. Christians are expected to incorporate justice and mercy into their economic calculations, discussed at length elsewhere in these pages. In addition, we are to support those who make spreading the gospel their full-time vocation, as well as other efforts to extend the work of faith. The matter is spiritual. It is not about money or other forms of wealth. It comes down to our attitude toward that wealth—the sense of whose wealth it is and what our roles as trustees of that wealth are to be.

Although basic economic concepts rival mathematics in the area of unalterable truth, the discipline is awash in theory. Hence, once past the numeric calculations, there is much room for Christian scholarship. In fact, there are few disciplines more in need of Christian input than economics, because it is the economic market that drives the nations of the industrial world. Basic economic concepts regarding scarcity, distribution, inflation, recession, and profit motives are to be studied thoroughly by the Christian for more than disinterested academic reasons. The Christian economist does well to examine economic trends in the context of how they advance or militate against societal justice and compassion for the poor. To be sure, Christian scholars will differ as to the effect of various economic factors, just as they do about certain doctrines. Nonetheless, there is a need to look at economic forces in the light of divine values.

Nowhere is there a more appropriate opportunity for a prophetic stance than in economics. Indeed, legendary figures in the discipline like Milton Friedman and John Kenneth Galbraith were genuine ideologues who came to their discipline with distinct philosophical biases. Therefore, Christian economists would do well to move beyond a comfortable acceptance of the capitalist status quo. Easy affirmations of middle-class values, the connotations of the Protestant ethic, right-wing economic policies, and even classical liberalism as they pertain to economics hardly seem sufficient, especially in the face of Christian history. Philip Yancey's statement, "Through the ages, Christian saints have chosen the most unDarwinian objects for their love," reminds us of how Christians have a heritage of being in the forefront of concern for "those without."[1]

Economic trends that emerge from social ideologies need to be examined. The effects of the Protestant ethic's highly prejudicial though unstated corollary—that if one is not successful, one has not worked hard—is an example. The millions of working poor, many of whom are believers, belie this corollary daily. Yet it lives on, suggesting that the sting of poverty is the result of laziness, constituting an ideological force implying that to be poor is one's own fault. Once this prejudice is institutionalized in the social system and internalized by the members of the society, it is a short step to a society's comfortable neglect of those at the bottom of its economic structure.

▸▸ Ethics

The most effective way to inject faith into economics is to probe beneath the descriptive level involving structures and measurement, into the area of societal impact and significance. Holmes advocates an ethical approach to faith and learning, one that involves relating facts to ethical concepts.[2] For example, one can associate economics (and particularly, business) with more value-oriented issues like fair wages and prices and a philosophical examination of the very meaning of work as part of the cultural mandate. Justice and compassion should be issues of major import to the Christian in economics because it is central to any Christian social system. There should be no escaping the centrality of these concepts in Christian thinking, with the Bible's emphasis on God's concern for justice and his love for the poor.[3] Yet millions of worshiping believers from a variety of traditions have heard nary a single sermon focusing on either of these concepts. The reason, perhaps, is because Christian leaders are uncomfortable in their own relationships with money and the issue of dealing with the poor and oppressed, and therefore even less comfortable with becoming prophetic with regard to these issues. Justice and compassion are immensely practical, rather than theoretical, elements, to which the life of the Reverend Martin Luther King Jr. is testimony. Indeed, these third-rail scriptural issues, if practiced conscientiously, would have great impact on any economic system and on the lifestyles of many Christians.

Ethics, defined in terms of the rightness or wrongness of human behavior and the positivity or negativity of motives and outcomes, has long been a thorny issue in the world of American business. More specifically, ethicists have turned to Kant's notion of the "categorical imperative" for guidance. The categorical imperative holds that one should engage in a given action only if he feels that the behavior is of sufficient moral purity that it could constitute a guideline by which to establish law. In addition, Kant asserted the concept of duty, meaning that one should perform one's duties for their own sake, rather than act to pursue rewards. The categorical imperative and the concept of duty fit well within deontology—the study of moral obligation in which one chooses his actions on a right-for-right's-sake basis in the context of universal statements of right and wrong, rather than in terms of their practical consequences for him.[4]

Over against deontology is utilitarianism, which emphasizes the greatest good for the greatest number. Utilitarianism is akin to exchange (cost/gain) theory in social psychology, the notion that people conduct themselves on the basis of maximizing gains and minimizing costs. Utilitarianism, however, is exchange theory with a wide-angle lens in that there is more than individual cost and gain involved. According to utilitarianism, an action is ethical if the total of its utilities for all is greater than an alternative action. Although versions of utilitarianism can degenerate into a pragmatic "What's in it for me" approach, a serious utilitarian approach is difficult to execute in business, because people in upper management have to make so many choices daily in a business. Deontology is therefore more suitable from an ethical standpoint, because it does not require a calculation for every decision.[5]

▸▸ Business

Business and ethics often do not hit it off much better than faith and learning do. In raw terms, economists see the purpose of businesses to be the maximization of profits. This notion, often regarded as libertarianism, holds that society benefits from profitable businesses in many ways: fuller employment, better wages, happy customers, and an increased tax base. This is an easy morality. There is no trace of altruism here. The maxim of the "social good" concept seems to be "Make as much money as humanly possible and everybody wins."[6]

The libertarian notion has some formidable advocates. Celebrated economist Milton Friedman argues that the primary social responsibility of any business is to generate profits. Again, the core of the argument is that profitable businesses employ people, generate revenue for them, pay taxes, and offer goods and/or services that the society values sufficiently to make the business profitable. The libertarian may argue that for business to seek any other goal defuses its very reason for existence. To deviate from its mission risks failure at generating what gives it life—profits. By this logic, not to make the generation of profits *the* goal would be unethical.[7]

Another approach, the social responsibility model, looks more directly at how a business makes choices and takes actions that help the society. The guiding principle is that business can and should take steps to ameliorate some of society's ills. More specifically, if businesses view certain demographic segments of the society as having a particular stake in the success of the organization, then the business needs to "give back" some of its success to those specific segments. This might include supporting local educational institutions, sponsoring community activities, or engaging in employee training. According to this approach, a business—whether multinational, national, or local—does not exist in a vacuum but is part of a larger community. Therefore, it makes being a corporate "good citizen" part of its identity. Businesses, however, sometimes pervert the social responsibility model, publicizing their noble deeds to gain goodwill and additional business in the marketplace.[8]

The social responsibility concept is a sticky one due to its subjective nature. It begs a series of questions. For example, what constitutes a valid contribution to the society? What should that include? How much is enough? And should a company profit from its good deeds by marketing itself as a good citizen? People differ sharply on these matters. Nonetheless, this school of thought does exist. Some firms are committed to this more wide-ranging approach, examining their legal, ethical, and discretionary responsibilities as well as their need to be profitable.

Still another school of thought centers on "virtue," emphasizing the proper treatment of employees and other organizations. If a business operates legally and treats fairly those that have a stake in its success, it is considered to be acting virtuously. The argument for virtue is that when people engage the challenges of business honestly, character is developed and they become better (more virtuous) members of society. The emphasis here is more on the character and development of the people the organization wishes to hire than on their specific conduct.[9]

Regardless of one's position, the research and dialogue on business ethics needs to continue. Ethics has a real place in business because the actions of a business profoundly affect the lives of its workers and the well-being of a capitalist society. Ethics provide a nonmaterial structure of rules within which the material enterprise of profit-seeking takes place. It sets boundaries separating healthy competition from conflict—achievement and excellence from rapacious aggression. A business cannot benefit the society of which it is a part if the business is driven solely by self-interest. Therefore, ethics are not merely a way of building image and promotion aimed at driving up profits; they must be integral to the character and identity of the business.

Donald Lester and Walter Padelford cite Charles Dickens's 1843 fable, *A Christmas Carol,* in offering another view of business ethics. Using the character of Ebenezer Scrooge, Dickens portrays the English industrialists of his day as greedy, exploitive, and uncaring. The English system was driven by raw power in which capitalists possessing economic leverage extracted the maximum from their employees. There is no morality in this depiction, only an economic version of the law of the jungle, in which the stronger species devour the weaker. Dickens appears to be arguing that humans, regardless of their station, should seek the common good by practicing mercy, charity, and kindness.[10]

Clearly, Dickens sees the libertarian view as a mere permission-giver for exploitation and the benefit of a few at the expense and pain of the masses. Moreover, the social responsibility notion is regarded as at best pandering in nature. For Dickens, social responsibility would have to entail more than a handout or a public relations effort at goodwill. His view was more comprehensive. He felt businesses ought to see themselves as being in the service of all humanity. This is close to a Christian view, one that is rooted in God's love for humanity.[11]

▸▸ Christian Businesses

Lester and Padelford make some thought-provoking points. They argue that deontology and utilitarianism are humanistic rather than Christian. They are descriptions of the ideal person or the ideal corporation. In short, glory goes to the people and to the businesses of which they are members. Although intent is important—the Christian faith is about the inner person's motivations and heart—their critique may be a bit extreme. Humanistic notions of just and ethical conduct do often cohere with Christian doctrines grounded in the "love your neighbor as yourself" commandment. Hence, businesses that take humanitarian approaches are to be commended, patronized, and deemed worthy for employment.

Nevertheless, for an organization to be unabashedly Christian, it needs to emulate the nature of God. The authors contend that chief among God's attributes are that he is holy, just, and loving. Though not defining *holy,* they imply that it refers to a reverence and adoration for God. Moreover, their definition of justice connotes a structure of fairness. In any case, their view squares with Micah 6:8, which speaks of the importance of being just and merciful and of living humbly before God.[12]

Alexander Hill has examined the concept of a Christian business. Hill sees holiness, justice, and mercy as key factors constituting a three-legged stool. Each leg is crucial to the stool because it helps balance the other two. A lack of mercy brings legalism and harshness, with rules and exacting standards becoming cold prods in an absence of personal affirmation. Without holiness, the business is predisposed toward prideful humanism and arrogance. The business and its leaders become the objects of veneration (and worship) rather than servants of God. As justice recedes, permissiveness emerges. Rules and their application put healthy boundaries around behavior that flows from imperfect people.

The businesses are cited as having definable Christian cultures characterized by a belief in transformation rather than past behavior predicting future conduct. There are daunting challenges facing the avowedly Christian business. Even if one were to hire only professing Christians, we are not capable of looking at a person's soul. The founder and leader of the business would have to be a role model of how a Christian business is to be run and an incarnate example of holiness, justice, and mercy. The company's mission statement would have to be a creed. Even having that in place, however, is no ultimate safeguard. The fallen nature of every person in an organization's employ will visit its effects on even the Christian business, which is certainly the case in the church. Still further, there are the challenges of having to recruit topflight talent, deal with government regulations, and function under the constant cloud of potential church/state lawsuits.[13]

But the Christian business concept does raise a number of perplexing questions for the Christian economist. How does one put together a Christian business in an era of open hiring and religious pluralism? Perhaps more important, should a Christian attempt to forge a Christian business? Is it Christian to deny or tilt employment opportunities away from nonbelievers? Are we not violating the precept of justice, suggesting that God rains only on the just? These are issues to discuss and provide avenues for further research. There are more questions than answers, and one can be sure that Christian business models will generate intense debate. Some who advocate the New Testament model of socialism will reject any profit-generating approach. Still others will argue that what might make a business Christian would be its treatment of the poor and the oppressed rather than the spiritual professions of its employees or the management team. Some will assert that the essence of a Christian business must be the active faith of those working there, believing that from people of faith will come godly business practices. Still others will argue that the business itself should be a mission field, and therefore, hiring below the managerial level should be open.

In any case, there is no keeping Christ out of the corporate boardroom. Though dubious in application, a hot topic for books on business and leadership in the new millennium is Jesus, according to theology professor Susan Ross. She found such titles as *Jesus on Leadership: Executive Lessons from the Servant Leader; Perfect Leader: Following Christ's Example to Learn Leadership Success; Jesus CEO: Using Ancient Wisdom for Visionary Leadership;* and *The 25 Most Common Problems in Business (and How Jesus Solved Them).*[14]

Ross assesses the nature of Jesus' leadership in the light of today's leadership criteria. She cites five characteristics in Jesus' communication style, each of which is defined as a successful leadership trait two thousand years later. She notes that Jesus listened to others sincerely and empathically. Moreover, because of the rapport he effected, he was able to get others to listen to him. Healthy relationships and authentic interactions emerged from this. Further, Jesus treated each person with equal respect. By the norms of the culture in which he lived, Christ was a social revolutionary in terms of his treatment of the poor, the minorities, and women. He practiced diversity in the best sense of the word. He also communicated the principle that institutions are to serve people rather than vice versa. Legalism was subordinated to divine purpose. Finally, Jesus presented a vision to his followers. He placed himself at the center of the community of God, not above it, and invited his followers to join him in that realm.[15]

Ross's research has solid potential for Christian scholars. The timeless relevance of Christ's leadership style serves as an apologetic for the validity of the faith. In addition, her work encourages us to follow the example of the Savior in secular as well as specifically spiritual realms. Finally, in examining the example of Jesus closely, we learn more about who he is and what it means to have the mind of Christ.

▸▸ Advertising

There is yet another major area of concern for the Christian economist: advertising. This subject is often treated in the social psychology literature because of its influential effect on mass behavior; however, it is actually an economic topic because it is aimed directly at generating money. Advertising is simply everywhere. The average American is exposed to more than a million advertisements by the time he reaches fifty years of age. "Yet there is no field of discourse in which advertising is treated Christianly," says Blamires rightly.[16] The problem with advertising goes beyond the exaggeration, dishonesty, and carnal nature of so much of it. The main problem is that it sends an entirely nonspiritual, secular message as to the essence of life. "It is not just that we are being seduced by the advertisers to buy X's chocolate instead of Y's," argues Blamires. "We, or our fellow-men, are being conditioned by advertisers to believe that such and such things constitute the fullness of life. An ideal of the full life is being hammered daily into the minds of our fellow-men—even our young, impressionable children. This ideal is cynically materialistic. We are being taught to treat worldly possessions as status symbols rather than as serviceable goods."[17]

Blamires insightfully detects a naturalistic foundation to advertising in its attempts to communicate the notion that the goods or services promoted have a near-fulfilling value. It is as if we viewers of a television spot are unsuccessful, unattractive, and unhappy. But wait! If we bought this car, wore this cologne, or consumed this brand of beer, we would suddenly be transformed into successful, attractive, and self-actualized creatures. By the doctrines of advertising, the really good life is not one of meaning and significance. It is not one of holiness, justice, and mercy. Rather, it is one filled with the latest technological conveniences and forms of entertainment. Materialism and wealth constitute a ladder of purpose and fulfillment.[18]

And it is cunning. The world commercialism portrays is a false and seductive vision of life, one that is not really part of human existence. "For in the world of advertisements no man ever grows older than thirty-five and no woman grows older than twenty-seven," notes Blamires. "It is a cosy picture of life, full of colour and ease. There is always plenty to eat and drink. The furniture never gets old and drab."[19]

It is also amoral. Whether it is rebellious behavior, cloaked violence, or lust, what is used is what sells. The sexual drive with its life-giving energy is among the most powerful of all forces. "It is precisely because it is such a fine, keen-edged instrument that it can be abused and exploited on an enormous scale, as it is today," says Blamires. "Every advertiser in the world knows that you have only to touch a sensitive man's eyes with lines and curves lyrical with sexual overtones, and you have won his attention."[20] In advertising, the end does not justify the means. The end—the successful manipulation of consumer behavior—is all that needs justification.

Not unlike the Christian artist in Wolterstorff's thinking, the believer in the world of business or promotion must be responsible to those to whom he appeals. Just as the artist's responsibility is not solely to the world of art, the Christian is not solely responsible to the corporation. There are many challenges and myriad moral dilemmas. Success and excellence, for example, are divine attributes to be pursued, if only to reflect the nature of our Maker. They are not, however, the only goals. So are honesty, responsibility, and ethical behavior. There is much to discuss and marvelous opportunities for research here.

The faith-and-learning effort in economics is wise to include economists, philosophers, and theologians. Such an alliance may balance the ideological forces in the matter. The economist, of course, is the central figure in the matrix. It is his field, and he will ground the discussion in an economic reality that does not compromise the integrity of the discipline; however, the philosophers and theologians may open value-based vistas to consider. In any case, that no Christian model of economics in general and business in particular is ever likely to approach consensus ought not to discourage Christian scholars from the task of theory building. As bottom-line as economics is, in the case of Christian theorizing, the process may be more important than the product. It moves students of economics toward meshing their faith with the operations of the national and global marketplace.

Notes

1. Philip Yancey, *What's So Amazing about Grace?* (Grand Rapids: Zondervan, 1997), 266.
2. Arthur F. Holmes, *The Idea of a Christian College* (Grand Rapids: Eerdmans, 1987), 50–52.
3. David Claerbaut, *Urban Ministry* (Grand Rapids: Zondervan, 1983), chap. 1.
4. O. C. Farrell and L. G. Gresham, "A Contingency Framework for Understanding Ethical Decision Making in Marketing," *Journal of Marketing* 49 (1985): 87–97; Donald L. Lester with Walton Padelford, "Christian Worldview and the World of Business," in *Shaping a Christian Worldview,* ed. David S. Dockery and Gregory Alan Thornbury (Nashville: Broadman and Holman, 2002), 336–38.
5. Lester with Padelford, "Christian Worldview and the World of Business," in Dockery and Thornbury, *Shaping a Christian Worldview,* 338.
6. Ibid., 336.
7. Milton Friedman, "The Social Responsibility of Business Is to Increase Its Profits," *New York Times,* September 13, 1970, 32ff.; Richard Nunan, "The Libertarian Conception of Corporate Property," *Journal of Business Ethics* 7 (1988): 891–906; Lester with Padelford, "Christian Worldview and the World of Business," in Dockery and Thornbury, *Shaping a Christian Worldview,* 337.
8. Lester with Padelford, "Christian Worldview and the World of Business," in Dockery and Thornbury, *Shaping a Christian Worldview,* 336–37.
9. Ibid., 336, 339.
10. Charles Dickens, *A Christmas Carol* (New York: Signet, 1987), 4; Lester with Padelford, "Christian Worldview and the World of Business," in Dockery and Thornbury, *Shaping a Christian Worldview,* 339–41.
11. Lester with Padelford, "Christian Worldview and the World of Business," in Dockery and Thornbury, *Shaping a Christian Worldview,* 339–41.
12. Ibid., 341–42.

13. Alexander Hill, *Just Business* (Downers Grove, IL: InterVarsity, 1997); Lester with Padelford, "Christian Worldview and the World of Business," in Dockery and Thornbury, *Shaping a Christian Worldview,* 342–45.

14. Susan Ross, "What Would Jesus Do?" *Loyola,* Summer 2001, 22.

15. Ibid., 22–23.

16. Harry Blamires, *The Christian Mind* (Ann Arbor, MI: Servant, 1997), 28.

17. Ibid., 29.

18. Ibid., 160–61.

19. Ibid., 74.

20. Ibid., 188.

CONCLUSION

The issue is clear and logical: Contemporary society is oligarchic. It is ruled by a few—shaped by leaders who come from the ranks of the formally educated. Hence, if Christians abandon the halls of mainstream academe to the secularists and allow even their Christian institutions of higher learning to loll in the complacency of compartmentalization, they will lose all impact on the future of Western culture.

I am not dismissing the centrality of the soul to Christian faith. No thinking Christian will do that. Basic to Christianity is the belief that the soul is eternal and belongs to Christ. Similarly, I am not questioning the importance of the spirit—the emotions—to the Christian life. It is our nature to be drawn to what feels good, and the gospel is the best of news. Moreover, when our emotions are aligned in a personal relationship with God, health and fullness of life result. There is much evidence that Christianity continues to focus effectively on the soul and the spirit.

Outside that inner world of soul and spirit, however, is an outer culture that is decaying spiritually. That culture is ever secularizing, ever denying the truth, and ever marginalizing the role of faith. Christianity must once again become an impact player in that culture. To do that, it cannot nurture only the soul and the spirit. It must also cultivate what Blamires calls the Christian mind. The Christian mind is one that learns in the context of faith. It affirms learning, progress, and intellectual development, but it does so with the aim of glorifying the God who is the author of all learning. It continuously combines faith and learning. Most important, the Christian mind interacts with the soul and the spirit. It completes the personal Christian trinity.

Faith and learning will never exist in an idyllic relationship on this side of the eternal boundary. Nothing—not even marriage—does. That, however, is no reason to abandon the endeavor or imagine it is of no consequence. Nor is it a reason to forge superficial, simplistic faith-and-learning interactions, ones that are unstimulating to the thinking believer, devoid of academic quality, and therefore irrelevant. With the future of humankind in part dependent upon it, faith and learning need to be taken to the edge.

For the Christian scholar, the call is to critique, develop, and refine. It is to *critique* by placing every bit of learning under the lens of Christ, examining it with the jeweler's eye of faith. It is to separate the wheat of reality from the chaff of secular speculation, to distill the gold of truth from the dross of illusion. It is to *develop* Christian models of thought and analyses—yes, even paradigms—and to present them with the boldness of Paul when he lectured in the intellectual centers of the first century and with the confidence of those that advocate special interest perspectives today. It is also to *refine* the models, modes of analysis, and paradigms, continuously with the aim of making them better vehicles of faith and learning, better exponents of God's truth.

The faith-and-learning challenge is not a matter of intellectual talent. There is much absolutely brilliant scholarly capacity present in the Christian community. It is a matter of passion, will, and vision. For the scholar, truly excellent faith and learning come from a passion to discover, and to contribute to the discovery of, academic knowledge in the genuine (rather than the artificial) light of the truth. For the administrator in the Christian institution, or the Christian activist in the mainstream, it comes from the will to endure in the face of resistance. For both, however, it comes from a vision, one that sees faith and learning, stimulating Christian models and analyses, built and refined both to cultivate the minds of believers and to shine the light of truth into the dim world of secularism.

NAME INDEX

Abbott, Edwin, 177
Abraham, 297
Addams, Jane, 43
Ahlem, Lloyd, 275–76
Allport, Gordon, 276
Anderson, Paul M., 148, 261
Angus, David, 19
Aquinas, Saint Thomas, 148
Aristotle, 196
Ashby, E. C., 259
Ayer, A. J., 195

Bahnsen, Greg, 103
Ballard, William, 64
Balmer, Randall, 106
Balzac, Honoré de, 304
Barker, Lewis, 69
Bartel, Roland, 198
Beals, Timothy, 194–97
Beaty, Michael, 89
Bechler, Johann, 36
Beckett, Samuel, 23
Behe, Michael, 67–68, 149
Bennett, Richard, 31–32, 101–2, 119, 149
Bennett, William, 181, 185
Berdyaev, Nicolas, 200
Bethell, Tom, 66
Blamires, Harry, 22–23, 26, 31, 60, 83–85, 100–101, 113–14, 146, 149, 153, 167, 174, 182–84, 186, 224, 253–54, 267, 283–84, 286–87, 303–4
Blumenfeld, Samuel, 43
Brett, R. L., 196
Briner, Bob, 87, 113, 131–32, 190–92
Brown, H. C., 259
Browning, Robert, 17

Bube, Richard, 171–72
Buber, Martin, 207–8, 280
Buckley, William F., Jr., 29, 37, 44, 56–57, 59, 118, 132, 196
Bultmann, Rudolf, 201
Bunyan, John, 215
Bush, George W., 67
Butterfield, Herbert, 239, 241

Calvin, John, 17
Camp, Ashby, 71
Campolo, Tony, 177, 202
Camus, Albert, 19
Carson, Verna Benner, 263, 276
Chain, Ernest, 165
Chaucer, Geoffrey, 14–15
Chenoweth, Mark, 73
Chiareli, Antonio, 43, 47, 49, 90, 100, 224, 252, 289–91
Clark, Mark T., 260
Clark, Robert, 290
Clouse, Robert, 234, 237, 241
Coles, Roger, 151
Colson, Charles, 18, 251
Comte, Auguste, 48, 214
Confucius, 60
Copernicus, Nicolas, 122
Creechan, Henry, 63
Cymbala, Jim, 252

Daniel, 132, 141
Darwin, Charles, 46, 63–69, 71, 149, 151
David, 103, 297
Davidman, Joy, 221
Davis, Jimmy, 36–37
Dawkins, Richard, 38, 77, 155, 157, 163

Dembski, William, 68–70, 149
Derrida, Jacques, 209, 229, 231
Descartes, René, 25
Dewey, John, 226, 231
Dickens, Charles, 301
Donne, John, 15
Dostoyevsky, Fyodor, 200–201
Durkheim, Emile, 282–84
Dyer, Wayne, 58

Eden, J. Gary, 149
Einstein, Albert, 151, 171, 177, 216
Eliot, Charles William, 33
Eliot, T. S., 43, 84
Elliott, Elisabeth, 236–37
Ellis, Albert, 158, 203, 266
Elzinga, Ken, 166, 225
Erikson, Erik, 258, 264–68, 275

Famaliel, 110
Finley, Darel Rex, 36–37, 63, 65, 69
Fish, Stanley, 37
Flaubert, Gustave, 188
Fleming, Ambrose, 165
Foucault, Michel, 209–10
Freud, Sigmund, 34, 68, 213–21, 270–72
Friedman, Milton, 43, 297–99
Fuller, Millard, 251
Futuyma, Douglas J., 68

Galbraith, John Kenneth, 43, 298
Galileo, 122
Gamaliel, 134
Gannon, Thomas, 19
Gini, Al, 43
Gould, Stephen Jay, 63–64, 68
Grant, Peter, 65
Grant, Rosemary, 65
Green, Brad, 121
Guenin, Louis, 65

Haeckel, Ernst, 64
Hatch, Nathan, 86, 89
Hawking, Stephen, 148
Hearn, Walter R., 45, 47, 72

Heeren, Fred, 68, 70
Heisenberg, Werner, 171
Hemingway, Ernest, 14, 116
Herberg, Will, 31
Hill, Alexander, 302
Hitler, Adolf, 27
Holmes, Arthur, 60, 96, 108–9, 112, 226–27
Hulett, Louisa, 260–61
Hull, David, 33
Hume, David, 34, 48, 93, 173
Hummel, Charles, 53

James, 189, 206, 262
James, William, 221
Jeffrey, David Lyle, 86, 89, 107, 198
Jennings, Willie, 126
Jesus, 26, 29, 92, 99, 101, 132, 166, 189,
    248, 249, 250, 252, 260, 262, 271, 296
John, 26, 112, 206, 262
Jones, Ernest, 218, 221
Joseph, 155, 295
Jung, Carl, 272–73

Kant, Immanuel, 217, 227, 231, 299
Keener, James, 148, 163, 165, 167–69, 225
Ketley, Martin, 194
Kettlewell, Bernard, 64–65
Kierkegaard, Søren, 204–7
King, Alec, 194
King, Martin Luther, Jr., 119, 298
Kohlberg, Michael, 197
Krishtalka, Leonard, 69
Kuhn, Thomas, 129–30

Lavoisier, Antoine, 37, 129
Lawrence, D. H., 23
Lazarus, 248, 295
Lee, Robert E., 196
Leslie, Bill, 120, 206
Lester, Donald, 301
Lewis, C. S., 95, 174, 192, 194, 197, 213–22,
    275
Litfin, Duane, 77
Loewen, Jacob, 34
Lowie, Robert, 34
Luther, Martin, 113

McConnell, Michael, 55, 59, 97
McGraw, Phillip, 205
MacKay, Donald M., 46
McMillin, Barbara, 197–98
Magee, Bill, 251
Marsch, Glenn, 45
Marsden, George, 28, 78–81, 87, 89, 95–97, 125, 127–28, 132–33, 140–41
Martha, 248, 295
Marx, Karl, 14, 68, 254, 284–85, 287–88
Mary, 248, 295–96
Maslow, Abraham, 258–59, 262–64, 267–68, 274
Matthew, 296
Matthews, Chris, 66–67
Mead, George Herbert, 279–82
Medved, Michael, 192
Merton, Robert K., 282–83
Miller, Henry, 23
Milton, John, 194, 219
Moberg, David, 44, 290
Morgenthau, Hans, 245
Morgenthau, Henry, 46
Morrison, Jim, 186
Mouw, Richard, 87
Mulder, Karen, 188–89, 191

Nagel, Thomas, 71–72
Naisbitt, John, 131
Neill, A. S., 227–28, 231
Newton, Isaac, 151, 172, 215
Nicholi, Armand, 213, 215, 265, 268
Niebuhr, Reinhold, 246
Nietzsche, Friedrich, 14, 157, 209, 250
Nisbet, Robert, 282
Noll, Mark, 86, 106

Olasky, Marvin, 35
Orr, James, 15
Orwell, George, 23

Padelford, Walter, 301
Patmore, Coventry, 183
Patrick, John, 147
Pattison, Mansell, 42

Paul, 16, 25, 34, 92, 94, 110, 112, 120, 121, 127, 128, 132, 134, 173, 202, 210, 225, 249, 271, 287, 296, 308
Paul, Pope John, II, 115
Pearcey, Nancy, 18
Pelikan, Jeroslav, 87
Peter, 110, 173, 206, 262, 296
Pfister, Oskar, 215–16
Picasso, Pablo, 188
Plantinga, Alvin, 36, 87, 89
Plato, 60, 119, 200, 229
Poe, Harry, 195
Porter, Katherine Anne, 198
Presley, Elvis, 186
Priestley, Joseph, 36, 37
Putnam, James Jackson, 218
Puttnam, David, 192

Reagan, Maureen, 157–58
Reagan, Ronald, 157
Reich, Charles, 53–54
Reiff, Patricia H., 151–52, 177
Reitsma, Carl, 119
Richardson, Michael, 64
Risman, Barbara, 82
Rogers, Carl, 274–75
Rosebrough, Thomas, 225
Ross, Susan, 303

Sagan, Carl, 38
St. Augustine, 121
St. Paul, 215
Sartre, Jean-Paul, 158, 202–4
Saunders, Cicely, 251
Sayers, Dorothy, 181
Schnur, Max, 221
Schrader, Paul, 184–85
Scott, Eugenie, 64, 69
Seamonds, David, 277
Seymour, Charles, 28–29
Singer, Marcus, 197
Skinner, B. F., 273–74
Sloan, Robert, 70
Smelser, Neil, 47
Smith, Fred, 261

Socrates, 119, 220
Solomon, 297
Stah, Georg, 36
Stalin, Joseph, 27
Stoner, Peter, 102
Stott, John, 291
Sunday, Billy, 107
Suppe, John, 260

Temple, William, 167
Teresa, Mother, 251
Thomas, Dylan, 186
Thornbury, Gregory Alan, 30
Tillich, Paul, 208–9, 285
Tinder, Glenn, 71, 200–201, 246–47
Tournier, Paul, 284
Trueblood, Elton, 192

Ugolnik, Anthony, 192

Van Til, Cornelius, 101, 103
Vanier, Jean, 251

Walkup, John F., 173–74
Weber, Lynn, 81–82
Weber, Max, 287–88
Weinberg, S. Kirson, 280–81
Wells, Jonathan, 63, 67
Wilder, Thornton, 267
Williams, Charles, 183
Wilson, Woodrow, 29
Wolfe, Alan, 86–88, 131
Wolterstorff, Nicholas, 25, 85, 87, 95,
    98–99, 102, 112, 115, 117, 122, 125,
    128, 130–31, 190–91, 268, 304

Yancey, Philip, 250, 298
Yandell, Keith, 201

Zacharias, Ravi, 35, 156, 164, 172–73

SUBJECT INDEX

Abolition of Man, The, 197
academic freedom, 56–57
academic mainstream, 58–60, 62–74, 77–91
actualizing theory, 274–75
advertising, 303–5
African American perspectives, 43, 57, 83, 126, 127, 128
agnosticism, 44, 255
Alcoholics Anonymous, 250
alienation, 282–84
American Baptist Convention, 30
American Museum of Natural History, 33
American Scientific Affiliation, 133
American Sociological Association (ASA), 82
anomie, 282–83
anti-Semitism, 218
arrogance, 134, 165–66
Art in Action, 190
artists, 188–93
arts, 53, 179–242
assimilation, 77–78
atheism, 44, 213–23

Baltimore Catechism, 55
Baylor University, 68, 70, 86, 89–90
behavioral sciences, 46–51, 129–30, 236, 243–306
behaviorism, 130, 273–74
Being a Christian in Science, 72
belief systems, 129–30
belongingness, 262
Bible, 30, 59, 92, 93, 99, 101, 102, 107, 108, 109, 251, 253, 287
Biblical Images in Literature, 198

biblical worldview, 18. *See also* Christian worldview
Blessed Assurance, 106
Boisi Center for Religion and American Public Life, 86
Boston College, 86
Boston Globe, 35
Brief History of Time, A, 148
Brothers Karamazov, The, 201
Bucknell University, 30
Buddhism, 251, 252, 289
bureaucracy, 287–88
business
    advertising, 303–5
    Christian businesses, 301–3
    and ethics, 299–301

California State University, 260
Calvin College, 87, 184
Calvinistic theology, 17, 55, 103
Calvinists, 176, 217
cardinal Christian concepts, 234–36
Chariots of Fire, 192
chemistry, 36–37, 129
Christian businesses, 301–3
Christian colleges, 13–30, 45–46, 73–74, 86–90, 107–8, 131–34
Christian community, 85
Christian compartmentalization, 85
Christian economics, 16, 129, 295–306
Christian education, 13–26, 42–43, 74, 86–90, 92–93, 169. *See also* Christian scholarship
Christian historian, 234–42
Christian mathematics, 129, 163, 169
Christian mental health models, 275–77

Christian mind, 22–24, 26, 90, 307
Christian psychology, 129
Christian scholarship
    and academic mainstream, 77–91
    challenge of, 135, 308
    and educational system, 25–26
    quality of, 95–98, 113–14
    reasons for, 25–26
    role of learning in, 106–14
    and value freedom, 44
    see also Christian education
Christian sociology, 16, 128–29, 279, 288–92
Christian thinking, 13–24, 113–14, 144
Christian View of God and the World, The, 15
Christian worldview, 18, 93–95, 102–4, 113, 129, 134, 238
Christianity, 55, 79–81, 92, 99–104, 150–51, 213–23, 250–53, 289, 307
Christianity Today, 89, 115
Christians in the Visual Arts (CIVA), 192
Christmas Carol, A, 301
Chronicle of Higher Education, 94, 95
Church of England, 106
church survival, 286–87
civil religion, 253
colleges, 13–24, 28–30, 45–46, 73–74, 86–90, 107–8, 131–34
commitment, 23, 96, 99, 202–9, 240
Communism, 253–54
communities, 85, 117
Company of the Committed, The, 192
complacency, 307
Conference on Christianity and Literature, 133
Conference on Faith and History, 133
conflict theory, 130, 285
contemporary society, 307
Control of Language, The, 194
Cosmos, 38
creation
    concept of, 101–2, 108–9, 146–59
    and designfulness, 149–51
    and logic, 151–53
    mastering, 111

    and origins, 147–48
    and purpose, 154–58
    view of, 37, 142
Crime and Punishment, 201
cultural relativism, 90, 289–90
culture, 32, 181, 307

"Darwin vs. Design: Evolutionists' New Battle," 68–69
Darwinian thinking, 28, 46, 63–69, 149, 151
Darwin's Black Box: The Biochemical Challenge to Evolution, 67–68
death, 220–22
death principle, 272
deconstruction, 55, 118, 229–30
deontology, 299, 301
Descent of Man, The, 65–66
Design Inference, 68
designfulness, 149–51
determinism, 288
developmental theory, 264–68
Devil, 30, 219
Deweyism, 226–27
dialogue, 139–45
Dictionary of Biblical Tradition in English Literature, A, 198
Discipline and Punish, 210
Do I Have to Be Me? 275

economics
    and business, 299–301
    and ethics, 298–99
    study of, 129, 297–98
    view of, 16, 295–306
education
    and deconstruction thinking, 229–30
    focus on, 231–32
    importance of, 25–26, 226–27
    and secularism, 224–25
    and Summerhill, 227–29
    teacher's role, 225–26
educational system, 13–32, 37–38, 42–43, 74, 86–90. *See also* Christian education; Christian scholarship

ego, 271, 272, 275–76
"Eight Stages of Man," 264
emotional life, 249–50
empiricism, 41, 46–49, 58, 94, 289, 291
emptiness, 205
Encyclopedia Britannica, 102
Enlightenment, 26–28, 38, 57, 58, 127
epistemology, 153–54
Essays on Moral Development, 197
estrangement, 208–9
ethics, 298–301
ethnomethodology, 237
evil, 216–18
Evolutionary Biology, 68
evolutionism, 37, 48, 62–72, 147–48, 163–64
excessive freedom, 204–7
existentialism, 201–9

faith and learning
    challenge of, 13–24, 307–8
    components of, 125–35
    and creation, 146–59
    criteria for, 141–43
    critiquing component, 125–27
    experiences of, 13–24
    importance of, 22–24, 307–8
    philosophical component, 125
    in physical sciences, 173–74
    relationship of, 141
    theory building, 127–33
    understanding, 92–105
faith and reason, 115–24
Fatal Skin, 219
feminist perspectives, 43, 81–83, 126, 127, 128, 130, 133
Fides et Ratio, 115
film, 183–86
Flatland, 177
Foundation for Individual Rights in Education, Inc. (FIRE), 82
freedom, 41–45, 204–7, 228–29, 232
Freudian theory, 213–21, 270–72
Fuller Seminary, 87
functionalism, 130, 285–87
fundamentalism, 106–8
Galapagos Islands, 65

gay perspectives, 43, 126, 127, 133
Generalization of Ethics, 197
Georgia Tech, 259
God
    attitude toward, 93–100, 263
    existence of, 99–104, 141–42, 213–16, 224, 291–92
    honoring, 253–55
    in nature, 177–78
    relationship with, 25, 111, 169–70, 231–32, 261, 281–82, 307
    totality of, 249
God and Man at Yale, 29
good and evil, 216–18
"Good Science, Bad Science: Teaching Evolution in the States," 63
gospel, 248–51, 263
gospel-embedded sociology, 292
Greening of America, The, 53
guilt, 263

Habitat for Humanity, 251
Handbook of Sociology, 47
Hardball, 66
Harvard University, 33, 65
healing ministries, 297
hierarchy of needs, 258–62
Hinduism, 251, 289
historian, 234–42
historical perspectives, 237
history
    concepts of, 234–36
    contraction of, 237
    expansion of, 236–37
    philosophy of, 238–39
    study of, 234–42
holistic sociology, 292
Holy Spirit, 99, 120, 121, 173, 249–52, 263, 271
hospice movement, 251
"How Apes Became Human," 67
human beings, 231–32, 235
human nature, 117, 142
humanism, 31, 90, 301
humanities, 46, 116–18, 130, 179–242
humility, 134

I-and-me relationship, 279–81
I-It relationship, 280, 285
I-Thou relationship, 207–8, 279–80
Icons of Evolution, 63, 64
id, 271
identity, 202–4, 210–11, 271, 275–76, 279–80
inclusion, 81–85
independent variable, 98–100
inferiority complex, 131–33
Institute for the Study of American Evangelicals, 133
Institute of Faith and Learning, 70
instrumentalism, 226–27
intellectual discrimination, 34–35
intellectual journey, 57–58
Islam, 251, 252, 289
isolation, 265

Jesus CEO: Using Ancient Wisdom for Visionary Leadership, 303
Jesus on Leadership: Executive Lessons from the Servant Leader, 303
Jungian therapy, 272–73
justice, 247–48
justice-in-shalom, 25, 168

Knox College, 260

l'Arche Movement, 251
Law of Conservation of Mass, 37
lay-aside rule, 139–40
learning, 106–14. *See also* Christian education; Christian scholarship; educational system
lesbian perspectives, 57
liberalism, 37–38, 55
libertarianism, 299–301
life, 154–58, 163–65
life choices, 264–65
Life Strategies, 205
Lilly Endowment, 133
limits, 118–19
literature
    definition of, 195–96
    evaluating, 196–97

guidelines for, 197–98
subjectivity of, 194–99
teaching, 195–99
view of, 53, 185–86
loneliness, 265–66
love, 182–83

Madame Bovary, 188
Madness and Civilization, 210
majority-minority relations, 77–79
manipulation, 208–9
Marine Corps, 260
Marxism, 55, 127, 128, 284–85
Maslow's pyramid, 258–59, 262, 263
material blessings, 297
materialism, 38, 90, 204–5, 208–9, 266–67, 283–85, 296–97, 304
mathematics, 129, 163, 169
meaning
    and commitment, 202–4
    and creation, 154–58
    in life, 204–7, 261
mental health models, 270–78
Mental Health Nursing, 263
mental life, 249–50
Mere Christianity, 197
metaphysical naturalism, 66
Millbrook School, 59
modern era, 53–54
moral development, 267
moral policy, 255
morality, 90, 156–57, 216–18, 232, 271, 273
Moses and Monotheism, 215
movies, 183–86
multiculturalism, 59, 78–79, 83, 95, 133, 230, 239–41
Muslims, 251

National Academy of Sciences, 65
National Center for Science Education, 64
nationalism, 253–54
naturalism, 36–38, 41–52, 58, 60–63, 66–68, 72, 74, 94, 133, 151, 154, 167, 231–32, 273–74, 279–94

Nature, 65
Nature, Man, and God, 167
Nearer, My God, 118
need theory, 258–64
New Testament, 92, 248, 250, 251, 261, 287
New York Times, 67, 68
New York University, 71
Newsweek, 67
non-Enlightenment, 210
"Noon Wine," 198
Northwestern University, 47
Notre Dame, 86, 87, 89

objectivity, 96, 239
Old Testament, 92, 101, 246, 249, 251
oligarchy, 307
On the Origin of Species, 151
operant conditioning, 273–74
Operation Smile, 251
origins, 147–48
Our Town, 267
Outrageous Idea of Christian Scholarship, The, 78

paganism, 59, 131
pain, 218–20
paradigmatic disciplines, 146–47
paradigms, 129–31, 308
Paradise Lost, 219
paradoxical apologetic, 167–68
Perfect Leader: Following Christ's Example to Learn Leadership Success, 303
personal fulfillment, 202–4
personality theory, 270–75
Pew Charitable Trust, 133
philosophy
    existentialist philosophy, 201–9
    postmodern philosophy, 209–11
    and truth, 117–18
    understanding of, 34
    value of, 115–16
    view of, 48, 55, 200–223
phlogiston theory, 36–37
physical life, 248–50

physical sciences
    attitude toward, 163
    Christian implications in, 163–78
    and mystery of life, 163–65
    and purpose, 168–70
    and time, 174–77
    view of, 47, 163–70
    and worship, 165–66
physics, 171–73, 176
Pilgrim's Progress, The, 215
pluralism, 78–81, 96–98, 301
political agenda, 68–72
political choice, 254
political science
    and Christianity, 32, 248, 250–53
    issues of, 129, 253–56
    and justice, 247–48
    and religion, 245–47
    and whole-person gospel, 248–51
Possessed, The, 201
postmodernism, 32, 53–63, 74, 81, 94, 118, 127, 198, 209–11, 229–30
poverty, 296, 298
Princeton University, 29, 103, 260
Principia, 151
Protestantism, 86, 89–90, 107, 238, 247
psychologism, 81
psychology
    developmental theory, 264–68
    study of, 258–69
    view of, 47, 129–30
Psychology and Alchemy, 273
psychotherapy, 272–73
Puritans, 235
purpose
    and commitment, 202–4
    and creation, 154–58
    in life, 204–7, 261
    and physical science, 168–70

quantum theory, 171–72
Question of God, The, 213

rationalization, 288
reality, 231
reason and faith, 115–24

Reason and Imagination, 196
reductionism, 41, 45–46, 58, 163–64, 286
relativism, 90, 289–90
religion classes, 13–24, 29, 89–90
repentance, 263
resistance, 20–22, 133–35
revelation, 108, 119–23, 177–78
Rice University, 151

St. Christopher's Hospice, 251
Satan, 30, 219
science, 42, 147–53, 164–65, 168, 258. See
    also behavioral sciences
scientific method, 33, 42, 43
scientism, 33–36, 66, 72
scientists, 36–37, 172–73
secessionism, 86–89, 128
secularism, 22–23, 28–35, 62–63, 72–74,
    83–84, 90, 97, 112–13, 133–34, 224–25,
    290, 296, 307, 308
self-actualization, 264, 267, 274–75
self-esteem, 259, 263–64, 267
self-identity, 202–4, 210–11, 271, 275–76,
    279–80
self-indulgence, 266–67
sexism, 50
sin, 118–19, 184–85, 263, 276–77
social movements, 252–53
social order, 156–57
social psychology, 279–82
social responsibility, 300
social sciences, 46–51, 129–30, 243–306
society, 117, 307
Society of Christian Philosophers, 133
sociologism, 49–51
sociology, 16, 47, 49–51, 128–29, 279–94
"Some Explorations of Milton's Lycidas,"
    194
Soul of the American University, The, 28
special interest groups, 43, 128, 237
sphere sovereignty, 17
spirit, 23, 173, 307
spiritual belonging, 262
Spiritual Dimensions of Nursing Practice, 263
spiritual life, 59, 117–18, 173–74, 248–50

structure-functionalism, 285–87
Structure of Scientific Revolutions, The, 129
suffering, 218–20
Summerhill, 227–29
superego, 271
symbolism, 55

teacher, role of, 225–26
*Teaching Sociological Concepts and the Sociology
    of Gender,* 82
technology, 168–69
temporal view, 84–85, 174–77, 283
Texas Tech, 173
theology, 48, 107
theories, 49–50, 143–44
Third World perspectives, 57
Time, 67
time theory, 174–77
Trinity, 120, 121, 307
truth
existence of, 100–102, 142, 210
knowledge as, 25
search for, 116–18, 173
*Twenty-Five Most Common Problems in Busi-
    ness (and How Jesus Solved Them),* 303

Union University, 36
universities. See colleges
University of California, 56, 98
University of Chicago, 43, 55, 68
University of Illinois, 37, 150
University of Kansas, 69
University of Massachusetts, 71
University of Michigan, 35
University of Minnesota-Duluth, 148, 261
University of Ottawa, 147
University of Texas, 35
University of Utah, 55, 148
utilitarianism, 299, 301

value freedom, 41–45
values, 142–43, 267
virtue, 300

Walden II, 273–74
wealth, 247, 296, 304

Western perversions, 253–54
Wheaton College, 77, 86, 128
whole-person gospel, 248–51, 263
Women's Studies Quarterly, 81

worship, 165–66

Yale, 28, 29, 53, 87
Your Quest for God, 31

We want to hear from you. Please send your comments about this book to us in care of zreview@zondervan.com. Thank you.

GRAND RAPIDS, MICHIGAN 49530 USA

WWW.ZONDERVAN.COM